BEYOND PSYCHOTHERAPY

In *Beyond Psychotherapy: On Becoming a (Radical) Psychoanalyst*, Barnaby B. Barratt illuminates a new perspective on what it means to open our awareness to the depths of psychic life and restores the radicality of genuinely psychoanalytic discourse as the unique science of healing.

Starting with an incisive critique of the ideological conformism of psychotherapy, Barratt defines the method of psychoanalysis against the conventional definition, which emphasizes the practice of arriving at useful interpretations about our personal existence. Instead, he shows how a negatively dialectical and deconstructive praxis successfully 'attacks' the self-enclosures of interpretation, allowing the speaking-listening subject to become existentially and spiritually open to hidden dimensions of our lived-experience. He also demonstrates how the erotic deathfulness of our being-in-the-world is the ultimate source of all the many resistances to genuinely psychoanalytic praxis, and the reason Freud's discipline has so frequently been reduced to various models of psychotherapeutic treatment. Focusing on the free-associative dimension of psychoanalysis, Barratt both explores what psychoanalytic processes can achieve that psychotherapeutic ones cannot, and considers the sociopolitical implications of the radical psychoanalytic 'take' on the human condition. The book also offers a detailed and compassionate pointer for those wanting to train as psychoanalysts, guiding them away from what Barratt calls the 'trade-school mentality' pervading most training institutes today.

Groundbreaking and inspiring, *Beyond Psychotherapy* will be essential reading for psychoanalysts, psychoanalytic psychotherapists and all other therapists seeking a radically innovative approach. It will also be a valuable text for scholars and students of psychoanalytic studies, social sciences, philosophy and the history of ideas.

Dr Barnaby B. Barratt is Director of Studies at the Parkmore Institute and Senior Research Associate at the WITS Institute for Social and Economic Research, University of Witwatersrand, South Africa. He is a Supervising Analyst with the Indian Psychoanalytic Society, as well as a Training Analyst with the South African Psychoanalytic Association, and was previously a Training Analyst with the American Psychoanalytic Association. His books include *What is Psychoanalysis?* and *Radical Psychoanalysis: An Essay on Free-Associative Praxis* (both Routledge).

BEYOND PSYCHOTHERAPY

On Becoming a (Radical) Psychoanalyst

Barnaby B. Barratt

Routledge
Taylor & Francis Group

LONDON AND NEW YORK

First published 2019
by Routledge
2 Park Square, Milton Park, Abingdon, Oxon OX14 4RN

and by Routledge
52 Vanderbilt Avenue, New York, NY 10017

Routledge is an imprint of the Taylor & Francis Group, an informa business

British Library Cataloguing-in-Publication Data
A catalogue record for this book is available from the British Library

Library of Congress Cataloging-in-Publication Data
Names: Barratt, Barnaby B., 1950- author.
Title: Beyond psychotherapy : on becoming a (radical) psychoanalyst /
Barnaby B. Barratt.
Description: 1 Edition. | New York : Routledge, 2019. | Includes
bibliographical references.
Identifiers: LCCN 2018054234 (print) | LCCN 2019007801 (ebook) |
ISBN 9780429432217 (Master eBook) | ISBN 9780429778322 (Adobe
Reader) | ISBN 9780429778308 (Mobipocket) | ISBN 9780429778315
(ePub) | ISBN 9781138362215 (hardback) | ISBN 9781138362222
(pbk.) | ISBN 9780429432217 (ebk)
Subjects: LCSH: Psychoanalysis. | Psychology–Philosophy.
Classification: LCC BF175 (ebook) | LCC BF175 .B278 2019 (print) |
DDC 150.19/5–dc23
LC record available at https://lccn.loc.gov/2018054234

ISBN: 978-1-138-36221-5 (hbk)
ISBN: 978-1-138-36222-2 (pbk)
ISBN: 978-0-429-43221-7 (ebk)

Typeset in Bembo
by Swales & Willis, Exeter, Devon, UK

Printed and bound by CPI Group (UK) Ltd, Croydon, CR0 4YY

May all beings be happy and free;
may these writings contribute
to the happiness and freedom of all beings.

CONTENTS

About the author   ix
Prefatory note   x

1   Introducing praxis: why 'radical' and why 'beyond'?   1
    Prolegomenal notes 2
    On the radicality of psychoanalysis 4
    On the project of going beyond 7
    On scurrilous histories 11
    What 'self' expresses itself? 16

2   Free-associative praxis *against* interpretation   20
    Exploring differences 21
    Defining psychoanalysis 22
    Against conventional approaches to lived-experience 25
    Free-associative 'attacks' on certitude 30
    The force of desire against the stases of repetition-compulsivity 35

3   Notes on becoming a psychoanalyst   46
    Against (trade) schooling 46
    Entering psychoanalysis 51
    Psychoanalysis and the sense of transition 54
    On functioning as a psychoanalyst 58
    On the vulnerability and fear in becoming a psychoanalyst 78

4   Psychoanalytic discoveries: sexuality and deathfulness   83
      Ontoethics before and beyond epistemology 83
      Lived-experience and libidinal energies 87
      On 'falling into' free-associative speaking 95
      Free-associative awareness and our polysexual humanity 102
      Free-associative listening, awareness and deathfulness 107

5   The psychoanalytic leap and the necessity of revolution   111
      Critique of the discourse of domination 114
      From transformative imprisonment to transmutative release 118
      On the nonviolent power of transgressive praxis 124

Notes   *130*
Bibliography   *165*
Index   *197*

ABOUT THE AUTHOR

Barnaby B. Barratt is currently Director of Studies at the Parkmore Institute, and was previously Professor of Family Medicine, Psychiatry and Behavioral Neurosciences at Wayne State University (Detroit). He serves as a Supervising Analyst in India, as well as a Training and Supervising Analyst in South Africa, and previously in Michigan. He is Senior Research Fellow at the University of Witwatersrand's Institute for Social and Economic Research. His previous books include *Psychic Reality and Psychoanalytic Knowing* (Routledge, 1984), *Psychoanalysis and the Postmodern Impulse* (Routledge, 1993), *What is Psychoanalysis?* (Routledge, 2013) and *Radical Psychoanalysis: An Essay on Free-Associative Praxis* (Routledge, 2016).

PREFATORY NOTE

In this trilogy – *What is Psychoanalysis? 100 Years after Freud's 'Secret Committee,'* *Radical Psychoanalysis: An Essay on Free-Associative Praxis* and *Beyond Psychotherapy: On Becoming a (Radical) Psychoanalyst* – I have developed the argument that psychoanalysis is the supreme discipline of listening to the multiplicity of 'voices' that constitute each person's psychic life. As such, it treats the human condition and heals it in a profound way that the practices of interpretation and reinterpretation cannot. Perhaps I should not write that it 'is' the supreme way, but rather that it 'might have been,' because psychoanalysis today – and through the course of the past one hundred years – has become lost amidst the production of various models of the mind and their associated sets of practices that are perhaps therapeutic (or perhaps not), but lack the radicality of a genuinely psychoanalytic praxis. Thus, the aim here is to restore a vision of psychoanalysis that has been obfuscated by all the various therapies that brand themselves 'psychoanalytic.' The aim is to argue for the profound ontoethical value of listening psychoanalytically – that is, free-associatively – because this is the praxis that breaks down the barriers that compulsively arrest the flow of desire. The thesis here is that only such a listening praxis can authentically free the truthfulness of what might be called the human 'spirit.' The diverse practices of interpretation and the search for new modes of interpreting the human condition can serve to *transform* our psychic life psychotherapeutically, whether for better or often, in what may be the case in some fundamental sense, for worse. By contrast, listening to the voices of our bodymind in a way that is deconstructive and negatively dialectical – the way of an ongoing and rigorous commitment to free-association – serves to *transmute* our psychic life in a manner that is often unsettling, but that is genuinely freeing and truthful.

1

INTRODUCING PRAXIS

Why 'radical' and why 'beyond'?

What is needed, for the human community as much as for each individual, is *psychoanalysis beyond psychotherapy*. This book will argue the significance of this statement, especially as it pertains to humanity's current epoch, characterized as it is by the burgeoning ideologies and globalized practices of rampant militarization, transnational corporatism, escalating fundamentalism and resurgent authoritarianism – all marked by so much violence against people and against the planet. To address the suffering of the human psyche at a basic level, what is required is not so much therapeutic palliation offered by some form of (re)interpretation of our lives, as significant as the latter may often be. Rather, the suffering of the psyche needs to be addressed by the challenging authenticity of *psychoanalysis* as a unique process of liberation – a radical praxis – that is both spiritual-existential and subversively political in its impact. This is not, of course, to suggest in any way that this is all that is needed, but radical psychoanalysis is, in a profound way, an exemplar of what is needed, because this is healing by a process of perpetual *listening-opening-changing/learning* that is in itself a liberatory movement against stultifying and compulsively repetitious modes of interpretation that imprison us. Moreover, it is the human propensity for repetition-compulsivity that sustains and recruits adherents to the ideologies of domination, fanaticism, exploitation and violence. The liberatory movement of discourse against repetition-compulsivity is the central dimension of *psychoanalysis-as-praxis*, which echoes Karl Marx's 1845 aphorism, 'philosophers have only interpreted the world … the point is to change it.' The discoveries of psychoanalysis indeed have deep and far-reaching implications for philosophy, but the discipline is not a philosophical-theoretical exercise, nor is it the enterprise of an applied science in the conventional sense. In making these assertions, I am not referring to just any 'psychoanalysis.' For nowadays the label is routinely appropriated for procedures that actually comprise psychotherapy practiced by someone who is nominally a 'psychoanalyst' or practiced as a set of techniques based on one of the models of mental functioning that have been promulgated since Sigmund Freud's lifetime (or even those that he developed during the last twenty-five years of his life). The latter are the so-called 'psychoanalytically-informed' or 'psychoanalytically-oriented' psychotherapies. As will be discussed, for the most part 'psychotherapy' of any variety involves a manipulative application of techniques derived from theoretical frameworks that purport to explain human functioning. Psychoanalysis is not like that. Rather, I am pointing to a radicalized process of changing-by-listening to the inner and outer conditions of what it means to be human and what it means to suffer as a human. That is, a praxis of listening-and-opening and changing-learning and then listening-and-opening again, *in perpetuum*. This is not unlike the notion of a permanent revolutionary movement as necessary to effect thoroughgoing, rather than transient, change.[1] Only such a praxis decenters our discourse in a way that frees us from the compulsive repetitiousness of our lives and that thus liberates us into becoming more *alive!*

Prolegomenal notes

This book expresses and explains my conviction that there are pronounced divergences, and perhaps contradictions, between procedures of discourse that are merely psychotherapeutic and the unique processes of *radical psychoanalysis*. One implication of this is that there are profound differences both in the tenets of healing or health that are encoded in each discourse and in the manner that the patient's lived-experience is facilitated in accordance with those tenets – herein I will use the term 'lived-experience,' borrowed in a modified way from Simone de Beauvoir, as elaborated by Eleanore Holveck and others, simply to emphasize the existential implications of psychoanalysis, for this discipline is, above all, about the ethical, experiential and experimental way in which we engage life. Radical psychoanalysis prioritizes a unique process of listening-and-opening inwards – the rigorous method of free-associative praxis – rather than the arrival at supposedly improved behavior, beliefs or feelings about one's place in the world. It is this praxis that – freed from therapeutic ambition, from biological prescriptions and even from the mandates of conventional psychology – comprises the healing at the heart and soul of any genuinely psychoanalytic process, which is about becoming *alive!*

On what basis am I advancing these claims? I have over forty years' experience doing psychoanalytic work. I am also qualified as a sexologist and a somatic psychologist or bodyworker (with both clinical and developmental training in psychology, as well as a rather wide-ranging education in the human sciences). Furthermore, it might be noted that I have been a consistently vigorous activist for causes of human rights, civil liberties and justice. In these decades, I have conversed with many patients – some in great depth over many years of treatment, others more briefly. Especially at the beginning of my career, many were engaged with me in the alleviative procedures of psychotherapy. As a somatic practitioner and specialist in sexuality, I have also learned much from hundreds of individuals, who did not become patients in psychotherapy, but who consulted me more briefly in relation to a wide range of painful life-issues. In the course of this vocation, my calling as a healer, gaining professional experience with patients and deepening the exploration of my own psyche, I have chosen to spend more and more of my time in the deeply illuminating processes of psychoanalysis. Such that today I no longer offer psychotherapy *except* as preparatory to psychoanalysis (which implies that this is a special and rather exceptional species of 'psychotherapy'). Currently, I see ten patients a day, each for four sessions per week of fifty-minutes duration. Almost all my patients are trainees in psychoanalysis; 80% are women and the group includes not only whites (of mixed gentile European, Lithuanian Jewish and Afrikaner descent), but also Zulu, Xhosa and individuals of South Asian origin. I do still offer brief consultations on focused topics (principally within the domain of sexology and somatic psychology), but I do not do what is ordinarily called psychotherapy *except* in so far as psychotherapeutic procedures are often a necessary preparation for the processes of psychoanalysis and are, as it were, a sort of way-station or set of preparatory procedures within the everyday course of a radical psychoanalytic treatment.

Radical psychoanalysis draws from Freudian roots, but is thoroughly contemporary and innovative, at least in the sense that it diverges significantly from that propounded by any of the prevalent schools that nominally characterize this discipline (as well as the practices that have followed from Adlerian and Jungian theorizing). As represented today in the International Psychoanalytic Association that Freud's colleagues founded in 1910, the three prevailing schools from which radical psychoanalysis diverges notably are: (i) the structural-functional or ego-psychological; (ii) the Kleinian or post-Kleinian and independently object-relational; (iii) the social, interpersonal-relational and self-psychological schools. More about these schools will be discussed in what follows. This list might also have included, with a rather different emphasis, the very important Lacanian and post-Lacanian schools. It is hard to imagine that the approach to radical psychoanalysis presented in this text could have been articulated without the influence of Jacques Lacan's multifarious writings. In this sense, my approach might be categorized as post-Lacanian. Yet it is rather unlikely that any brassbound devotee of Lacan's work would concede that there is much of any merit to what is expounded in this text (Lacanians, with whose vantage-point I shall take serious issue, tend to be deeply wedded to theoretical speculation, whereas, in addition to other profound divergences, the emphasis in this trilogy is on psychoanalysis as spiritual-existential and sociopolitical praxis). My specific focus herein will be on the way in which radical psychoanalytic praxis differentiates itself from the psychotherapeutic procedures, as propounded by three main schools – the structural-functional, the object-relational and the social/self-psychological. All this will become clear in the course of the text.

On the radicality of psychoanalysis

The calling to which I am committed is psychoanalytically *radical*, not only in the sense that it deviates from the hegemonic schools of this discipline, but also in that it returns to the roots of the discipline of psychoanalysis as a *method* or *praxis* that uniquely explores and heals the interiority of being human *beyond* what can typically be accomplished in a psychotherapeutic discourse. This is a return to, as well as a somewhat original refinding and refueling of, Freudian insights that have almost been lost. The world in which something called 'psychoanalysis' is clinically practiced (that is to say, now on every continent of the globe, to some degree, with the exception of Antarctica) identifies this discipline both with a model of mental functioning and with clinical procedures that exploit the transformative properties of (re)interpretation. The theoretical models, on which such interpretative enterprises depend, may emphasize, to greater or lesser degree, the ego organization, the inner theater of object-relations, or the self and its social embeddedness. But the commonality of these approaches is that these sorts of theoretical framework govern clinical techniques that manipulate the patient's functioning to achieve an improved degree of adaptation, maturation, adjustment, integration or personal contentment (which are themselves theoretical terms that are rarely, if ever, sufficiently examined critically, or unpacked deconstructively). Against these procedures, the radicality of the mode of psychoanalysis to be discussed herein is at least threefold.

(i) It lies in its centering, not on a theoretical model that is then applied to clinical labors with the patient, but rather on *method-as-praxis*. As will be discussed, this is a method that is radically decentering of the subject (or more accurately that acknowledges and addresses a subject that is already decentered from itself but does not know it), and in which theorizing occurs only as the *ad hoc* operation of provisional or 'auxiliary notions' (Freud's *Hilfsvorstellungen*). Psychoanalysis is scientific, but it is not a psychology in any ordinary sense of this term (and it is certainly not an adjunct to the empirical enterprises of neuroscience). Indeed, it is not scientific in the mode of an objectifying investigation. It is defined by its method and not by the grand generalities of theoretical propositions about how our human being-in-the-world supposedly functions (generalities that are often alleged to hold across historical epochs and cultural diversities). This statement requires some qualification, as will be discussed in the course of what follows, because psychoanalysis does make some generalizable discoveries about the way our being-in-the-world is constituted (by the semiotics of enigmatic messages and by the symbolic system of language itself) and about the rupturing effects of the 'repression-barrier' and the incest taboo within our psychic life (the repression-barrier is the intrapsychic inscription of the incest taboo, as will later be elaborated). However, radical psychoanalysis is to be understood primarily and centrally as this method of listening-and-opening to the interiority (and thence to the exteriority) of our being-in-the-world. It is an inquiry that is neither subjectivistic (like phenomenologies are typically supposed to be), nor objectivistic (like mainstream sciences are supposed to be). Unlike conventional ways of thinking about what it means to know something scientifically or to illuminate something hermeneutically, this method depends neither on the *a priori* theorizing of possibilities nor on a schematic conceptual system *about* the object under scrutiny. In short, radical psychoanalysis is not the application of a theoretical model of mental functioning, nor is it concerned with the *a posteriori* development of such models. Its method of listening is not engaged in order to develop a generalized understanding about how humans operate and, most significantly, it produces nothing that could be considered 'data' for the generation of such theory. Rather, it is engaged as the praxis of change that is both *changing-by-listening* and *understanding-by-changing* – a process which is neither subjectivistic nor objectivistic, and for which theoretical conceptualization or the collection of 'data' toward the construction of theoretical edifices, is irrelevant.

Thus, as mentioned, psychoanalysis is not a psychology, if we define that discipline as the enterprise that formulates models of mental functioning and human behavior on the basis of the collecting of objective data (including data consisting of subjective accounts). And very definitely this radicalized psychoanalysis has nothing to do with Kraepelinian psychiatry as horrifically exemplified by the American Psychiatric Association's *Diagnostic and Statistical Manual of Mental Disorders* (DSM). That is, a psychiatry that serves the *status quo* by categorizing individuals so that they may then be manipulated pharmacologically, genetically and behaviorally (or even, once in a while, offered some understanding form of psychotherapy) so that they may become more 'normal' – in this context, radical psychoanalysis is resolutely 'anti-psychiatry.'[2] Obviously, there are psychological and psychodynamic models of mental life that claim – with varying degrees of plausibility – to have been derived from the theorist's experience with some sort of psychoanalysis. In addition to Freud's various efforts in this direction (notably between the 1914 essay on narcissism and his 1926 text, *Inhibitions, Symptoms and Anxiety*), several schools, each with rather different models of human functioning and indeed assumptions about what it means to be human, have already been mentioned (ego-organizational, object-relational, self-psychological). But the crucial point I want to make here is that these models are not, in any way, a necessary or primarily important feature of psychoanalysis itself. Indeed, such models are far less significant or interesting than, and indeed virtually impertinent to, a unique method that cares about the interiority of lived-experience. In short, the healing method of radical psychoanalysis is singularly scientific, but the discipline is neither a science nor a hermeneutic system in any ordinary sense.

(ii) The radicality of psychoanalysis as presented in this book is also evident in the manner by which the method somewhat engages, but then proceeds decisively *beyond*, the endeavors of psychotherapy. Such endeavors aim for the individual's improved adjustment and the rationale for their engagement ceases when adjustment of some sort is achieved. The criteria for this are various, but inevitably conceived, overtly or covertly, in terms that are somewhat external to the individual's internal journey. This is the case even when the languaging of the psychotherapeutic goal is 'personal contentment,' because such a seemingly monadological criterion is inevitably tied to conventions external to the individual.

I have been told that Jean Laplanche once said, 'from the beginning, we are all muddled up with others in ways that we are never able to grasp.' In an aphoristic sense, riffing on the adages of Donald Winnicott in 1965 ('there is no such thing as a baby') and of André Green in 1991 ('there is no such thing as a mother-infant relationship'), it might be said that there is no such thing as an individual psyche. In Félix Guattari's famous formulation, 'we are all groupuscles' – the individual is culturally and sociopolitically constituted via representationality that is always structured like a language. There is a serious and profound sense in which individuality is a cultural and sociopolitical construct, more than a reality of psychic life. This is because both in its particular contents and its structure (the rules and regulations of 'making-sense'), the representational system that comprises the fabric of each of our psychic lives is not authored by us, so much as authored by the whole system within which it is acculturated (and only within this system is there latitude for what may be studied as 'individual differences').[3] Such dicta point not only to the way in which the signifier 'I' and all its movements are determined by the rules and regulations of linguistically-structured representationality (by which I mean representational systems that are always structured like a language), but also to the many ways in which the entire internality of our being-in-the-world is mixed up with external forces (that bombard us as enigmatic messages coming from 'outside' our organismic status). The criteria of psychotherapeutic success, appraised in terms of improved adaptation, maturation, adjustment, integration or contentment, are inevitably ensconced in a web of ideas and ideological values around these tricky concepts. Any appearance of harmony, integration or wholeness within an individual's functioning is culturally and sociopolitically contextualized. Thus, in some sense, it is external to the individual. It is also saturated in ideologies that preserve the *status quo*, and that assume the benefits of an apparent congruence between the particular and the system in which it operates.

We must surely ask what it really means to be adjusted, contented, or 'maturely adapted' when the current circumstances and the history of human existence are characterized by all sorts of venality and dehumanization, exploitation, brutality, genocide, ecocide and cyclical horror? We live in a world in which all human relations are infected with the afflictions of oppression, both internally and externally. In such a world, almost all sources of comfort – emotional and material – can only be acquired at the expense of others, as well as at the expense of truthfulness and the pursuit of freedom. Within the world we live in today, the goals of psychotherapy are inherently anodyne – emolliative, tranquilizing and analgesic.

(iii) These ideas comprise a 'leftist' notion of healing that is difficult for anyone, who has not stayed the radical course of psychoanalytic engagement, to grasp. Thus, the final aspect of the radicality of psychoanalysis is that its method, which deconstructs (or engages in a 'negatively dialectical' manner) the forces of suppression and repression that are inscribed within us, necessarily issues into a momentum that is anti-ideological. Sooner or later, the praxis of radical psychoanalysis implies a critique of the ideologies of domination and exploitation – oppression – that are everywhere around us. One cannot engage radically in psychoanalysis without becoming aware of all the various positions we adopt within systems of human relations that are endemically oppressive. Overtly or covertly, positions of domination/ subordination-subjugation and exploitation are inherent in every instance of human conduct. Tragically, there are no opportunities to 'opt out' or 'drop out' of the system in which we are all, without exception, perpetrators of oppression, collusive bystanders and victims. The awareness that accrues from an ongoing engagement with the method of psychoanalysis may not be pleasant in that it prompts us to dissent from all that is hegemonical, but the 'negatively dialectical' or deconstructive character that is at the heart and soul of its discourse ethically empowers us in a liberatory direction – spiritually, existentially and sociopolitically.

These are some of the coordinates of what is, in a sense, a 'guide' to its method-as-praxis as the process of going *beyond psychotherapeutics*. This text does not merely reiterate the material of two previous books (the 2013 *What is Psychoanalysis?* or the 2016 *Radical Psychoanalysis: An Essay on Free-Associative Praxis*). Rather, in a somewhat different but related vein, this guide aims not only to sketch what radical psychoanalysis is, but also to offer *not* formulae, but rather provocative ideas, as to how to engage its distinctive method. In that sense, this is part of a trilogy.

On the project of going beyond

Psychotherapists are notoriously reluctant to face questions about what exactly it means to adjust to a world that is characterized by the motif of mastery as domination-subordination-subjugation with all the suffering that results. For example, to consider the implications of personal adjustment to the alienating cultural, sociopolitical and economic conditions of the now globalized military-industrial-academic

complex.[4] Yet encoded within the procedures of psychotherapy are notions of healing and health not only as the avoidance of pain and the avoidance of death, but
also as the cultivation of the conformity exemplified by the 'happy citizen' (and the
phony conceit of the legendary *belle âme*, who, as Georg Hegel described in 1807,
revels in a fatuous sense of self-certainty that actually lacks substance). As was
insightfully suggested by Leszek Kolakowski in 1972, the philosophies and practices
of analgesic palliation necessarily negate the liberatory value of experientially knowing how and why one suffers, in order that the systems that cause unnecessary suffering might be changed. All too often, reformist opportunism stifles the revolution
that would heal a system more profoundly, as Rosa Luxemburg famously argued
(although not with reference to therapeutics). In this sense, the assumption that pain
avoidance, death avoidance and happy citizenship are genuinely *healing* is not only
bogus. It is a denial both of the reality of suffering, its actual conditions and of the
hope for authentic liberation. The philosophies and practices of alleviation thus represent a flight into delusion and illusion. This is a flight away from the praxis of
truthfulness and the genuine dynamics of freedom, which is – as will be discussed –
the praxis embraced by radical psychoanalysis as the ethicality of compassion, appreciation and grace.

To advocate going beyond an endeavor is not to be entirely against that
endeavor, but it is, unequivocally, to be against terminating when the ends of
that endeavor are met. In short, the mandate to go beyond the enterprise of
psychotherapy is an insistence on the *ethical and sociopolitical necessity* of transcend-
ing – in the sense of superceding or surpassing by sublation – the ends of that
enterprise. Thus, although radical psychoanalysis subsumes some of the procedures of psychotherapy, it shares neither the chimerical ambitions nor the ideologies that invariably pervade such procedures.

As I have elaborated previously, the psychoanalytic method of free-association
discovers two unsurpassable ruptures in the constitution of our humanity: Between
the biology of our body and what I shall call our psychic energies of *desire*, and
between our *desire* and the representational system (our thoughts, feelings, wishes,
fantasies and motives) that we commonly call our 'mind.' Suffering is inevitable
because of these dynamic 'disjunctures' (ruptures within the formation of our
being-in-the-world) that cannot be undone or surpassed (and certainly not by epistemological contrivances).[5] Psychoanalysis thus endorses at least one of the 'noble
truths' or realities (*catvāri āryasatyāni*) taught by Gautama Buddha some two-and-a-
half millennia before Freud's birth.[6] However, the inevitability of suffering does
not imply that it must be endured in the compulsively repetitious fashion that is customary (and that, in a profound way, psychotherapy so often promotes). It does not
have to be endured by the legerdemain of comforting delusions and illusions.
Rather, as a path – praxis – of truthfulness and freedom, radical psychoanalysis
makes our suffering less burdensome, for it opens 'timespace' within us to *love,
work, play*, even while unflinchingly facing the horrors of human chaos and cruelty.

How could anyone be against psychotherapy? If we define this venture as
a special mode of dyadic conversation with the intent of alleviating emotional

discomfort or cognitive confusion (and I will later discuss the limitations and qualifications that should accompany this definition), it might seem that opposition to it would only amount to a masochistic idealization of those very conditions of discomfort and confusion. It is obvious that one surely would not oppose the use of acetylsalicylic acid (aspirin) by someone wishing to relieve a painful headache. Yet is this so obvious? Or is it, as Ronald Laing suggested in 1968, a situation in which the 'obvious' serves to obscure an important dimension of the truthfulness underlying the situation? To be sure, one does not wish for the onset of a headache or for its prolongation. But when one arises, there is an important sense in which it might convey a message about one's being-in-the-world in relation to one's psyche or lived-experience. For example, perhaps one has been physically taxed in ways that are deleterious or perhaps there are thoughts and feelings that have been suppressed. The headache might be indicative of inhumane or discordant conditions of employment. It might intimate that recent interactions in a close relationship are not as emotionally unproblematic as they might seem. These are, in a sense, conflictual meanings that the beleaguered individual has probably not sufficiently considered or has considered but feels helpless to change (as when the only available employment involves inhumane or discordant conditions). Such meanings are now signaled symptomatically. Of course, it might simply be that the person was badly inebriated the previous evening. But even this is far from a simple explanation: Why is s/he inflicting such toxicity on her/himself? Approached in this manner, a headache is never just a headache. Rather, it is, so to speak, a 'call' to understand its potential meaningfulness (and surely such an event could never be other than meaningful) and indeed a 'call' for change in one's life. A headache is just one example. There is a sense in which every phenomenon of our lived-experience, every seemingly new event, can be taken as a 'call' to explore its potential – and often hidden – meaningfulness.

The point here is that the rush to alleviate an unpleasant event – the impulse to swallow the aspirin and forget the experience – can all too easily result in the event's significance continuing to be ignored. So, indeed, it may be 'obvious' that relief from pain is a worthy aspiration. But, if the rush for relief obscures the truthfulness about our lived-experience that the headache might convey to us, were it to be interrogated properly, then perhaps the aspiration is not so worthy. This is the problem of our culture of analgesia. It is not so much that the tactics of alleviation should be entirely renounced. Rather, it is essential *not* to use analgesic tactics in the service of ongoing ignorance – ignorance as to what the obvious advantages of alleviating pain can actually be used to obscure. In our today's globalized culture, the 'obvious' very often – perhaps always – serves to hide a dimension of truthfulness that then remains recondite.

It is too tempting, and not entirely irrelevant, to offer an analogy from the cultural and sociopolitical sphere. We all know that when despots arrange for their militia to gun down citizens who have gathered in the streets to protest the deprivation of their basic rights, the tactic does not address the prevailing mechanisms that ensure they are deprived. Rather the 'problem' of this civil unrest is 'taken care of' with surgical military exactitude, precisely so that existing sociopolitical arrangements (in which it is ensured that some prosper by means of the deprivation of others) can be maintained. And we all know that when the powerful and wealthy offer the weak and the poor some ameliorative reforms in the social system, more often than not the reforms serve mostly to stabilize and perpetuate a system in which the powerful and the wealthy are able to sustain and expand their advantages. This was the conundrum cogently addressed by Rosa Luxemburg in 1899 as she faced the question of whether to push for reforms in a corrupt system or strive instead to overthrow the system itself. She questioned to what extent reforms, which may well have humane effects, also have the unfortunate consequences of impeding those radical measures that are ultimately needed. As is well known, she posed this issue dichotomously – either 'reform or revolution.'

Such cultural and sociopolitical analogies may seem overly dramatic. But I think not. Because there are serious issues here – issues all too frequently overlooked. Surely no one would deprive any individual seeking psychotherapy of its benefits. As I already indicated, no one should oppose the individual's right to seek the alleviation of emotional discomfort or cognitive confusion. So this is not a matter of being against psychotherapy (especially when it is conducted on psychodynamic and humanistic lines). Indeed, the discourse of psychotherapy occurs within every genuinely psychoanalytic treatment because, as previously mentioned, such discourse is a sort of way-station or set of preparatory procedures on the way to the uniquely critical discourse of psychoanalysis. However, the question to be raised concerns the extent to which the obvious palliative benefits of psychotherapy for any particular individual nevertheless hide a dimension of truthfulness pertaining to that individual's lived-experience. That is, one must be *against* psychotherapeutic discourse that fails to examine its own ethical and sociopolitical positioning – that is, a discursive procedure that presumes the criteria of improved adjustment and takes them as the end of the psychotherapeutic enterprise. In short, as a psychoanalyst, one must be ceaselessly vigilant that the process or procedure one is facilitating or invigilating does not devolve, sliding back, into the unctuous but reassuring 'truthlessness' – that is, the ideologically conditioned and constrained truth – of psychotherapy.

What is to be considered here is that psychotherapy involves interpretation and that there is a profound sense in which all interpretive ventures are inherently normalizing in that – directly or indirectly, even inversely – they foster the individual's capacity for suppression and repression in the service of accommodation to an oppressive world. That is, fostering the capacity to appear 'normal' or alienated in some 'adaptive' sense. In short, the alleviation of emotional discomfort and cognitive confusion may be admirable goals, but not if they serve the individual's further alienation (since his/her adjustment to an oppressive world is inherently the condition of alienation). The argument to be considered here is that the antidote to the inherent tendencies of psychotherapy toward alienated conformism is only to be found in the liberatory way in which the free-associative discourse of psychoanalysis frees the psyche from its repetition-compulsivity (and from what I have previously named the 'narratological-imperative') by acknowledging and addressing its inevitable estrangement from itself. It is in this way that psychoanalysis proceeds, as it should, *beyond* the mandate of psychotherapy. It is in this way that its discourse diverges profoundly and distinctively from procedures that are merely psychotherapeutic.

On scurrilous histories

So to explore further this *beyond* of psychoanalysis (which might also be dubbed *behind, beneath* or *beside*), the general philosophy and sociopolitics of psychotherapy must be briefly discussed. I will start with an overview of the history of psychotherapy, emphasizing how it evolved alongside coercive procedures by which individual differences were classified or categorized and then manipulatively compelled toward normalization. This will provide background for an understanding of the way in which 'talking cures' – by means of their ideologies of interpretation – can also serve the mandate of sociopolitical and cultural reproduction at the expense of individual liberation.

My working definition of psychotherapy – '*a special mode of dyadic conversation with the intent of alleviating emotional discomfort or cognitive confusion*' – presents an interestingly polemical challenge in that it immediately highlights the extent to which 'psychotherapy' might have potentially problematic connections with other modes of discourse. Most notably, it intersects with the ritualized interpretations traditionally offered as one aspect of shamanic practices.[7] However, leaving aside the equivalence between many shamanic traditions and the lineage of contemporary psychotherapy, there are other more immediate challenges. If indeed psychotherapy is a 'special mode' of discourse designed to change at least one of its participants, then surely we should be able to specify what distinguishes its processes from modes of discourse such as: the influence of advice-giving on the part of a teacher (or some other sort of self-appointed educator); the encouraging exhortations of a professional counselor (or a sports coach or your favorite role model); the expiatory impact of the confessional (or of prayer to a deity who may, or may not, seem to answer); the persuasive blandishments of a seductively successful salesperson (or anyone who flirts in order to obtain sexual or other favors); or, for that matter, the techniques implemented by the official in charge of a torture chamber (for, as we all know, a proficient torturer achieves not just compliance, but conviction that occurs through the conversation that accompanies the threat of pain). All these 'modalities' involve the skill of the agent administering the protocol – supporting the limited self-expression of the recipient and then the exchange of interpretations pertaining to the event. Although lopsidedly authoritarian to a greater or lesser degree, all are conversational and all aim at the modification of behavior, which in turn is an effect of, or must have an effect upon, the recipient's emotional state and cognitive repertoire. These are commonplace and frequently successful procedures that have the intent to change the recipient in the direction of their contextual reintegration, even if only for a briefer duration or perhaps with a different scope, than is typically the ambition of psychotherapy.

If we focus on psychotherapy as a formal professional practice that claims to differentiate itself from all the 'modalities' listed above, psychotherapy can be said to have emerged during the Islamic Golden Age from the eighth to the thirteenth centuries and was centered on Baghdad. This emergence is specifically associated with the prolific labors of Abū al-Rāzī at the end of the nineth century and Ibn Sīnā (known as Avicenna) at the beginning of the eleventh century. However, some historians have also emphasized the later influence of such writers as Rūmī in the thirteenth century and Hafez in the fourteenth century in opening attitudes toward 'madness' (at least within their predominantly middle-eastern sphere of influence). Other historians have claimed that procedures similar to psychotherapy were operative even earlier, tracing them back to Patañjali's yogic practices in the fourth or fifth century B.C.E. or to Guru Rinpoche's (also known as Padmasambhava) medical practices in eighth century Tibet.

However, as an elaborated formal procedure, with professional designations and literatures on technique, psychotherapy is usually reckoned to be a phenomenon of twentieth century Europe and America, with its inauguration marked by Freud's turn to 'talking cures' as they were dubbed by Bertha Pappenheim (Josef Breuer's patient, 'Anna O,' whose treatment was documented by Freud in the 1895 *Studies on Hysteria*). If Lacanian and post-Lacanian treatments are set aside, the history of psychotherapy subsequent to Freud's pioneering steps is usually described in terms of the development of three major 'psychoanalytically-informed' (or 'psychoanalytically-oriented') lineages. As already mentioned, these are: (i) the *ego-psychological* or structural-functional (focusing on the cognitive and affective ways in which the ego organization manages the conflicts it experiences between impulses, reality and constraint of internalized values causing guilt and shame); (ii) the *object-relational*, which includes Kleinian, independent and post-Kleinian or neo-Kleinian formulations (focusing on the cognitive and affective ways in which the inner representational world of 'objects,' including those pertaining to the self, is organized); and (iii) the *self-psychological* or social-relational, which includes many variants after the writings of Harry Stack Sullivan, including self-psychology and interpersonalist or intersubjectivist approaches (focusing on the cognitive and affective ways in which the self relates to others in its milieu).[8] After the initiatives of these schools, the practices of psychotherapy come to cover all manner of counseling and humanistic therapies, such as the person-centered, rational-emotive and many other approaches.[9] However, this definition of psychotherapy as 'talking cure' focuses techniques that are notably *ideocentric* (and *ideogenic* in their understanding of what it means to be human), which leaves out the special case of the modalities of 'body psychotherapy' that are *somatocentric* and *somatogenically* grounded. I will return to this distinction later for not only are the 'body psychotherapies' or 'bodymind therapies' of great importance for the future, but also the way in which radical psychoanalysis is a somatocentric discipline will need to be explored.[10] Thus, my emphasis in these essays will be a critique of psychodynamic psychotherapies, particularly the so-called 'psychoanalytically-informed' versions that appear to be closest to psychoanalysis itself. Also, the discussion will be limited to these special modes of dialogue involving two adults, a patient and a practitioner, and thus excluded, at least for the time being, are child therapy, adolescent therapy, couple therapy and group therapy.

My definition demarcates psychotherapy as a procedure for changing the patient's thinking and feeling by a conversation *about* thinking and feeling – a discourse or, more precisely, a sort of dialogue, even if a lopsided one, with the purpose of changing the *psyche* or lived-experience of at least one of the participants, presumably for at least some duration beyond the conversation itself. Potentially this seems like a comparatively humane enterprise. However, it is relevant to note how psychotherapy both developed in the wake of, and alongside, far less humane procedures for managing individuals designated as 'mad,' and developed integrally with programs for classifying and diagnosing individuals in order to achieve more effective mechanisms of social control.

The idea of a special mode of talking as the means by which to rehabilitate the individual within her/his social world is, in some sense, an extension of less sophisticated 'treatments' that operate not by dialogue, but by direct or indirect manipulation of the patient's physical circumstances and wellbeing. As documented in Franz Alexander's 1966 book and elsewhere, these include such 'therapeutic' enterprises as: incarceration (used somewhat systematically since the ninth century); cold showers or 'crisis induction' and various forms of hydrotherapy (known since ancient Egypt, but revived systematically in the eighteenth century); mesmerism (as an energetic procedure developed in the late eighteenth century); hypnosis and other induced altered states (known for centuries, but introduced systematically as a treatment modality by Étienne de Cuvillers in the early nineteenth century); 'rest cures' for the wealthy in specialized sanatoria; lobotomy (developed as a psychiatric treatment in the early twentieth century by António Moniz); insulin shock therapy (introduced in the 1920s by Manfred Sakel); and electroconvulsive therapy (known since the early nineteenth century but popularized in the 1930s by Ladislas Meduna). Other more sophisticated techniques of manipulative and coercive 'persuasion' also emerged in the twentieth century, notably behavior modification or 'applied behavior analysis' and cognitive behavior therapy, as well as the alleged 'wonders' of contemporary psychopharmacology that has burgeoned in the past fifty years and that dominates today's 'mental health' industry. This 'brave new world' also now offers the prospect of neuroscientific advances (to say nothing of 'neuropsychoanalytic' ones) that will enable medical professionals to intervene directly upon specific cortical structures (by stimulating or by extinguishing their functioning) in order to achieve particular behavioral, cognitive and emotional effects. As one young psychiatrist recently told me, 'soon we will be able to cure what people call "existential problems" not only pharmacologically but also by highly sophisticated manipulation of neural networks.'

The point of my listing this rather scurrilous family of 'mental health' treatments is to sharpen an appreciation of some critical issues pertaining to psychotherapy in relation to the contestable sociopolitical mandate that, for the sake of the preservation of extant cultural arrangements, deviance must be controlled (and punished). We cannot shrink from considering to what extent, and in what sense, conversational psychotherapy might be the liberalized extension of, for example, hydrotherapy and electroconvulsive therapy, and psychopharmacology along with neurosurgery (their neoliberal, and not so liberal, successors). This was Thomas Szasz' 1988 charge that psychotherapy merely amounts to a liberalized rhetoric of repressive persuasion. To consider such challenges, it is also important to note the historical complicity of the development of schemes by which to classify individual differences and the development of modes of 'treatment' for those designated 'abnormal.'

The systematic *categorization* of group and individual differences in emotion, cognition and motivation – the study of temperament and the like – has a strikingly lengthy history. In a 'western' context, one thinks immediately of the diagnostics of Hippocrates, of Galen's study of humors and of a lineage that extends to Franz Gall's promotion of phrenology, William Sheldon's somatotyping, the Jungian 'type indicator' developed by Katharine Briggs and her daughter Isabel Myers and Hans Eysenck's multifactorial research. In an 'eastern' context, one would think of ancient systems of classification such as both the diagnostics of yin-yang (and the five-phases) that date back to the Shang Dynasty of the second millennium B.C.E., and the wisdom of the Vedas, also dating back to the second millennium B.C.E., from which emerged the ayurvedic classification according to the three doshas (and the five great elements), as is notably articulated in the *Charaka Samhita* of the third century B.C.E. One could also think of many other eastern sources, such as those Carl Jung appropriated in the development of his archetypal vision.

Some of these sorts of endeavors may have been motivated by pure curiosity as to how personalities vary. But frequently such investigation has involved vested material interest. Those who can afford the ministration of professionals need to be healed of their ailments and, for many physicians, diagnosis determines the selected remedy (or at least appears to do so). Moreover for the powerful and wealthy, the capacity to differentiate between those of their minions likely to fight or flee, to work or to abscond, to obey or to rebel, has significant advantage. In the nineteenth century, studies of 'inferior personalities' burgeoned as an attempt to justify the racism of colonialist domination (as it had earlier done for the practices of outright slavery).[11] The contemporary field of 'psychological assessment' – armed with personality tests, interview protocols and sophisticated statistical techniques – then burgeoned in the twentieth century funded by the military-industrial complex and largely implemented under the auspices of academia. The corporations invested in 'human relations' departments charged with predicting who will contribute to the profit margin in what position, and who must be weeded out. The military needed to know who will function most effectively in what strategic positions, especially as warfare became more technologically sophisticated. In short, whereas the philosophical rationale for investigating and classifying people according to their individual and group differences may be broadcast as scientific interest, rarely if ever has this enterprise been without sociopolitical motive. This verdict extends to the development of the *Diagnostic and Statistical Manual of Mental Disorders*, which began in 1952 with a list of only 106 disorders but today, in its fifth edition, boasts over 300 categories and subcategories. The development of psychotherapies is quite deeply entangled with this history of psychological classification and psychiatric diagnosis. This form of psychological and psychiatric science may have made impressive advances. If so, they have been generated not so much on the basis of liberatory aspiration, but more on the ambition to predict and control the 'other' (as well, in the case of the DSM, as the pharmacology industry's greed for its escalating profitability). The rather fatuous proposition that one 'knows' a human phenomenon if one is able to predict and control its activities continues to reign within the discipline of 'scientific psychology.' In short, understanding the human condition and its suffering is not the issue underlying these developments.

Most psychotherapists would find this historical sketch and its implications quite objectionable or abhorrent. They tend to refute these comparisons in three ways. First, it is claimed that the *intent* of psychotherapeutic discourse is not self-serving on the part of the administering agent. Rather, it is rather designed in terms of the patient's best interests and offered only with the patient's voluntary cooperation. This defense is actually quite weak, invoking theoretical concepts such as goals of psychotherapy being the patient's adaptation, maturation, adjustment, integration or contentment – all of which will shortly be called into question. Second is the tenet that psychotherapeutic discourse is, at least in some versions, *co-constructed* by the practitioner and the patient in concert – the discourse of psychotherapy is dialogic, rather than a protocol imposed upon the patient regardless of the latter's wishes. This defense of democratization might have some validity were it not for the fact that both participants bring their explicit or implicit precepts to the conversation, and the contestive character of their engagement has to be elided. That is, both participants concede to a tacit set of rules as to what is 'obvious' and their dialogue is circumscribed by an agreement to make matters more and more obvious. Third, it is claimed that the distinction of psychotherapy is that it is based on *theorizing* – even scientific theorizing – about the human condition and how it may be transformed. This is a charmingly naïve defense and one that is ultimately bogus. Not only do those other practitioners (who advise, persuade, seduce, persecute, manipulate and coerce) all have techniques that refer to some implicit theory as to how to change their selected target, but most psychotherapists (and one can only express this as a rather rude generalization) do not have much awareness of the theory they are utilizing and next to no awareness as to the grounds on which this theory has been generated.

Procedures of categorization are not equivalent to procedures of intentional change. Yet the influence of the instrumentalist model of medical treatment – in which diagnosis must precede and preside over the techniques of treatment – has caused the progress of psychotherapy to be partially contingent on developments in medicine. Psychotherapy is inherently a transformative venture, and ignorance as to how the ailment might be categorized or conceptualized does not necessarily impede the effectiveness of its processes. Arguably the priority of psychotherapy is not classification, but *change*. As will be discussed, one can make the case that healing the *psyche* or 'soul' does not require that one knows in advance what or how it is to be healed. Indeed, in psychoanalysis, the medical model (diagnosis before intervention and the technical application of *a priori* theory), in which the practitioner must know something about the patient before treatment can proceed, is entirely irrelevant. Psychotherapy, as a conversational craft, can well proceed in the sort of atheoretical manner intimated in Paul Feyerabend's writings. However, in practice – in 'reality' – all psychotherapies are committed to interpretation, including those that vaunt their supposedly 'nonjudgmental' techniques. Only radical psychoanalysis is actually, by means of the deconstructive commitment of free-associative praxis, a genuinely atheoretical method. By contrast, the ideocentric psychotherapies are, almost by definition, deeply committed to the instrumentalist application of implicit and explicit theorizing. In short, they prioritize change as a procedure in which the patient's interpretations of self and world are expressed and then subjected to reinterpretation.

What 'self' expresses itself?

The value of self-expression in healing is 'obvious' – can anyone oppose the beneficial effects of expressing oneself? For this very reason, the proposition must be scrutinized critically. Known since Aristotle, 'catharsis' – the paradigm of expressivity – has always been understood as a purgative mode of purification by which toxins, as substances or as emotions, are to be expelled. The salubrious implications of this notion might seem self-evident, except for the fact that what 'toxins' can be expressed, where and how, is strongly contingent on the values of the surrounding community. Legions of what would seem to be spontaneously creative individuals have expressed themselves, only to be censored – muzzled or killed – for it. Clearly, the matter is not so simple that self-expression can be endorsed without deeper investigation. The conversational treatments of psychotherapy involve a particular mode of self-expression. Namely, the utterances of a 'self' are presumed not only to have an inner world of personalized meanings, but one that it would be somehow to the individual's advantage to express aloud or even in public. In short, the idea of psychotherapy becomes linked to the project of 'telling one's own story' – and to the procedure of having it 'corrected.'

It has been argued that this sort of 'self' is 'modern' and 'western' (that is, especially characteristic of post-medieval cultures of the North Atlantic). But this should *not* be taken as suggesting that there is no such 'self' elsewhere (which would be a ridiculous assertion). Rather, it is to point out that it is the colonialist cultures – cultures that have typically implemented enslavement or genocide toward whoever is 'other' – that have paraded the sort of individualist values that aggrandize this sort of 'self.' This is illustrated by the history of autobiography, as a genre of reflective writing in which the author assumes that the inner meanings of her/his world have – superior – qualities that would make them of interest to others and therefore to warrant publication. To write autobiographically also, in some sense, presumes not only the interest of one's 'self' but also the notion that one has, to at least some degree, determined who one is. It presupposes the significance of self-formation or self-cultivation (as articulated in the literary tradition of *Bildungsroman* and in Wilhelm von Humboldt's philosophy of education of the 1790s). Thus, autobiography, as distinguished from sociopolitical memoirs or confessional *apologia pro vita sua*, is a comparatively recent – and notably bourgeois – genre that blossomed in the west only since the early nineteenth century and notably in the wake of such mid-eighteenth-century luminaries as Jean-Jacques Rousseau and Johann Wolfgang von Goethe.[12]

The tenet that there is a 'self' with an inner personalized theater of lived-experience that might be worthy of reflection and dissemination – in writing or in other forms of art – is, in many respects, recent and it opened three ways of thinking about healing. First, it implies that our inner theater might be, at least to some degree, self-directed, self-formed or self-cultivated. That is, the person's destiny might not rest with the deities, or in the stars, but be a matter of self-determination. The individual is understood as, at the very least, having a share in the creation of her/his own meanings, and hence is empowered to modify or re-create these meanings. Second, the tenet entails the possibility that the personalized theater of meaningfulness is susceptible to interpretation and reinterpretation (either by the self or by another agency with whom these meanings are expressively shared) and this becomes key to the idea that a 'self' could be re-created advantageously. Third, with this comes the notion that the sharing of personalized experience expressively might have a specifically psychotherapeutic value. And this is precisely because there is no self-expression without (re) interpretation.

Freud's contemporary, Émile Durkheim, in his 1912 work on religious life, analyzed the social value of emotional sharing and emphasized how such cathartic or self-expressive procedures integrate individuals with their community and, by this means, offer them renewed strength of purpose and self-confidence. Catharsis and self-expression are thus appropriated as a means of socialization wherein the individual's idiographic meanings are reinterpreted in alignment with those of the community. As one of the three founders of contemporary social science, Durkheim was concerned with the way in which what he called the 'elementary forms of religious life' promote acculturation collectively, and less preoccupied with the internal effects of cathartic procedures on the individual. However, his research highlights the inherently (re)interpretive effects of self-expressive activities. Arguably, if one 'tells one's own story' to oneself, in writings that are never read or by speaking in the absence of an audience, the revision of interpretations that one has of oneself is likely to be tightly circular (similar to Anselm of Aosta's hermeneutic circle of faith in that one believes in the 'I' that understands and that therefore understands what it believes). However, as soon as there is an audience – even one that is wordless with its only ostensible intervention being its presence – we know clinically that a complex process of dialogical reinterpreting of oneself is set in motion. The interpretations of the audience impact the self-understanding of s/he who expresses her/himself, and these interpretations are driven by the audience's implicit or explicit theorizing.

This last point may be contentious, because some psychotherapists – for example, Carl Rogers in his writings from the late 1940s until the early 1980s, as well as other promoters of 'humanistic psychotherapy' – have prided themselves on developing conversational techniques that purport to be 'nonjudgmental.' These are techniques of psychotherapy that break with the psychodynamic tradition's proclivity toward offering patients – sometimes with alarming largesse – judgmental interpretations of their stories. In one or another vocabulary, practitioners such as Rogers propose that the individual's 'self-actualizing growth' can be facilitated by the provision of a psychotherapeutic relationship in which the practitioner warmly responds to the patient's stories with genuineness (the therapist's 'congruence'), acceptance ('unconditional positive regard') and accurate empathic understanding (a complex and much-debated concept, equivalent neither to endorsement nor to sympathy, yet having both flavors). However, much as the Rogers' solution might seem a salutary remedy to the browbeating tendencies of – shoddily conducted – 'psychoanalytically-informed' psychotherapies, the issues raised by the interpretive and reinterpretive dialogue are not resolved by the appearance of abstinence or non-interference. Genuinely expressed acceptance and empathy, as responses to the patient's self-expressed story-telling, are nonetheless interpretations of a certain sort, and the patient is likely to react to them as such. Compared with the licentious proffering of purported 'insights' that are the stock-in-trade of 'psychoanalytically-informed' practitioners ('perhaps you acted that way to avoid feeling guilt' or 'perhaps you feel your girlfriend is a little too like your mother'), the Rogerian stance of *laissez-faire* concern seems benign. However, seemingly nonjudgmental warmth – to give just one instance – slides into approval (*laissez-faire* can also mean *let's do it*), which is as much an interpretation as outright disapproval. The same claim of non-interpretation is sometimes articulated by art therapists, dance therapists and body psychotherapists. If it appears that I'm simply 'dancing my dance,' it may seem that my expressivity is without interpretive activity, but this is not the case. Not only am I aware of my performance, but I am also aware of my psychotherapist observing it. So although words may never be exchanged, a complex dialogue of unspoken interpretations is actually in motion. This is not to disparage the power of dance therapy (which I have greatly enjoyed), nor of the family of body psychotherapies (from which I have also felt great benefit), but rather to dispel the notion that it, or any other mode of self-expression, somehow escapes the problematic of interpretive processes.

The complicity of self-expression and interpretation is inescapable, especially if the performance is in any sense public. Even when self-expression is private or privy only to a psychotherapist, any act of 'telling one's own story' – even in a wordless modality, such as bodywork – relocates the actor within a community of meanings. The actor, the act and the audience, are subject to what I have named the 'narratological-imperative' (in my 1993 discussion of the way this system creates its subjects as subjected to it, created by it). Interpretation, within which I include all representationality, is ubiquitous and rarely, if ever, 'under our control.' Indeed, it is suggested that the 'nonjudgmental' modalities of psychotherapy may potentially be all the more hazardous to the extent that their judgments are denied or rendered obscure by their attachments to what is 'obvious.'

Thus, the thesis to be highlighted here is: (i) that psychotherapy requires the patient's voluntary self-expression (lest it collapse into a blatantly manipulative and clearly coercive modality, like cognitive behavior therapy); (ii) that, whenever self-expression occurs in the presence of an 'other' (or even without this presence), it is always, explicitly or implicitly, the subject of, or more accurately *subjected to*, interpretation, which thereby relocates the subject within a narratological community; and (iii) that all interpretation is inherently acculturating or sociopolitical, in that it integrates, smoothly or jarringly, the individual into a community of meanings.

The conversational passage of 'talky' psychotherapy (and even the non-conversational passage of psychotherapies that claim to be 'purely expressive') is inherently normalizing. Any treatment in which interpretations are enunciated and exchanged in a procedure of reinterpretation – that is, a procedure of thinking, feeling, expressing, with the intent that the subjects involved should come to think, feel and express themselves differently – participates in a movement of socialization. That is, a movement which implicitly or explicitly reproduces the prevailing social (cultural, political and economic) order. This justifies the venture of going *beyond* the mandate of psychotherapy. It is the praxis of radical psychoanalysis that claims to do this, simply because its deconstructive momentum interrogates the very law and order by which interpretations are generated.

2

FREE-ASSOCIATIVE PRAXIS *AGAINST* INTERPRETATION

If psychoanalysis, when engaged radically, goes beyond the mandate and the purview of psychotherapy, then it must be concluded that many treatments branded as 'psychoanalysis' are actually a prolonged course of 'psychoanalytic-ally-informed' psychotherapy that never engages an authentically psychoanalytic process. That is, a procedure that stops short of the radicality of psychoanalysis as engaging, almost relentlessly, the praxis of free-association. If this might be the case, then we need to be open to the possibility that there is something vitally important at issue here – a dimension of psychoanalysis virtually lost in the fog and mist of the discipline's history of just thirteen decades. Opening to this possibility is perhaps facilitated by the consideration of questions such as these:

- What if there are modes of meaningfulness that impact our lived-experience dynamically, yet cannot be known in the epistemological sense that a representation of them can express or capture their existence? That is, for example, a vital force that eludes representation yet impacts our capacity for representationality.
- Are we so confident in the sort of Hegelian assumption that everything that *is* – everything that we experience – can sooner or later be known repre-sentationally? That is, confidence in the assumption that all knowing must be confined by its articulation – that interpretation has the capacity ultim-ately to capture 'all that is' of our lived-experience.
- Could it not be possible that, for example, as Heraclitus would have it, movement precedes the existence of that which moves, and contradictori-ness flourishes dynamically within us in a way that takes precedence over the meaningfulness of the particular items that appear to 'contradict' each

other? Must we accept those aspects of the eleatic metaphysics intimated by Parmenides that posits the dichotomous appearance of 'being' and 'non-being' such that there can be no intermediary conditions (and the manifest presentations of our reality are either true or false)? Are we assured by the western metaphysics that prioritizes presence over absence?

- What if praxis as a method of listening to ontic occurrences – that are unthinkable, yet move within us – is a journey of liberatory healing? That is, a journey too quickly preempted by ratiocination, referential thinking and the narratological-imperative to understand and organize our lived-experience representationally?

- What if psychotherapeutic maneuvers within the realm of representational-ity – our attachment to understanding as the act of interpretation – actually retard the profundity of psychoanalytic exploration? That is, what if 'making-sense' actually forecloses listening to the restless forces of desire within us – desire that eludes the law and order that governs 'making-sense'?

Such questions may seem obscure, but this is surely because they highlight dimensions of the psychoanalytic process that are, so to speak, both pre-Socratic and postmodern. As such they elude the assumptions that have girded 'western' reflection for several centuries. However, these questions are germane to the issue of healing and to grasping psychoanalysis as beyond psychotherapy.

Exploring differences

As is well known, the usual way of thinking about the difference between psychoanalysis and those psychotherapies that are 'psychoanalytically-informed' is that the former is: (i) more intense both in terms of the frequency of sessions and the relationship between the practitioner and the patient; (ii) more thorough in terms of its investigative coverage of any and all aspects of the patient's personality; (iii) more likely to go 'deeper' in terms of those influential fantasies and motives of the patient that are, descriptively speaking, 'unconscious.' All this may be correct, but it is – from my point of view – an entirely insufficient and indeed misleading way to think about the differences between these modes of discourse. My point of emphasis is that the discourse of psychotherapy (which is subject/object, theory/application, governed by models of mental functioning, oriented to the reinterpretation of the patient's lived-experience, and so forth) is profoundly different from the discourse of psychoanalysis (which is negatively dialectical, deconstructive, prioritizing an ongoing commitment to listening free-associatively to the enigmatic and extraordinary motions and commotions of interminably recondite desire, and so forth).

Although I do not believe that engagement in the discourse of psycho-analysis is ever likely to be accomplished without the intensity of at least three sessions each week with at least forty working weeks in each year, the frequency of sessions does not, in and of itself, ensure that a psychoanalytic process will eventuate. There are treatments with as many or more frequent sessions that never get beyond the framework of psychotherapy. In terms of the intensity of the relationship between the practitioner and the patient, acute or immoderate emotional reactions can sometimes be evoked as much by infrequent sessions as by frequent ones. The advantage of frequency is that such reactions may be easier to address in a way that is helpful to both participants. In terms of the thoroughness and the 'depth' with which the patient comes to be understood and to achieve greater self-understanding, there can be little doubt that, by and large, the average expectable course of psychoanalytic treatment is both more efficacious and more effective than the average expectable course of psychotherapy. That is, more efficacious in terms of the eventuation of wide-ranging and 'deep' effects (but not necessarily in terms of the individual's fitting within her/his cultural and sociopolitical circumstances). Greater frequency can be more effective, if not in terms of the financial investment, at least in the sense that – to give a single example – a four-year course of four-times-per-week psychoanalysis is likely to impact the patient's life more dramatically than an eight-year course of twice-weekly psychotherapy.

However, these points are tangential to the more fundamental issue that *psychoanalysis and psychotherapy differ in their mode of discourse*, most notably in the manner in which they treat the stases of interpretation and thus also in the directionality of their cultural and sociopolitical impact. In this chapter, I will review the discursive process that is distinctive of psychoanalysis – at least when it is engaged in the radical manner that prioritizes free-associative praxis above all else – and discuss how it is different from any mode of discourse that is solely or simply psychotherapeutic. I will then suggest how psychoanalysis, unlike any discourse that is psychotherapeutic, uniquely empowers us to listen to the voicing of our erotic embodiment and to the deathfulness that lies deep within every moment of our lived-experience, our human being-in-the-world.

However, there is a crucial qualifier to this thesis. In the day to day praxis of psychoanalysis – however radically it is engaged – psychotherapeutic procedures necessarily occur. Indeed, any psychoanalytic session will almost certainly involve moments of friendly conversation and moments that are psychotherapeutic (and possibly informed by, or oriented to, some or other 'psychoanalytic' model of mental functioning), but it will also involve extensive periods that are genuinely and purely psychoanalytic. It is these that are crucial for understanding the necessity of going *beyond* psychotherapy.

Defining psychoanalysis

With these considerations in focus, my concise definition of (radical) psychoanalysis can now be rendered:

Psychoanalysis is a unique method of listening to the living and lived-experience of being human, the experience of our being-in-the-world. As spiritual-existential and sociopolitical praxis, it is a liberatory process that facilitates the freeing and the truthfulness of each individual via a dynamically deconstructive and negatively dia-lectical exploration of her/his psyche. The psychoanalytic method is that of the patient's free-associative speaking in a setting that offers the psychoanalyst and the patient optimal opportunities to engage in the workplay of listening together to the multi-dimensional meaningfulness of the various 'voices' that impact upon and reside within each of us, including the elusive, enigmatic, excessive, extraordin-ary, exuberant and unrepresentable voicing of desire that is repressed.

In this sense, psychoanalysis is not – the normalizing, theory-driven and ideo-logically steeped practice of – psychotherapy that priorities adjustive procedures of interpretation and thereby repositions the patient within the imprisonment of repetition-compulsivity and the narratological-imperative. Rather, it incorporates many of the operations of psychotherapeutic endeavors but, in ways that cru-cially need to be appreciated, psychoanalysis goes beyond psychotherapy. This is, at the very least, what differentiates radical psychoanalysis from the rather frac-tious 'family' of psychotherapies that today call themselves 'psychoanalytic' (and that house themselves within the International Psychoanalytic Association and other such organizations). Let us continue this journey of describing and explor-ing how radical psychoanalysis goes beyond therapy by noticing several critical implications of the above definitional paragraph.

In the italicized definition, the emphasis is on listening as spiritual-existential praxis (which inevitably has cultural and sociopolitical implications). This is a process of listening to the 'voicing' of aspects, levels and dimensions of lived-experience, some of which may be familiar but much of which may be 'strange' – alienated or estranged – from and within the domain of all that is familiar. I will later discuss the significance of the distinction between lived-experience as dynamically estranged or as alienated in stasis (the distinction introduced in my 1993 book). Note also that the emphasis of the definition on listening is deliberately not on understanding, interpreting or manipulating what is heard. Rather, whatever changes occur in radical psychoanalysis (and they are typically profound) are not only transformations but also transmutations that inhere to the very process of listening in this unfamiliar and unfamiliarizing manner. Again, I will later develop the distinction between a transformative and a transmutative change (which was discussed in my 2013 and 2016 books and echoed here in my previous allusions to the difference between reformism and 'per-petual revolution'). One fundamental aspect of this distinction is that transmutative change only occurs when the narratological-imperative, with its assumption that all that 'is' must be representable and thence captured by the repetition-compulsivity of interpretation, is methodically relinquished or suspended. But it must be empha-sized that the vocal release of thinking from the ordering of thought by the narrato-logical-imperative is not to be equated with some sort of regression into pathological thought-disorder. Rather, it brings speaking into a greater alignment with the energetic forces of our embodied being-in-the-world (as will be later explained). Here we must note how listening – in this radicalized manner – defies, subverts or abolishes the customary distinctions between inner and outer, within and without, subject and object. As will be shortly discussed, this is why, going beyond anything that psychotherapeutic discourse can achieve, psychoanalysis enables us to listen to messages that are *otherwise* than those that can be represented – the messages of our polysexuality and our pluritemporality.

Thus, psychoanalysis is not a discourse that is, implicitly or explicitly, directed by the values of understanding, interpreting or manipulating. It is not a discourse directed toward goals such as improved adjustment, adaptation, maturation, integration or contentment. Rather, the radical discourse of free-associative speaking-and-listening (praxis as changing-by-learning and learning-by-changing) frees truthfulness from its frozen state of obfuscated *alienation*, propelling it into a fluid dynamic of *estrangement* (again, this distinction will be elaborated later).

Notice also in this italicized definition that 'freeing' is a verb, an ongoing emancipative process. It is not some utopian endstate of 'freedom' (let alone the delusion or illusion of complete relief from all internally generated and perpetuated suffering). Later I will discuss the specifically psychoanalytic meaning of this notion in terms of freeing the patient from alienated repetition-compulsivity in psychic life – the freeing of desire from its semiotic entrapments. 'Truthfulness' is also an actively ongoing process of disclosure and acceptance or letting-go, facilitated by what might be called 'deconstructive critique' (which might be compared with the interesting discussion of these issues provided by Nikolas Kompridis). It is not some delusional or illusory arrival at 'truth,' as if it were a fixed and terminal state (of correctness, of correspondence, of coherence, or whatever). In what follows, these notions will be elaborated in terms of the psychoanalytic discovery that, whether we embrace our dynamics or not, we all interminably face conflictual and contradictory 'voices' within us, including the embodied 'voicing' of desire that cannot be adequately articulated as representation or ideation (and thus can never be properly subjected to interpretation).

Thus, we may notice how the emphasis of my definition is both on *inviting lived-experience to speak in the discourse of free-association* (that is, more fully than can possibly be spoken under the rules and regulations of logical and rhetorical transformation) and on *listening to lived-experience and its multi-dimensional meaningfulness* as the praxis of transmutative change. The implication of such precepts is that 'meaningfulness' can itself be a healing movement that frees the truthfulness of our being-in-the-world (but not in order for the motions and commotions of our desirous being to be ushered into the stases of representation). This truthfulness is found to be both erotically-embodied and subversive of the unilinear metaphysics of temporality. In short, this is a movement that undoes – and is to be contrasted with – the maneuvers of suppression, repression and oppression, which operate on the conquest of, annihilation of, or dominative mastery over, moments of potential meaningfulness that are objectionable to stability as the

stases of repetition-compulsivity and the narratological-imperative (which constitute the ideological reproduction of the status quo). The de-repressive momentum of freeing and the truthfulness of our being-in-the-world requires a method
that operates precisely against repetition-compulsivity and the narratological-
imperative. The latter are what binds the representational system together,
whereas free-association 'attacks' these bindings so that the kinesis of desire may
be freed, and one may *listen more fully* to it (a process which is profoundly different from the enforced procedures of hearing-to-understand).

It seems relevant here to recall that Freud insisted on calling his discipline psycho*analysis* and he explicitly argued against the notion of psycho*synthesis*. He did
not mean analysis in the sense of a logical analysis (contrary to the message conveyed by many ego psychologists), but in the sense of the 'analysis' done by
chemists wherein a compound is broken down into its elements in order for
them to be free to rearrange themselves.

In sum, the central implication of this definition is that radical psychoanalysis
is characterized by its prioritization both of *free-associative speaking* that counter-
acts repetition-compulsivity (along with the narratological-imperative) and of the
'workplay' of a conjoint, albeit lopsided, *specialized process of listening* both to the
flow and ebb of the patient's speech and precisely to the moments in which
speech does not, and cannot, 'make-sense.' As has been discussed, this is quite
unlike psychotherapeutic procedures that prioritize the role of interpretation, of
'making-sense' of that which is expressed by the patient, and indeed of 'making-
sense' in a way that rehabilitates the patient to a community of interpretation,
thereby improving this individual's adjustment to the dominant culture. I coin
the term 'workplay' because this process is challenging and often painful work,
yet not in the ordinary sense of a goal-directed task. It is also characterized by
the spontaneity and *en-*joyment (the 'finding joy in') of play, yet not in the conventional definitions of the term that refer either to a pastime governed by rules
and repetitions or to a nugatory exertion devoid of any ontological significance.
The significance of free-associative speaking, as what Freud consistently asserted
is the *sine qua non* of his discipline, warrants detailed examination.[13]

Against conventional approaches to lived-experience

One useful mode of access to such an examination is to consider the merits (and
demerits) of first-person, second-person and third-person approaches to the
study of lived-experience.

Third-person accounts comprise the normative objectivistic way of understanding the world. As is well known, the methodological commitment of mainstream
science is a sustained effort to describe and explain the world in a manner that is
independent of subjectivity. Indeed, many contemporary philosophers – one might
think here of a lineage from Wilfrid Sellars and Willard Quine to Daniel Dennett –
defend the opinion that *only* this way of viewing the world constitutes scientifically
valid knowledge. In this mode, the phenomena of lived-experience can only be

addressed scientifically if subjective accounts of experience are treated objectivistically as 'data' for observation and inference. However, objectivity is comprised of the – culturally determined – collectivity or consensuality of first-person and second-person viewpoints. In this sense, the third-person perspective is incisively described by Thomas Nagel as 'a view from nowhere' – indeed one that consistently hides its cultural and sociopolitical determinants.

Moreover, even within a particular cultural context, there is a crucially significant hiatus between the subject's actual experience and the objective account of it when treated as 'data.' Although not acknowledged by the hegemonic advocates of objectivism, the import of this hiatus is even more significant when the processes of suppression and repression are taken into consideration – as will be evident from what follows. In short, the third-person approach to the study of lived-experience has serious limitations – limitations that have been articulated by writers such as Edmund Husserl in 1935 and many others subsequently. In recent years, the general claims of objectivism have generally been under attack.[14] Specifically in relation to the exploration or understanding of lived-experience (as contrasted with the manipulation of behavior), the limitations of objectivism are conspicuous and profoundly significant. Indeed, the arguments against attempts to study lived-experience by means of objectivistic procedures are strengthened when we consider how lived-experience is riven by the processes of repression and what Freud called the 'repression-barrier.' The latter implies that subjective accounts are always ideologically distorted versions of the actually multiplicious meaningfulness of our being-in-the-world and this is necessarily the case if indeed the repressed eludes representation that might be shared and scrutinized objectivistically.

This issue – of the elusiveness of the repressed dimensions of our lived-experience in relation to what can be shared via linguistically-structured representationality – also indicates the limitations of second-person methodologies. Such approaches to the understanding of psychic life are fundamentally dialogical. They depend on some sort of a 'me-you' conversation aimed at the arrival at – or construction of – a shared set of meanings. Particularly in the last decades of the twentieth century, many 'psychoanalysts' acknowledged the difficulties in validating certain psychoanalytic tenets, notably that of repression, by empirical methodologies (despite valiant efforts to do so) and consequently resorted to hermeneutic and dialogical justifications for their discipline.[15] However, the problem here is that, while the me-you format of dialogical exploration, clarification and interpretation may elucidate those aspects or dimensions of lived-experience that can be shared, that which cannot be expressed in linguistically-structured forms of representation (by which is meant, that which is repressed) is entirely elided. The significance of this point, which will shortly be further discussed, is complex but essential to comprehend. Freud's first two decades of clinical experience with free-associative discourse intimated how a representation that is subjected to repression decomposes into the non-representational form of a 'thing-presentation,' which remains psychically active.

That is, thing-presentations persist and insist as traces, sparks or waves, *embodied motions or commotions of psychic energy*, which can be named *desire*. They 'persist' in the sense that they do not become inactive but continue to meaningfully disrupt the law and order of representable meaning, and they 'insist' as if demanding their 'voice' within the conscious and preconscious world of representationality. In relation to the latter, we must note that, in his 1915 essay on *Triebeschicksale,* Freud defined desire or 'drive' as a force that perpetually imposes a 'demand for work' (*Arbeitsanforderung*) on our psychic life. That is, desire compels transformations in the representational system, by a shifting of energetic investment from one representation to the next (despite the fact that no representation can ever capture or fulfill the excessive and exuberant longings of desire). In this sense, transformations concurrently involve the flowing (presencing or lifefulness) and the ebbing (absencing or deathfulness) of desire into successive representational formations. The important point here is that, if repression is indeed a decomposition of meaningfulness into embodied motions or commotions of psychic energy or desire, then a commitment to understandings achieved dialogically preempts the possibility of listening to meaningfulness that is repressed.

'Psychoanalysts' today almost invariably fail to consider this point, and thus they have abandoned Freud's distinctive discovery of the unconscious-as-repressed. Green, however, lucidly understood the significance of the issue, when he stated in a 1999 interview with Gregorio Kohon that 'in the preconscious you have words and thoughts, but in the unconscious you are not supposed to have words and thoughts, you only have thing-presentations … something that for us is very important.' The crucial significance of this issue must not be missed for it implies that when a hermeneutic, dialogical or intersubjective approach to treatment is adopted, the 'unconscious' that is thereby illuminated or expounded is not actually that of the repressed. Rather, it is the descriptive 'unconscious' that was known long before Freud's labors (as Henri Ellenberger and others have demonstrated). It is an 'unconscious' of suppressed representations that can, potentially, be fully brought into conscious awareness and explicated accordingly. It would be preferable, as I have suggested previously, to call this 'unconscious' the domain of representations that are preconscious or 'deeply-preconscious' (the latter is a term I have coined for representations that are either strongly suppressed from self-consciousness or that are yet-to-be-constructed and thus inaccessible to its current self-reflectivity). These considerations not only indict the dialogical tradition of interpersonal-relational theorizing, but they also call into question the Kleinian notion of 'unconscious phantasies' (as was suggested in my 2017 paper questioning Kleinian psychology). For example, Suzanne Isaacs' famous 1948 paper on 'phantasy' addresses psychic formations which, with the maieutic aid of the clinician, can be brought into conscious representation, implying that they were already in some sense represented or representable. That is, they were not repressed but deeply-preconscious. Green's 1974 paper offers a tactful critique of this notion of 'unconscious phantasy' formations. When the notion of repression is sidelined and the 'unconscious' reduced to its descriptive usage, what is the discipline that is being practiced? As Freud suggested in 1914, there is a sense in which psycho-analysis is coterminous with its teachings about the repressive constitution of human self-consciousness.

As is well known, Paul Ricoeur branded psychoanalysis a 'hermeneutics of suspicion' – thus amplifying, or perhaps vitiating, Freud's notion of 'analysis' as a mode of 'breaking-down.' Ricoeur's text did perhaps serve to indicate Freud's methodical departure from any dialogical practice that merely aims toward agreement between two persons as to the interpretation of their lived-experience after they have explored it together conversationally. Yet unable to confront the rupturing of psychic life between the domain of representationality and that which is repressed from it, the proponents of a second-person approach to lived-experience (the 'psychoanalysts' who embrace the model of interpersonal, relational or intersubjective treatment) necessarily ablate key psychoanalytic discoveries. They nostalgically adopt an otiose preference for a pre-Freudian 'hermeneutics of inquiry' and 'curiosity' – as Polly Young-Eisendrath explicitly proposed. That is, for a conversation that reflectively and dialogically explores the interiority of thoughts, feelings, wishes and motives. However, a discussion of these phenomena, as valuable as it might be, is not equivalent to a process of listening to the unconscious-as-repressed (and never can be). Rather, it constitutes a preference for cozy agreements and the investigation entailed by self-expression accompanied by the arrival at increasingly coherent story-telling and procedures of 'making-sense' that are dyadically concordant. From a radically psychoanalytic standpoint, this is surely a resistance to the rigors of suspicion implied by an ongoing commitment to free-associative interrogation. It is a historically regressive tactic that eradicates the key coordinates of psychoanalytic discourse.

If third-person and second-person approaches fail to do justice to the complex challenge of unveiling the interiority of lived-experience and the dynamic conditions of our being-in-the-world, if indeed such approaches perpetuate or leave untouched the repressiveness of representationality within our psychic life, then the first-person approach must be considered. What can the subject, the reflective 'I' of self-consciousness, know about its own constitution and momentum? But here, perhaps paradoxically, psychoanalysis encounters yet greater adversity, principally coming from the claims of phenomenology. Leaving aside the Hegelian usage of this term to refer to the dialectical method by which philosophy might grasp the absolute, logical, ontological and metaphysical 'spirit' underlying all phenomena, It is Husserl who launches phenomenology in the manner that it is ordinarily understood today. For him, it is a transcendental-idealist method of philosophical inquiry, by which the subject might arrive at the foundations of its own operations. It eventually comes to designate a sort of self-reflective study of and by the 'I' of self-consciousness that aims, for example, to elucidate the structures and contents of consciousness in their 'intentionality' (the latter is a term dating from medieval scholasticism, but revived by Franz Brentano, who taught philosophy and 'psychognosy' to both Husserl and Freud).

Husserl's phenomenology starts with first-person intuition and proceeds by 'bracketing out' (the technique of epoché or 'phenomenological reduction') all third-person and second-person information. Once all theoretical assumptions and received ideas are suspended in this manner, the subject is supposedly able to proceed from a descriptive psychology to a transcendental phenomenology. Thus it is alleged or assumed to have the capacity to comprehend its own foundations. That is, to grasp the essence of consciousness, the essential properties and structures of lived-experience – our perceptions, judgments and emotions.[16] However, if psychoanalysis is indeed insightful in finding that the psyche is doubly ruptured (both between biological mechanisms and desire, and between desire and our representational system) and if the subject of consciousness is thus, so to speak, always deferred or displaced from itself, then this subject's certainties about itself are surely not the vantage-point from which to embark upon an inquiry into the composition and the movement of lived-experience. Indeed, from a psychoanalytic standpoint, although one can only approach an inquiry into lived-experience by 'starting' with the subject, the 'I' of self-consciousness, one immediately goes astray if one treats this subject's apodicticity with any method other than that of an interrogatory of suspicion. In short, starting with consciousness preempts the possibility of listening to the meaningfulness of the representationally 'decamped' – exiled yet alive – dimension of our being that is repressed. Phenomenology is thus an egology without ontology. Radical psychoanalysis, by contrast, is *praxis*, understanding-by-changing such that the event that is understood is no longer. It thus prioritizes *being* and transmutative change in our lived-experience over the epistemological stance of knowing an 'object' (or the 'subject') in a manner that is ultimately static or repetitious.

Yet there is now a voluminous literature attempting to marry phenomenology and psychoanalysis.[17] It is a literature that bleeds over into approaches to 'psychoanalysis' that are hermeneutic, dialogical, constructionist, interpersonal-relational and intersubjective, as well as social-phenomenological, dialectical-phenomenological and indeed even 'heterophenomenological' or 'lone-wolf autophenomenological' (as discussed by Dennett in 1991). It is a literature that cannot but be, ultimately and from its starting-point, flawed (as I believe I demonstrated in my 1984 critique of Husserlian readings of Freud's discipline). Phenomenology of whatever ilk starts with the unity and integrity of the 'I-Now-Is' that will proceed to inquire upon its own characteristics and foundations. That is, it starts with the identitarian assumption that 'I is I' (no more and no less), located within the unilinearity of narratological temporality that secures the 'now' as if it were without the determinants of multiple 'past-futures' inhering to it, and it assumes the substantive significance ('is') of what might be no more than a roving signifier that is subjected to the law and order of the representational system (tossed about by displacements, condensations and reversals or negations). In short, phenomenology treats the subject as if it could be considered 'outside' the world, an assumption which leads to Jacques Derrida's dismissal of phenomenology in 1967.

Contrary to this 'I' that is not of the world, the subject that expresses itself is consti-tuted by and within the system of representationality (thus it is, from its inception, generated culturally and sociopolitically). The Husserlian project starts with metaphys-ical assumptions about the presence or the 'I-Now-Is' (or, in more Freudian termin-ology, the integrity of the manifest text) that psychoanalysis, via the rigors of its commitment to free-associative discourse, subverts. So in response to the question how the subject, the reflective 'I' of self-consciousness, can come to understand its own constitution and momentum, psychoanalysis answers that it cannot possibly do so by accepting or affirming itself 'as is.'

Free-associative 'attacks' on certitude

The self-certainty of the reflective 'I' of self-consciousness is 'attacked' by the discourse of free-association. This subject can only come to understand its own constitution and momentum by allowing itself to fall into – Freud's notion of *freier Einfall* – the flow that indicates the inherency of its own perpetual deferral or displacement from itself. To allow this requires that one accepts, at least pro-visionally, a double possibility. This is the possibility *both* that the subject of self-consciousness is never merely when and where it thinks it is *and* that the system of representationality, which spawns this subject, not only *suppresses* some ideas and wishes such that they are less than likely to emerge pristinely in conscious-ness (they emerge only via condensations, displacements, reversals and neg-ations), but also *represses* some ideas and wishes into the condition of a meaningful but unrepresentable dimension of our being-in-the-world. This is the possibility both that the 'I-Now-Is' as the presence that has beguiled 'west-ern' metaphysics might actually not be identitarian, and that the meaningfulness repressed from and by our self-consciousness into a condition of embodied psy-chic energy remains insistent and persistent within our lived-experience. *Provi-sional acceptance of this twin possibility allows the subject to give itself over to the discourse of free-association and experience with this discourse, and then more than vindi-cates these tenets of the subject's deferral and displacement from itself, as well as the doc-trine of systemic repression.*

To express this differently, one does not free-associate unless one accedes to a certain sort of ethical openness both to what is *other* and, more radically, to what is *otherwise* than what self-consciousness knows (as discussed in my 2017 essay). That is, an accedence (submission, surrender or releasement) to the way in which the errant stream of self-consciousness throws the 'I' perpetually into question, unveiling the way in which this subject is always deferred or displaced from itself. Thus, psychoanalysis 'starts' dialectically contradicting the pretensions of Humpty-Dumpty, who (in Lewis Carroll's rendition of 1872) had the author-ial power to know *exactly* what he was talking about (*this*, no more and no less), but who (it should always be remembered) ends up irreparably shattered into pieces. It 'starts' with the disquieting supposition that the subject of self-consciousness can *never* be sure of itself (and can never become sure of itself by any procedure of self-amplification). This is partly because, as psychoanalysis then discloses, it is little more than a transient signifier perpetually produced by the system of linguistically-structured representationality, but also because (as again psychoanalysis then discloses) this system not only suppresses certain representations within itself but also represses certain ideas and wishes from itself. This 'starting' with radical suspicion of any appearance of self-certainty is betokened by the maxim 'that which is cannot be true' (coined by Ernst Bloch in 1961 and ably discussed by Herbert Marcuse in 1964). This is the initiatory insight of psychoanalysis and is thus the *modus operandum* of its free-associative method of suspicion. To achieve a psychoanalytic process, not just the ego's organization but the 'I' itself must perpetually place itself under suspicion, calling itself into question not just epistemologically but ontologically and ethically.

Psychoanalysis cannot be aligned with any third-person, second-person or first-person approach to understanding our lived-experience, our psyche or being-in-the-world. Of course, it has aspects of both first-person and second-person applications, but it proceeds in an unconventional direction by its commitment to free-associative discourse. Starting with expressivity, description and a modicum of reflection, it proceeds by the momentum of its flow (in the sense of Heraclitus, more than the notion popularized by Mihaly Csikszentmihalyi) to call into question the face value, the 'manifest content,' of whatever the subject utters in the presence of the psychoanalyst. In this context, 'calling into question' means that, instead of pausing to make-sense of this content, the subject is invited to accede to the stream of consciousness – the chaining of representations – by uttering whatever comes next. Fundamentally – and this is perhaps the contentious key to the radicality of psychoanalysis – the healing power of this discourse is *not* due to its provision of enriched material for self-reflection and interpretation, but rather due to the way in unlocks the repetition-compulsive procedures and structures of self-reflection and interpretation, thus inviting renewed psychic energy into the subject's movement, rendering our psychic life more *alive!*

However, before this fundamental conclusion can be elaborated, we need to step back – at the risk of reiteration – in order to define the discourse of free-association, for there is a dual misunderstanding that pervades the disciplinary literature.

A major misunderstanding is the assumption that the sole purpose of free-associative speaking is as a 'data-gathering' means toward an interpretive end.[18] That is, free-association is conceived as the means by which information about the interiority of the patient's experiences may be collected in order for it to be treated as 'data' that can be interpreted – the idea that the content of free-associative expressivity is, in Marita Torsti-Hagman's terms, to be 'harvested' and thence organized into the syntheses of interpretation. Toward the goal of effective interpretation, such data can be addressed in three ways. First, it can be used for the patient's own self-reflection and interpretation. This is enshrined in the rather misleading notion of 'self-analysis' that was launched in Freud's correspondence with Wilhelm Fliess and later with Sándor Ferenczi (and is well discussed by Didier Anzieu). It operates on the egological premise that the subject of self-consciousness can come to gain adequate and sufficient understandings *about* that which it has repressed. The notion is elevated to a necessary component of treatment, especially after Richard Sterba's 1934 paper on the patient's capacity for 'self-analytic' functioning, and it is later enshrined in the writings of contemporary clinicians such as Fred Busch. Second, free-associative data can be used for dyadic interrogation in a second-person mode. For example, the interpersonalist clinician responds to a patient's statement by asking what further 'comes to mind' about the issue, and uses the additional material to discuss with the patient and thence interpret the significance of these contents. Third, such data can similarly be used for objectivistic third-person observation and inference, as if the virtues of psychoanalysis are to be proven by empirical investigations located outside the psychoanalytic process itself.

In this regard, there is now a history of research using recordings or transcripts of sessions as data for objectivistic research, by methodologies such as thematic analysis, examination of rhetorical structures, assessment of word frequency and so forth. This sort of research is well documented in a rather outdated anthology by Hartvig Dahl and his colleagues, which nonetheless gives some sense of this early history of investigation. Summaries of more recent investigations in the field of 'psychoanalytically-informed' psychotherapy are provided in anthologies by Raymond Levy and his colleagues. These lines of empirical research have proceeded despite Freud's blatant assertion (in the introductory lectures that he penned in 1915 or shortly thereafter) that the talk involved in a psychoanalytic process is necessarily wholly private and entirely confidential – it 'does not allow an audience and cannot be demonstrated.' In what follows, I shall defend Freud's pronouncement and even extend it by arguing more boldly *both* that free-associative process requires the presence of the psychoanalyst (that is, cannot be adequately accomplished by an individual alone) *and* that it cannot occur if third-parties are present in any form (that is, when notes are taken for consultative purposes, when recording devices are in the consulting room and so forth).

However, at this juncture, my emphasis is on an insistence *both* that the importance of the free-associative process is precisely not its provision of data for interpretation, despite the fact that one might try to use it in this manner, *and* indeed that psychoanalysis is not principally about the interpretation of data, whether in the form of recordings of what seems to be free-associative talking or any other mode of self-expression (projective story-telling, inkblot protocols, squiggle games, sandbox stagings, or psychodramatic scenarios). If the process of psychoanalysis were principally about arriving at effective interpretations, then indeed such techniques could be substituted for the labors of free-association (as has been argued by Peter Fonagy and many others). However, whereas such techniques may elucidate thoughts and wishes that have been suppressed and are preconscious or deeply-preconscious, they do not, and cannot, constitute a method or praxis for listening to the otherwise 'voicing' of the repressed, precisely because the repressed does not express its meaningfulness in representable form but rather expresses itself in disruptions to the representable stream of consciousness. To be sure, interpretation is prioritized in any psychotherapeutic procedure that manipulates such data in the service of the development of more adaptive, mature, adjusted, integrated or personally contented functioning. However, as I have already argued, this is not psychoanalysis, precisely because the free-associative process lies in the transmutative momentum with which desire is mobilized, rather than its use in providing material for transformative interpretation.

Another misunderstanding needs to be addressed, namely that free-associative speaking is merely a matter of uncensored story-telling or even 'free talking' as Christopher Bollas perhaps would insist.[19] This is also a crucial point. Free-association is actually more than a matter of speaking without censorship. As a means by which to introduce my specific definition of the distinctiveness of free-associative discourse, I will briefly review some of Freud's statements on the topic. The idea of psychoanalysis having a 'fundamental principle' (*Grundsatze*) emerges more or less as soon as Freud discovered his distinctive method and is very clearly illuminated in his classic 1900 text on how to excavate the meaningfulness of dreams. In his 1910 lectures, Freud refers to the patient's commitment to free-association as the 'main rule' (*Hauptregel*) and a little later as the 'fundamental rule' (*Grundregel*) of his discipline. Translating liberally from Freud's 1913 paper on beginning a treatment (and with my italics, as well as an interpolated comment about 'transferential material'), the following is the manner in which the 'rule' is to be conveyed to patients:

> The basic rule that the patient must follow needs to be explained right from the start: 'Before you begin, know that ours will not be an ordinary conversation. *Ordinarily you try to maintain a connecting thread as you converse* and you ignore all intrusive thoughts, feelings, or side-issues, in order to stick to the point – *you should not do that here* [my italics]. As you speak here, you will notice all sorts of occurrences that you want to reject. You will be tempted to tell yourself that they do not belong here, that they are unimportant, that they do not make-sense, and so you will be inclined not to speak them [here I would add: 'This will include all sorts of thoughts and feelings about me, positive and negative, as we proceed together']. Please do not give in to this censorship and speak them anyway, especially if you feel averse or reticent to do so. You will eventually understand the reason for this practice, which is really the only "rule" that you need to follow in the course of our conversations. So please try always to say *everything* that occurs within you, and try never to omit something because you are uncomfortable with it [here I would add: 'If you do at times find the rule impossible to follow, as most patients occasionally do, then let us use the experience to discuss together why it seems impossible to say certain things aloud'].

As is well known, in the introductory 'lectures' published in 1917, Freud addressed quite extensively both the necessity of this 'rule' and the ways in which patients *invariably* resist it. Interestingly, it is at this point that he refers to the patient's obligation as the 'sacred rule' (*der heiligen Regel*) of his discipline. However, by the time of his 1923 encyclopedia article, Freud almost seems to have softened the presentation of his *Grundregel*, simply telling the patient 'not to hold back any idea from communication, even if (i) he feels that it is too disagreeable or if (ii) he judges that it is nonsensical or (iii) too unimportant or (iv) irrelevant … '

From the standpoint of a radicalized praxis, there is a crucial omission in this later text, namely the instruction to the patient *not* to 'try to maintain a connecting thread as you converse' and this perhaps highlights the way in which free-associative speaking in the presence of a psychoanalyst engages a process that is more than a mere lack of censorship. Rather, it is an 'attack' on repetition-compulsivity and the narratological-imperative.

If one speaks without censorship in circumstances of complete privacy, there is a pronounced tendency to observe the rules and regulations that I have called the narratological-imperative. That is, the discourse moves – as one representation is transformed into the next by condensations, displacements and reversals – from one more or less coherent story to the next. Thus, an individual alone, who is trying to speak aloud the stream of consciousness, may indeed talk without censorship (at least to a certain extent) but will nevertheless 'make-sense.' A 'connecting thread' will be maintained (and thus a discourse is produced that perpetuates the repression of 'otherwise' meaningfulness). Similarly, if an individual is speaking in the presence of any audience *other than the psychoanalyst* (that is, in the presence of third-parties, such as observers, recording devices and the like) simply talking without censorship will not be equivalent to free-association as I am about to define it, because again a 'connecting thread' will be maintained. The unique power of free-associative discourse lies *both* in that it is uncensored *and* that it occurs in the presence of the psychoanalyst (and in her/his presence alone). From this radical standpoint, I will now define free-association concisely but in a way that radically extends standard definitions:

> *Free-associative discourse is the complexly dynamic process in which the individual voices, aloud and without any censorship, her/his streaming of consciousness in the silent presence of a psychoanalyst.*

The former part of this definition is generally uncontentious, although I have borrowed William James' 1890 terminology of a 'stream of consciousness.' Interestingly, Freud used this term in 1901, writing of the 'uninhibited flow' or 'stream of free-associations' (*der ungehemmte Fluß der Assoziationen*), but seems to have dropped it thereafter, favoring the notion of a 'train' or 'chaining' of conscious representations. However, the latter part of my definition – that the process requires the silent presence of a psychoanalyst – is often not considered.

The reason that a genuinely free-associative process occurs *only* in the presence of a psychoanalyst (and without any other audience) is not merely because this practitioner is there to address the patient's inevitable resistances to ongoing free-associative discourse and aid her/him in relinquishing them. It is also because there is a quality to the very being and presence of a psychoanalyst, as well as the ground or setting that s/he establishes for the patient, which invites the desire of the repressed into the patient's enunciations and utterances. It is as if, in the presence of the psychoanalyst and the ambiance of the psychoanalytic setting, the patient's repressed unconscious becomes more activated and the patient's defenses are more prone to allow the unconscious to disclose itself both in its opening and in its closing.[20] The very 'absenting-presence' of the psychoanalyst unsettles the hegemony of the narratological-imperative (and secures the passage of free-associative speaking from being anything like a regression into thought-disordered psychosis).

This double feature of the psychoanalyst's presence and its necessity for the patient's free-associative trajectory will be discussed later in this text. However, at this juncture, several considerations must be mentioned. In (radical) psychoanalysis, the only interpretive interventions required of the psychoanalyst are those that facilitate the patient's ongoing free-associative discourse and address the latter's invariably extensive repertoire of resistances to ongoing free-association. The implication of this is that there is no such thing as 'psychoanalytic technique' in so far as this term, which is derived from the Greek *technê*, implies both a craft of *application* (in this case of a model of mental functioning such as the structural-functional theory) and a *manipulation* of the objectivistically treated material toward a predetermined goal or endstate. Additionally, it must be noted that there is something almost mystical or magical about the being and presence of the psychoanalyst, as well as the setting in which s/he functions – not just for reasons of transferential processes, which I will later discuss, the psychoanalyst's 'absenting-presence' is unsettling in a unique manner that is essential to the psychoanalytic process. This is not believable unless one has been in psychoanalysis and it is what I will call *the otherwise otherness of the psychoanalyst* (which, as I will later discuss, is a significant deviation from the Lacan's writings on the psychoanalyst as functioning in the position of the *Grand Autre*). It is precisely this feature of the psychoanalyst that enables the patient to abandon the maintenance of a 'connecting thread' as s/he speaks. In normal discourse, whether talking to oneself or speaking to an ordinary 'other' or 'others' as one's audience, such an abdication of the narratological-imperative is not feasible.

The force of desire against the stases of repetition-compulsivity

Once the narratological-imperative of cogency, coherence, continuity, as well as all the rules and regulations of plotline and of 'making-sense' is, as far as possible, abolished or at least partially relinquished, the patient's discourse opens to what is otherwise than representationality – the motions and commotions of the repressed – and with this 'attack' on the subject's imprisonment by repetition-compulsivity, desire enters discourse with greater vivacity. At the risk of over-simplification, the issue can be presented as follows. To the extent that the patient cannot possibly abandon entirely the connectivity between what Freud called the train or row (*Assoziationsreihe*), chaining or concatenation (*Verkettung* or *Assoziationskette*) of the free-associative stream, the discourse remains within the rules and regulations of the linguistically-structured representational system. To this extent (which the literature has discussed in terms of the obvious point that there is no such thing as fully 'free' association), the patient's discourse remains within the realm of psychotherapeutic interpretation and the psychoanalyst must assist by addressing the patient's difficulties with, or resistances to, her/his commitment to the rigors of free-association. But to the extent that the patient relinquishes the connectivity mandated by the narratological-imperative, the grip of repetition-compulsivity is loosened and the repressed surfaces more vigorously within the manifest textual stream of self-consciousness. Desire is thereby restored to the patient's discourse. The implication is that, whether it comes from the patient or the psychoanalyst, interpretation (unless it is of the patient's resistances to ongoing free-association) is always an effort to close-down the streaming or flooding of desire into the patient's discourse.

To reiterate these points somewhat simplistically: If patients are merely engaged in uncensored talking, their speaking moves from one story to the next and themes emerge as each step in the sequence by condensation and displacement (which are the operations of metaphor and metonym, as discussed by Roman Jakobson) simultaneously both reveals and conceals latent meanings *other* than that which is in the patient's awareness. To some extent, the narratological-imperative is preserved and what is concurrently revealed and concealed within every transformative step from one story to the next are representable meanings that are held to be (or have been) preconscious or deeply-preconscious. However, if patients fall into free-association (Freud's *freier Einfall*), their speaking not only moves from one narrated item to the next, but also becomes more conspicuously punctuated, *as if randomly*, by the eruptions of seemingly irrelevant and meaningless signs or signifiers – a mode of semiosis enunciated by bodily phenomena or within speech.[21] Again, it must be emphasized that the apparent randomness of free-associative speaking is responsive to embodied forces, and thus is in no way equivalent to or similar to the expressions of thought-disorder. Rather, as I have indicated, the 'disordered' expressions of free-associative speaking are meaningful in a mode that is *otherwise* than that which is representable, and Freud clearly suggested that they are to be understood as the *'thing-presentations' of repressed desire*. That is, traces that persist within the embodiment of lived-experience yet are insistent upon the sense-making of representationality, like sparks or waves that are the embodied motions or commotions of psychic energy.

This is almost impossible to illustrate, let alone demonstrate or prove, except from within the radical process of free-associative discourse. I attempted to portray the process more fully in my 2016 *Radical Psychoanalysis*, in which a patient is described whose movement from one story to the next elucidated an unconscious theme (that is, 'unconscious' but only in the descriptive sense of preconscious or deeply-preconscious representations that are *other* than those owned within the purview of self-consciousness). The theme could be roughly summarized as 'If I am angry, s/he will abandon me.' However, the stream of this patient's discourse also intimated, in strange eruptions, a darker meaningfulness that cannot be articulated – meanings *otherwise* than those that can be represented. It is the capacity to listen to these, even while they cannot 'make-sense' that takes psychoanalysis beyond any psychotherapy. That is, what is now also voiced is not a representationally meaningful theme but the meaningfulness of desire, which can only be clumsily and entirely inadequately indicated (similar to, as Buddhist wisdom teaches, the finger pointing to the moon that must not be taken to be the moon itself) as a momentum both of the erotic impulses (and the polysexualities) and of the deathfulness (and the pluritemporalities) that lie at the heart of our being, our lived-experience.

What psychoanalysis discovers – that could only have been discovered by an ongoing commitment to the praxis of free-association – is that the representational system, which we commonly call our 'mind,' *both* suppresses meanings *within* its organization, rendering them 'other' than those within the purview of reflective consciousness *and* also, as it were, keeps the meaningfulness of desire repressed *without* representation in a condition 'otherwise' than that which can be articulated. Yet this condition of repressed desire remains active, embodied within our being-in-the-world. As Freud kept asserting, it never deteriorates into irrelevance. Indeed, it is the brio of our desire, and this is why we may think of the psychoanalytic method as *negatively dialectical* (as I discussed in my 1984 book) or *deconstructive* (as I discussed in my 1993 book) in relation to the representational system and its organizational law and order.

Leaving aside the rich lineage elaborated within the diverse traditions of Sanātana Dharma, in the history of 'western' philosophy the notion of dialectics emerges in association with the Socratic method, but was given its most systematic treatment in Hegel's writings, along with Johann Fichte's *Wissenschaftslehre*. At the risk of oversimplification, the positing of a contrary or contradiction initiates a process of sublation (transcendence or synthesis, by the Hegelian *Aufhebung*) from which a new position emerges that *both* abolishes *and* preserves the 'values' established previously. The Hegelian dialectic is thus a progressively upward and affirmative movement. In his challenging 1966 text, *Negative Dialectics* (which I consider one of the most significant and intrepid works of twentieth century philosophy), Theodor Adorno sought to flout this tradition by freeing dialectics from its affirmative conditions without foregoing its power or determinacy (that is, the way in which dialectical movement involves transmutative shifts not just in what is known and knowable but in the very *being* that undertakes such praxis). My argument has been that this is one important way to appreciate what free-associative praxis achieves. Free-association is, so to speak, a dialectical 'attack' on the law and order of representationality. As the self-validated certainty – the referential confidence that a representation means just what it is supposed to mean, no more and no less – of the representational system or 'ego organization,' which establishes what is known and knowable, is contradicted, there is a 'voicing' of something as if 'new.' However, except when preconscious or deeply-preconscious thoughts, feelings and wishes are brought into the reflective awareness of self-consciousness (and there is thus an expansion of the known), this 'new' is *not* an upward synthesis of representations (amplifying or expanding the known). Rather, the movement is 'negative' in relation to the known and knowable of representationality – a 'downward' rather than 'upward' momentum. However, it is a momentum that opens us to listen to an otherwise voicing of what is within us. That is, the negatively dialectical movement of free-associative discourse opens us to the enlivening (as contrasted with the dulling repetition-compulsive operations of the representational system) voicing of repressed desire.

The significance of free-associative praxis can also be considered in terms of deconstruction, the Derridean 'method' that critically attacks the metaphysical assumption of an identitarian relationship between text and meaning. This is another important way to appreciate what free-associative praxis achieves. This method refuses to embrace the self-certainty of the 'I-Now-Is' that is repeatedly posited or established in consciousness. It refuses to accept that the subject merely means what it believes it means, no more and no less (recall here the suspicion instantiated by Bloch's maxim 'that which is cannot be true'). Rather, it casts this identity into Heraclitus' river such that all the repetitious positions it enunciates are exposed for their nonidentity. The referential meaning of one story is belied by the next. As has been discussed, free-association is an 'attack' on repetition-compulsivity and, not unlike the critique involved in a textual deconstruction (which is heir to the Heideggerian *Destruktion* of ontological conceptuality), free-associative praxis thus exposes how there is always a mode of meaningfulness that eludes, exceeds and exuberates, in ways that are enigmatic and extraordinary, the domain of representable meanings and transformations of representable meaningfulness. This is the repressed momentum of desire that animates representationality but can never be adequately translated into representation. The radical praxis of psychoanalysis thus exposes the nonidentity of the 'I-Now-Is' – in its immediacy and in its compulsive repetitiousness – as well as the polysexuality or psychic energy of the 'is' and the pluritemporality of the 'now.'

The discovery of the free-associative method led inexorably to the doctrine of repression, as it exposes the eruptions of 'thing-presentations' within the streaming of consciousness. The praxis discloses how there is far more meaningfulness within our enunciations and utterances than the concealing and revealing of themes *other* than those that are consciously intended. However significant these latent meanings (preconscious and deeply-preconscious) may be, they do not exhaust the meaningfulness of our expressivity, for there are *otherwise* meanings – the recondite energies of thing-presentations that cannot be represented yet are deeply significant to our being-in-the-world. Repression is thus the unique discovery and the doctrine on which – as Freud expressed it in his 1914 'History' – the entire adventure of psychoanalysis is founded, because only by free-associative praxis can one listen to the voicing of 'thing-presentations' expressing the psychic energy of desire that is inexorably otherwise than representationality. However, what is unique to free-associative discovery does not stop there. Experience with this method leads us to dual conclusions about the meaningfulness of the repressed both that the energies of the repressed occur as the embodied desire of libidinality and that its motions or commotions are not subject to the organization of unilinear time. Both these features warrant further discussion.

Experience with free-association required Freud to assert that psychic life is not only composed of the inner representational theater of thoughts, feelings and wishes, along with its biological substrate. It is animated by the energies of *Trieb* or desire that operates momentously as if in between the materiality of biology and the representationality that we are accustomed to call our 'mind.' This discovery of the repressed as thing-presentations and the roiling motion and commotion of psychic energy – desire, *Trieb*, or libidinality – is thus a further aspect of psychoanalysis that is incomprehensible outside the lived-experience of free-associative discourse. The idea that psychic life is animated by the movements of desire (that can never be adequately or sufficiently realized by representationality and its transformations) prompts Freud's portrayal of psychic life as inevitably and irrevocably ruptured *both* between the material substrate of biological operations and what we are calling the psychic energies of desire or libidinality, *and* between the elusive, excessive or exuberant movements of desire and the representational system (our thoughts, feelings, wishes, fantasies and motives) that we commonly call our 'mind.' Desire or libidinality – 'drive' as Freud discussed it in 1915 – comes to be defined as a force that demands the transformation of representations from one to the next (Freud's notion of the *Arbeitsanforderung* of the 'drive'), but is never exhausted within representationality. Thus, there is a sense in which desire is inexhaustible unto death, thrives on its own insatiability and is – in Lacan's formulation – always 'desire for unsatisfied desire.' In this context (which defines desire in fleshly terms that Lacanian theorizing precludes), *libidinality reigns throughout our psychic life*. It is the roiling investment (*Lebenstrieb*) and divestment or dis-investment (*Todestrieb*) governing shifts within the representational system. These are the 'lifefulness' and 'deathfulness' principles that describe the movements by which representations are either *Besetzt* (occupied or invested) or *Unbesetzt* (vacated or drained of) with psychic energy respectively. Thus, experience with free-association invariably not only leads us to a deepening awareness of the voicing of our embodied messages throughout our psychic life, but it also leads us to insist – in line with Freud – that there is no psychoanalysis without awareness of the fundamentality of erotically-embodied experientiality in the composition of our human being-in-the-world. Whereas ordinary thinking maintains its attachment to the narratological-imperative, free-associative discourse allows a radically different mode of embodied meaningfulness to have its voice.

Contrary to the impression given by most 'psychoanalysts,' the discipline is not ideocentric and ideogenic. Rather, *psychoanalysis is profoundly somatocentric and somatogenic*, although not in the sense that could possibly permit the hegemony of any neuroscientific findings.[22] Free-associative praxis invites a special mode of listening to that which is otherwise than representation. But this otherwise expresses a meaningfulness that is recondite to representationality yet not equivalent to the materiality of biological operations. The repressed is – as Laplanche has so well formulated – composed semiotically of enigmatic messages that 'lean-on' (Freud's notion of *Anlehnung*) biological determinants but are not identical with them. This is the semiosis of libidinality or psychic energy, which leads to Freud's 1905 insistence both on the ubiquity and the polymorphous potential of our sexual life that I have termed our *polysexuality* or polysexual potential. We are born ready for any and every sort of erotic pleasure, for libidinal energy is literally everywhere – or at least, in the context of Freud's ambiguous insistence on its endogenous containment, everywhere within us.[23]

Tightly associated with the notion of the polysexuality of our being-in-the-world is the yet more daring notion of the *pluritemporality* of our lived-experience – this is the discovery that our psychic life is not simply divided into 'before' and 'after' with the presence of the 'I-Now-Is' poised tremulously between those ontological zones. What free-associative discourse exposes is the way in which the security of the present (the apparent certitude of the 'I-Now-Is') is actually rendered only by the repetition-compulsivity of the representational system. The 'I-Now-Is' comes to be exposed as being infused with multiple past-futures. The motions and commotions of psychic energy render the 'time of the mind' otherwise than that of chronology. The representational system indeed appears to inscribe our being within the narratological regimentation of clocktime. There is a past, a present and an anticipatory future. Every story must have its beginning, its middle and sooner or later its end. In our ordinary thinking, these have an ontological status such that we cannot conceive of them getting mixed up or alchemically conjured.

However, if indeed the salience of representations in relation to our self-consciousness depends on the motions and commotions of psychic energy, what appears in the present can be a past that is reconfigured or reinvested with the elusive, enigmatic, excessive, extraordinary, exuberant and unrepresentable voicing of repressed desire. Moreover, anticipation can literally be 'made real' as with the processes of dreamwork that Freud discussed in 1900, wherein past-futures palpably infuse the 'present.' If past-futures infuse the presentness of the dream, this surely occurs, albeit in a more occluded manner, in the constructions and organization of our waking life. Through experience with free-associative discourse, the temporality of psychic life is found to be multiple. The 'time of the mind' only appears Newtonian – as a single arrow, moving equably – when it is presented representationally, with repetition-compulsivity seeming to assure us of the probity of the 'I-Now-Is' and the narratological-imperative seeming to assure us that 'the past is the past' and the future is 'yet to be.' Against this simplistic metaphysics, the psychoanalytic method suggests how otherwise temporalities inspire psychic life flowing in ripples, waves, eddies, spirals and reversals.

In a certain sense, Freud first announced this discovery in his 1895 exegesis of the conflicts of his patient, Emma, for whom an innocent childhood experience became traumatic some years after its occurrence. This notion of *Nachträglichkeit* (elaborated over two decades later in his 1918 report on the childhood genesis of the disturbed experiences of the so-called 'Wolf Man') pointed to the way in which the significance of the past can be redone. Only the objectivism of a third-person approach to lived-experience – the hegemony of shared representationality – insists that this cannot be so. As is well known, Friedrich Nietzsche somewhat anticipates Freud in opening up this topic with his 1882 doctrine of 'eternal recurrence' (which greatly influenced Karl Jaspers' later work on temporality) and thereafter, in his 1927 *opus magnum*, Martin Heidegger famously shows us how temporality is a complex ontological issue that surpasses epistemological capture (issues admirably expanded upon, albeit in a rather different vein, by Emmanuel Levinas and others).

Specifically in relation to Freud's germinal notion, we owe much to Lacan's 1964 discussion of the Wolf Man's case. However, as Laplanche's writings indicate, the matter must be taken further. In addition to its general significance in understanding how our lived-experience embraces multiple movements of time, we may think of this discovery of *Nachträglichkeit* or 'afterwardsness' (*après coup*) as being a step toward a realization that Freud intimated, infamously and perhaps rather confusingly, in his 1920 essay, under the influence of Sabina Spielrein's 1912 paper, which was in turn influenced by Nietzsche and Jung. In the 1920 essay, Freud speculates about what are presented as two new 'drives' of life, *Lebenstrieb*, and death, *Todestrieb*. The speculation has caused almost endless consternation for those who seemed to follow in Freud's footsteps. For example, in the 1930s, it provoked Paul Federn to postulate a suicidal drive, *Mortido*, and Eduardo Weiss to propose a destructive drive, *Destrudo*. The latter seems quite congruent with the Kleinian interpretation of *Todestrieb* that emerged in the 1930s and 1940s as indicative of innate aggressivity, destructiveness and primal envy. However, it can be argued that Freud's speculations should be understood as leaning heavily, although not in a way that was adequately acknowledged, on Spielrein's writing. Although the idea of *Thanatos* had been discussed in psychoanalytic circles prior to 1920 (for example, in a 1916 note by Leonard Blumgart), it is Spielrein who wrote of the complicity of moments of destruction and creation in every eventuality of becoming. In line with this, Laplanche suggests that, when Freud posited what seem to be two new 'drives' within his vision of our psychic life, these should preferably be understood as the dual principles by which desire or drive operates. *Lebenstrieb* refers to the principle of *lifefulness* in which psychic energy is invested in our representational repertoire, whereas *Todestrieb* refers to the principle of *deathfulness* in which psychic energy drains away from representationality.[24]

This insight goes to the very heart of radical psychoanalysis, conjoining its discoveries concerning repression, the ubiquity of libidinal kinesis and the plurality of time. It is not only that human subjectivity is – to borrow from Alphonso Lingis' writings in the 1980s – 'deathbound' but that *deathfulness* pervades every moment of representational instantiation. The brio of self-consciousness – the streaming of thoughts and feelings in our awareness – is a manifestation of the flow and ebb of psychic energies. Every moment of investment requires a complicit moment of divestment or dis-investment – the deathfulness of life itself. What feels to us most certain, the apparent rectitude of the 'I-Now-Is,' pivots perpetually on the deathful kinesis of libidinality within us and does so until we reach the *terminus ad quem*. Experience with free-associative praxis suggests that only in the embrace of this truthfulness of our being-in-the-world do we become fully *alive!*

* * *

Let us summarize how the scope and the effects of psychotherapy are limited by its commitment to – its prioritization of – the conventions of epistemology. That is, limited in so far as its definitional procedures involve re-experiencing and reinterpretive understanding within the context of a novel dyadic relationship that has the aim, implicitly or explicitly, of the patient's improved adjustment in terms of the relations (meaningful links or connections) that characterize her/his both internal and external worlds. The emphasis of these procedures may vary according to the theory that is applied to the practice. Some psychotherapies focus on the relationships within the individual's functioning (for example, those involved in the ego organization's repetitive formation of compromises between the forces of id, superego and reality). Others focus on the relationships between the individual's internal representation of its 'objects' and 'self' (for example, those animating the individual's repetitious reenactment of patterns of dissatisfied longing and rage that inevitably come to color the transference/counter-transference interaction); others on the patterns of external relationships in which the individual is repetitively engaged (for example, between the patient and his social world, which now includes the relationship with the understanding practitioner). In short, psychotherapy involves understanding relationships within the context of a 'new' and allegedly different relationship with the practitioner. This indicates their limitations.

Understanding entails the interpretation or reinterpretation of relations between entities that are representable. It requires the capacity of both practitioner and patient to listen to what is *other* than that which the patient already knows self-reflectively (and acts upon routinely). This other is expressed only by indirection (that is, the meanings that are suppressed from the reflectivity of the patient's self-conscious discourse). Patients' symptoms or, if the presenting issue is more characterological, their 'ego-syntonic' sets of symptoms (which is a rough definition of 'character') already involve the reinterpretation of events from their formative past. In the context of a novel relationship (the novelty of which is somewhat differently conceived by adherents to ego-psychological, object-relational, interpersonal-relational and self-psychological models), the psychotherapist and the patient listen to the latter's expression of her/his thoughts, feelings, wishes, fantasies and motives, in order to reinterpret them in a way that has transformative effects. The transformative shift from one interpretation to one that is, in some sense, 'better' involves acts of translation conveyed in the course of the dyadic conversation or dialogue. This general description both intimates the power of psychotherapeutic procedures, but also their triple limitation.

The first limitation is that the procedure is profoundly impacted by the personage of the practitioner. This is the inevitable limitation of any dyadic interaction and it applies to psychoanalysis as well as to psychotherapy. However, there are perhaps far-reaching differences *both* in terms of the way in which the psychotherapeutic practitioner conceives of her/himself (for example, as exegetical expert who knows how patients could or should better conduct their lives, or as a more 'mature' individual whose maturity enables him/her to 'hold' patients interpretively so that they too can progress to greater maturity, or as an adjusted individual who can explore with patients their parameters of emotional and social 'maladjustment') *and* in terms of the way in which the practitioner does (in psychoanalysis) or does not (in many types of 'psychoanalytically-informed' psychotherapy) conceive of her/his task as one of voiding her/himself (as will be discussed in Chapter 3).

The second limitation of psychotherapeutic understanding – meaning the procedures of interpretation and reinterpretation of internal and external events – is that it is inevitably steeped in ideology. As indicated in Chapter 1, expression and interpretation are complicit (there is no instance of self-expression that is not already an interpretation, even if only implicitly so) and the act of reinterpreting or 'reconstructing' an interpretation is always, to greater or lesser extent, one in which the individual's idiographic meanings are re-aligned with those of the general community. That is, the community of discourse sets the – mostly undisclosed – rules and regulations of translation from one interpretation to another. The latter are ideological in the sense that they necessarily serve (again to greater or lesser extent) in the reproduction of the community's social arrangements and relations, including those that are inherently oppressive (characterized by domination and subordination-subjugation). Chapter 3 will offer a further discussion of this.

The third limitation of procedures of interpretation and reinterpretation is that they can only engage phenomena that are representable. Psychotherapy concerns relationships between entities (whether these existents are conceived as internal or external to the individual) and these entities must be rendered representationally for them to be reinterpreted (with transformation being entailed by the reinterpretation). These entities and the relations between them may be *other* than those available self-consciously to the patient's reflectivity prior to psychotherapeutic treatment. Indeed, this is the maieutic power of psychotherapeutic elucidation. However, the free-associative praxis of psychoanalysis involves not only listening to these other meanings and then reinterpreting them in a way that is transformative, but goes beyond psychotherapy in a process of listening to a meaningfulness that is *otherwise* than that which can be adequately or sufficiently translated into representation. Psychoanalysis not only elucidates representable meaningfulness but exposes movements within the patient's lived-experience or being-in-the-world (as well as the psychoanalyst's) that are neither readily nor ever adequately translatable into the transformations of representationality. Such a process implies that its power is not only *transformative* but also *transmutative* of the repressed dimensions of our being that perpetually evade representation. This is the transmutative impact of a de-repressive praxis (contrasted with the more limited transformative impact of a discourse that only addresses conscious, preconscious and deeply-preconscious material that is already represented or representable). In short, psychotherapeutic procedures address relationships within the realm of representationality, relationships that have been suppressed from the individual's self-consciousness, whereas psychoanalysis engages a de-repressive praxis that enlivens the individual by exposing unknown and unknowable energies that are within the 'beingness' of our being-in-the-world.

Can healers of the psyche afford to limit themselves to understanding only that which is representable and (re)interpretable, that which can be transformed as such? The answer, which is a central rationale for this trilogy, is that they cannot.

To achieve personal transformation through effective reinterpretations of our lived-experience is the Holy Grail of psychotherapy. It rehabilitates the subject but – as discussed in the previous chapters – all too often amounts to the personal adjustment of lived-experience to accommodate the reproduction of an oppressive world, the extant world of domination and subordination-subjugation. In a profound sense, the goals of reinterpretation are inherently and necessarily conservative – a powerful procedure of sociopolitical engineering that harmonizes the subject, as patient, to a profoundly dysfunctional world. This is psychotherapy – a series of transformations that cannot but remain within the imprisonment of repetition-compulsivity. By contrast, an ongoing commitment to the negatively dialectical or deconstructive impact of free-associative discourse subverts the transformative goal of interpretation, opening the subject to a transmutative process that invites the 'voicing' of desire and enables our listening to this recondite voicing within us. This is psychoanalysis going beyond psychotherapy.

Borrowing, with some modification, from insights offered in Lacan's *Écrits*, it is surely fair to conclude that because they understand, or believe they understand, a lot of things, psychotherapists imagine that to understand is an end in itself and that it can only be a reasonably 'happy ending.' A perfectly interpreted world of lived-experience, the sangraal of psychotherapy, would offer an individual the best possible life in the 'reality' of present circumstances. But this is an act of compliance to ideological falsities and it is not the directionality of psychoanalysis. The commitment to ongoing free-associative praxis is not *in order to* achieve this myth of perfect adjustment through interpretation. Rather, this commitment is to listen to, and to free the truthfulness of, the recondite voicing of desire. This is not so much a reinterpretation as it is a re-vivification of our lived-experience that operates against the deadening force of the repetition-compulsivity that sustains the representational system.

Thus, one should not necessarily expect the psychoanalytic patient to be wiser than the average expectable product of a reasonably conducted psychotherapy – one should not necessarily expect this patient to 'know more,' in the sense of 'knowing' exemplified by the knowledge we now have of the dark side of the moon – but one should indeed expect this patient to be more *alive!*

3

NOTES ON BECOMING A PSYCHOANALYST

There is a very serious question – although one which most 'psychoanalysts' will probably condemn as mere stupidity – with which we must begin these notes. Do psychoanalytic organizations, with all their procedures for the authorization of training institutes, actually promote psychoanalysis or suffocate it? The question must be entertained, even if one cannot arrive at a definitive answer. My personal impression, based on experience with a number of training institutes (both inside and outside the International Psychoanalytic Association that Freud founded around 1910), is that such training often does harm to the discipline as much as, or more than, it serves to facilitate the formation of caring, yet suspicious and free-thinking, practitioners. And can any genuine psychoanalyst be other than committed to being consistently caring, suspicious and free-thinking?

Against (trade) schooling

The advent of professional associations for psychoanalytic practitioners predated the development of formal 'standards of training' by a couple of decades. The most notable benchmark for the latter was the promulgation of the 'Eitingdon Model' in the early 1920s, which was gradually elaborated into the current tripartite scheme that, to greater of lesser extent, characterizes the majority of training institutes internationally. The scheme stipulates that for candidates to graduate as a 'psychoanalyst' they must successfully pass through: (i) a personal 'training analysis'; (ii) the supervision of several 'control cases' which means patients that the candidate sees in psychoanalysis; and (iii) a series of seminars based on reading the extant literature by which the candidate must learn the discipline. I will briefly discuss each of these in reverse order, because what I want to emphasize most clearly is how the ideology by which this tripartite model is implemented is almost always thoroughly and egregiously *pedagogic* – children are to be taught the values and practices of the preceding generation.

Surely no one disputes that it would be, at the very least, challenging to enter this field without doing some reading. But what is to be read and how? We are long since past the period in which Anna Freud could blithely, but sincerely, advocate that the trainee should read the 'psychoanalytic literature' in its entirety. Today such a recommendation would not only challenge the candidate with an almost impossible task and, even if the candidate were sufficiently voracious, the task would constitute an act of idiocy. The contemporary 'literature' spans at least over fifty scientific and professional journals as well as thousands of books, across at least four major languages (German, English, French and Spanish). But more pertinently, it must be added that this 'literature' is so riddled with banality and irrelevancy that one would seriously question the judgment of any candidate who undertook such an obsessively Herculean task. So the disciplinary literature is to be read selectively, but who makes the selection and how?

It is not unfair to conclude that many, if not all, training institutes across the globe have – since the 1940s – become fiefdoms with far too little interest in any impetus toward cross-fertilization. At North American institutes, the traditions of ego-psychological or structural-functional psychologies, together with social, self-psychological and interpersonalist approaches, have traditionally prevailed. In European and South American institutes, the object-relational (Kleinian, independent and post-Kleinian or neo-Kleinian), as well as more recently the Lacanian, formulations have traditionally been propounded with an equally exclusionary vigor. If Asian institutes are surveyed, one currently finds that they tend to adhere dogmatically to whichever European or North American organization nurtured their initial establishment (India and Australia look to the United Kingdom, Japan and China to the USA and so on). Not only does an external observer rightly question the nature of a discipline that is so fragmented. Theoretical physicists, botanists and electrical engineers, to give just a few examples, do not seem to segregate themselves into clubs and cults that routinely fail to read each other's publications. We must also question which, if any, of these *psychological models* of mental functioning (structural-functional, object-relational, interpersonal-relational and so forth) has much to do with *psychoanalytic praxis*, as I have radically defined it.

We might also consider how training institutes across the globe determine what sorts of individuals, in terms of their educational backgrounds, should be accepted as candidates.[25] In his 1926 essay on 'lay' psychoanalysis, Freud was very clear that the appropriate educational background for an individual entering the field would be the humanities – as specific examples, he mentions knowledge of the history of civilization, of mythology, of the psychology of religion and of the 'science of literature.' Indeed, the individual should – surely – have a passionate curiosity about the human condition in all its existential, spiritual, cultural and sociopolitical aspects. Ideally, the individual would be, like Freud himself, a *gebildeter Mensch* – the term used for someone with diverse intellectual interests and pronounced literary and philosophical sophistication. In this same essay, knowing that the medical model is objectivistic with a distinct tendency to treat the human being as a set of anatomical structures and physiological functions (a set that is hopefully, but not invariably, still alive), Freud effectively cautioned *against* medicine as a preparation for psychoanalysis. Yet, as is well known, what has been for most of the twentieth century the main organization in the United States, in its befuddled arrogance, barred non-physicians from training. The ban was eventually challenged – on legalistic rather than educational grounds – and this association has had to relinquish its guild interests.

But I ask: How long will it be before we challenge the educational appropriateness of psychology as a preparation for psychoanalytic training? One does not wish to condemn a discipline by generalization, but the rise of psychology through the twentieth century is a somewhat tawdry history (as I indicated in Chapter 1). It has been propelled more by the requirements of the military-industrial complex, even when implemented in academia, and it has been focused more on its technical capacity to predict and control humanity than by any ideal of emancipating the human 'spirit' from internal and external conditions of oppression. Its clinical arm has been the handmaiden of the discipline of psychiatry – the problems with which I discussed earlier – and its commitment to psychotherapy has all too readily been co-opted not only by instrumentalism (theories whose power lies not in an unveiling of truthfulness, but more in their ability to manipulate the object), but also by the ambitions of conformism and contented or quasi-contented adjustment to extant cultural and sociopolitical circumstances.

Taking a more general perspective, we might also note that the qualitative value of most university degrees has deteriorated since Freud's epoch (leading commentators like Richard Hofstadter and Russell Jacoby, as well as others subsequently, to protest about the decline of intellectuality). Today there is a yawning gap between the disappearing ideal of academia as challenging and facilitating the individual's 'spirit' of self-formation or self-cultivation (from the late 18th century, this was von Humboldt's notion of *Bildung* as promoting capacities to think critically about the sorts of topics that Freud mentioned in his 1926 essay) *versus* the reality of contemporary academia as the industry that produces individuals suited to the managerial and technical requirements of advanced capitalist production and consumption. The latter comprises what Paolo Freire robustly condemned as the 'banking system' of education, in which students are to be filled with information and technical skills that enable them to take their place as a serviceable cog within capitalism's economic and sociopolitical arrangements – structures that globally perpetuate exploitation and impoverishment. As Ivan Illich, Henry Giroux, Jacques Rancière, Bell Hooks and many others such as Jan Matthews – in addition to, or following, Freire – have demonstrated in different ways, such a system of education not only fails to address the needs of the disenfranchised and the oppressed, it actually bypasses the lived-experience of any and every student and, all too readily, it reinforces the mechanisms of oppression. In short, we are now at the point where universities have mostly become trade-schools and, as Adorno wrote as long ago as 1963, the human sciences have become so preoccupied with the scientistic delivery of the commodities of skilled labor and information (techniques and data required by extant cultural, economic and sociopolitical organizations) that they have lost sight of the human 'spirit' and its desperate cry for emancipation.[26]

Thus, there is a very serious challenge here. I believe it would shake up almost every training organization, with which I am familiar, if it were to assess the extent to which it has become a trade-school. All too frequently it appears that the central and most ardent concern of these institutes for 'training in psychoanalysis' is to perpetuate their own organization.[27] That is, to produce graduates who will secure and advance the institute itself. By their very constitution, trade-schools inculcate techniques – colloquially, a 'bag of tricks' – as well as objectivistic theories or instrumental models that are to be applied to the object's manipulation. This is *not* equivalent to any concern for the elucidation of the truthfulness of the object, let alone for the process of freeing it from its imprisonments.

Although I have argued that psychoanalysis should be understood neither as a set of techniques nor as an objectivistic model of human functioning, even if one does not accept my argument surely it is warranted to ask: Is the ethos of a trade-school really the way to facilitate individuals in their formation as psychoanalysts? One might hope that the answer to this question would be resoundingly negative. Psychoanalysis cannot be taught, only experienced (and thus assimilated). If anyone 'teaches' psychoanalysis, it must surely be on the model of Rancière's 'ignorant schoolmaster,' whose virtue of 'ignorance' serves the processes of genuinely emancipative education. Yet in all too many institutes across the globe, the attitude tacitly conveyed in reading courses and seminars is all too frequently 'you are not here to think or grow, you are here to learn our ways of doing things.'

This sort of problem is replicated in the second component of the usual structure of training, the supervision of several 'control cases' of patients that the candidate sees in 'psychoanalysis' – the procedure in which candidates review with a more experienced colleague their initial experiences being in the position of a psychoanalyst with a patient. Surely no one disputes that it would be profoundly and perhaps terrifyingly unethical to present oneself as a psychoanalyst to any prospective patient without a serious course of such supervisory consultations (although Freud's 1910 paper on 'wild' practices and his 1912 paper on recommendations for doctors practicing psychoanalysis are not entirely discouraging of such eventualities, as Todd Dean has discussed). Whereas in the first decades of the discipline, 'supervision' might amount to no more than a casual chat with Freud himself or with another of the early practitioners, today it has become a systematized practice.

In my experience, supervisory consultations range between two poles. At one end are supervisors whose attitude is that they know *the* best, if not the only, way to conduct what they think of as a psychoanalytic treatment. Accordingly they assume that the candidate's job is to learn to do it their way. At the other end there are supervisors whose attitude is that their job is to facilitate the candidate in becoming the best 'psychoanalyst' that s/he is destined to be (and perhaps to cue the transition into psychoanalytic functioning out of whatever previous training the candidate might have had psychotherapeutically). For the candidate, the former attitude demands processes of identification and mimicry, sincere or insincere. Such processes are, surely, rampantly anti-psychoanalytic. The latter attitude risks a deterioration of the discipline into the state that is already all too prevalent, in which 'anything goes' and any conversation between two people that explores thoughts, feelings and wishes, counts as 'psychoanalysis' (a recent study by Kate Schecter indicates that many 'psychoanalysts' are quite unable to define their discipline as anything more than such a conversation).

There is probably no ready solution to the inherent difficulties of the supervisory relationship. Perhaps one piece of a solution is for every candidate to have several different supervisors and for a course of consultation with any one supervisor never to last more than a year or two of weekly meetings. Perhaps another piece would to encourage more open discussion about the dangers of identification (even if this injures the narcissism of senior practitioners).

Training in psychoanalysis is necessary. I am not arguing otherwise. But it is crucially important for the discipline that it ceases to be pedagogically-oriented training. Rather, *psychoanalytic training should be thoroughly andragogic* – in both conceptualization and its implementation. The notion of andragogy, which was coined by Alexander Kapp in 1833 and principally developed in the twentieth century by Malcolm Knowles, is precisely important for its differentiation from the notion of pedagogy. The latter is a matter of leading children, whereas andragogy is a matter of allowing adults to lead – adults who are already seasoned learners in life itself – and, in this context, to allow candidates to lead themselves onto the path of becoming psychoanalysts. Andragogy is the process in which sophisticated learners question the assumptions on which they operate and surely whatever else 'psychoanalysis' might be held to be, it is the process of calling onself into question. Is there really any place in psychoanalysis for received 'wisdom' that supposedly has to be transmitted pedagogically?

In previous publications, I have written about the way in which *the main limitation to any psychoanalytic treatment comes from the practitioner's narcissism*. That is, treatments stall less from the intractable resistances of the patient, more from the insufficiently analyzed narcissism of the person who has assumed the position of the psychoanalyst. Narcissism is, in a certain sense, a failure to call oneself into question, whereas psychoanalysis – *analysis* – especially as radically conducted, is a process of breaking-down assumptions. That is, of perpetually being willing to call oneself into question. Unlike the syntheses of interpretation, this is 'analysis' as a breaking-down into elements so that they may be free to rearrange themselves. The 'psychoanalysts,' who are smug in their own assumptions, both that they know what's what about the process and that they know themselves, perpetually betray the discipline (despite whatever their qualifications as efficacious and effective psychotherapists). The process of becoming a psychoanalyst is, as much as anything, a process of coming-into-the-freedom to break oneself down. But this, like any other genuine freedom, cannot be bestowed by those who place themselves on high. Rather, it must be grasped from below and from within. In sum, the denting of the candidate's narcissism, which is a necessary dimension of training, should never be used as an excuse to treat candidates as children.

Genuine education (as in the latinate *e-ducere*) is a leading out of oneself, not a matter of being filled up – surely this precept is as, or more, valid for psychoanalytic training than for any other discipline. Surely in psychoanalysis, more than any other pursuit one can imagine, there is no place for received wisdom and no place for anything but a radical questioning that includes a challenge to all existing cultural and sociopolitical structures and movements – including whatever is represented by the ancestors and the elders. In this context, one must ask: What, if anything, would be lost if candidates in training were given license to forage through the psychoanalytic literature in whatever way they saw fit? What, if anything, would be lost if the only supervisory requirement were that candidates must meet weekly with at least five different supervisors, each for at least a year but for no more than two, over a period of a decade? These are merely suggestions, for the fundamental point is that the pitfalls of contemporary training urgently need examination.

The third component of training, the personal psychoanalytic treatment, is the most essential and the most significant. What makes a psychoanalyst is the travail of being fully a patient in psychoanalysis, and nothing less. With some caution and qualification, we might consider adding 'and nothing (necessarily) more.' Of course, this begs the issue as to what exactly it means to be a patient in psychoanalysis and for how long being a patient in psychoanalysis actual requires the participation of a senior 'training psychoanalyst.' The process of being a patient is – or should be – perpetual, whereas the initial period of having a senior practitioner listening alongside usually terminates after some years (even if 'going back into' treatment with a practitioner after the initial psychoanalytic treatment is, more often than not, necessary). Thus far, I have also begged the issue of training in radical psychoanalysis as profoundly different from training in some mode of 'psychoanalytically-informed' psychotherapy. I will return to these issues shortly. But in line with the plea for andragogic training rather than pedagogic, let us consider the point that Laplanche ably intimated in 1999. Namely, the notion of a 'training analysis' is oxymoronic: For to start 'psychoanalysis' *in order to* train would be like starting free-association with the intent to cover certain topics. The discipline is betrayed before even the pretense of embarkation. One only enters psychoanalysis because one suffers – a suffering inflected with a sense 'that which is cannot be true.'

Entering psychoanalysis

Whether one eventually becomes a psychoanalyst or pursues another line of commitment, entering psychoanalysis starts with the awareness of one's own suffering, no more and no less. In as much as no individual ever genuinely entered psychoanalytic treatment *in order to* train to become a practitioner, there is something inherently spurious about 'filling out an application' to be accepted into a training institute. One way to grasp this point is to insist that psychoanalysis is *not* a career (nor in many respects a profession). *Psychoanalysis is a calling* – a calling to a unique way of life.

This notion of a 'calling' is complex and requires qualification. Traditionally, the term seems tied to the priesthood and the authoritarianism in which almost all clerical training is steeped. The value of the term is the implication that one is 'called' *as if from elsewhere*. Priests – pastors, rabbis, imams and all manner of non-Abrahamic practitioners – are supposedly 'called' to their life's travail by the deity, even when such a 'calling' seems pedestrian rather than epiphanous. One is 'called' into psychoanalysis fundamentally by a sense of one's innermost suffering that comes as if from 'elsewhere.' But this is a special sort of 'elsewhere' because, if one is convinced that 'someone or something else is to blame,' then one should avoid entering the psychoanalyst's consulting room. Indeed, if one merely wants to be a 'happier soul' – the *belle âme* or 'good citizen' – whose adjustment, adaptation, maturation, integration and general contentment need to be, and hopefully will eventually have been, improved by some mode of intervention, one goes into psychotherapy *and* one ensures that it never becomes too psychoanalytic!

Psychoanalysis is a challenging path of truthfulness as a momentum of freeing. It is scarcely pabulum for contentment within a world assumed to remain 'as it is.' As I have discussed previously, there are five criteria to be met before starting a psychoanalytic treatment and it is the task of the psychoanalyst to assess whether the prospective patient meets them.[28] Only when one's – initial – psychoanalytic treatment nears some point of termination can one possibly know in any real way whether one is 'called.' In this sense, the only significant issue in determining who becomes a psychoanalyst and who does not is the *ethical integrity* of those who claim to be called to this path. This is, of course, largely the sort of issue that almost entirely evades external assessment – which is why one might be skeptical of so many institutional 'admissions procedures.'

In terms of affiliation with a training institute, if there then has to be some sort of application interview, I would suggest that applicants be asked to account for their 'calling' exclusively by describing its determinants at the generational level of their grandparents. This is an interesting exercise – everyone has or had at least four grandparents, even if one never met them, and who they are or were has much to tell about each of us, particularly in relation to any 'explanation' as to why we need to become psychoanalysts. The proverbial 'Tom, Dick and Harry' can always expatiate on the shortcomings of their parental caretakers and the traumas of their childhood. But to understand how the suffering of psychic life has passed to them intergenerationally – and is now being perpetuated by each of us internally – is a challenge that elicits the capacity, or lack of capacity, to think about the realities of psychic life in a way that might permit functioning as a psychoanalyst. Are there other criteria to be assessed in such an interview? I would suggest three:

(i) That the applicant offer substantial evidence of strong curiosity not only about her/his intrapsychic and interpersonal life, but about all the behavioral varieties of human life including – most of all – the many varieties of human erotics. Perhaps every applicant should be able to present an extended personal response to Thich Nhat Hanh's memorable poem, 'Call Me by my True Names.'[29] I specifically would not accept any applicant who seems sexually inhibited – for example to the point where s/he seems reluctant to contemplate the possibility of finding any particular erotic impulse within her/himself.

(ii) That – whatever their bourgeois background – applicants should have performed manual labor for at least a year. I do not mean this facetiously. There is something about any avoidance of those tasks that are the daily burden of the working-class that seems to ensconce 'psychoanalysts' in value systems that are an anathema to psychoanalytic practice. Perhaps the same principle formulated more broadly would be that applicants should be committed to freeing themselves from tribal affiliations (even though most of us retain, hopefully with a sense of dis-ease, the residue of nostalgia for such attachments). Just as I would be very wary, to say the least, of any applicant who seems avariciously committed to bourgeois life, I would vote against individuals who are unquestioning of, or in any way comfortable with, their patriotic sentiments, their religious dogmas, or their ethnic and racial allegiances.

(iii) That the applicant offer substantial evidence of strong curiosity about what are loosely called altered or different 'states of consciousness.' By this I mean not only the madness within each of us, as well as that of those who are condemned as mad (and customarily confined or incarcerated for this reason), but also a curiosity about states of consciousness that are accessible in other ways. I would be suspicious of any applicant who has not tried to experiment with different modes of artistic or sensual expression (whatever the wealth or paucity of the results of such experimentation). In our contemporary world, I might even be suspicious of any applicant who has not, out of fear, experimented at least minimally with drug-induced states (from alcohol to hallucinogens), as well as different modes of meditation. However, the addict in active practice is unlikely to succeed as a psychoanalyst. As an aside, it must surely be noted that the most pernicious and prevalent human addiction is arguably our attachment to what can aptly be called our 'egotism.' Almost all of us are still tied, to greater or lesser degree, to this addiction and it is the one that most commonly impedes success in psychoanalysis. In any event, I would also be suspicious of any applicant who does not enter with enthusiasm into experiences such as occasional states of reverie, the opportunity to do 'improv' and other forms of acting that invite us to 'get out of ourselves,' or the dissolutive states that occur when one spends an hour in a sensory-deprivation tank. I suggest these merely as a few examples.

To return to my emphasis on psychoanalysis as a calling, it must be noted that no ordination is relevant. Graduation from a training institute does not make one a psychoanalyst. From this standpoint, there are many who graduate, few who grasp the profound difference between 'psychoanalytically-informed' psychotherapy and psychoanalysis. Equally, there may be psychoanalysts who never graduated from an institute training – individuals who underwent a full course of psychoanalysis, who sought supervision from senior practitioners, and who directed their own curriculum of study. It is important to acknowledge this, because authorization to become a psychoanalyst is not, and cannot be, the prerogative merely of a convocation of those who regard themselves as 'Training Analysts,' nor of any organization such as the International Psychoanalytic Association, the International Federation of Psychoanalytic Societies, the World Association of Psychoanalysis and so forth.

Perhaps one can become a 'psychoanalytically-informed' psychotherapist by book learning. Perhaps one can become an aficionado of all the theoretical models that comprise the field of 'psychoanalytically-oriented' psychology. But one cannot become a psychoanalyst by these means. In sum, at this juncture, there is a threefold conclusion:

(i) The process of becoming a psychoanalyst is a calling as if from 'elsewhere.' That is, from the depths of psychic life. The calling only occurs in the course of being a psychoanalytic patient and thereafter it has no point of arrival, because the process of being a psychoanalyst is the perpetual movement of becoming a psychoanalyst.

(ii) Becoming a psychoanalyst is not to be considered a matter of training in the manner that one trains to be an electrician, a literary critic or an astrophysicist – again precisely because it is a calling.

(iii) One responds to this calling but only refers to oneself as a psychoanalyst as an internal process transitions from being a patient in psychoanalysis to being a psychoanalytic patient who is now ready to function as a psychoanalyst. This warrants further discussion.

Psychoanalysis and the sense of transition

I have questioned the pedagogic commitments of training under the auspices of authorized institutes and concomitantly I have challenged the authoritarian precept that one becomes a psychoanalyst by the judgment of the elders or the ancestors. As will be discussed shortly, I also oppose (although not without some sympathy) the idea that anyone should be able to claim this title or that candidates should imagine they have the consciously-held and thus inevitably narcisstically-driven authority to graduate themselves. But all these arguments pivot on questions about what it means to undertake a personal psychoanalysis that – while not being the delusional or illusory entity often called a 'training analysis' – is nevertheless a process of being a patient that eventuates in becoming, or more accurately starting-to-become, a psychoanalyst. At the risk of reiterating ideas that have been covered earlier in this text (as well as in previous two volumes of this trilogy), we should focus here on what is essential *experientially* to the process of undertaking and perpetually re-undertaking the challenge of being a patient in psychoanalysis.

I have emphasized that, unlike psychotherapy, psychoanalysis is not a procedure of coming to believe that one knows something definitive about oneself. Rather, it proceeds through the psychotherapeutic domain into a process *beyond*, in which one is willing to call oneself perpetually into question. To riff on T. S. Eliot's *Little Gidding*, anything that appears as an interpretive end is merely the beginning of further interrogation. In sum (if one were to explain psychoanalysis to lay persons), one would *not* say that psychoanalysis is the way of coming to know the unconscious because the unconscious can never be represented (although indeed we do get to know themes that are preconscious and deeply so). Rather, one would say that psychoanalysis is the unique way of listening to profoundly significant voices within oneself that decline to be heard (that are elusive, enigmatic, excessive, extraordinary, exuberant in relation to that which can be heard, in the sense of represented). Psychoanalysis is a radical mode of listening to what is other and otherwise than the formulations of self-consciousness and, as such, is profoundly different from the logical and rhetorical procedure of 'hearing-to-understand.' It is this unique process of listening that takes (radical) psychoanalysis beyond, indeed way beyond, the prerogatives of what can be heard, represented and thus allegedly comprehended. It is to this that one is called.

It is, of course, the individual's experience in psychoanalysis that may, or may not, facilitate her/his becoming a psychoanalyst. In the course of psychoanalysis, there is — for some but not all — a sense of transitioning from simply being a patient in psychoanalysis to being a psychoanalytic patient on the path of becoming a psychoanalyst. In short, one starts as patient, one finds oneself a patient-candidate and one eventually becomes a patient-psychoanalyst (my emphasis on the interminability of understanding oneself as a patient in the process is deliberate). In this trajectory, so much depends on who the individual's psychoanalysts, the 'Training Analysts' (obviously there is sometimes only one, although many trainees find themselves engaged in more than one personal treatment), are and how they conduct themselves in relation to their patient. What seems crucial is *both* the Training Analyst's grasp of the difference between psychoanalysis and 'psychoanalytically-informed' psychotherapy (many who hold the title of 'Training Analyst' have long since lost any grip they ever had on this distinction), *and* her/his latent attitudes toward the patient as a prospective candidate and thence as a prospective psychoanalyst, who may become a collegial peer.[30]

One is in psychoanalysis and one is — perhaps — called to become a practitioner. These internal — although discussable — processes of subtle transition should be distinguished from the infamous but brief Lacanian experiment with the *'passe'* (the step of declaring one's desire to be a psychoanalyst). Brought into effect in 1967, shortly after the founding of the *École Freudienne de Paris* in 1964, the *passe* was essentially a mechanism that permitted candidates to decide when to graduate themselves. As I have already indicated, the major millstone that limits the power of psychoanalysis is the unanalyzed narcissism of the psychoanalyst. Becoming a psychoanalyst is or should be, in large measure, the beginning of a perpetual process of breaking-down assumptions that are the fabric of narcissism. However, the wiles of human narcissism are devious and almost almighty. So, although it is disastrously anti-psychoanalytic to imagine that the power to graduate candidates should lie merely within the authority of some 'graduation committee' of designated 'Training Analysts,' it is perhaps an even greater disaster to imagine that the power to 'graduate' should rest with candidates themselves. The Lacanian experiment, however righteously conceived in the optimism of giddily revolutionary times throughout Europe and North America, is and was – perhaps predictably – a failure.

Nonetheless, there is a crucial internal process involved in moving from being a patient in psychoanalysis to being a psychoanalytic patient who becomes ready to function as a psychoanalyst. For the sake of the future of the discipline, it needs far more discussion than it has yet received (by which I mean not only in this trilogy, but by and between all of those who cherish the discipline). I suggest that this process cannot be the '*passe*,' although perhaps it is not entirely unlike the internal developments that this mechanism was intended to mark. What happens as patient becomes patient-candidate is more like a process of *ça te fait venir!* That is, *it happens!* (at least to some). Again the calling is *as if from elsewhere*. It is as if from 'elsewhere' that the patient and the psychoanalyst come to know, most mysteriously and almost mystically, that the former, the patient, is ready to take the chair behind her/his own patients on the couch. But before this can be discussed in any further detail, more must be said – even at the risk of reiteration – about the experience of being a psychoanalytic patient as contrasted with that of being in a 'psychoanalytically-informed' psychotherapy.

As has been expounded, whereas psychotherapies involve theories of mental functioning associated with techniques that can be taught, psychoanalysis involves neither such theoretical constructions nor techniques. Although a treatment may pass through all sorts of phases that are psychotherapeutic, if it is really psychoanalysis (in the radical sense expounded in this trilogy), the patient will sooner or later realize that the process is more about the problematization of whatever is taken to be self-knowledge, more about the free-associative dismantling of understanding and more about listening to the restless motions and commotions of desire, than it is about any arrival at interpretations. Psychotherapeutic discourse aims to arrive and is thus inherently normalizing. The repetition-compulsivity of interpretation is required and serves to reposition the subject within a community of interpretation (as discussed in Chapter 1). By contrast, psychoanalysis is a spiritual-existential process of opening to the recondite depths of our lived-experience, by the deconstructive or negatively dialectical impact of free-associative discourse, and listening (opening-and-listening-and ...) not only to what is other, but also and perhaps more significantly to what is otherwise than the interpretable. In psychoanalysis, there is no fantasy about 'normality' that is not to be called into question.[31]

It should be again noted here how psychoanalysis stands against psychosynthesis (as Freud wrote unequivocally to Jung on April 16th 1909), and an interpretation is by definition an integrative mode of synthesis. Freud following this declaration by explaining, in his 1919 paper by suggesting how, in their 'workplaying' together, the psychoanalyst and the patient need not concern themselves with matters of synthesis. Psychoanalysis is a journey of decomposition that frees the 'elements,' as it were, to rearrange themselves. Although never elaborated in his writings, Freud (at least in the first two decades of his psychoanalytic praxis) can be read as intimating a clear sense of the distinction between psychoanalysis and psychotherapy. Even in the undelivered lectures of 1933, while hailing the successes of psychoanalysis, he announced that he had 'never been a therapeutic enthusiast' and one can only wonder what the full implications of such a statement may have been. However, a reading of his two main essays in 1937, written as he approached his death, suggests that by that time he had more or less lost any sense of the possible distinction between psychoanalysis and psychotherapy.

So, the answer to the crucial question (which is, 'what occurs when a psychoanalytic patient transitions to being a candidate in psychoanalysis and then to being a psychoanalyst who will perpetually understand her/himself as a patient?') has to refer to the process in which the patient her/himself comes to sense the difference between the process of psychoanalysis and whatever psychotherapeutic maneuvers may have preceded it. The transition from patient to patient-candidate entails the deep assimilation of an awareness of the profound difference between the free-associative praxis of psychoanalysis and the maneuvers of psychotherapy. This is usually a transition in which s/he realizes the joy and the terror of psychoanalytic processes, yet grasps them whole-heartedly. This is, I suggest, the 'calling' – the moment or moments in which *ça te fait venir!*

Potentially, it is surely at this point, or at some time thereafter, that the individual in psychoanalysis is ready for her/his first psychoanalytic patient to come. That is, uncontaminated by the residues of oedipalized rivalries with her/his own Training Analyst, the patient is ready to assume the position of the psychoanalyst. Indeed this is very much what happens in many, but not all, psychoanalytic processes, but it is far from a matter in which 'that's that.' Rather, as if coming from the unconscious depths of our humanity, it is a critical moment of deepening in what will be a life-long calling, an endless process of becoming a psychoanalyst. If this readiness is genuine, it will be accompanied not by arrogance, but rather will be undertaken with – to borrow from Søren Kierkegaard – a profound sense of fear and trembling.

It is a little too much to suggest that patients only come when the patient-candidate is ready, but the suggestion carries some weight. Only in the early days of the discipline (as recounted for example in Sterba's *Reminiscences*) did many patients arrive in a patient-candidate's consulting room expressly wanting psychoanalysis. Nowadays patients typically arrive seeking psychotherapy and the patient-candidate, who surely should announce her/his intentions to conduct a psychoanalytic treatment, necessarily commences in a mode that is wholly that of 'psychoanalytically-informed' psychotherapy. Cases are, as often as not, 'conversions' in this manner. This raises very complex issues of method and of ethicality. For just as patients should never be cajoled or coaxed – let alone coerced or compelled – into any form of psychotherapeutic treatment, there are serious challenges involved in facilitating a psychoanalytic process with a patient who thought they were bargaining for a more ameliorative treatment. In terms of method, this has to be done with care, consideration and caution. In terms of ethics, this cannot be done with any sort of guile – complete candor and confidentiality must always pertain between patient and psychoanalyst – and yet, however much the practitioner is sure the patient will benefit from psychoanalytic praxis, the patient cannot know in advance a process that they have yet to experience. Perhaps the most salient feature of 'conversion cases' is that, starting in the mode of 'psychoanalytically-informed' psychotherapy and attempting to move the treatment toward a psychoanalytic process is challenging. The patient-candidates have, in large measure, to rely on the experiences they themselves had with their Training Analyst. This, of course, implies that if the Training Analyst did not appreciate the difference between psychotherapeutic procedures and psychoanalytic processes, it is unlikely that the patient-candidate will know how to facilitate the treatment's movement beyond psychotherapy. Additionally, since many institutes have relaxed the requirement that the treatments conducted by candidates must proceed to full termination (and indeed sometimes only require that the training cases be of a couple of years duration), it is almost certain that a large percentage of candidates currently graduate from their training without a strong – or perhaps without any – sense of the vital distinction between psychotherapy and the radicality of psychoanalytic processes. In this context, it is not exaggerative to suggest that appreciation of the significance of free-associative praxis – and thus psychoanalysis itself – may be waning, even while 'psychoanalytic' organizations trumpet their expanding horizons.

The genuine calling to the path of radical psychoanalysis – the *ça te fait venir* – demands of the patient great generosity of spirit, because the path of the psychoanalyst is one that requires an incessant commitment to the free-associative dismantling of what I will call our 'egotism.' The term is convenient as inclusive not only of the 'I-Now-Is', as a 'rock' perpetually 'attacked' by free-associative praxis, but also of all the self-preoccupations that might be marshaled under the notion of narcissism.[32] In a sense, becoming a psychoanalyst is no less than a process of relinquishing one's attachment to egotism – as if for the sake of the other and the otherwise. If free-association is, as Freud once expressed it, the 'sacred rule,' then surely to be seated behind a psychoanalytic patient is to take up a function that is sacrosanct.

On functioning as a psychoanalyst

It surely should be with fear and trembling that patient-candidates take up the position of being the psychoanalyst for their first patients. The patient-candidate surely has, by now, some sense of what it means to function as someone's psy-choanalyst – a sense gained only through the experience of being in psycho-analysis. Indeed, the patient-candidate should – but perhaps rarely does – have some ideas about the issues raised earlier, when I insisted that *free-association can only occur in the presence of a psychoanalyst.* That is, both cannot occur in the ear-shot of any third-parties (recordings and so forth) and cannot occur in the absence of a psychoanalyst (although there are special meanings of the notion of 'absence' here, as will be discussed). These considerations are surely the most fundamental key to the question: Why is the psychoanalyst necessary?

If the free-associative method is about freeing the truthfulness of the body-mind, it is obvious why it cannot be done to one person by another, like a sur-gical procedure or military strategy or even a game of chess – even though Freud suggested each of these mistaken analogies.[33] Against the idealized image conveyed throughout the Abrahamic tradition, the practitioner is no shepherd. In psychoanalysis, person *A* cannot change person *B* instrumentally or even directively, like a shepherd corralling the sheep or a sherpa showing a hapless tourist the way to ascend a mountainside. Freeing truthfulness is surely not a directive process that can be imposed, compelled or even persuaded. However, in what sense cannot it be done by an individual alone? Although commonly attributed to Bob Marley's *Redemption Song,* it was actually the great anti-racist freedom-fighter Marcus Garvey, who famously instructed us that 'none but our-selves can free our minds.' Yet only implicit in this instruction is the insight that the process has also to be shared – a communal process even if pertaining only to a dyad. Psychoanalysis shows why. It is not only because the structures of oppression operate societally and globally, but also because the operations of repression and suppression are effected by the individualized representational system as a systemic whole within which we think. Whereas the solo individual can engage experiences that loosen the bonds of suppression (at least to some degree), the subject produced by the representational system that represses is almost powerless to act de-repressively. In a sense, to grasp this is to compre-hend the radicality of psychoanalysis.

The possibility of autonomous self-emancipation is somewhat mythical. I mentioned in Chapter 1 how the idea of 'self-analysis' – attributed to Freud's considerable labors with himself, since he was the 'first psychoanalyst' – is some-what misleading. This is not only because Freud had interlocutors of a quite unusual variety, but also because the idea assumes that Freud was able to deploy the insights he gained into himself to remobilize desire.[34] To express this differ-ently with just a single example, we surely know that Freud's own 'psychoanaly-sis' was far from exemplary in that he never managed to deconstruct his quite intense attachment to being an authoritarian leader in the image of Moses and Hannibal (whether he was remotely fulfilled in his sexuality is an additional question that has understandably entertained historians). In short, the egological project, which assumes the possibility that the subject of self-consciousness can come to gain adequate and sufficient understandings *about* that which it has suppressed, let alone repressed, is false. On its own recognizance, self-consciousness cannot come to listen to that which is otherwise than representationality, the motions and commotions of desire.

There are three prevailing models of the functioning of the 'psychoanalytically-informed' psychotherapist – none of them particularly pertinent to the processes of psychoanalysis.

First, there is the model of the practitioner as wielding an – epistemologically – interpretive authority over the psychic life of the patient. Sooner or later, the 'psychoanalytically-informed' psychotherapist knows best. This practitioner comprehends external reality more accurately than the patient does. On the basis of the 'data' provided by the patient, this practitioner comes to comprehend the internal conflicts in which the patient's ego organization is embroiled more lucidly than the patient does. Perhaps most importantly, this practitioner comprehends better than the patient how the patient's life could be conducted more adaptively. This description may fit how much of the public as well as many 'psychoanalysts' understand the role of the practitioner, but it is not that of a psychoanalytic process. In relation to this, the principal delusion or illusion that the patient-candidate must relinquish is surely that of believing that s/he possesses some sort of epistemological superiority over the patient and thus knows how the latter's life should be better conducted.

The second model also positions the practitioner as another sort of – ontologically – interpretive authority, but here the emphasis is less on adaptation, more on an ideal image of the organization and maturation of the patient's theater of object-relations. The prototype of this ideal is the patient's progression from chaotic 'paranoid-schizoid' states of inner disorganization toward more organized 'depressive-reparative' states. With the latter, the patient becomes sadder, wiser and more accepting of harsh realities. These realities are both inner (followers of Klein depict the infant as born with almost unbearably destructive tendencies) and outer (more independent object-relational theorists emphasize aggression only as a response to the frustrations and mis-attunements that invariably characterize infancy). Thus, there are some fanciful variants to the scheme of a progression from paranoid-schizoid to depressive-reparative conditions. For example, the patient should mature from an inner world of 'transitional objects' to one in which 'objects' are experienced more realistically, yet the capacities to love, work and to engage in imaginative play are preserved. In all such scenarios, there is an indisputable 'reality' to human development; namely that the trajectory of psychic life demands that every individual bear a succession of painful losses – loss of split-off or idealized 'good objects' and then an entire sequence of additional 'object' losses. What varies in these depictions of life's journey is the notion of the 'reality' or 'realities' that propel this trajectory. As just mentioned, there is the alleged 'reality' of each individual's innate endowment of a horrendous proclivity toward aggressivity, destructiveness and primal envy (for which there is little if any evidence, direct or indirect). There is the indubitable reality of the frustrations and empathic misalignments that every individual must bear, and without which there would be no development. Then there is the reality of the incest taboo that is effectively inscribed intrapsychically as the repression-barrier and which precipitates oedipality (a dimension of psychic life that much psychotherapeutic theorizing, even of the brands that are 'psychoanalytically-informed,' downplays with crippling results).[35] Finally there is the 'reality' of the 'ways of the world' – economic, cultural and sociopolitical arrangements – that psychotherapists egregiously treat as matters to which the patient must be encouraged to adjust.

This second model differs from the first in that it does not boast a spurious objectivism. By and large, the ego-psychological or structural-functional model treats the patient as a source of 'data' for the computational practitioners' procedures of observation and inference, which are to be followed by the delivery of interpretations designed to transform the patient. By contradistinction, the object-relational model elevates practitioners' emotional engagement and responsivity to the patient. There are at least two versions of this: *Either* the psychotherapist poses as an 'empty container' (and can do so thanks to her/his own treatment), who receives internally and thus interpretively contains the patient's emotional communications, *or* the psychotherapist brings her/his own emotional life into a responsive reciprocity with that of the patient in a way that enables the former to interpret the patient's communications usefully (that is, toward greater maturity). In either case, these 'psychoanalytically-informed' practitioners own an interpretive authority based not so much on computational skills (including the ability to make instrumentally useful inferences on the basis of theoretical application), but more on the premise that they are more mature than the patient with whom they are empathically engaged. Their emotional life is *prima facie* better organized than the patient's (precisely because they have been in 'psychoanalysis' and the patient has not). In this context, another principal illusion that the patient-candidate must relinquish is surely that of believing that s/he possesses some sort of emotional superiority over the patient and thus knows how the latter's life should be better conducted.

Third, there is the model of the practitioner less as an interpretive authority and more as a democratic interlocutor whose role is to talk with the patient in a manner that fosters the latter's normalization. This is where the psychotherapist typically finds it difficult to distinguish the craft from an everyday conversation about thoughts, feelings and wishes, conducted with the intention of making-sense of them. In Kate Schechter's ethnography, the confusion and disillusionment of many 'psychoanalysts' is documented with scholarly precision. Faced with the question *what is not psychoanalysis?*, one senior practitioner responds 'if you put it that way, I can't think of anything.' Thus, psychotherapy (rendered indistinct from psychoanalysis by many of the latter's card-carrying practitioners) becomes the sort of conversation that one might have had with one's Great Aunt. Perhaps more sophisticated, perhaps not. Psychotherapists make a career of such conversations and therefore – one might hope – possess a certain sort of professionalized sophistication. From the writings of Harry Stack Sullivan to those of the current aficionados of interpersonalist and relational approaches, they have thought extensively about whatever typifies the life journey of the average – North American, more often than not – citizen and they have considered quite deeply many of the nuances of its emotional and interpersonal features. They have studied empathy and are practiced in its vicissitudes. They cherish the way patients 'tell their story' (at least up to the point where it can still 'make-sense') and they are eager to help them amplify it, extend its reflective purview and render it more cogent, coherent and cohesive. The practices of palliative elucidation have replaced emancipative excavation, and an eviscerated ethos of circumscribed curiosity has long since replaced the stringencies of Freud's school of suspicion – all in the interests of their patients' greater contentment and 'good citizenship.' Such psychotherapy may shine a light into the patient's imprisonment in repetition-compulsivity (even while it certainly reinforces the prison bars), but psychoanalysis ventures to break-down the prison walls. Reading their literature, it often seems as if interpersonal or relational practitioners, and their many colleagues, can scarcely explain how their craft differs from what Szasz called a 'rhetoric of persuasion.' They have long since lost any ability to grasp the unconscious-as-repressed. Moreover their notion of the libidinality and the ubiquitous energies of the human condition amounts to little more than the sanitary acclaim of the missionary position – sexuality is merely one category of behavior among many. Grievously, this is today how much of what is called 'psychoanalysis' comprehends sexuality, perhaps especially in North America.

The Lacanian 'take' on the function of the psychoanalyst has much to teach us, especially given the problems with the three prevailing models.[36] The Lacanian psychoanalyst is theatrically positioned, in the patient's anticipatory purview, as the *sujet supposé savoir*. That is, 'He who is supposed to know' (I will deliberately reference the Lacanian psychoanalyst in the capitalized masculine, given not only Lacan's notorious sexism personally, but more importantly the inherent phallocentricity of his methods and his theoretical assumptions). The psychoanalyst poses as if occupying the abstract locus of the grand 'Phallus,' the symbolic position of the 'dead father' that sustains, abstractly and centripetally, the operations by which the symbolic order (the *Grand Autre* or capitalized Other) makes representable meaningfulness, even while it produces and reproduces the interminable *méconnaissance* of the speaking subject (the reflectivity of self-consciousness that never really knows 'where it is at'). Thus, the Lacanian psychoanalyst absents himself from any and all ordinary discourse (see Endnote 20). Cadaverizing himself while seated in the chair behind the patient, he is exclusively 'interested' in the patient's inability to 'make-sense,' as evidenced by the occurrence of errant signifiers, slips, scansions, mistaken punctuation, malapropisms, syllepses, catachreses and so forth (including, perhaps, disruptive bodily phenomena, although this is less than clear from Lacan's own accounts). In order to emphasize appreciatively the potentially liberatory value of what might seem a bizarre procedure, I will leave aside, for the moment, the notorious delivery of this treatment in 'sessions' that might last the customary fifty minutes, but are more likely to last only a few. The virtue of what the Lacanian psychoanalyst offers his patients is surely the realization that their speech comes from 'elsewhere.' That is, from the unconscious as (the capitalized) 'Other' and not the authorial pretensions of the 'I' that thinks it knows of what it speaks. In this realization, it is as if what I have called the narratological-imperative gives way to what Lacan calls the 'Real' in a moment of rupture. The speaking subject comes to 'realize' – for want of a better term – that all its stories are 'just stories.' This is the realization that all the transferences the patient might have attributed to the psychoanalyst, including the most powerful assumption that *He* must really be the one 'in the know' (the one in the locus of the grand 'Phallus' as the originative mark of all linguistic representationality) are empty delusions or illusions. In such a theater, desire is reclaimed in the impossibility of comprehension.

The account of the function of the psychoanalyst that is involved in radical psychoanalysis draws from the three models discussed above (although only in so far as every psychoanalysis includes phases that are those of 'psychoanalytically-informed' psychotherapy), and then, as the psychoanalytic process intensifies, it diverges from them markedly, albeit in a manner decisively different from that of the Lacanian 'clinic.' There are three dimensions to the function of the radical psychoanalyst.

Establishing the psychoanalytic relationship: The psychoanalyst is responsible for establishing and maintaining what is sometimes called the 'frame' of the treatment. It often takes around a year of sessions for patients to come to know, as if in their bones, that they are in a thoroughly reliable relationship of unparalleled safety, intimacy and freedom (as Adam Limentani discussed so ably). It is the task of the psychoanalyst to facilitate the patient's relaxation into this experience – the secure establishment of what is, basically, a unique mode of friendship, albeit a lopsided one.[37] The psychoanalyst is foremost the patient's friend, for as Pythagoras stated 'friends are as companions on a journey, who ought to aid each other in persevering on the road to a happier life' (although in this respect Derrida's 1994 discussion of the notion of accompaniment is important). For psychoanalysis, this is a unique blend of *érōs, agápē,* and *philía.* The psychoanalyst offers friendship as love of a certain specific blend and also the most enigmatic and extraordinary mode of hospitality – the psychoanalyst must be genuinely hospitable and indeed humble in relation to the awesome complexity of the patient. Unlike the conventional notion of friendship and hospitality, this both seduces (in the latinate sense of *seducere*) the patient and disrupts the patient's equanimity (I will return shortly to the notion of the *caress* as a seductive act warmly received). The lopsidedness of this friendship is threefold. The psychoanalyst is (i) a friend who is unaccepting of what the patient takes to be her/his realities, (ii) a friend who disturbs the patient's equilibrium that is achieved largely through the operation of resistances and (iii) a friend whose stance is that there are mysteries to the patient's psychic life that the patient does not want to hear. A diligently careful, patient and persistent, 'setting of the frame' is essential to the psychoanalyst's capacity to deliver such friendship and, in this context, there are three aspects that almost invariably call for the psychoanalyst to educate the patient.

The first is the 'sacred rule' of free-association. If psychoanalysis is to be attempted from the start, this will need to be immediately introduced to the patient. If the treatment is to segue from procedures that are prevalently those of 'psychoanalytically-informed' psychotherapy into the processes of psychoanalysis, then this introduction may have to be more gradual and more frequently reasserted. Riffing on Freud's suggestions in his 1913 paper, I suggested (in Chapter 2) how such an educational intervention might be worded. Of central importance for the psychoanalyst's attention is to be aware that the 'rule' is impossible for the patient to follow – this will be addressed shortly in terms of the practitioner's role in facilitating the dissolution of the patient's inevitable resistances to free-associative praxis.

Second, the patient almost always needs education as to the psychoanalytic way of workplaying with dreams (as discussed in my 2016 text). This is not only because many patients have very nonpsychoanalytic, indeed anti-psychoanalytic, ways of treating their dream-life, but also because the lure of the manifest content of the dream is very difficult for almost everyone to avoid (including Freud, as is evident if one studies his own struggle with the *My friend R was my uncle* dream, as described in Chapter 4 of his 1900 text).

The third aspect of workplaying psychoanalytically in which the patient usually requires education concerns the way of listening to bodily disruptions in the patient's discourse. This is discussed in my 2013 paper, 'Free-Associating with the Bodymind,' and does not require reiteration here.

Other aspects of 'setting the frame' include arrangements for location, money and time. I will briefly discuss each of these in turn.

In his 1955 paper on regression, Winnicott wisely described why psychoanalysis cannot be done in a passageway or corridor. What he called the 'holding environment' of the treatment needs to feel exactly that. For the sake of the patient, the psychoanalytic consulting room needs to be consistent and containing, with the couch as comfortable as possible. For the sake of the psychoanalyst, it needs to be comfortable and familiar (decorated authentically by the practitioner, rather than unfamiliar or antiseptic), with a capacious chair that holds her/him steadily upright. For the sake of both, it needs to be quiet (as little possible noise from outside, and not ticking clocks or whirring machines inside), preferably with natural lighting but definitely without any lighting that is harsh, overhead or variable, and without any likelihood of violations of confidentiality or intrusions. That is, no shared waiting rooms, no secretaries making the appointments, no possibility of being overheard (even if the patient shouts), no possibility of anyone barging into the space, and so on.

In relation to money, it must be emphasized that payment of a reasonable fee is an essential ingredient of the psychoanalytic relationship – the patient has to know that s/he is making a realistic contribution to the psychoanalyst's livelihood. There is no treatment *gratis* and even somewhat moderated fees can jeopardize the process. One cannot be psychoanalyzed by a practitioner to whom one feels beholden – for example, on whose monetarily-equivalent generosity the treatment is dependent. This is because, apart from several other considerations, the full force of negative transferences (hatred of and rage at the practitioner) must be able to be freely and fully expressed.[38] The payment can be made weekly or monthly and, whichever agreement is adopted, it must be paid in full, on time and in person (by which I mean it is strongly preferable that, at the end of each week or month, the patient hands the psychoanalyst the payment in cash or as a bank cheque). The reason for this is simple. It is deleterious to the development of a psychoanalytic process if the patient (or the psychoanalyst) attempt to deny or in any way conceal this essential ingredient of the relationship. This is evident from the fact that it is around the issues of payment and time that so many patients enact their initial resistances to the treatment.

Despite some excellent contributions to the topic, we still understand far too little about the temporal constitution of psychic life (as I indicated in discussing the pluritemporality of the psyche in Chapter 2). On a pragmatic level, psychoanalytic experience shows that it is imperative that sessions begin precisely at the appointed time and end exactly fifty minutes later. The reliability of this routine is essential to the patient's experience of safety in the relationship with the psychoanalyst and thus also of intimacy and freedom. Practitioners, who waiver from the punctuality with which sessions must begin, inadvertently (or perhaps with an unconscious sadism) communicate to the patient either their lack of commitment to the process or feelings about the patient that urgently need examination (in the psychoanalyst's own travail as a patient). Some psychoanalysts will extend a session even by a few minutes – often imagining that they do so out of a kindness – because the patient is saying something 'so interesting' or something 'so distressing' that the practitioner decides it must be brought to some sort of closure before the patient is required to depart. This is a mistake, not only because there is nothing 'so interesting' that it cannot be addressed in the next session, but also, more importantly, because the extension communicates to patients that the psychoanalyst doubts their capacity to regulate and moderate their own distress – and such a capacity, even in periods of regressive stress, is essential to functioning as a psychoanalytic patient.

As is well known, much brouhaha was stirred by Lacan's experiment with variable length sessions (an experiment that many Lacanians continue today and believe is necessary to their practice). Aside from all the aspersions cast about this practice – the financial advantage accrued by seeing, for example, twenty or more patients a day each for a reduced 'session' but for a full fee – the rationale given by Lacan seems seriously flawed. At one point, Lacan boasts how ending a session prematurely (supposedly because the obsessive patient was droning on repetitively) was 'successful' because it provoked in the following session the patient's fantasy of anal penetration. This is surely a naïve justification for the practice of variable length sessions. The patient's fantasies need to surface when they are ready to do so, no sooner and no later. It is quite easy to provoke fantasies. After an intemperate police interrogation, many if not all people will experience fantasies of being violated. After being approached seductively by someone who seems very sexy, many if not all people will experience fantasies of an erotic character. So what? Fantasies that are coerced or provoked in this manner are rarely amenable to being psychoanalytically interrogated in a manner that contributes usefully to the freeing of truthfulness that characterizes psychoanalysis.

This triad of practicalities that 'set the frame' of a psychoanalytic treatment – the consulting room, the financial arrangements and the issues of time and timing – constitute procedural rituals that it is the responsibility of the psychoanalyst to insist upon and to maintain assiduously. They make possible the authentic spontaneity of the patient and the patient's willingness to allow her/ himself to have her/his equilibrium perturbed, if not entirely deranged, by the course of the treatment.

*Interpreting resistances to free-associative speaking:*The emphasis of radical psychoanalysis is that the praxis is not about arriving at substantive interpretations about psychic life. Rather it is about reanimating psychic life free-associatively, freeing its truthfulness from repetition-compulsivity by listening anew to the energies of desire. Psychotherapy may be accomplished by the delivery of contentful interpretations about the patient's psychic life, but by contrast a psychoanalytic process is usually impeded by the practitioner who imagines this is the prime task, or even an aspect of her/his tasks. This implies that the only significant interpretive activity of the psychoanalyst is directed toward the dissolution of the patient's resistances to speaking free-associatively. To phrase this simplistically, unlike the psychotherapist, the psychoanalyst is not so very concerned with the content of the patient's psychic life (its references to the past or to future aspirations), only with its intrapsychic and interpersonal processes as they pertain to the patient's resistances to ongoing free-association.

Freud's term, resistances (*Widerstande*), was perhaps unfortunately chosen since it has always suffered its martial connotations (although the French translation, *résistance*, has some quite favorable resonance). For whatever reason, Freud chose not to adopt terms such as *Hindernis* or *Obstruktion*. His choice instigated an early theme in the literature in which the psychoanalyst's role in 'overcoming' the patient's resistances was phrased in the decidedly combative language of direct warfare. The term was used, with almost equal fervor, to refer both to the patient's reluctance to accept or assimilate the practitioner's substantive interpretations (as well as the public's general resistances to psychoanalysis itself) and to the patient's difficulties in following the essential *Grundregel* that s/he must free-associate. In the former case, the practitioner's efforts would often devolve into the crafts of persuasion or propaganda, marshalling evidence in lawyerlike fashion, browbeating or even threatening the patient (we might wonder how many of the early 'psychoanalysts' would stoop to communications such as 'if you can't accept this, you might as well leave now'). Not least because the radical psychoanalyst is not engaged in offering substantive interpretations, this sort of crass coercion need not even be a temptation for the practitioner. In the latter case, confrontations with the patient's failure to comply with (at least a facsimile of) the mandate to free-associate would typically be more critical than empathic – at least as it was theorized through the first decades of the discipline. The practitioner's charge was described as one of overcoming, conquering, vanquishing and generally wrestling into submission any such difficulties or reluctance that the patient might manifest. For example, Freud's 1926 essay, despite its launch of a more sophisticated description of the ego organization and its anxieties, is almost blood-curdling, with references to 'our fight against resistances' and our task 'to overcome the enemy's resistance,' as well as its reminder that 'such battles call for time.' Until sometime in the mid-1930s, the temptation was always, and continues to be, the slide into an authoritarian approach, along with tactics analogous to direct combat. For example, Wilhelm Reich's 1933 classic, *Character Analysis* (which continues to be reading recommended to every practitioner), was and is invaluable for its role in keeping the erotic energies of our embodied experience within the discipline's purview, but it too retained the emphasis on direct interventions against the patient's defenses. The approach was certainly prevalent through the 1920s and for many practitioners it continued long thereafter.

Only in the later 1930s, with some increased understanding of the operations of the ego organization, did practitioners come to realize that resistances are necessary in terms of the patient's equanimity and perhaps even survival. Resistances are the 'patient's friend' (as one of my teachers very appropriately told me) and no one should be without friends. However, as just mentioned, psychoanalysts are also the 'patient's friend' – and therefore they must treat the patient's other 'friends' – her/his resistances – with courtesy at the very least! Anna Freud, perhaps because of her experience with children, had a substantial influence on this salutary development. The realization that patients need their resistances, or at least believe that they do, instigated a profoundly important shift toward the precept that resistances are not to be attacked but rather to be dissolved with tact and indirection. Indeed, efforts to attack can be expected to have consequences that are the reverse of what is intended by the practitioner. The dynamics of psychic life are such that the patient's resistances to free-association appearing to have been overcome coercively almost always reappear with redoubled strength elsewhere.

At the risk of reiteration, this second of the three functions of the radical psychoanalyst is indeed not the proffering of substantive interpretations about the content of the patient's psychic life, but is most saliently the dissipative interpretation of her/his resistances, which are, by definition, processive. Nothing psychoanalytic is served by grand interpretations of the patient's thoughts, feelings, wishes and fantasies (although this is what passes as 'psychoanalytically-informed' psychotherapy). But it is also crucially important to understand that nothing psychoanalytic is served by an interpretation of resistances to free-association that does not respect the value of those resistances for the patient's equilibrium (even while the interpretation is going to cause that equilibrium to wobble and hopefully to dissipate). Obviously, the psychoanalyst can never be 'on the side' of the patient's resistances to free-association, but direct warfare against them is *never* the appropriate method. Rather – and with some qualification – a useful analogy might be that *the radical psychoanalyst is a friendly guerilla* operating empathically within the patient's ego organization as it ubiquitously manifests its many and varied resistances to free-association.[39] The point of this analogy to the friendly guerilla (which is made in all seriousness, even with some qualifications to be mentioned momentarily) is as follows. In addressing resistances, the psychoanalyst is essentially and necessarily identifying loci within the patient's suppressive and repressive representational system (effectively the patient's ego organization) that will allow the system to change, transformatively and transmutatively, *as if spontaneously* or, colloquially, as if 'of its own volition.'[40] Resistances are to be dissolved, dissipated, dismantled or decomposed, rather than combated in a more direct or coercive manner.

There is a pragmatic sense in which the patient's resistances to ongoing free-associative exploration manifest themselves intrapsychically ('there is something on the horizon that I don't want to think about') or interpersonally ('there is something on the horizon that I do not want to speak aloud for my psychoanalyst to hear'). The interpretive function of psychoanalysts involves their skill both in addressing the multifaceted forms of resistance – which are ongoing – and in doing so 'on the side of the ego organization.' Again, this implies that the interpretation will be empathic in relation to the patient's conviction that s/he needs the resistance and that the interpretation will be respectful, tactful and tactical – the activities of a friendly guerilla not a combatant in direct warfare.

As Ralph Greenson warned, interpretation *that* there is a resistance is not a useful tactic unless one can also interpret for the patient both the 'how' and the 'why' of the resistance. However, an inclusive interpretation that covers all these aspects might be applauded by Greenson, but all too often it is, for the patient, indigestible in three ways.

(i) If the interpretation touches too heavily upon the patient's 'signal anxiety' – to use the term Freud started to develop in 1926 – and indeed all interpretations are more or less of no avail unless they do so, then the patient cannot possibly immediately assimilate anything but the briefest message. To reinforce this point, we might note that experimentation in cognitive psychology has proved it fulsomely.

(ii) Interpretations that address a resistance comprehensively – by which I mean inclusively in the '*that, how and why*' sense – not only tend to be 'too much' for the patient, but they also propel the treatment toward intellectuality. As is well known, this is all too often the disastrous outcome of many 'psychoanalytically-informed' psychotherapies. The sizable, intellectualized interpretation cannot be immediately assimilated, so most patients miss any impact it might have had. However, some compliant patients will carry the interpretation around after the session, like so much 'academic' (in the pejorative sense) baggage; out of some form of anxiety, the 'good' patient feels it is her/his duty to identify with the pronouncements of the practitioner. Interpretations of resistance are only effective if they touch on – caress – the patient's affect and (signal) anxiety, but to some extent they should always be 'little and light,' titrated according to the patient's readiness to hear them in their immediacy.

(iii)   The Greenson approach to interpreting resistances (which I am using in a somewhat caricatured manner) sets the psychoanalyst up as having epistemological authority over the patient – a problem I discussed earlier. Practitioners about to make any such interpretations should surely stop to ask themselves why the patient hasn't already arrived at the insight. Such a momentary pause to reflect before addressing the patient usually results in the realization that the resistance about to be addressed should not actually be the next resistance to be addressed. For example, the patient, who repeatedly stops free-associating just as she is about to say something about her sexual dissatisfactions with her partner, does not need to hear the practitioner tell her something like 'you don't want to think about or tell me about how disappointed you are sexually with your partner, because you fear that to explore the issue will lead you to want to have an affair, which is against your consciously-held values, so you try instead to distract yourself by focusing on the benefits of being with him.' Such is the belaboring of – mediocre – psychotherapy. The patient in psychoanalysis does not need them, because the prior question, as it were, is why she hasn't thought exactly this herself and indeed shared the insight with the practitioner. Surely it would have been preferable – to give just one of a large range of possibilities – if, as the patient fell silent, the psychoanalyst had simply said 'ouch.'

Skilled psychoanalysts use sentences less and less – and interpretations *about* events less and less – as the workplay with each particular patient goes deeper and its mobility becomes livelier. Inexperienced practitioners imagine that they have to make a lot of sense to the patient about the events in her/his psychic life. They imagine that their interpretations need to be literal and referential. This is far from the case. Nonverbal interpretations – deliberate noises emanating from behind the couch – can be very effective interpretations of resistance. Moreover, *the most effective 'weapon' in the interpretation of resistances is the use of tropes, perhaps especially irony.* So celebrated by the Jena romantic school of poetic philosophy and in Kierkegaard's writings, irony (not to mention other devices such as humor, litotes, meiosis, apophasis and so forth) is perhaps the supreme method by which to express the interpretation of resistances in ways that avoid the difficulties in what I am characterizing as Greenson's approach.[41]

Although not, in a strict sense, an example of irony, Freud gives a very pertinent example of the way in which psychoanalytic discourse must unmask hypocrisy and pretention. In his 1910 paper on the future prospects of his discipline, he imagines how, when the bourgeoisie go on picnics in the countryside, the ladies might have an understanding that, if one of them needed to urinate or defecate, she should simple announce she was going off to 'pick some flowers.' Freud then imagines the effect a *Boshafter* – a mischief maker – might provoke by distributing flyers that read something like 'Ladies who want to piss or shit should announce that they are going to pick flowers.' The façade of bourgeois niceties might thereby implode, since no 'lady' could now make use of this flowery pretext and Freud – perhaps rather optimistically – concludes that thereafter natural requirements would be freely accepted.

I have made much – perhaps too much – of the image of the psychoanalyst's interpretation of the patient's multiple and multifaceted resistances to ongoing free-associative speaking as the act of a 'friendly guerilla.' The guerilla acts in ways that the conservative forces within a system do not anticipate. That is, acts within the system at those loci that will allow the system to change. In psychoanalysis, free-association exposes such loci and all the friendly guerilla must do is to facilitate, in a supportive and empathic manner, the patient's capacity for ongoing free-associative speaking and listening. This is guerilla warfare as in the nonviolent mode of *ahimsā* and *satyāgraha* – not unlike Mohandas Gandhi's notion of *love* as ethical yet vigorously confrontational action that discloses *truthfulness*. I offer the analogy of the friendly guerilla as antidote to the pugnacity of Freud's imagery of the clinical encounter as warfare. It is necessary for the psychoanalyst to move combatively against the patient's resistances to free-associative discourse. But also the psychoanalyst must actually be expressively and empathically understanding of the patient's need to resist, even as s/he is unwaveringly 'against' such resistances. There are better analogies. One would be to suggest that psychoanalysis be conducted in the manner Lao-Tzu recommended that adversaries be treated. There is indeed much that the psychoanalyst can learn from Taoic teachings.[42] Another would be to suggest that the interpretation of resistances must be the act of a – verbal – caress. Consider these features: The caress intends a certain sort of shift in the beloved recipient; it expresses a wish for the recipient's increased openness and responsivity; it is inherently light, considerate and caring; and it is willingly received by the recipient, even while it brings about a momentum of changes in response to it.[43] Much of the issue here pivots on the way in which interpretations of resistances can or cannot be listened to, and effectively heard (I will return to the issue of psychoanalytic listening shortly).

Being an 'absenting-presence' for the patient: The psychoanalyst takes responsibility for the 'frame' of the treatment process and offers the patient an unflagging devotion not only to the patient as a person but to the caressive interpretations of her/his resistances to ongoing free-associative expression. There is a third function of the psychoanalyst, which is perhaps most complex to elaborate, because it involves a unique process of being both present for the patient yet simultaneously absenting. It is comparatively easy to distinguish my notion of this 'absenting-presence' function of the psychoanalyst from the three extant ways of thinking about the operation of the 'psychoanalytically-informed' psychotherapist (the computational model of the objectively interpreting practitioner, the emotionally engaged model of the containing-by-interpreting practitioner, and mutually co-constructing model of the reciprocal learner-teacher practitioner). It is less easy, but profoundly important, to differentiate the absenting-presence of the psychoanalyst from the Lacanian model that positions the practitioner in the symbolic place of the dead father, the position of the grand 'Phallus' that is the authorial centerpoint of the *Grand Autre* (the primordial 'mark of marks' as the originary difference that, in previous writings, I compared with Shiva's lingam in South Asian mythology).

The initial point of differentiation is that the radical psychoanalyst is – unashamedly – engaged emotionally with the patient, indeed passionately so, as well as being a palpable emotional and energetic 'presence' for the patient. The traditions of ego-psychology, object-relations and interpersonal-relational psychotherapy have always vacillated around the issue of what the patient is supposed to mean emotionally to the psychoanalyst. In terms of the emotional connection the practitioner has with the patient, at one pole is the outdated image of the white-coated, objectivistically disdainful, medical-model practitioner – the patient is the 'thing' to be treated. At another pole is the more contemporary fashion for a dialogically 'intersubjective' practitioner, who does have her/his own feelings for the patient *but* only the 'proper' sort of feelings that one might have for a professional 'client' (or, if 'improper' ones emerge, the practitioner refrains from utilizing them, let alone disclosing them, in the course of the treatment; if s/he cannot excise them from her/his enactive repertoire, then it is only professionally responsible to abort the treatment). Somewhere in between these poles is the neo-Kleinian practitioner whose feelings during a session may be 'improper,' but who seems comfortable to attribute them entirely the patient, who has 'deposited' them there by the mechanism of 'projective identification' (a standpoint I criticized in my 2017 paper). For example, practitioners who feel enraged with the patient, then must address with the patient why s/he is so – unconsciously – enraged and enraging. There are important differentiations to be made from both these poles and from the many variants that have been promulgated in between them.

Contrasted with these standpoints, the radical psychoanalyst experiences, without inhibition or reservation, any and all sorts of feelings for the patient – love, hate and 'forbidden' erotic urgings – but s/he functions psychoanalytically only by consistently and zealously *voiding* her/his own narcissistic longings for emotional gratification from the patient. It is essential to comprehend the character and conditions of this 'voiding,' especially because, as I indicated earlier the main limitation to any psychoanalytic treatment comes from the practitioner's narcissism. Here 'voiding' does not mean evacuation, suppression or repression; nor does it mean sublimation or condemnation in quite the ways that most of the literature uses these terms (and certainly it does not mean simply attributing these 'counter-transferences' to the patient's psychodynamics and then interpreting the patient's psychic life accordingly).

However, sublimation and condemnation probably cover Freud's ideas about what the psychoanalyst should do with her/his feelings for the patient. Sublimation (*Sublimierung*) was a term introduced by Freud in 1908 and it was never well developed in his writings subsequently, perhaps because Freud assumed a knowledge of the major European philosophical writings on the philosophy of the sublime from Edmund Burke in 1756 and Immanuel Kant in 1764 to Arthur Schopenhauer's *The World as Will and as Representation* (a major influence on Freud's thinking, and possibly his contemporary Rudolf Otto. In their 1967 *Language of Psychoanalysis*, Laplanche and Jean-Bertrand Pontalis also remind us that Freud was very familiar with the usage of 'sublimation' in chemistry, wherein a substance passes from a solid to a gas without an intervening liquid phase. In the context of this discussion, sublimation implies that the psychoanalyst has converted her/his erotic energies into those that can fuel the activities of a psychoanalytic practitioner (for example, into curiosity, inferential capacities, appropriate caring for patients and the like). Freud's image of this suggests that the psychoanalyst is the ultimate 'civilized man' (the male pronoun is deliberate), who has harnessed his emotionality to the cause of rationality.[44] In part this may be a useful description, mostly it is not.

Condemnation (*Verurteilung* or *Urteilsverwerfung*), a profoundly important notion which Freud developed in a rather scattered manner in his writings on repression and negation (beginning in 1909 with the formula 'psychoanalysis replaces repression with condemnation'), implies that the psychoanalyst knows fully what his urges are but refrains from their enactment; for example, knowing about anger or lust toward a patient but holding in abeyance the wish to enact the feeling. This is partly a useful description of the practitioner's functioning but, to the extent that it is drastically oversimplified, it is not.

To some extent these two terms fail to convey the active usefulness of the psychoanalyst's passionate engagement with the patient. The psychoanalyst, who is passionately engaged emotionally with the patient, voids her/his narcissistic longings for gratification from the patient by a process that might best be understood in terms of Derrida's notion of 'under erasure' (as in ~~mother, hate~~ or ~~fuck~~, which both are and are not present here as the words, *mother, hate* and *fuck*). In psychoanalysis, the erasure or voiding has special significance. The thought or feeling, wish or fantasy, is in no way suppressed by the psychoanalyst, but deployed within the function of interpreting the patient's resistances to ongoing free-association. This 'deployment' has an ambiguity that is all too often evaded in the discussions of this matter that are offered by the extant literature. Importantly, the psychoanalyst's function as an absenting-presence is to silently free-associate along with the patient. The content of her/his free-associative concatenations is indicative of resistances in the patient – it is *as if* the patient has evoked this stream of thoughts and feelings within the psychoanalyst – but it is also indicative of dynamics within the practitioner. Expressed simply, the psycho-analyst's free-associations are used for their responsiveness to the patient's resistances to free-association, rather than for what their content might say *about* the content of the patient's psychic life.

In the literature, there are ambiguities to what is taught about the psychoana-lyst's own 'deployment' of what occurs internally while listening to the patient. There was a tendency in the classic literature to suggest that whatever occurred within the practitioner that was not clearly about the patient (that is, other than the practitioner's observations and inferences about the patient) amounted to a counter-transferential interference. That is, a residue of the practitioner's own dynamics that have been 'insufficiently analyzed.' There is a contrary tendency in the neo-Kleinian literature to suggest that everything that occurs within the practitioner during the session is actually 'deposited' there by the patient (that is, the practitioner is like an empty container without her/his own dynamics). Clearly, both standpoints have merit and both are mistaken if taken to their extremes. As I have suggested, one mode of exit from this ambiguity is to sug-gest that psychoanalysts must treat what occurs within themselves not so much for its relevance to the *content* of the patient's material or to the content of their own dynamics, but rather as indicative of *process*, namely of the pressures, coming from within themselves and coming from the patient, to resist ongoing free-associative praxis.[45]

One probably should not speak of the psychoanalyst's altruism, mostly because it is – despite writings such as Mathieu Ricard's – a notion laden with religious sentiment and pop psychology. No one genuinely enters psychoanalysis 'for the sake of others.' One enters as a patient because of one's own suffering, and only later comes the authentic calling to become a psychoanalyst oneself and devote oneself to the relief of other's suffering. The prime motivation is suffering and the practitioner is aware of it foremost within her/himself. Thus, there is indeed a sense in which the psychoanalyst's most passionate commitment is truthfulness and freeing, which accounts for her/his focus on facilitating the patient's ongoing free-associative expression as a uniquely de-repressive praxis. In this context, truthfulness does not mean the correctness or the correspondence of representations with whatever they purport to represent, nor does it mean the cogency, coherence or continuity, of the stories that patients have about them-selves, nor does it mean the pragmatic utility of these constructions in enabling patients to master the worlds they inhabit. Rather, truthfulness entails a freeing from repetition-compulsivity, a de-repressive praxis that reinvigorates the patient by accessing the kinesis of desire.

To pursue the patient's truthfulness in this manner, the psychoanalyst must be experienced by the patient as a very alive and involved presence. In a personal conversation, Sterba (who was a member of the original Wednesday Evening Meetings and one of the first two graduates of the Vienna Psychoanalytic Soci-ety, who were the only ones to have their diplomas signed by Freud himself) once told me that Freud's earliest patients typically spoke of how intensely they felt his presence behind the couch. One does not know if this intensity was only an expression of his commitment to healing or as much the ferocity with which he pursued his discipline (one also wonders about the pungency of cigar smoke). In any event, the presence of the radical psychoanalyst must be experienced as one of unswerving and unconditional *caring* ('freely given care') and this presence must be maintained by the practitioner consistently and zealously voiding her/his own narcissistic longings, as has been discussed here. This 'absenting-presence' of the psychoanalyst renders her/him into the personage of a sort of void into which patients speak their longings and their fears. These are the repetition-compulsive stories that traditionally fall under the heading of 'transference.'

Being the recipient of the patient's transferences (or 'transferencing' as an active verb) certainly does not mean that psychoanalysts have to be some sort of 'non-person' or 'blank slate' for the sake of the patient's psychoanalytic process (a rather ludicrous idea that the practitioner could or should shroud his personality by almost total non-disclosure, the most standardized 'look' of bourgeois professionalism, and an office without decoration). Rather, it implies that whatever the patient's reactions to the person of the psychoanalyst (including, and perhaps most of all, to whatever the practitioner discloses about her/himself), they will be subjected to free-associative interrogation. It is this freedom to interrogate spontaneously and without reservation in this manner that is the axis of the patient's emancipation from the imprisonments of transference paradigms.

The literature on transference is voluminous and its review outside the scope of this text. Transference implies expression of the patient's intrapsychic and interpersonal templates in the relationship with the psychoanalyst. Each template involves a tripartite representation of the self, the other and the actions or affects pertaining between them. Typically, each patient will, in the course of any psychoanalysis, express with great intensity maternal transferences, paternal transferences, sibling transferences and transferences that concern the primal scene (the relationship between female and male figures, as well as other configurations of sexual partnering). What is often not emphasized in the literature is the way in which multiple transferences usually occur simultaneously, with one transference serving to occlude another that is also active (recall that the operations of preconsciousness are multi-layered). In an event, all transferences are sooner or later to be subjected to deconstructive or negatively dialectical interrogation by free-association and eventually – colloquially speaking – they 'lose their steam.'

Here the deviation of psychoanalysis from 'psychoanalytically-informed' psychotherapy is evident. For the latter practices typically advocate a seemingly neutral interpretation of transference (for example, 'you are expecting me to treat you in the manner that you experienced your father when he disapproved of your sexual inclinations') or its manipulative interpretation. The latter is conceptualized as the salutary disconfirmation of a transferential pattern (for example, 'you expect me, like your father, to disapprove of your sexuality but actually I don't feel that way') or as providing a 'new' and more healthy object-relational experience (from Franz Alexander's notion of the 'corrective emotional experience' in the early 1940s as discussed in his 1963 book, to the psychodramatic techniques prevalent since the 1960s, some of which border upon sheer idiocy).

The psychoanalyst is the willing recipient of all the many and varied configurations of transference that the patient projects onto him/her. But unlike the 'psychoanalytically-informed' psychotherapist, the psychoanalyst does not seek to interpret these configurations, nor to confirm or disconfirm them by her/his activities and interventions. The psychoanalyst is, so to speak, a void into which the patient speaks her/his multiple fears or longings and the very setting of the psychoanalytic 'frame' – as well as the practitioner's diligent interpretation of the patient's resistances to free-associative speaking – ensures that the transferential content of their relationship will be starkly illuminated. But this is not brought about in order that transferencing may be interpreted and understood in terms of its content as referencing previous relationships (maternal, paternal and so forth). As Freud suggested in his 1912 paper on the dynamics of transference, such interpretation may be the vehicle and the mode of whatever healing is brought about by 'psychoanalytically-informed' psychotherapies, but in psychoanalysis transference is '*the most powerful resistance*' to the treatment and the 'strongest weapon of resistance' (the italicized emphasis is Freud's). Although in that paper, Freud professes to finding this a puzzle, it is surely because transference immediately interferes with the patient's commitment to ongoing free-associative speaking. That is, transferences are 'positionalities' experienced compulsively by the patient – repetitive configurations of thoughts, feelings, wishes and fantasies that keep him/her preoccupied with the personage of the practitioner – and as such the patient finds that they constrict or derail her/his readiness to engage fully in the free-associative process. Thus, contrary to the procedures of psychotherapy, in psychoanalysis, transferences have to be interrogated free-associatively as if solely for their significance in the here-and-now of the relationship. In effect, the psychoanalyst is concerned exclusively with the present and what patients make of her/his 'absenting-presence.'

Everyone knows the present is historically constituted, that the 'now' is 'of the past' (as Roger Kennedy cutely phrased it) and that this 'now' determines the possibility of futures. But none of these well-worn insights should be taken to imply that the key purpose of psychoanalytic treatment is to understand, in an interpretively referential manner, how the past created the patient's present circumstances. That may be the task of 'psychoanalytically-informed' psychotherapy, but it is not (radical) psychoanalysis. The phenomena of the present, including transferential reactions very notably, represent innumerable 'past-futures' expressed in terms of the repetition-compulsivity of our thoughts, feelings, wishes and fantasies (as discussed in Chapter 2 and in my previous books). The movement of psychoanalytic change involves their deconstruction or negatively dialectical sublation and *not* the arrival at referential interpretations about their constitution. Such interpretations merely freeze the subject in a different form of repetition-compulsivity (as if symptoms might be converted into insights about the past, equally bound by repetition-compulsivity). The commitment of psychoanalysis to free-associative praxis is precisely as an unfreezing of the subject's intrapsychic and interpersonal repertoire.

Hanna Segal wrote about how, as patients end the 'initial phase' and enter the 'middle phase' of treatment (which might be taken to mean that the patient segues from the procedures of 'psychoanalytically-informed' psychotherapy toward a more psychoanalytic process), they come to realize how their relationship in the here-and-now with the psychoanalyst (their various modes of transferencing) reflects and refracts both their present relationships with people other than their psychoanalyst and all their past relationships, perhaps especially the more salient and conflictive ones. In this respect, once the patient is fully engaged in a psychoanalytic relationship, it is as if there is no need for the conversation to focus on the conflicts of past relationships or on the hopes for better relationships in the future. As what has been called the 'transference neurosis' develops, the patient accepts the profound sense that only the present relationship in which s/he is deeply engaged with the psychoanalyst (and the psychoanalyst with her/him) is relevant and, with this development, all the resistances to free-associative speaking are likely to coagulate around the patient's thoughts, feelings, wishes and fantasies, pertaining to the here-and-now of this relationship.

At the risk of reiteration, it must be emphasized how, contrary to prevailing wisdom, the patient is not going to be relieved of her/his entrapment in the repetition-compulsivity of transferencing by knowing about how experiences in the present are repetitions of the past. Knowing *about* the significance of present experiences does not free the subject from its imprisonment in compulsive repetitiousness (herein lies the significance of the little understood process of working-through, Freud's *Durcharbeitung*, which he first discussed in 1893 and then more extensively in 1914). But the free-associative interrogation of such repetitions as they appear in the here-and-now of the psychoanalytic relationship does effect such a freeing process. The absenting-presence of the psychoanalyst is a void that eventually frees the patient to confront her/his aloneness and to face new relationships with the spontaneity of desire. However, in a manner not unlike the Lacanian description of the 'cure,' the patient does come to realize that all the fear and longings experienced in relation to the absenting-presence of the psychoanalyst are indeed 'just stories.' The realization is powerfully disconcerting for it brings the patient face-to-face – in a Levinasian sense – with the principle of deathfulness that pervades every moment of her/his life and with the ubiquity of the kinesis of libidinal energies that drain away from the subject in the very moment that they enliven his lived-experience. Such is, as will be discussed, the vulnerability and the fear involved in becoming a psychoanalyst.

Finally, it is only to the extent that the psychoanalyst functions as an absenting-presence for the patient that the repressed can fully 'come forth' – its voicing becoming more accessible to the listening dyad. It is only if the psycho-analyst functions in this manner, with her/his own narcissism voided and her/his need to 'make-sense' of things set aside, that the unique mode of psychoanalytic listening can be fully engaged. This is a mode of listening with which the psy-choanalyst has facility and the patient sooner or later engages. Psychoanalytic lis-tening is not about 'making-sense' and not even so much about inferring the latent preconscious themes that might be expressed as the patient moves from one item that 'makes sense' to the next (as discussed in Chapter 2). Rather, psy-choanalytic listening is primarily a listening for what does not 'make-sense' (again, this is not the same as 'hearing-to-make-sense' or hearing-to-understand). That is, the occurrence of errant signifiers, slips, scansions, mistaken punctuation, malapropisms, syllepses, catachreses and so forth, as well as disruptive bodily phenomena. In psychoanalysis, the ûr, the ŭm, the stutter and all the syncopa-tions of speech – to give just a few examples – are far more significant than the story that the subject believes s/he is trying to tell. For these are the irruptions of the unrepresentable psychic energy of desire and are also source of the patient's resistances to free-associative speaking. For similar reasons, psychoana-lytic listening is uniquely attuned to the unrepresentable messages that come from the patient's (and the psychoanalyst's) embodiment. The disruptive 'voi-cing' of leg or arm pain, abdominal cramping, borborygmic noises, genital engorgement or lubrication, tightening or grinding of the jaw, tensing of the anal sphincter, erythemic flushing, burping or belching, thoracic constrictions, flatulence, muscular twitchings and so forth, are far more significant than the story they interrupt (as indicated in my 2013 paper on 'Free-Associating with the Bodymind'). This is again because these are the irruptions of the unrepresen-table psychic energy of desire. It is *not* so much that errant signifiers, stutters or stomach rumbles are to be 'made-sense' of – by the belabored procedures of forced and utterly inadequate or insufficient translation into representation. Rather, their spontaneities of expression are to by listened to 'in their own right' – so to speak.

Here we come to the key to radical psychoanalysis. The creation of a free-associative mode of relating (both within and lopsidedly between the two parti-cipants) invites the remobilization of libidinality within and through the patient's speech. This can only occur if the premium on 'making-sense of the patient's stories' is relinquished by both participants, and instead the unique listening pro-cess is engaged with what does not, and will not, make-sense within the repre-sentable domain occupied by the narratological-imperative. The implication of this is, as I have indicated previously, that the subject becomes less governed by repetition-compulsivity and consequently more *alive!*

With the commitment to ongoing free-associative praxis, the patient becomes aware of the restless motions and commotions of psychic energies. This has dual implications. The patient becomes more aware of her/his libidinality, the erotic messages within her/his embodiment. Free-association invites the surfacing of body memories, and this is a vitally significant – often 'regressive' – aspect of its effects. In this respect, the praxis renders the discipline somatocentric. It leads – as it were – back to the body and its recondite wisdom. It does so in a way that cannot possibly be achieved by the ideocentric procedures of 'psychoanalytic-ally-informed' psychotherapy, the mandate of which is to make-sense represen-tationally, under the aegis of the narratological-imperative. Moreover, every movement of psychic energy involves simultaneously *both* the lifefulness prin-ciple of investment *and* the deathfulness principle of divestment or dis-invest-ment, the draining away of libidinality. Because of this, the patient becomes more aware not only of her/his liveliness – and indeed becomes more *alive!* – but also of the deathfulness that pervades every instantiation of the 'I-Now-Is.' Again, such awareness is almost mystical and certainly cannot be achieved by psychotherapeutic procedures that maneuver within the domain of representa-tionality, under the aegis of the narratological-imperative – within this domain all death can mean is the end of the story. Only the deconstructive and nega-tively dialectical impact of free-associative discourse brings with it the awareness of the inherency of deathfulness within life itself.

Here we begin to grasp the reasons why psychoanalysis has been so regularly betrayed, even by those who are its ostensible proponents. We begin to grasp why so many 'psychoanalysts' actually remain within the realm of 'psychoanalytically-informed' psychotherapy. The radicality of the free-associative method, as de-repressive praxis, is that it brings with it a unique awareness of sexuality and death. Consequently, becoming a psychoanalyst is a matter of considerable trepidation.

On the vulnerability and fear in becoming a psychoanalyst

Through the twentieth century to the present, there has been – quite predict-ably – much *sturm und drang* over psychoanalysis. After all, as I argued in my 1993 book, psychoanalytic praxis is a revolutionary discovery that indicts the ideologies of modern thinking and is the harbinger of other possible – perhaps 'postmodern' – ways of pursuing wisdom and healing. But to any thoughtful observer, it is evident that, whereas other disciplines usually seem to chug along quietly, occasionally announcing new and exciting discoveries, psychoanalysis has, from the start, been a battlefield. Its advent is itself more than a mere 'para-digm shift' in Thomas Kuhn's terms. Rather, it comprises an 'epistemic rupture' in our understanding of what it means to be human (to use the preferable and more powerful ideas developed by Gaston Bachelard and Louis Althusser). Con-sequently, as seems to happen in the aftermath of such ruptures, the discipline is much misunderstood, much vilified, and – the most slickly and seemingly effect-ive way to ignore profound challenges to predominant modes of thinking – often treated as if it were already passé.

By and large, through the course of the twentieth century, the public's attitude toward psychoanalysis – often based on a mixture of sensationalized curiosity, deri-sion and dismissiveness, but always catalyzed by considerable misunderstanding – has been fluctuating in its ambivalence. Within academia, a veritable gang of professional philosophers have made their careers by attacking its precepts with great virulence, while almost invariably avoiding the possibility of actually experiencing its discourse. Especially since the 1950s, innumerable psychologists and psychotherapists have announced – usually having hardly sampled its literature and definitely having avoided its praxis – that psychoanalysis is now nothing more than a historical curiosity and they claim that their endeavors have long since overtaken much, perhaps all, that Freud might have had to contribute. And so on.

Despite these varied modes of opposition, it has to be concluded that the most powerful and pernicious resistance to psychoanalysis has always come from 'psychoanalysts' themselves – not only all the alleged practitioners and wannabe practitioners, but also those who have, ignoring the necessity of free-associative praxis, seized upon one aspect of the several theoretical models of the mind that Freud constructed after 1914 and then sought to amplify or modify these metapsychological speculations into their own model for the practice of 'psychoanalytically-informed' psychotherapy. Here I am not so much referring to all the famous break-aways from the auspices of the organization founded by Freud – Alfred Adler, Carl Jung, Wilhelm Stekel, Otto Rank and perhaps even Sándor Ferenczi. I might as well be referring to Freud's own error in imagining that his discipline should be protected by a 'Secret Committee' and later his mistaken determination to claim that psychoanalysis might be an objectivistic science 'like any other.' What has to be faced is that, both within Freud's own journey and in the varied undertakings of those who claim to be his followers, the praxis of psychoanalysis has been abandoned in favor of the far less threatening enterprise of psychotherapy guided by an objectivistic model of mental functioning (ego-psychological, object-relational, self-psychological, interpersonal-relational and so forth).

In the two previous volumes in this trilogy, I have discussed Freud's shift around 1914. Although he continued throughout his life to state clearly that free-association is the *sine qua non* of psychoanalysis, during and after World War I, his actual commitment to this praxis became occluded by his preoccupation with speculative theorizing (the mythmaking 'witch metapsychology' that, as he hinted, might be discarded without loss to the discipline's method). By this, I mean the construction of complex models of mental functioning – notably, ego-psychology and object-relations – that can be used to govern the conduct of 'psychoanalytically-informed' psychotherapy, but are a departure from psychoanalysis as radically defined herein. Psychotherapies guided by ego-psychological or structural-functional, by object-relational, by self-psychological or by interpersonal-relational models of the mind do not require the free-associative method. Consequently, in various ways that I have discussed previously, they modify fundamentally the notion of the dynamic unconscious-as-repressed, the notion of the ubiquity of libidinal psychic energy or polysexuality, and the notion of the pluritemporality of psychic life – all of which are integral to the discovery of free-associative praxis. It is these objectivistic or dialogical models of psychotherapy that have now appropriated the title of 'psychoanalysis.'

This is why it can be concluded that the greatest resistance to psychoanalysis comes from those who claim it to be their own discipline. Why has there been this pervasive retreat from psychoanalysis as free-associative praxis? The answer has to be that *the rigors of an ongoing commitment to this praxis are fearsome*, not least because – as I have indicated and will elaborate in Chapter 4 – free-associative discourse, pursued in the manner I have described, leads the patient and the psychoanalyst listening to the pervasiveness of libidinality and the inherency of deathfulness within every moment of our subjectivity. Moreover, this is, as I have argued, a calling or way of life. As Freud stated in his undelivered 'lectures' of 1933, 'psychoanalytic activity is arduous and exacting; it cannot well be handled like a pair of glasses that one puts on for reading and takes off when one goes for a walk.' Thus, the slide back into psychotherapy is invariably and constantly a temptation. It is in this context that one must understand the deepest roots of what Nathan Kravis and others have aptly begun to explore as the psychoanalyst's antipathy toward her/his own discipline, for it is because of this antipathy that so many treatments conducted by 'psychoanalysts' never go beyond 'psychoanalytically-informed' psychotherapy. The workplay of psychoanalysis makes a threefold demand upon the practitioner.

First, it is inherently unsettling to listen psychoanalytically and, if this is indeed what being a psychoanalyst involves, then it is perhaps understandable why so many practitioners take refuge in assuming a position of epistemological or ontological authority. But such retreats imply a departure from psychoanalysis which is, primarily, an *ethical* praxis of opening to what is other and otherwise – a spiritual-existential venture that shakes the foundations of what we take to be most foundational about our subjectivity and self-consciousness. I have written previously that *the psychoanalyst is one for whom everything is strange and nothing is alien*. Psychoanalysts cannot distance themselves from any human phenomenon. They cannot pretend that anything that is human could not be part of themselves or that they could not identify with it (recall Thich Nhat Hanh's poem in Endnote 27). Nothing human can be treated as alien, and yet everything must be treated as strange, including – or perhaps most of all – the psychoanalyst her/himself. This is a source of profound vulnerability.

Second, the psychoanalyst befriends the patient but cannot be befriended and must set aside any and all gratifications that might be accrued from the patient's transferences. On the basis of one's own experiences as a patient, to become a psychoanalyst one must know, *as if in one's bones*, that the patient's transferences are just that, the products of a compulsively repetitious need to express transferentially. One may – should – love the patient. But not even after the treatment appears to be terminated, can one fully receive her/his friendship without considerable misgiving. There appear to have been occasional exceptions (Marie Langer disclosed how she became a friend of the Sterba family long after her personal treatment with him in Vienna), but it is an open question whether such friendships can ever transcend the sheer oddity of their beginning. For the most part, the practitioner must accept and indeed never forget for a moment that s/he is, for the patient, a function. This implies that *the psychoanalyst must accept, without any prospect of relief, a deep and far-reaching sense of aloneness.* This is perhaps why, in his 1964 'Founding Act,' Lacan suggested that every psychoanalyst should affiliate her/himself with a cell of three to five practitioners (with membership of each cell periodically changing). In any event the aloneness cannot, and should not, be evaded and it too is a source of profound vulnerability.

Third, becoming a psychoanalyst is, or should be, the most profound and incessant blow to the practitioner's narcissism. Much has now been written about the problems of the patient's narcissism as the strongest force of resistance to psychoanalysis. Initially, this literature focused on the patient, but more recently there has been some attention to the ways in which the practitioner's narcissism limits the potential of psychoanalytic treatment. I wrote in 1984 that the psychoanalyst's narcissism is the major impediment to any psychoanalysis and there have been subsequent contributions along these lines (for example, Judith Chused's in 2012). Thus, *the psychoanalyst must perpetually call his narcissistic proclivities into question*, and submit her/himself to the psychoanalytic process which requires that s/he, as the practitioner, engage in a continual and rigorous process of self-voiding. This self-voiding required of every moment of the workplay involved in functioning as a psychoanalyst is exacting and contributes much to the vulnerability and fear that is necessarily at the heart of this calling.

Why then become a psychoanalyst? The slide into doing 'psychoanalytically-informed' psychotherapy is pervasively and incessantly enticing. Doing psychoanalysis may, indeed should, provide the practitioner with a livelihood, but it would be absurd to list this as a motivation; except for a brief mid-twentieth century period in the United States, it has always been the case that psychotherapy is a far more lucrative mode of employment. Earning a living is surely the least of three benefits that the psychoanalyst may accrue. One key to the joy of becoming a psychoanalyst is that it offers one an unparalleled intimacy with people from many, if not all, 'walks of life.' This is surely an awesome and humbling experience, as well as a source of deep joy and great responsibility. Psychoanalysts do indeed come to 'understand a lot of things' although this leads to the significant danger that they come to imagine that 'to understand is an end in itself' that will necessarily have a 'happy ending' (see Endnote 20). The psychoanalyst's refined understanding of much about the human condition is often as much or more of an obstacle to the psychoanalytic process of listening. So this source of pleasure in being a psychoanalyst is also one to be guarded against – its indulgence slides the practitioner back into psychotherapy. The other key to the joy of becoming a psychoanalyst may well lie in William Hazlitt's much quoted aphorism from 1821, 'the soul of a journey is liberty.' One enters psychoanalysis because of one's own suffering and one continues the journey into becoming a psychoanalyst for reasons that have a similar root, but are now, in a certain sense, thoroughly different. Even while – or more accurately, because of – constantly voiding oneself as a practitioner, the journey of becoming a psychoanalyst is a lifelong trajectory of freeing one's own truthfulness. It is not as simple – or as crass – as that one 'uses' the patient for one's own growth, but every encounter with every patient provokes the psychoanalyst deeply to challenge her/himself and in this sense the joy of the calling to become a psychoanalyst is the profound joy of knowing and being on one's own journey of freeing one's own truthfulness.

Yet the truthfulness that is freed brings the psychoanalyst face-to-face with the human constitution in the forces of sexuality and death.

4

PSYCHOANALYTIC DISCOVERIES

Sexuality and deathfulness

The diverse enterprises of psychotherapy march under the tripartite banner of epistemology, morally-regulated relationships (that is, relationships that are perceptibly or imperceptibly ideologically-governed) and the pragmatics of personal adjustment. Psychotherapy is epistemological in that it concerns a subject that knows its 'objects' (its self or parts of itself, as 'object' of inquiry and representations of other people, material entities, ideas and feelings as such 'objects,' as well as the nexus of intersubjectivities). Its capacity for epistemological change (knowing and the application of knowing) is limited to the transformation of that which can be known, that which can be represented, interpreted and reinterpreted. It is entirely about relationships between entities (intrapsychic or interpersonal) and can only transform them via discursive procedures that honor and obey the apparent 'reality' of 'what is' or what appears to be. It does so by means of judging the appropriate or inappropriate courses of action within the context of this 'reality' (that is, according to some implicit or explicit moral code).[46] Under a variety of conceptualizations, adjustment is ultimately the 'name of the game' in every form of psychotherapeutic endeavor. It may be varyingly conceived as adjustment between different parts or aspects of the psyche, or as adjustment between the individual and other persons, and foremost between the individual and the 'outside world.'

Ontoethics before and beyond epistemology

Psychoanalysis reaches beyond knowing – beyond not only the known but also the knowable – and thus beyond the epistemological limitations of any and every psychotherapy. Its distinctiveness lies in its exposure of these limitations via the method of free-association. What free-associative discourse exhibits is the way in which, even when an epistemological procedure interrogates itself, questioning its own conditions of knowledge and its gaps of nonknowing (all of which are assumed to be able to be domesticated within the potential purview of whatever is or can be captured by self-reflectivity, the self-conscious knowing of what is knowable), there is actually an exuberant excess. There is a 'remainder' of *being-as-becoming*, an ontological residue untouched by epistemological operations. This is an erotically-embodied surfeit of lived-experience that Freud declared to be the core or 'heart' of our being. In a qualified sense, this might be formulated as 'I am the surfeit of all that I think, or could ever think, I am' ('we are the surfeit of all that we think, or could ever think, we are'). This is the eruptivity of the desirous energies of our lived-experience that cannot be, or refuse to be, subjected to, or captured by the existing schemes of knowledge or within the existing rules and regulations of representational form. Such energies may be required for representational formation and transformation, fueling them but never captured by them. This is the key to Freud's free-associative discovery of an energetic 'core' to our psychic being and becoming – a force that is not merely biological and that eludes the ratiocinative grasp of our mentation.

It perhaps comes as a surprise – going against the current of conventional teaching about what is confusingly called 'psychoanalytic psychology' – that psychoanalysis is not primarily about knowing. Rather, at least in its radical rebirth, it ultimately prioritizes not any arrival at interpretation, but rather 'free-associative listening' to the brio of the unknown and unknowable dimension of our being-becoming. That is, it privileges a commitment to such listening over any arrival at the potentially deceptive and foreclosing appearances of interpretive knowing. One way to appreciate this is to insist that a genuinely psychoanalytic process only occurs when it is driven foremost by *principles* – the necessary central 'root' principle being that of an ethical commitment to free-associative praxis. This is because, as articulated by Guy Thompson in *The Ethic of Honesty*, 'a principle has priority over theory because theories are derived from the experiences that principles presuppose.' The principle that drives radical psychoanalytic process is an ethical one, namely the drastic commitment to a militant method of openness that is not merely an openness to other ways of knowing but to the otherwise dimension of our being-becoming. This is a prioritization of the fullness – the ontological multidimensionality – of our lived-experience, over the conventions of epistemology that assume the positionalities of a subject and its objects of investigation (and thus take-off from metaphysical assumptions about the beingness of these entities). Ethics, in this sense, necessarily entails ontology. Thus, reaching beyond what epistemologies allow us to understand (especially in relation to their dualistic and rationalistic underpinnings) and what they empower us to change instrumentally, *psychoanalysis as free-associative praxis is an ontoethical discipline* that I am also describing as the *spiritual-existential praxis of liberation*.[47]

The priority of ethics and ontology over epistemological concerns may be understood in this manner. We cannot appreciate relationships unless we primarily approach them ethically because, if we do not do this, everything that is other and otherwise can only either be assimilated to the same (sooner or later), or remain unaddressed. We cannot appreciate the 'beingness' of our existence unless we are willing to relinquish the metaphysical assumption that our human essence lies in our capacity to think and thus that all that 'is' can eventually be captured in our logical and rhetorical maneuvers of representationality. This is because there are ontological modes by which we discover ourselves and our world that are prior to, and must take a certain sort of priority over, that which can be encapsulated in the epistemology of subject/object relations. This is, I propose, precisely what Freud discovered through the radicality of his discursive method. Engagement with the de-repressive method of free-associative discourse – the process of listening to the 'voicing' of that which cannot be translated into representation – is foremost an ethical and ontological praxis, rather than an epistemological one. This process of psychoanalysis, as opening us to the otherwise otherness that resides animatively within our being-in-the-world, transmutes our lived-experience beyond what can be accomplished by the procedures of knowing about ourselves.

Thus, to those who endorse the metaphysical assumption that everything composing the meaningfulness of our being-in-the-world either can potentially be coherently *reflected-on* within the purview of the subject's logical and rhetorical transformations, or can potentially be *known-about* by the subject's correspondent representations of the world of objects that are other than itself, the proposals advanced in my writings can only seem absurd. Such metaphysicians, imbued with the confidence of naturalistic commonsense, live in the – psychoanalytically mistaken – surety that what composes a human being is 'mental' and/or 'material.' That is, any event may potentially be adequately and sufficiently represented either in terms of a description of our thoughts (from percepts to concepts and judgments), feelings, wishes, fantasies and motives, or in terms of a description of the physical operations of our biology, our anatomical structures and physiological functions. As is well known, this sort of dualistic scheme generates a history of debate over the relations between the mental and the material (concomitancy or William Whewell's idea of 'consilience' are the currently fashionable designations for this relationship, since both notions appear to sidestep the charge of intemperate reductionism). Moreover, it is almost always assumed that the events occurring in one mode of discourse (for example, the physical) can potentially be adequately and sufficiently translated into those occurring in another mode of discourse (for example, the mental) and vice versa. However, if one adheres to such assumptions, much of the vision of our humanity that Freud discovered is effectively obliterated, because the notion of repression and of de-repressive praxis implies the operation of a discourse that is, so to speak, both physical and mental, yet neither purely physical nor purely mental. It is thus fundamentally ontoethical, not epistemological.

This is what is at stake metaphysically in appreciating the radicality of psychoanalysis. Freud's experience with free-associative discourse led him to posit the existence of a psychoenergetic force operating as the (dis)associative copula *between* the psychology of representational discourse and the biological discourse of anatomical and physiological structures and functions. In 1913 he wrote that 'we cannot avoid "drive" as a boundary notion for what mediates the psychological and the biological ... psychoanalysis operates in a realm between psychology and biology.' The realm he called *Trieb* or 'drive' is that of psychic energy, which is characterized herein as desire or libidinality. What is proposed here is that, if psychoanalysis does not disappear into the hegemony of psychotherapeutic theorizing, it will eventually be understood that Freud's central discovery is that of psychic energy. It is quite 'reasonable' to dispense with this notion as unproveable – that is, to return our understanding of the human being to the binarism of mind/body – *but* if one does so, the radicality of psychoanalysis and the coordinates of Freud's originality are actually forfeited and there is no healing science beyond the logical and rhetorical maneuverings of psychotherapy.

In this context, free-association comprises the praxis of thinking and feeling that proceeds beyond the known and knowable, as if endorsing Heidegger's aphorism of 1943 that 'thinking begins only when we have come to know that reason, glorified for centuries, is the most stiff-necked adversary of thought.' Thus, if we were to insist (very reasonably and very much in line with the hegemonic discourse of the 'modern era') that, for psychoanalysis to be legitimate as a science of healing, its foundations and the totality of its processes must be epistemological, then we would fail to appreciate the revolutionary character of its discourse as foundationally ethical and ontological.[48]

As is well known, ontology traditionally addresses what *'is'* more emphatically than it addresses what *'might be'* (against which Heidegger insisted in 1927 that 'the possible ranks higher than the actual'). In the course of the modern era, the master discourse of post-Copernican science obscures (although with the contemporary advent of the so-called 'new sciences' this concealment becomes piecemeal) the way in which ontological considerations have ethical-political significance and constitute obstacles, opacities and limits to any and every epistemological endeavor. As I have indicated, epistemological enterprises presume the ethical and ontological ground on which they operate and discussion of this ground is relegated to the realm of 'metaphysics' (which some of the advocates of epistemology, notably from David Hume to Rudolf Carnap, claim it has surpassed). Whatever process claims to open itself concretely to this realm is typically derided as mysticism (at least within the modern 'western' zeitgeist). Against this, Levinas (who develops a line of philosophy that is discernible from the pre-Socratics to such writers as Gottfried Leibniz and Henri Bergson) emphasizes and demonstrates not only the complicity of ethics, ontology and politics, but most strikingly the priority of ethics as 'first philosophy' (see Endnotes 46 and 47).

This is the radical path of psychoanalysis, wherein its praxis is foremost an ontoethical discipline that frees the truthfulness of our lived-experience (and is thus also subversively political). Prioritizing the ethicality of discourse, the ontology of psychoanalysis concerns what traditional metaphysical philosophy has less frequently addressed, namely not only *being* as such, but the character, conditions and *process of being-as-becoming* (which I earlier suggested might amount to the seemingly preposterous claim that movement precedes the existence of that which moves).

As I have indicated, psychoanalysis joins – or, more precisely, fuels, albeit indirectly, the initiation of – a current of thinking that calls into question the modern era's emphasis on, and prioritization of, the rules and regulations of epistemology that have been systematically developed and multiply contested under the auspices of Platonism, Cartesianism and Hegelianism, as well as the more contemporary exponents of analytic-referential (logical-empiricist) and hermeneutic discourses (see Endnote 14). Contemporaneous with and subsequent to the advent of psychoanalysis, this movement links a raft of profound and quite diverse philosophical thinkers. This includes Nietzsche, Bergson, Heidegger, Adorno, Levinas, Derrida and perhaps most notably (given his interest in amending the discipline of psychoanalysis) Gilles Deleuze. In a different vein, the movement has certain potential ties with the writings of many quantum scientists (from Erwin Schrödinger and Werner Heisenberg to Richard Feynman). If psychoanalysis is a discipline, a method or praxis, that – by deconstructing the establishment of self-consciousness – uniquely opens our awareness to its own ontological process as the dynamics of being-becoming, then what is revolutionary about this discipline is precisely the way it opens our thinking and feeling to the composition of our lived-experience, our being-in-the-world. That is, the way it opens the horizon of our lived-experience to dimensions of its meaningfulness that are incomprehensible to an epistemological reasoning operating on the assumptions of dualism (and rationalism).

Lived-experience and libidinal energies

Free-association led Freud to some remarkable discoveries, the implications of which are still too little appreciated. Experience with this praxis required him to posit notions that are, in a certain sense, auxiliary to the method itself. These are his 'helpful ideas' (*Hilfsvorstellungen*) that are the fundamental coordinates of his discipline.[49] In these developments, the central notion is that dangerous ideas can not only be suppressed from our self-consciousness, but also *repressed* as if exiled beyond a barrier that prevents translation back into representational form. Beyond the repression-barrier, such ideas persist as flashes, fluxes, traces, sparks or waves of turbulent energy – termed 'thing-presentations' in 1915 – that insistently fuel, eruptively and disruptively, the transformation of representations from one to the next in our stream of consciousness. Thus, the discovery of the free-associative method required Freud not only to develop Johann Herbart's 1824 notion of repression (and to think about the operation of a 'barrier,' an ontological rupture of translatability between the repressed and the representable), but also to consider the psyche as being composed of, and by, energetic forces that are themselves recondite. It then led Freud to the polysexuality and pluritemporality of psychic life, as well as to the repression-barrier being established formatively as the intrapsychic inscription of the universal taboo against incest and hence to the universality of oedipal complexities.[50] However, at this juncture we need to focus on the boldness with which Freud asserts the ubiquity of psychic energy.

'Stirring up the underworld' as he experimented with free-associative praxis (in 1900 he characterized his labors in this manner), Freud is compelled to declare in 1913 that the notion of *Trieb* cannot be avoided as a frontier or limiting notion (*Grenzbegriff*), and that his discipline operates *between* biological and psychological standpoints (*welch ausgiebige Vermittlung zwischen der Biologie und der Psychologie durch die Psychoanalyse hergestellt wird*). From the mid-1890s and for the rest of his career, Freud posits what I am calling a notion-for-praxis (*Hilfvorstellung*), which is that of a specifically *psychic* energy. By 1915, he will argue that this is the force that demands the labor (*Arbeitsanforderung*) of representational formation and transformation in the stream of consciousness, even while its meaningfulness cannot be captured by conscious and preconscious representationality. Psychic energy – desire – cannot be adequately and sufficiently represented because repression is, as Freud defined it in 1896, a 'failure of translation.' Psychic energy always remains exuberantly excessive in relation to the system of representationality, precisely because of the irreparability or insuperability of this failure.

The essential and most provocative point here is as follows. It is the point about psychoanalysis that is perhaps most misunderstood, then being invoked as the reason to turn away from this discipline and to turn toward some disempowered form of psychology, psychotherapy or neurobiology. Psychic energies are events that occur *between* the realm of biology and the domain of representationality. They are, as it were, both material and immaterial (neither material like a physical entity that is demonstrable, nor purely immaterial, 'mental' or representational). The psychic energy of desire is meaningful in that its motions and commotions seem to follow paths of pleasure/unpleasure (*Lust/Unlust*), yet it is meaningless *if* (and only if) by this it is implied that eventually it could be adequately or sufficiently represented. It fuels representationality but also disrupts its narratological cogency, coherence, continuity and completion through the stream of consciousness. Even in the 1890s, Freud understood that ideas which have been oedipally subjected to 'literal' or 'actual repression' (*eigentliche Verdrängung*) decompose into psychic energy. By 1915, he added that there must be an originary process of 'primal repression' (*Urverdrängung*) in infancy that generates psychic energy (libidinality or desire) from out of biological processes (on which it leans, as suggested by Freud's notion of *Anlehnung*) and thus partitions psychic energy from even the inchoate formations of representationality. As elaborated by Laplanche, this primal repression implies that psychic energy is generated leaning-on, propped-upon or following-from (*Anlehnung*) biological operations but becomes infused with enigmatic messages that bombard the infant from out-side (the 'seduction' that Laplanche calls our 'fundamental anthropological situation'). Thus, it is crucial to grasp how it is that, after primal repression, oedipality (which entails the toddler's induction into the symbolic register of language and the attendant encounter with taboo or the symbolic *No!*) involves dynamics in which representations may be formed but then decomposed back into the enigmatic 'protolanguage' of psychic energy by processes of actual repression. In short, there is a rupture between biological operations and desire or psychic energy, as well as between the latter and the representational world it fuels.

Thus, critical to understanding the necessity of free-association for any genu-ine psychoanalytic process is this notion-for-praxis of psychic energy, desire or libidinality.[51] Yet what can it mean to suggest that there might be such an 'intermediary' (*Vermittler*), imperfectly linking the material mechanisms of our biology and the mentality of the representational world we inhabit (indeed, link-ing them with an insuperable 'imperfection' that is itself meaningful as the dynamically constitutive bio of our lived-experience)? Moreover, how important is it that Freud asserts the nonidenticality – the imperfectability or impossibility of full and complete translatability – of the discourses of this mediating force of desire and the world of representations? And what are the implications of sug-gesting that, as elaborated by Laplanche, this energetic force arises with or from the semiotic (signaled meanings that are enigmatic and incomprehensible in terms of the comprehension afforded by symbolic language and its narratological formations) bombardment of the infant, such that it draws upon (leans-on, is propped-upon or follows-from) biological operations but is not, and cannot be, identical with them?

In raising these questions, Freud's psychology challenges, or collides with, the entire 'western' tradition – Platonic, Cartesian, Hegelian – that in various ways addresses matter and mind dichotomously. Whether he was aware of it or not (and he can be read as vacillating on the ontological status of psychic energy), Freud joins, or perhaps more precisely he anticipates, the further development of an undercurrent of philosophical thinking, a wayward lineage, which compre-hends the universe in terms of what Elizabeth Grosz calls *incorporeality*.

For example, Stoicism (such as articulated by Zeno, Cleanthes and Chrysip-pus) draws on the pre-Socratic philosophy of Anaximander, Herclitus and Empedocles, in refusing the binarization of matter and idea.[52] The Stoics develop practices predicated on a vitalistic cosmology in which every element of the universe is animated by a fiery breath or 'pneuma.' Humans can master nei-ther matter nor thought, but must submit to this universal force and somehow make it their own. In this way, ethicality comes to be at the center of Stoic philosophy. Operating actively or passively in relation to the various forms and processes of being, pneuma is an incorporeal (*asomata*) force that subsists throughout all existence. It does not itself exist, but it is not nonexistent. Per-haps, in this respect, it is much like a doctrine of subtle energy that is required for the movements of both physicality and ideation, yet is never manifested apart from these existents that it animates.

Baruch Spinoza's 1677 *Ethics* (as well perhaps as some of the contemporaneous writings of Leibniz on the notion of the 'fold' whereby considerations of ontology, ethics and the politics of collective life are conjoined) develops the Stoic's early efforts to expound a philosophy of immanence. Spinoza seeks to attack – indeed at times he lampoons – the influential philosophy of mind/body dualism that had been articulated a few decades earlier by René Descartes. As is well known (especially since Spinoza has become fashionable with the rise of so-called 'neuropsychoanalysis' and the writings of scientists such as Antonio Damasio), Spinoza refutes the idea that there are different types of being – as in the Cartesian dichotomy of *res extensa* and *res cogitans* – arguing that these are two attributes of a single substance. Such a 'substance' is the uncaused causal force that makes each kind of 'event' (material and mental), and that is the totality of all there is. The attributes of matter or mind (and there might be other attributes of which we are entirely unaware) are *in* this substance and are expressions of this substance – they are, so to speak, ways in which substance is involved with itself and expresses itself.[53]

Although many 'psychoanalysts' are now resorting to Spinoza's ideas (and the fashionable enthusiasm for 'neuropsychoanalysis' that follows Damasio and his many colleagues), one must not jump over Freud's contemporary (to whom he declared a certain sort of *homage*). Nietzsche asserted quite powerfully that whatever order the world manifests is (behind, beneath or beyond the way in which we try to extract principles of its regularities) primarily chaotic, contradictory, excessive and open-ended. That is, not controlled by 'things-in-themselves' but to be understood as the material effects of forces and force fields. For Nietzsche, as for Spinoza, life is pure immanence. His notion of the 'will-to-power' (which should not be confused with psychological traits such as having a powerful will or being a willing power) differentiates Nietzsche from Spinoza. Whereas the latter propounded *amor dei intellectualis*, Nietzsche advances the notion of *amor fati*, the love of destiny that overcomes the present to embrace the 'eternal return.'[54] Nietzsche advances a notion far more like the Stoic's fiery pneuma than Spinoza's immanentist notion of substance, the operations of which are deducible. Concurrent with Freud's notion of psychic power, Nietzsche argues that 'all driving force is will-to-power ... there is no other physical, dynamic or psychical force except this.'[55] One can open oneself to this power, but it remains chaotic, contradictory, excessive and open-ended – it forever evades our fantasies of mastery, domination and control.

What is pneuma for the Stoics, the immanence of substance for Spinoza and the will-to-power for Nietzsche, is discussed by Deleuze and Guattari as the 'plane of immanence.' Through a sequence of works on Nietzsche, Bergson, Spinoza and Leibniz, as well as his collaboration with Guattari, Deleuze advances his own attack on the impossible division of the material and the immaterial, arguing that such a disjunctive concept masks the complicity of the disjunctive terms in what are actually conjunctive relations as phases of becoming. Influenced by philosophers such as Georges Bataille and Roger Caillois, Deleuze thus joins his contemporaries (such as Foucault, Derrida and Luce Irigaray) in developing thinking that demonstrates the extent and the way in which such binary divisions are unsettled. It is a line of philosophizing that was, in Grosz' words, 'nascent in the pre-Socratics, self-consciously developed in the Stoics, fully systematized and philosophically ordered in Spinoza, and given blood and life in the writings (and life) of Nietzsche.' Like Levinas, Deleuze makes ethics implicitly or explicitly central in all his writings. Notably, this is ethicality outside and beyond the prescriptive configurations of moral codes. Rather, it is the ethics of engagement with – or even an amplification of – ontological forces that support life itself. This is an ethics that does not impose regulative judgments, but rather one that seeks principles that are immanent to the being-becoming of lived-experience. Thus, it is both ethics of ontology and ontology of ethics. Deleuze develops ontoethics both as a way of grasping the world and as an ethical stance by which to live in it (and it might be noted that he also deals extensively with aesthetics and with the ways in which lived-experience enhances and expresses its own 'style' of being-in-the-world).

Pivotal to this venture is Deleuze's notion of the plane of immanence, which he elaborates most clearly in his writings with Guattari (notably *A Thousand Plateaus* and *What is Philosophy?*). This plane is, in many ways, a rereading of Spinoza's notion of substance, without the latter's totalizing implications. As an aside, it may be noted that this is contrary to Alain Badiou's critique of Deleuze as another philosopher of '*the one*' (which is precisely the reason that Jaspers, pursuing his theological interests, celebrated Spinoza's philosophy). As is very competently explored and discussed by Grosz, Deleuze was also influenced not only by Jakob von Uexküll's ideas about the co-constitution of *Lebenswelt* and *Umwelt*, but also more contemporaneously both by the work of Gilbert Simondon on individuation and ontogenesis, and by that of Raymond Ruyer on embryogenesis. There are several planes in Deleuze's ontology, yet perhaps the importance of the plane of immanence – at least from a psychoanalytic standpoint – is that it is an incorporeal force, like that discussed by Spinoza and Nietzsche, which addresses the mode of encounter between entities, including concepts, and does so in a way that is unlike any transcendental or teleological mode of organization. The plane of immanence is not itself representational (neither discursive nor propositional, neither intentional nor referential). Indeed, it seems that representationality hides or betrays the plane of immanence, which is why Deleuze and Guattari seem to favor paradoxical and nonsensical expressionism. As a sort of virtuality, the plane *becomes* even while, as incorporeal, it lacks specifiable historical and geographical location. It is thus the un-conceptualized (and un-conceptualizable) condition of conceptuality, the un-narratable condition of narrative, defined by its exponents as 'the image thought gives itself of what it means to think.' It may be stretching a point of comparison, but it is striking that for Freud, psychic energy is – in a manner not entirely dissimilar to the plane of immanence – the unthinkable precondition of thoughts, the force that makes thoughts possible and animates their coordinates.

Schopenhauer's *The World as Will and Representation* is known to have been a significant influence on the three contemporaries, Nietzsche, Freud and Bergson.[56] Schopenhauer argues that all natural and human events are expressions of an insatiable *will-to-life*. This 'will' can also be appropriately translated as desire or urge, and it bears a striking comparison to some of Freud's pronouncements about *Trieb* or psychic energy. As most commentators agree, Schopenhauer was profoundly influenced by the teachings of Sanātana Dharma, notably both Vedantic Hinduism and Mahāyāna Buddhism. In multifarious ways, such teachings posit a universal force of subtle energy as animative of 'all that is.' Unlike Schopenhauer, Freud's interest in Asian thinking was cautious, perhaps ambivalent (the ambivalence probably motivated by his determination to appear 'scientific'). Nevertheless, I have written previously on the way in which, at least in some sense, the strange – enigmatic, extraordinary – notion of desire or libidinality as psychic energy seems to bear comparison with longstanding notions in Asian cosmology, both Dharmic and Taoic.[57] Here, at the very least, one must consider the dharmic lineage's notion of *prānā* (as cosmic energy that operates within our embodiment as well as all around it) and the Chinese teachings about *ch'i* (or *qi*, which is *ki* in Japanese, *lom* in Thai). Also there are the notions of *mana* in certain oceanic cultures, *orenda* for some native American groups, and *od* in ancient Germanic cultures (of which Freud undoubtedly had some knowledge). Although this set of doctrines is not monolithic, these ancient wisdom traditions point to the subtle invisible energy of a lifeforce – an incorporeality in Grosz' terminology – pervading the entire universe, animate and inanimate. The flow of this lifeforce is essential to both material and immaterial beings, coming between and thus linking the body and the mind, as well as weaving and circulating all around our *bodymind*.

Polemically, one might argue that *either* there is value in accepting the reality – even as a mythematic reality or virtuality – of the existence of such an incorporeal force, the eventuation of which is a quasi-chaotic or minimally predictable flow between the operations of biology and the domain of representationality with all its transformations, *or* one returns to the Cartesian dichotomy which posits the function of the pineal gland in linking matter and mind. Contemporary neuroscience tends to talk about the way in which an ensemble of cerebral devices maps the body, the external world and the brain's own functioning, and then how this forms a 'proto-self' that permits the formation of a 'core-self' as well as 'core consciousness' that then allows the creation of an 'autobiographical self' and 'extended consciousness' with reflectivity and so forth. But as seductive as such talk is (emblematized by the vacuous idea that there must be a 'consilience' between the data of brain functions and that of psychological phenomena), it is as mythematic as anything else. The mythic quality is persuasively buried in verbs such as *maps, forms, permits* and *allows* that describe these processes of emergence (among others, this has been trenchantly argued by Catherine Malabou, along with Adrian Johnston). As comic as we might nowadays find Descartes' belief about the labor of the pineal gland, in effect these verbs perform the same labor (now more diffusely located). These mythemes of emergence may be more parsimonious than the notion of an incorporeal force that operates between or throughout both matter and mind, but the latter is aligned with lived-experience, especially as it is exposed by free-associative praxis.

I am definitely not advancing any simplistic proposition about the equivalence of the notions mentioned here – the Stoics' pneuma, Spinoza's substance, Schopenhauer's will-to-life, Nietzsche's will-to-power, Bergson's élan vital, Deleuze and Guattari's plane of immanence, or the cosmologies of prānā, ch'i and the like. What I am suggesting is threefold.

First, Freud's notion of psychic energy – *Trieb*, desire or libidinality – decisively sabotages, overturns or breaks with hegemonic assumptions about ontological dichotomies. This subversion is not to be dismissed cavalierly, because it is, in various ways, supported both by a marginalized thread in the history of 'western' ontological philosophy and by a central thread in eastern cosmology. It is a thread that problematizes the ontology of conventional dualisms (and thus problematizes the priority of epistemological labor and the prevalent dichotomizing of rationality/irrationality), and that does so by positing some sort of subtle force between, or pervasively throughout, the material and the immaterial.

Second, Freud's version of subtle energy actually deviates somewhat from the more cosmological depictions of this force because, by and large, he adheres to the endogenous/exogenous distinction and writes of psychic energy as if it were solely created within, and operative within, the individual's body (as a closed energy system modeled on the ideas of Hermann von Helmholtz). However, although Freud did publish two conservatively toned and moderately skeptical professional essays about telepathy in 1920 and 1921, these did not intimate the actual strength of his personal convictions about such phenomena (see Endnote 23). He believed in telepathy even while trying to keep this conviction more or less secret, writing as much to Ernest Jones on March 7th, 1926, in a letter insisting that 'my acceptance of telepathy is my own affair' and that 'the subject of telepathy is not related to' psychoanalysis. The former part of this insistence is, of course, questionable, the latter is an absurdity. If telepathy is the transmission of information – thoughts or feelings – from one person to another without any ostensible communication, then how could such a phenomena possibly occur unless they involved some sort of movement of some sort of invisible energy? Clearly, Freud's assertion of the endogenous character of psychic energy was, by his own almost clandestine admissions, called into question, for he seemed to hold possible the operation of some sort of subtle energy outside the individual's embodiment. In this context, it is far from clear how Freud could maintain what seems to be his general opinion that psychic energy is created from and operates exclusively within the individual's embodiment. Freud's sparse writing on the notion of *Anlehnung* can be read as assuming that libidinality emerges from the self-preservative operations of biological mechanisms such as the sucking reflex (although as Laplanche and Pontalis stated in 1967 his ideas on this matter have 'not yet been fully extricated,' partly due to their entanglement with his emphasis on early 'object-choice'). However, his classic 1905 *Essays* are a sustained three-part thesis designed to show how our libidinal 'patterning' – the recondite meaningfulness of the turbulence of our desire – is not simply determined biologically, as *Instinkt* or the modal action patterns discussed by ethologists, but rather shaped semiotically by life experiences. That is, psychic energy, the incessant motions and commotions of desire, leans-on, is propped-upon or follows-from (*Anlehnung*) biological mechanisms and operations, but is never identical with them, precisely because infants are, as it were, 'hailed into being' psychically by the 'voices,' the enigmatic messages, that bombard them. Thus, desire is never simply concordant with the physical events on which it depends, precisely because it develops from the infant's semiotic bombardment with enigmatic messages from outside – messages associated with physical events, but ones that the individual cannot process representationally.[58] In short, between biology and psychic energy there is an ongoing dynamic rupture, as has been brilliantly expounded by Laplanche (and very competently elaborated by Ilka Quindeau).

Third, Freud's version of subtle energy deviates in another way from most of these cosmological depictions of this incorporeal force, precisely because of the notion of rupture or nonidenticality necessary to account for the lived-experience of free-associative discourse. As I have indicated, the notion-for-praxis of psychic energy entails a rupture between biological events and the movements of desire. What has been called the 'libidinal economy' of psychic energy may have been the conceptual heir to the 'economics of nerve force' that Freud wrote to Fliess about in April 1895.[59] But there is strong reason why Freud discontinued this neurological talk after his *Entwurf* of that same year and developed a notion of energy different from any biological operation (just as the 1905 *Essays* are precisely structured to show the difference between sexuality, as the libidinal patterning of the motions and commotions of desire, and its biological substrate). There is also nonidenticality between the movements of desire (the 'libidinal economy') and the representational system (commonly considered our 'mind'). As I have argued, this rupture is intimated by the discovery of the repressiveness of self-consciousness with the notion-for-praxis that, once repressed, an 'idea' only persists as a thing-presentation (as flashes, fluxes, traces, sparks or waves of turbulent energy) that insistently fuel, eruptively and disruptively, the formation and transformation of representations, but cannot be translated adequately or sufficiently into representational form. Desire is, as discussed previously, an elusive, enigmatic, excessive, extraordinary and exuberant voicing of an energetic dimension – or dimensions – of meaningfulness within our lived-experience that can never be fully represented. Thus, contrary to the mistaken aspirations of so-called neuropsychoanalysis, Freud's discipline cannot be assimilated to a philosophy such as Spinoza's, under the banner of 'consilience.'[60]

Spinoza posits one substance with – at least – two attributes, mind and matter. This would seem to allow no room for considering the ontological contradictoriness or dynamic of nonidenticality that psychoanalysis finds both between biology and desire, and between desire and representationality. The same might hold for the Stoic notion of pneuma, or for several of the eastern cosmological notions which seem closer to Freud's psychic energy than Spinoza's substance – the dynamics of nonidenticality do not seem readily able to be assimilated to such ontologies. The same may not hold for Deleuze and Guattari's notion of the plane of immanence, because they suggest that immanence is not the only such 'plane' – although again, the relations between them seem obscure, at least to the extent they are addressed in the 1991 discussion provided by these authors.

Psychic energy as the dynamic force of 'all there is' – mediating matter and mind in a manner that is assured momentum by its nonidenticality or contradict-oriness – is a necessary notion-for-praxis that is uniquely psychoanalytic. It thereby gives the lie to all the twentieth century enterprises that have attempted to subordinate psychoanalysis to some other discipline (such as cognitive psych-ology, textual hermeneutics or neuroscience).[61] In short, central to the ontoethi-cal discipline of psychoanalysis is this notion of psychic energy – *Trieb*, desire or libidinality. Its centrality is not only as permeating and mediating the matter of our biological physicality and the representationality of our mind, but also with the tenet that this force is dynamically nonidentical with both matter and mind (here nonidenticality implies that these modes of discourse are not inter-translat-able but are in a potentially dynamic relation). The different or *différant* 'voicing' of desire can be attended to – given expression in the speech that speaks the stream of consciousness – or listened to, and indeed such speaking and listening has transmutative effects. But this does not permit the reduction of one to the other. The nonidenticality of biology and psychic energy – obscurely articulated in the doctrine of *Urverdrängung*, our 'fundamental anthropological situation' as Laplanche describes it – implies that the events of biology and the occurrences of desire or libidinality cannot be inter-translated. To reiterate, the nonidentical-ity of psychic energy and representationality, which is the foremost finding of free-associative discourse, implies that desire and its representation can never be fully – adequately or sufficiently – translated one into the other, and thus desire remains an exuberant excess in relation to the transformations of our thinking. In short, if one insists that there should be inter-translatability, one misses entirely the revolutionary significance of psychoanalysis. One returns to the epis-temology of psychotherapy. The richness of our lived-experience is thereby falsely rendered 'one-dimensional' (to borrow Marcuse's phrase from 1964). That amounts, ultimately, to the tawdry task of adjusting one's thinking and feeling to an oppressive world – the task of making our alienated condition appear to function more smoothly.

On 'falling into' free-associative speaking

Adjustment, the watchword of psychotherapy, involves the challenge of rethinking (re-feeling, re-wishing, re-fantasizing and re-motivating) the nexus of relations, both intrapsychic and interpersonal, within which and by which each individual is formed and constantly involved. It is about relationships – about connections or linkages, and about 'correcting' those connections and linkages according to some implicit or explicit criteria. Its practice requires a modicum of self-disclosure on the part of the patient, as well as the clinician's ability to engage with what is disclosed and offer (re)interpretations of its significance according to an acknowledged or unacknowledged theoretical framework (and the sense of 'reality' to which the practitioner subscribes). For such ventures, the 'fundamental rule' of free-association, with its commitment to a sincere effort to speak aloud anything and everything that 'comes to mind' (and accordingly to an ethical relationship of absolute honesty), can be discarded. For psychotherapy, free-association is but one – dispensable – tool among many. It is considered inessential and typically resisted. As I have argued, the application of a 'theory of the mind' – in a relationship that prioritizes the transformative effects of interpretation and reinterpretation – can obstruct or negate the genuine discourse of psychoanalysis as free-associative praxis. Psychoanalysis is thereby abandoned in favor of psychotherapy.[62] Yet for psychoanalysis, free-association remains the *sine qua non*.

To some extent, even Freud may have participated in this betrayal of the radicality of his discipline. From 1896 to 1914, his priority can be described almost wholly in terms of his commitment to experimenting with free-associative praxis. With the advent of World War I, there was a shift or 'caesura' (as Green names it) in his writing. The prioritization of free-associative discourse seems to have receded (despite his continued assertion that this method is essential to the discipline he founded). Freud's main preoccupation turned to the construction of objectivistic models of mental functioning (as described in the two previous volumes of this trilogy). As I indicated earlier, when writing on psychoanalytic methods in 1913, Freud told his patients that they should *not* do what everyone does ordinarily, namely 'try to maintain a connecting thread' as they speak 'in order to stick to the point.' Yet by 1923, he describes his *Grundregel* somewhat differently, merely telling his patients 'not to hold back any idea from communication' just because it might be disagreeable or judged nonsensical, unimportant or irrelevant. I suggest that this seemingly slight shift is actually profoundly significant. It might entail the difference between the radical notion of free-association as *speaking the stream of consciousness* and a bastardized definition of this discourse as a more or less uncensored sequence of story-telling.[63] Another way of considering this is as follows. To the extent that speaking observes the narratological-imperative, the speaker usually continues to experience the 'mineness' of his or her speech, whereas with a more radical commitment to free-association, the speaker's words tend to lose their 'mineness' and s/he feels more as if s/he is ventriloquizing a borrowed discourse. Thus, with a freer mode of free-association (as it were), the speaker's discourse seems to be less her/his own and more that of others or of forces that are otherwise. In Nietzsche's characterization, *it speaks me*, or as Georg Groddeck, whom Freud admired, wrote *wir werde von unserem Es gelebt* ('we become lived by our It'). This radical notion of free-association, with its clear injunction that the subject is both to abandon the narratological-imperative encoded in the idea of 'connecting threads' or having a 'point to the story' and thus to speak the stream of consciousness, thereby opens awareness to listen to the − unrepresentable − otherwiseness of the repressed. By contradistinction, an uncensored sequence of story-telling merely provides the practitioner and patient with uncensored material for interpretation and reinterpretation (see Endnote 19). That is, translations and transformations of what is representable yet other than what is immediately available to self-consciousness. In this latter mode of speaking, the narratological-imperative still holds sway, and under its aegis, the voice of the untranslatable otherwise goes unattended.

The demotion of free-associative praxis − let us call it what it really is, the deep and tenacious resistance to this praxis because of all the anxiety that it elicits − has been embraced vigorously both during Freud's lifetime and even more thereafter. The resistance has taken the form of several sorts of argument: (i) that the free-associative method can by replaced by other techniques of 'data-gathering' to suit the purposes of interpretation and reinterpretation; (ii) that the products of 'active imagination' are equivalent to free-association; (iii) that inter-pretation of 'deep' conflicts around anxiety and affect can proceed without regard for the patient's readiness and these conflicts therefore do not have to have sur-faced free-associatively; (iv) that what counts is the patient being coercively thrown off balance, even violently destabilized, for example by 'short sessions,' so that new previously 'unconscious' material is evoked; and (v) that the back-and-forth of transference and counter-transference phenomena is equivalent to the flow of free-association and can substitute for free-association (thereby limiting the discourse to meanings that can be represented) and finally, in a similar vein, that dialogue can substitute for the workplay of free-association. This last view, the premise that one might dialogue one's way into the unconscious, is prevalent across a broad spectrum of psychotherapies. That a technique may be efficacious − contributing to the patient's adjustment and readjustment − does not of course make it psychoanalytic.[64] Compared with a commitment to the workplay of ongoing free-association, it is comparatively easy to access the descriptive uncon-scious and imagine erroneously that it is the repressed. Such tactics are ultimately deluded. Indeed, the motor of their efficacy may signify an ongoing reinforcement of the repressiveness of self-consciousness. Such are the consequences of any treat-ment that abandons the free-associative method.

Here it is not going to be suggested that the resistance to free-association is, to any great extent, due to a mistranslation or misunderstanding of Freud's terminology. Nevertheless it is useful to consider how this resistance has been supported by the focus on *freie Assoziation* rather than the other term used by Freud, *freier Einfall* (which has the connotation not only of a falling-into, but also of a touching, an incursive incident or even a benign invasion). I will dis-cuss the latter notion momentarily, but before doing so we must note how Freud alludes to the difference between these terms (for example, both in the second lecture of 1910 and in his 1920 note on psychoanalysis' prehistory), but regrettably never expounds its significance. 'Association' surfaces in the 1890s when Freud would often ask patients for the first item that 'comes to mind' in response to a particular thought (which he himself might have introduced to the patient). This use of the term was encouraged by Jung's early publication of his studies in which a word would be presented to an experimental subject, who would produce an 'association,' the content of which as well as the alacrity of response would then be investigated. Freud's augmentation of the notion of association with the modifier *freie* thus seemed appropriate for a method (which Freud continued problematically to refer to as a 'technique') in which no stimulus idea would be presented, but the patient would be required to speak, throughout the treatment session, whatever next 'comes to mind.'

Historically, the concept of free-association immediately sparked a lengthy debate, in part because the deterministic cast of psychoanalytic theorizing implied that no psychic event can be considered 'free' even if it appears with relative spontaneity, but also because what is of clinical interest about an 'association' is largely the way in which it deviates – seemingly to dissociate – from the semantic and pragmatic rules and regulations that govern ordinary meaningfulness and everyday conversation. Moreover, from the standpoint expounded in this trilogy, the unfortunate aspect of the notion of free-association is that it falls short, in its connotations, of opening our thinking to the possibility that thinking could open itself to the forces of a dimension of meaningfulness that is unrepresentable. Rather, it encourages the perspective that the 'point' of an item expressed free-associatively is that it can be treated as the object of inquiry by an epistemological subject. If a patient says 'mother' in response to 'spider,' we can set about figuring out why she came up with such an idea. If a patient talks about his uncle's visit and then, as if absent-mindedly, proceeds to speak about a newspaper article documenting Donald Trump's latest abuses of power, then we can set about exploring the significance of this linkage in terms of the ways the patient experienced his uncle and how these experiences have affected him. Thus epistemological subjects (the psychotherapist and the patient's 'self-observing ego') will now tinker with the 'data' that the free-association has provided. But this is not how the expressions of free-associative discourse should be listened to, and thus the term 'free-association' is unfortunate to the extent that it fails to convey the way in which, in a genuinely psychoanalytic process, free-associative speaking has, sooner or later, to be accompanied by a special mode of free-associative listening. By this, I do not so much mean 'listening with the third-ear' in the sense that Theodor Reik expounded in so masterfully (in 1937 as well as 1948), but rather the mode of listening that opens itself to whatever falls into awareness, even while the meaningfulness of such an incidence might be entirely unrepresentable. To open thinking and speaking to whatever falls into awareness is to open awareness to what is otherwise than representationality. It is a praxis of following the stream of consciousness out loud that dislodges the hegemony of representational – ordinary – thinking and speaking.

This crucial point can be further illustrated by examining the extent to which telling a sequence of stories, in a comparatively uncensored fashion, is not free-association (despite frequently being so labeled). For example, a patient who comes into a session, gives a more or less cogent description of his experiences watching a film the previous evening, proceeds to offer a more or less coherent account of how it reminded him of a childhood memory of his mother's fits of rage, and then continues to explain how grateful he is for the softly caring and considerate attitudes of the woman with whom he currently feels he is falling in love, is not fully engaged in free-associating. Similarly, a female patient who begins her session recalling a childhood act of stealing one of her brother's toys, proceeds to talk about a fantasy of her husband becoming disabled, and then speaks of her reactions to her son's penis, is producing very useful material from a psychotherapeutic standpoint. However, we should be very cautious about claiming that she is fully engaged in free-association, precisely because each 'moment' in the sequence is clearly bound to the narratological-imperative. Each 'moment' has a certain internal coherence and a 'point' – whereas a more radical adherence to speaking the stream of consciousness would doubtless be far less cogent and continuous. Yet, such vignettes are routinely described in clinical seminars, for they provide material which epistemological subjects can inspect in order to infer underlying or 'latent' themes. But such vignettes inevitably fall short of disclosing the richness and the depth of genuinely free-associative discourse. Here we must note how it is extremely implausible that a patient who is genuinely free-associating could produce a sequence of stories with such a degree of cogency, coherence and continuity. As I just described them (and of course in actuality this is merely a synoptic description from my memory), these patients are doing precisely what Freud in 1913 instructed them *not* to bother to do, namely they are maintaining a 'connecting thread' as they speak 'in order to stick to the point' – and they are doing so, despite the fact that they are almost certainly unaware, in terms of their reflective self-consciousness, what this 'point' actually is. Indeed, they may believe that the 'point' of their discourse is entirely different from that inferred by the exegetical audience – the inference of 'latent themes' usually requires the aid of an attentive clinician, who may then introduce the interpretation into the self-consciousness of the speaker. Although these simulacra of free-association are invaluable for the psychotherapeutic elucidation of latent themes that are 'other' than that which the patient is reflectively aware, they fall short of a method that facilitates listening to what is otherwise than that which can be, sooner or later, brought to representation.

A full commitment to free-association is jarringly disruptive of the cogency, coherence and continuity of sequentially uncensored story-telling, because, if one speaks the stream of consciousness authentically, no narrative is going to be enunciated without insistent and persistent interruptions. Moreover, in large measure, such interruptions come from the embodied voicing of our excessive and exuberant psychic energy, desire or libidinality. For want of a better term, 'straight-talk' – the prerogative of computers that stick within the law and order of their discourse, precisely because they lack the sheer fleshliness, the naked eroticality, of being human – is insistently and persistently disrupted by seemingly irrelevant sounds that come from within, erratic phonemes or misplaced words, strange locutions, as well as micro-moments of amnesia, pauses and so forth. These are the linguistic aspects of the patient's free-associative speech that violate the narratological-imperative. Then there are also the multiple 'distractions' of our body's capacity to 'talk.'

Moreover, unlike the techniques of purportedly 'free' dialogue, free-associative speaking invariably allows embodied experience to 'join in the conversation,' in a manner specifically precluded by discourse that obeys, even to a small degree, the narratological-imperative. 'Joining the conversation' is how Freud expressed these phenomena in the 1893 account of his work with Elizabeth von R, whose leg pains regularly expressed a different – *différant* in Derrida's sense – meaningfulness that interrupted the continuity of her speaking to the clinician. The actuality of the stream of consciousness rarely *if ever* 'sticks to the point.' Rather, it inevitably includes not only the awareness of visual stimuli (even if the eyes are closed), but also of leg or arm pain, abdominal cramping often with borborygmic noises, stiffening of the shoulder muscles, genital engorgement or lubrication, tightening or grinding of the jaw, tensing of the anal sphincter, erythemic flushing, burping or belching, thoracic constrictions, flatulence, muscular twitchings, transient (or more prolonged) headache and so forth.[65] As I argued in my 2013 paper on the bodymind in psychoanalysis, it would be a serious mistake not to embrace these occurrences as meaningful expressions of psychic energy manifesting themselves in an unrepresentable fashion. That is, manifesting themselves in a manner that transgresses the narratological-imperative. After all, contrary to popular belief, psychoanalysis is not an ideocentric and ideogenic discipline, it is prototypically a somatocentric and somatogenic one.

The occurrences listed above may be major or minor, but they comprise profoundly significant moments within the streaming of our awareness, because these moments are meaningful expressions of the motions and commotions of psychic energy within us. In this way, the importance of free-associative praxis is not merely because it as an excellent way of listening to the relationships, intrapsychic and interpersonal, that comprise the patient's being-in-the-world – the *other* meanings that psychotherapeutic methods or dialogue might well address. Going beyond that purview, the full commitment to the radically free-associative discourse is essential precisely because it is the supreme way of listening to movements of psychic energy within the patient's lived-experience – an *otherwise* meaningfulness that cannot be accessed by the talk of psychotherapeutic technique. Here psychoanalysis joins with some aspects of the treatments provided by 'body psychotherapy' or bodymind healing, as well as longstanding methods of 'meditating with the body' that are mostly associative with tantric lineages of spiritual practice.[66]

Some of the confusions about the concept of free-association might have been avoided if Freud had stuck to the notion of – and his translators coined a term for – *freier Einfall*. For this notion has far less the implication that one item determinatively (albeit spontaneously) leads to the next (with linkages that must necessarily be governed, at least to some extent, by the law and order of representationality, the narratological-imperative and being expressive of under-lying or 'latent' themes that are representable).[67] The notion has more the nuance of 'allowing things to fall into' awareness. That is, 'things' as presenta-tions that might be moved from outside the law and order of representationality and the narratological-imperative. This implies that free-associative speaking must be understood as involving a special mode of *receptivity* that I call 'free-associative listening.'

This issue of receptivity to what is otherwise can be introduced by the notion of *Gelassenheit*, which is a term that Freud never used but which is elaborated by Heidegger (although in a fashion that psychoanalysis must necessarily qualify or contest). For us to relinquish our resistances to the processes of *freier Einfall* necessitates the attitude of *Gelassenheit*, which denotes equanimity or calmness, serenity or tranquility, but it also, especially since the writings of Meister Eckhart, implies a certain attitude of yieldedness, letting-be, openness or submission.[68] In the 'Conversation' portion of his *Discourse on Thinking*, Heideg-ger suggests that what distinguishes humanity is thinking and that 'the essence of this nature, namely the nature of thinking, can be seen only by looking away from thinking.' Thinking, as defined traditionally, involves the willing of re-pre-senting, so to grasp the essence of thinking would seem to require the willing-ness to renounce thinking; 'willingly to renounce willing' (as one of Heidegger's figures expresses the matter). That is, a 'looking away' involving 'a non-willing in the sense of this, perhaps paradoxical renunciation, so that we may release, or at least prepare to release, ourselves to the sought-for essence of a thinking that is not a willing' (here 'willing' implies, I would suggest, the transformative force of representationality). This *releasement* is *Gelassenheit*, which is not exactly 'caused' in the usual sense, but rather 'let-in' from elsewhere. It does not belong to the domain of the will and yet, in a perhaps seemingly paradoxical manner, it is essential for us to keep 'awake for releasement.' Heidegger calls thinking with this releasement 'meditative' (although some might prefer to call it contemplative).[69] In short, this receptivity, or releasement from (and therefore negative in relation to) the law and order of thinking about thinking, contrasts dramatically with the motif of mastery that Freud enjoined us to consider central to the delusionality and illusionality of the ego.

Heidegger's notion of releasement points to – but perhaps does no more than point to – an exit from the hegemony of what he calls 'thinking in the trad-itional way as re-presenting.' That is, an exit from ordinary or traditional think-ing, which is governed by repetition-compulsivity and the narratological-imperative (although this is not Heidegger's terminology). He teaches us that 'releasement does *not* belong to the domain of the will' and enjoins us to 'wean ourselves from willing,' thus 'keeping awake for releasement.' From a psycho-analytic standpoint, Heidegger says strikingly little about *how* one might proceed from the attitude of ordinary thinking, cogitation, to that of 'meditative think-ing,' contemplation or *Gelassenheit*. The exit is indicated, as it were, but no method by which to proceed toward it is specified. Nevertheless Heidegger's ideas seem profoundly pertinent to an appraisal of Freud's achievement just a few decades even before his earliest major work in 1927 (and several decades before the notion of *Gelassenheit* was discussed). In this respect, Heidegger's disavowal of psychoanalysis is most regrettable. For surely free-association is the praxis of such a process of releasement and of listening of that which 'voices' itself from elsewhere in the otherwiseness of enigmatic messages that are not accessible via ordinary thinking. Certainly in relation to the repressed dimension of psychic life, this praxis of releasement and yieldedness (letting-be, openness, submission) is only achievable by the dissolution of our resistances to ongoing free-associative speaking and listening. Free-association and the dissolutive addressing of our resistances to its ongoing momentum constitute the key method of *Gelassenheit* (that Heidegger seems to have foresworn), because such discourse facilitates our receptivity to that which is otherwise than representational thinking. Again, this is precisely because the free-associative method acts against the suppressiveness and repressiveness of ordinary discourse in a manner that can be described as negatively dialectical or deconstructive.[70] Free-association proactively subverts the hegemony of 'ordinary' or traditional thinking as representationality with all its suppressive and repressive functions, thus opening us to what is otherwise than representation. In this sense, psychoanalysis is the praxis of receptivity to the messages that inform us and animate us from behind, beneath or beyond, the systematic of representational thinking – although this is rather far from where Heidegger proceeds with the issue.

All these considerations perhaps provide the route to an explanation as to why there is all this conspicuous and considerable resistance to Freud's singular and revolutionary discovery – the discovery of free-associative speaking and listening. The answer is surely that whereas other techniques keep the discourse of treatment safely within the bounds of the narratological-imperative (addressing relationships and trying to make-sense of them), psychoanalysis does not. Whereas psychotherapy examines and addresses connections or linkages, intrapsychic and interpersonal, and does so under the governance of the narratological-imperative, psychoanalysis assimilates and proceeds beyond the practice of transforming this domain. In so doing, it facilitates awareness of the sensuality-sexuality and inherent deathfulness of our being-in-the-world. This is surely the source of our resistance to free-associative speaking and listening. As must now be discussed, the profound vulnerability and fear of surrendering to the process of radical psychoanalysis – the terror of being and becoming a psychoanalyst – is that we are now, as it were, confronted with the polysexuality and the incessant mortality of our lived-experience, but only in living such ongoing confrontations can we become truly *alive!*

Free-associative awareness and our polysexual humanity

Whereas the talk of psychotherapy dwells on relationships, intrapsychic and interpersonal, the talk of psychoanalysis indeed addresses all these relationships but then, going beyond psychotherapy, it engages the expression of, and is receptive to, the enigmatic meaningfulness of our sensuality-sexuality and the ongoing deathfulness of our being-becoming – the otherwise dimension of our lived-experience. As will now be discussed, the erotics and the deathfulness of our lived-experience comprise the dual source of our fear of free-associative praxis. In short, they threaten the extant state of the 'ego organization' that has brought about their 'otherwiseness' and that will inevitably resist listening to their voicing. Moreover, both are forces or 'topoi' – for want of a better term – that psychotherapy necessarily avoids and is comfortable doing so, even when it appears not to do so.[71]

Thus, central here is *the healing value of psychoanalytic praxis in taking us back into living our embodied experience* – the dimension of our being, the voicing of which our ego organization seeks only to dominate and control. This is experience that germinates with the incessant flow of our erotic energies (and with the deathfulness of their ebb) within and even around our embodiment. Discourse that observes the narratological-imperative inevitably takes awareness decisively away from the embodied dimensionality of our lived-experience, precisely because it is the system of representationality with its law and order (including its narratological-imperative) that keeps the repressed in its energetic condition of untranslatability. By contrast, free-associative praxis tends ineluctably to move into the somatogenic and somatocentric processes of our being-in-the-world, precisely because it operates de-repressively. As I have described it, radical psychoanalysis is a fundamentally somatic discipline that validates Freud's theorizing the polysexuality of the human condition. That is, free-associative speaking and listening *returns us* to our lived-experience as embodied awareness, animated by the incessantly seething movements of psychic energy guided only by patterns or pathways of pleasure and unpleasure (Freud's *Lust/Unlust*) and the principles of lifefulness and deathfulness. Here we must pause at this notion of 'returning us' to consider what sort of self-consciousness, awakening or awareness, might be involved as we release ourselves free-associatively from the hegemonic governance of repetition-compulsivity and the narratological-imperative.

The history of psychoanalysis has been dogged by the assumption that to be conscious of something is to be able to 'hold it in mind' – by which is implied the capacity to represent it, or formulate it interpretively, within the reflectivity of our self-consciousness. Indeed, 'holding it in mind' reflectively is all too often taken to entail a certain sort of mastery, domination or control, over the object of thought (and thence of the body to which it might refer). This attitude contrasts dramatically with the 'attitude' that I am calling *ontoethical receptivity*. Under the assumption that equates consciousness with its secondary formations of 'holding in mind,' the potential for receptive awareness (such as an awareness that listens to the meaningfulness of thing-presentations that cannot be represented) appears to be subsumed by interpretive reflection, and healing is thereby envisioned as requiring the expansion of insightfulness and understanding rendered as formulations *about* lived-experience.

A full discussion of the range of philosophical ideas about consciousness would, of course, be way beyond the scope of this essay. Not only would it require a comprehensive review of 'western' philosophy and of the findings of contemporary neuroscience, but it would also call for an exploration of the many forms of consciousness described and documented in the Dharmic and Taoic traditions.[72] However, for my present purposes, we might usefully consider Gerald Edelman's widely accepted distinction between primal or primary consciousness and secondary consciousness, which I refer to as the distinction between awareness and the representational reflectivity of self-consciousness (the former has been variously discussed as pre-representation, proto-representational or para-representational). This is a distinction that has routinely been discounted or obliterated in all the 'psychoanalytic' literatures that have surfaced since Freud's innovations. Yet it is crucial, not least because it is surely the discovery of psychoanalytic praxis that 'secondary' self-consciousness (reflectively thinking *about* ourselves) systematically precludes or distorts, in operations that are suppressive and repressive, our receptiveness to the potential meaningfulness of 'primal' consciousness (which would include the enigmatic messaging of 'thing-presentations'). What psychoanalysis demonstrates, at least in its radicalized mode, is that any exploration of ourselves, of our lived-experience or our being-in-the-world, that starts in a Cartesian or quasi-Cartesian fashion with self-consciousness – that is with any sort of reasoning, reasonable method, or technique of 'thinking about thinking' – is doomed to perpetuate the masterful delusion or illusion of the 'I' that it can ascertain its own essence.[73] It is doomed not least because it precludes the possibility of a releasement from the law and order of thinking so as to become able to listen to that which is meaningful but otherwise than representationally. Herein lies the core significance of psychoanalytic discovery for the human condition – the finding that self-consciousness systematically distorts or occludes the messaging of awareness.

Definitionally, self-consciousness is exemplified by our human capacity to 'think about thinking' – in this respect, consciousness is the entire domain of that which can reflectively be thought-about *re*-presentationally. In the clinical terminology of psychoanalysis, it includes not only that which is immediately conscious to us (you are conscious of yourself reading these sentences), but also that which is preconscious and what I call 'deeply-preconscious' (or descriptively unconscious). All such contents – all these domains – of our psyche are representational, even if selectively unattended in the immediacy of the here-and-now. While this realm of potential reflectivity defines 'secondary' consciousness (and is always structured linguistically, even if not necessarily being formed and framed in a particular language), it is more challenging to define awareness (not least because all definitions are founded within the domain of representationality). It is all too easy to slip into an understanding that colludes with the hegemonic subsumption of awareness within the categories of representationality and that thereby precludes consideration of the extent to which, and the ways in which, self-consciousness actually represses awareness. The 'aware' consciousness has much to do with what might be considered a primary or primal way of being-becoming.[74] That is, with our sensuous connectedness with everything around us (as *life!*), and with what David Abram, somewhat in the vein of Maurice Merleau-Ponty's philosophy, called the 'mindful life of the body.' Awareness could be considered by analogies to the 'feminine' receptivity of the caress, a notion described by Levinas in 1961 (and criticized by Irigaray in 1984 for, in a certain sense, insufficiently freeing itself from patriarchal reasoning).[75]

The fear of free-associative discourse is due to the way in which it relinquishes 'making-sense' and facilitates a special sort of listening to the enigmatic messaging of our embodied experience. This messaging presents itself as the incessant motion and commotion of erotic energies within us, and perhaps also around us – that is, a semiotic field we sense only as being chaotically 'guided' by inchoate and enigmatic pathways of pleasure (*Lust*) and unpleasure (*Unlust*, which is not to be equated with pain). With a commitment to free-associative praxis, we come to experience the bodymind (not as self, or personhood, or network of cognitive and cognizable productions) but as spatiotemporally existent within a field of incessant movements of energy. This sensuous yet para/enigmatic semiosis of desire (psychic energy, libido or *Trieb*) is an individualized field of energetic events that can only be considered as a subfield within a universal plane (to borrow Deleuzean terminology) of immanence or becoming. We come to experience or 'know' these movements as disorganizing of the law and order of representationality. But it perpetually remains our fate that we cannot 'know about' them in so far as their meaningfulness remains excessive and exuberant in relation to the instantiations and transformations of representationality. This voicing of desire thus remains elusive, enigmatic and extraordinary. Yet, free-associative praxis brings us into, or releases us into, a receptive awareness of this voicing, in what might be considered an ecstatic – *ex-stasis*, as a releasing from repetition-compulsivity – momentum that is egologically terrifying.

Despite the misguided efforts of some of Freud's followers to rescue his teachings from what they – mistakenly – considered the errors pansexualism, the bodymind as a field of energy movements must nevertheless be considered psychoanalytically as *sexual*. In part this stems from Freud's apt insistence that the notion of sexuality has to be understood as involving far more than behaviors that implicate the genitals (and thus the term 'sensuality' is rightly disfavored as entailing an avoidant account of the full impact Freudian discoveries). In part this is also because we sense that the motions and commotions of psychic energies are erotic both in that they are experienced by us through our embodiment, and in that they are, in a somewhat paradoxical fashion, formlessly conveyed along incipient 'pathways' of pleasure and unpleasure. To grasp the latter aspect, it must be recalled that psychic energy is generated when enigmatic messages from outside bombard (are imposed on, implanted within) the infant in the course of processes that lean-on, are propped-upon or follow-from (Laplanche's interpretation of Freud's *Anlehnung*) our biological structures, functions and mechanisms. Recall that desire or psychic energy is thus both nonidentical with what we understand to be the anatomical structures and physiological functions of our physicality (which nevertheless constitute its substrate), and nonidentical with the operations of thinking as re-presentationality. In this way, psychoanalysis conceives of the entire bodymind as a field of erotic energy. In this regard, it is neither ostensibly physical nor representationally graspable.

Here we might pause to note how this links to what I have called the psychoanalytic discovery of the human condition as being that of *polysexual potentiality*.[76] Despite differences in our hormonal constitution, we are not born with this or that disposition as to how we will experience ourselves in pleasure or unpleasure (not, for example, with any genetic predisposition to be heterosexual, homosexual, asexual or whatever). Our 'lovemaps' or 'sexual patterning' – as eminent sexologists such as John Money or Robert Francoeur have called it – are not inscribed in our biological endowment.[77] Rather, we are born with a polysexual potential to experience any and all erotic pleasures (or unpleasures). Our 'orientation' as it is called (and for that matter our sense of gender) develops *both* from a 'thousand-and-one' enigmatic messages imposed upon us from outside our biologically organismic constitution in the genesis and the shaping of our erotic energies, *and* latterly from more ostensible, even flagrant and decipherable messages that instigate the suppression and oedipalized repression of impulses that are sociopolitically condemned or even persecuted.

This implies the unpredictability and the plasticity of our sexual patterning. Starting with his 1896 letters to Fliess and then in publications from 1900 onwards, Freud called this our 'original bisexuality' (*ursprünglichen Bisexualität*) and later, in 1923, each 'individual's constitutional bisexuality' (*konstitutionelle Bisexualität des Individuums*). The latter term is perhaps regrettable, since 'constitutional' is often taken to imply chromosomal causation, which we can be sure that Freud did not intend (since his 1905 essays painstakingly chart the molding of our prepubescent libidinality). Rather, his assertion is precisely that whatever position one occupies on the homo/hetero continuum (at any particular time, in fantasy or behavior) is *not* a matter of biological endowment. It is a process involving the ongoing suppression of impulses repudiated as 'other.' For example, overtly heterosexual proclivities develop on the basis of the suppression of homosexual impulses, and vice versa (and, as is well known, suppressed impulses are always expressed in some fashion, often by disgust and denunciation). Indeed, in suggesting that Freud's notion that we all start life 'polymorphously peverse' should be reframed as the polysexuality of the human condition, what is asserted is that all human beings begin their erotic trajectory with the potential to experience any and every variant of erotic fantasy and behavior. The development of our sexuality is thus a matter both of the evocation and sculpting of our libidinality by a bombardment of enigmatic messages and of the ongoing suppression of various lines of expression in our erotic potential (in the course of what is commonly called our 'socialization'). It is not, as Gayle Rubin amusingly phrased it, a 'teleology of the missionary position' driven by chromosomal or other biological determinants. It is this polysexuality of our being-in-the-world to which psychoanalysis opens our awareness.

Free-associative praxis thus returns us to our embodied experience and its wisdom. That is, to awareness different from the self-consciousness of that which can be captured within the representationality of reflective consciousness. This awareness engages the messaging of our embodied experience as a field of erotic energy movements. This is the mindfulness of our experiential embodiment, the lived-experience of the bodymind as an energetic field of desire or libidinality. It is thus an awareness that returns us to the sensuous basis of our being-in-the-world.[78] We come to appreciate psychoanalysis as an ontoethical praxis that (against the Lacanian reading of Freud's significance) poses a revolutionary ontology of sexuality, as the pervasive movement of subtle energies in pleasure and unpleasure that sustains the being-becoming of 'all that is' and 'is not.'[79]

Free-associative listening, awareness and deathfulness

As discussed previously, it is the task of psychotherapy that relationships, both intrapsychic and interpersonal, are ultimately required to 'make-sense' within the representational realm of realism and rationality, and thus to be ordered and re-ordered, contained and constrained, within the governance of repetition-compulsivity and the narratological-imperative. However, desire defies capture or containment within this system of law and order. The unique process of listening to the roiling motion and commotion of embodied psychic energy – desire, *Trieb*, libidinality – thus makes psychoanalytic discourse more or less incomprehensible to the endeavors of 'making-sense.' This radicality of the psychoanalytic processes involves a unique mode of listening that necessarily seems somewhat 'mad' outside its own lived-experience of free-associative praxis. As I have argued, psychoanalysis proceeds beyond the discussion and (re)interpretation of relationships, which is the concrete hallmark of psychotherapeutic enterprises, and its distinctiveness lies in the way that it opens our awareness to empower us to listen to the voicing of 'energy-messages' (or thing-presentations) whose meaningfulness is otherwise than that which can be represented.[80] This is, in a certain sense, the mystical or esoteric – spiritual and existential – impetus of psychoanalysis. But this is not to imply that its processes are ethereal, intangible or otherworldly, for psychoanalysis fundamentally concerns the flowing and ebbing of the bodymind's erotic energies that presents us with the meaningfulness of an inchoate and incomprehensible semiosis – the enigmatic messages that constitute the genesis of desire, as leaning-on but not identical with the needs of biological origination.

As I have indicated, when fully committed to free-associative praxis, we become aware of ourselves as spatiotemporally existent, individualized – at least in a certain sense – within a semiotic field comprised of an incessant movement of energetic events on the universal plane of immanence or becoming. It might be noted here how the historical development of various comparable methods of esoteric awareness (perhaps with some similarities to free-associative discourse yet markedly different) has often brought with it the aspiration to map the bodymind in terms of the movements of subtle energy, conceived, for example, as *prāṇā* or *ch'i*. Although often derided within the hegemonic ideologies of 'western science,' it would surely be foolish to dismiss ways of knowing that originate in a diversity of Asian cultures or to ignore their subtle energy teachings – and the associated doctrines of healing – that have been experientially honed over centuries, or even millennia, of clinical practice. Such teachings map the bodymind as a set of special channels – *nādis* in South Asia, *meridians* in East Asia – that are especially concentrated in networks or plexuses. These focal points are the *chakras*, of which seven major ones are usually depicted in South Asian healing practices as approximately corresponding to the regions of the coccyx (*Mūlādhāra-chakra*), the pelvis or genitals (*Svādhiṣṭhāna-chakra*), the navel or solar plexus (*Maṇipūra-chakra*), the heart (*Anāhata-chakra*), the throat (*Viśuddha-chakra*), the so-called 'third eye' (*Ājñā-chakra*, which is around the middle of the forehead, slightly above the junction of the eyebrows), and the crown (*Sahasrāra-chakra* or *Mahasukha*). There are also many minor chakras – as well as, in some schemes, chakras that are external to the body. Traditional East Asian acupuncture documents no less than 361 network points along the meridians, as well as numerous additional 'extraordinary' points. In short, an enormously complex vision of the prevailing movements of subtle energy within (and around) the human bodymind has been articulated in these maps.[81]

At this juncture, my point is not one of advocacy for Asian healing practices (although I am not averse to so doing, my expertise in these areas is insufficient). Rather, my intent is both to point to the ubiquity of human experience with subtle energies (across cultures and over millennia) and to illustrate how prevalent is the ambition to map pathways of subtle energy movement within and around our bodymind. That is, to highlight the possible paradox of asserting that subtle energies are everywhere in all entities and then to suggest that nevertheless their movements tend to adhere to complex patterns within us. Moreover, from the standpoint of thinking about the development of psychoanalytic theorizing, it might be added that, in a certain sense, Freud was not immune from the ambition to specify the particularity of drive pathways. His speculations about 'erotogenic zones' (from his 1896 letters to Fliess onwards) and about 'component instincts' (from 1905 onwards) testify to his insistence not only that 'drive energies' lean-on, are propped-upon or follow-from biological structures, functions or mechanisms that are demonstrable (and thus that such energies are endogenous, despite his private belief in telepathy), but also that there are patterns of order governing a force within us that is only known to our reflective consciousness by its defiance of the order, the rules and regulations, of representationality. In parallel with Albert Einstein's notorious resistance to the idea that the universe functions by aleatory whimsy, Freud ultimately – at least in this context – seems to hold to an unprovable faith in the lawfulness of every dimension of our lived-experience.

There is, however, an aspect of all these doctrines to which Freud can be read as contributing in a quite remarkable manner, which concerns his principle of the deathfulness – *Todestrieb* – that inheres to every moment of life itself. Here we might ask what it means to become aware of the movement of energetic events – within us, let alone around us – that are an incessant process of becoming. To be aware of energy is to sense its movement, its motions and commotions – its comings and goings, flow and ebb – its presentation or presencing as an inchoate and incomprehensible meaningfulness and then the dissipation or absencing of such meaningfulness, as if in an entropic vaporization. If there were such a condition as 'static energy' within us, it seems unlikely that one could possibly have any sense of it. So, the awareness of subtle energies is both of their flowing – that is, their investment in representations that makes them a salient presence in our awareness, their eruptive disruptiveness within the law and order of representationality and of the narratological-imperative, their insistence on aberrant modes of expression and so forth – and then of their ebbing or absencing from our awareness. As discussed preliminarily at the end of Chapter 2, this awareness of the ebbing of subtle energies – that is complicit with the flowing of energies into different formations – brings us to consider the deeper significance of Freud's articulation of *Todestrieb*, the principle of deathfulness within our lived-experience.

Death is normally considered as the endpoint, the *terminus ad quem*, of life itself. In this sense, it is perhaps paradoxically both unthinkable and terrifying.[82] It is considered the negation of life itself, the ultimate depletion of meaningfulness against which is projected a plenitude of myth and religious doctrine. However, Freud in 1920 and Heidegger in 1927 break with the notion of death as occurring outside of life itself (it may be noted that, in relation to the negativity of death, Giorgio Agamben's 1980 book provides a sophisticated discussion, which is beyond the scope of this text). What Freud proposes in his essay is that death or deathfulness is a fundamental motion *within* life itself – a draining or dissipative motion that shapes life ontologically. As is well known, the reading of this 1920 essay has been problematic and controversial.[83] It can be argued that many, if not all of these difficulties stem from Freud's triple insistence: (i) on maintaining his commitment to a dualistic vision of the drives; (ii) from his confusing and perhaps confused effort both to make an argument about the dissipation of desire (the so-called 'Nirvana Principle,' to use the term Freud borrowed from Barbara Low) and at the same time to make an argument about the genesis of aggressivity and destructiveness; and (iii) from his failure to recognize that what he was proposing was not two 'new' drives, but rather 'principles' on which the drives he previously articulated actually operate. Although this last point is best discussed by Laplanche, here we can again argue that *Lebenstrieb* or 'lifefulness' is the process in which desire or psychic energy is invested in representations and their transformations (the moment of an event that Spielrein dubbed creative) and *Todestrieb* or 'deathfulness' is the necessarily concomitant or complected process, the quasi-destructive moment in which psychic energy is drained from other representations. If drives are defined as forces that impose a 'demand for work' (*Arbeitsanforderung*) on our psychic life (that is, a demand for the transformation of representations), then it is evident that deathfulness is not a drive, but rather the quasi-entropic motion of psychic energy or desire away from that in which it was invested.

Breaking with the longstanding tradition that dichotomizes life and death, Freud thus offers us a depiction of the inherency of deathfulness within life itself. With awareness we come to sense the lifefulness of desire as it moves into new formations, fueling their salience within us, and we sense the draining of desire from other formations as their salience recedes. Jones may have intimated the significance of this when he argued in 1927 that what we fear is not so much 'castration' (the realization that we cannot be both *this/m* and *that/f*, and/or that we are not masters of our own meaningfulness and can never be), but rather *aphanisis*. This means the fading (literally disappearance) of desire or the extinction of the possibility of pleasure.[84] In the manner I am advancing these two principles, there is no conflict or contradiction between lifefulness and deathfulness. Rather, they are co-implicative within every movement of desire – the momentum of psychic energy within us and perhaps around us. Together 'they' compel the transformations of representationality and so, despite the structuring of the representational system in terms of repetition-compulsivity and the narratological-imperative, these motions and commotions of desire open the possibility of liberation from the stagnating conditions in which we are imprisoned in the name of realism and rationality. These motions and commotions that are equally those of lifefulness and deathfulness – since these principles are inseparable unto death itself – ensure that we are *alive!*

The praxis of free-associative discourse promotes the awareness of the energetic movements of desire within our embodied experience. Sexuality is the name given for these movements, and their polysexual potential is the ubiquitous condition of our humanity. With such awareness we sense the comings and goings of desire – psychic energy or libido – within us, and perhaps even around us. The comings, the presencing flows of desire, that are its principle of lifefulness, impel new investments in representationality, new transformations. This principle makes us alive, even though desire – incessantly elusive, enigmatic, excessive, extraordinary, exuberant and seemingly inexhaustible unto death – can never be fulfilled, never be satiated in the thoughts and actions that are constituted representationally. The goings, the absencing ebbs of desire, that are its principle of deathfulness, open the temporality of our psyche to the possibility of further life and provide us with a momentum of release from the imprisonment of repetition-compulsivity and the narratological-imperative.[85] The question of pleasure is complex, not only because we know that pain can become pleasurable under certain vicissitudes of lived-experience, but because the pathways of pleasure embrace both the lifefulness and the deathfulness of being *alive!* The fading of desire, the facing of the abyss that is both within us and that inevitably awaits us, may frequently be terrifying. But we also know that orgasmic intensities, in which it seems as if the 'ego organization' will never again return to its conditions of stagnant stability, are unquestionably of spiritual-existential significance in their momentum of ecstatic – *ex-stasis* – liberatory release.[86]

5

THE PSYCHOANALYTIC LEAP AND THE NECESSITY OF REVOLUTION

Perhaps the fuller title of this closing chapter should be: 'On the backwards-forwards leap of psychoanalytic discovery and the emancipative critique of everyday oppression.' The nub of the thesis that has been adumbrated in the course of this trilogy is that, through an ongoing commitment to the rigors of free-associative praxis, the representational enclosures of logical and rhetorical thinking are opened such that we become aware of the anarchic movements of desire within our lived-experience. Correspondingly, we also come to appreciate the suppressive and repressive character of our self-conscious – reflective – knowledge. Thus, 'becoming aware' is a process profoundly different from the maneuvers of ordinary or conventional self-consciousness with its laborious efforts at hearing-to-understand and interpretive formulation (efforts that perhaps, from an ethical-spiritual standpoint, operate under the inevitable penumbra of futility). In radical psychoanalysis, we become aware how desire subsists as the perpetual flow and ebb of subtle energies that both pervasively mediate and yet are otherwise than both the material realm of things and the immaterial domain of thoughts (the representational forum of cognition, affect and conation). In this praxis, we become aware of 'things' presenting themselves meaningfully within us – 'things' that cannot be captured, translated, or transfixed within the domain of representational sense-making and indeed that are actively exiled from the purview of the self-consciousness that is furnished within this domain. The process is profoundly enlivening.

The awareness this praxis facilitates – of the motions and commotions of drive, desire, libidinality or psychic energy – is surely a rediscovery of ancient wisdom that is still prevalent in so many cultures outside the modern episteme. In this respect, Freud's discoveries are *a momentous leap backwards*. That is, a retrieval and a vindication of insights eclipsed by the rise of the analytic-referential masterdiscourse that is the hallmark of the modern era (particularly through the political hegemony of North Atlantic cultures). However, the inauguration of the free-associative method is not coterminous with an atavistic return to indigenous lessons about subtle energy. That is, teachings subverting the detrimentally captivating dichotomy of mind/body (a subversion of Eurocentric assumptions that psychoanalysis achieves decisively). In arguing that experience with the radical praxis of psychoanalysis necessitates the doctrines of repression (both *eigentliche Verdrängung* and *Urverdrängung*), Freud not only points to the threefold constitution of our lived-experience, but also illuminates how our humanity consists of an inescapable double nonidenticality (ontological contradictoriness or failure of translatability). That is, *both* experientially between representationality and desire, *and* then speculatively-inferentially between desire and the operations of our biology. Of course, the ancients appreciated that the movements of subtle energy are not accessible to − cannot be captured by − the logical and rhetorical transformations of thinking. They were aware that, even in the highest forms of reflective and ratiocinative self-consciousness, thinking comprises an irremovable veil over the realities of 'spirit' − the veil of *māyā*, for example. But for a veil to be cast over a reality, such that, as Paul the Apostle (Saul of Tarsus) wrote to the Corinthians, we can 'only see through a glass darkly,' is not equivalent to a process in which the obscured reality is actively exiled, rendered unknowable, by the metaphoric and metonymic transformations of thinking itself (including the 'seeing' that thinking permits). Yet this is how the free-associative method compels us to consider the operations of repression, with their implication that self-consciousness is inherently repressive. Thus, in experientially and speculatively-inferentially disclosing the double rupture of the human condition, its irreparable and insuperable nonidenticalities, Freud's discoveries are *a momentous leap forwards*. That is, a prospective leap beyond the westernized episteme of the 'modern era,' with all its technological accomplishments. Psychoanalysis is thus the harbinger of an ontoethical journey that might aptly be appreciated as a trajectory of 'postmodern' impulses. This is ancient wisdom propelled well beyond what was commonly envisaged by the ancients, and now enhanced by an approach to accessing − listening to − the desirous reality of subtle energy movements that justifiably claim the transmutative status of methodical scientificity.

How might such a leap backwards-forwards change profoundly our general apprehension of human affairs? In these closing remarks, I want to consider, in what is admittedly a very preliminary and sketchy fashion, a partisan question no less urgent than the appraisal of Freud's discipline as the clinical modality specifically performed by the psychoanalyst and patient as a duo.[87] The question is: What are, or should be, some of the main implications of radical psychoanalysis for cultural and political praxis?

Surely no one can doubt the dire need for radical change worldwide in the economic, sociopolitical, cultural and ecological practices by which human relations are arranged. Capitalism has sustained itself, indeed bloated itself, well beyond Marx's optimistic yet sober prediction that the class, which labors productively and rarely or minimally enjoys the alleged 'rights' of ownership, would demand – and, through the momentous forces of historical materialism, eventually ascend to – its just place in the governance of human affairs. Although this socialist-communist vision has not been realized, we surely know nevertheless that capitalism is a self-terminating system. Being based on profitability, the accumulation of property and its accoutrements on the part of the few, by means of the immiseration and impoverishment of the majority (and at the ecological expense of the planet), the future of this system is necessarily limited. To this extent, Marxists correctly foresee its end, while others cynically continue to benefit or have already had their critical capacity for clear thinking ideologically squeezed out of them (on this point, Terry Eagleton's writings are among those that are interesting). Transnational capitalism today pervades every corner of the globe, whether controlled by the kleptocratic apparatus of nation states or more privately by the plutocratic interests of the corporate boardroom. Despite the totalizing power of this system (and a longevity that Marx could not have foreseen), it is nevertheless evident that we are, as Slavoj Žižek puts it, 'living in the endtimes.' It is utterly preposterous to think that today a mere handful of individuals control more wealth than the entire bottom billion (or 13%) of humanity; that 5% own more than the sum of all the rest (and so on, as has been documented by so many chilling statistics). However, this monstrous situation is not actually why capitalism is bound to implode, although it is unquestionably why capitalism frequently faces crises of dissatisfaction and always seems to proceed, sooner or later, in increasingly totalitarian and militaristic directions. Rather, even with global overpopulation (which handily assures those in control of a steady supply of cheap labor, the surplus-value of which can be coercively appropriated), a system based on the expansion of opportunities for the wealthy to accumulate and exploit cannot simply continue indefinitely, especially given the exhaustible limits of planetary resources (of fertile fields to farm, of unpolluted oceans to fish and of mines from which to extract, as well as the paucity of 'new frontiers' offering any pragmatic promise of salvation). In short, we know for sure that capitalism is not sustainable, and may even be imminently implosive.

Yet no one, or scarcely anyone, seems able to envisage, let alone strategize, a realistic exit (in the sense of one that is plausible, able to be implemented) from these 'endtimes.' At present, the satisfactions and dissatisfactions of the masses are either skillfully controlled by ideological mechanisms empowered by new technologies (the ubiquity of the internet and its array of 'social media' being one of the latest and most potent) or, when these fail to deliver the docility of those without power or privilege, genocidal violence remains an alarmingly available option. From the mid-nineteenth century to today, there has been an increasingly frequent resort to genocidal strategies (although exact statistics are often difficult to ascertain, it has been suggested that more have died of genocide in that period than in the entire prior history of humanity). In this context, the hope for transnational revolution in the interests of the disenfranchised seems, to say the least, dim. Žižek, arguably a leading philosopher of the contemporary left, who is well versed in the insights of political economy yet trapped in the conservatism and fatalism of a Lacanian understanding of the human condition, admits his hopelessness and merely suggests that we should engage in 'demanding the impossible' (and presumably also accept that any significant emancipative or liberatory movement is improbable).

Indeed, given that its structures and mechanisms are not going to reform themselves in the direction of freedom, justice, ecological sanity and equitable opportunities for all to have a sufficient livelihood and a life without material or psychosocial oppression, wherein lies our future after capitalism? In today's world, the overall success of social democratic movements has come to seem almost trifling; the values (and platitudes) of liberal humanism flicker, as if snuffable at any moment. All around us (and proliferating over the dozen or so decades since Freud began his labors), we witness at least five horrendous phenomena: the rise of violently intolerant fundamentalisms (and a racist nostalgia for tribal purity); frequent surges of totalitarianism (as well as what Alexander Ross and others have termed 'fascist creep' within those regimes that are allegedly democratic); the insidious entrenchment of sexist modes of oppression (against women, children and minorities of sexuality or gender); warfare on a scale now magnified by technological 'advances' (nuclear, chemical and biological); and the ecological acceleration of irreversible devastation to the planet. In short, it seems what will follow the zenith of capitalism perhaps can only be imagined as escalating barbarity.

How could have – should have – the psychoanalytic inauguration of fresh insight into the human condition contributed to the revolution in human affairs that is so urgently needed (or to what extent has it done so, or could it still do so)? Here I want to suggest three deeply interlinked ways of thinking about change in human practices and also about resistance to change in these practices that might be further considered (which is *not* to disrespect all those commentators who have already engaged this crucial challenge, and whose contributions are too extensive to be reviewed in any detail in this final chapter).

Critique of the discourse of domination

It is very evident that the motif of domination/subordination-subjugation, although refined and rationalized by the philosophies of the modern era, has characterized human conduct ubiquitously and disastrously. Here we can think of exploiting/exploited, abusive/abused, wealthy/impoverished, powerful/powerless, man/woman, adult/child, white/black, mine-ours/other, normal/abnormal and – prototypically – master/slave. What is to be suggested here is that psychoanalysis has contributed immensely (and could still more) to our understanding of the relations of domination, not only it its grasp of the narcissism by which individuals establish their 'self-esteem' by means of the denigration – chauvinistic and prejudicial – of the 'other' that actually defines the 'one' that dominates, but also both in its grasp of the way in which the representationality of thinking (structured like a language, in Lacanian terms) systemically underpins these relations and in its exegesis of oedipality (which I shall come to shortly).

In the context of the modern era of North Atlantic philosophy, it is Hegel who sets the stage for these contributions, offering a characterization of the master/slave dialectic in terms of the way in which the formation of self-consciousness requires the recognition of an equally self-conscious 'other' that it can then attempt to subordinate-subjugate in order to sustain or advance itself. We not only owe much to Hegel's *Phänomenologie des Geistes* in understanding the apparent necessity of conquest in the unfolding of the 'spirit' through self-consciousness, but also to the work of Alexandre Kojève (and Jean Hyppolite) in further explicating how the life-and-death struggle, in which master and slave are locked, is one of 'desire.' Each 'desires' to appropriate the life-blood, as it were, of the other. Here this term refers to intentionality, wishes, ambitions or aspirations (rather than the way it has been used in this trilogy to intimate the momentous operation of subtle energies within and around us). The struggle is such that each of the *dramatis personae* – or human groupings – desires to appropriate the desire of the 'other.'[88] The master wishes to own the aspirations of the slave. The master's position – mastery – actually depends on the existence and the enslavement of the slave. The latter, in longing for a certain sort of 'freedom,' intends to overthrow and thus assume both the position and the ambitions of the master.[89] Eventually the slave must prevail, almost inevitably becoming, it would seem, a simulacrum of the new master.[90] Hegel's account of this struggle is nuanced and complex (as many competent commentaries, in addition to Kojève's, attest). Hegel does then suggest how self-consciousness might escape – transcend – its imprisonment in the master/slave struggle. However, this section of his writing, comprising Hegel's distinctive and highly sophisticated riff on stoicism, skepticism and the 'unhappy consciousness,' remains one of the most challenging of his entire text. Although Hegel introduces the importance of a 'third relationship' in eventually promoting the possibility of 'freedom of self-consciousness,' this crucial moment of transcendence – in which self-consciousness might release itself from being imprisoned in a dominative struggle to define itself and empower itself against its 'other' – begs for elaboration in terms of what might, very crudely, be termed its 'applicability' or directions for praxis. This is where, as a few critical thinkers of the twentieth century have suggested (and I also will suggest), psychoanalysis might powerfully augment Hegelian insight, even though the potential impact of this narrative for our understanding political change, its perils and its limitations, cannot be overestimated.[91]

In the past century, our appreciation for the inescapable power of the master/slave dialectic in human affairs was enormously enhanced by the so-called 'linguistic-turn' in philosophy. I refer to this 'turn' as exemplified not so much by Heidegger (whose later writing, embraces formulations such as 'language speaks us' that almost seem to echo Nietzsche and Groddeck), nor by the followers of

Ludwig Wittgenstein's later work, but rather in relation to the advent of structuralist thinking in the social sciences and, as far as psychoanalysis is concerned, specifically its Lacanian development. Although Lacan's theoretical framework is ultimately a *cul-de-sac* for psychoanalysis (as I will shortly argue), one cannot today grasp this discipline theoretically without seriously addressing his standpoint, although, as I have already argued, one can well grasp the praxis of psychoanalysis without all the elaborate and formalistic theorizing, in which Lacan seems to delight. This is important, especially to the extent that other theoretical elaborations (the structural-functional or ego-psychological, the Kleinian or post-Kleinian and independently object-relational, and the social, interpersonal-relational or self-psychological schools) have in very fundamental, albeit deceptive, ways long since lost track of what it means to engage the praxis of psychoanalysis.

Lacan alerts us to the power of 'language' to generate the subject of discourse (the signifier 'I') and to govern its possible transformations. As is well known, the 'structuralism' of this approach (in which the transformation of elements can only be understood in relation to the operations of the systemic totality) began inchoately with Ferdinand de Saussure's linguistics and blossomed into the structuralist movement of Claude Lévi-Strauss (preceded by Marcel Mauss' theorizing the conditions of gifting and Maurice Leenhardt's notion, in the tradition of Durkheim, of the 'total social fact'). Lacanian theorizing takes this representational system as *phallogocentric*. The term is Derrida's contraction of 'phallocentric' (meaning organized as if around a central originary mark, the grand 'Phallus,' as introduced in Chapter 3) and 'logocentric' (Ludwig Klages' term for the way signs appear to privilege presence over the absencing on which they depend).

Although a sign, operating within the network of signs that comprises a representational system, has always to be part of a triangulated construction (as Charles Sanders Peirce demonstrated, the meaning of any sign requires at least two 'other' signs that can be related to each other), signs invariably appear to us as if their meaning is always constituted in terms of dualities of superordinate/subordinate relations. That is, for example, x/not-x or (very contentiously and most regrettably) *man/wo-man*. The definition of the one depends on the definition of its 'other' and at least notionally the 'other' always appears subordinate. In short, language itself makes it impossible, without laborious qualifications (that inevitably have a diminished emotional impact), to think of anything without positioning it in a network of superordinate/subordinate relations. This is the phallocentricity of language, as a network of such relations that must be centered on an abstract originary mark of difference that has been, perhaps regrettably, called the Phallus (which is *not* equivalent to the penis, although often confused as such). In relation to this, consider now the fragility of the subject of 'my' discourse ('I-Now-Is' as merely a roving signifier, tossed about by displacements, condensations and reversals or negations, which are the transformations governed by the law and order, the rules and regulations, of the representational system). To express the matter very colloquially (and in an unacceptably anthropomorphic manner), given the fragility of the 'I' (to say nothing of the 'Now' and the 'Is'), it is surely no surprise that humans are compelled, by repetition-compulsivity and the narratological-imperative, both to generate a constellation of 'me' representations in relation to those that are 'other' and to articulate these constellations in relations of dominance and subordination-subjugation. It is as if, for 'me' to be 'me' (and any grouping with which I identify), I must locate my sense of self in dominant/subordinate-subjugate relations with all sorts of representations of 'not-me' and the demands of my narcissism (or 'egotism') require that these others are treated in a chauvinistic, prejudicial, or denigratory manner. Under duress or under the grandeur of omnipotent thinking, such a manner readily amplifies itself into structural, institutional and tribal practices of exclusion, marginalization, brutalization and dehumanization. Here surely is the key problem underlying all elitist, sexist, racist (and so forth), explotative and oppression-generating thinking.

The representational system within which our thoughts (feelings, wishes, fantasies and motives) are produced compels us into relations of domination/subordination-subjugation. To step out of this system (as if such an exit were possible, for this can only be a fantasy) would be to take ourselves beyond the pale of humanity. The solution to the ubiquity of thinking in terms of oppressor/oppressed requires new ways to approaching the hegemony of representationality and the narratological-imperative. Here we must understand the crucial role of oedipality – as discovered by Freud through his commitment to the method of free-association – in rendering us human and we must understand the association of oedipality and the advent of representationality, in the sense of language or the symbolic order.

We are all familiar with the notion that psychoanalysis conjures each individual's induction into humanity in terms of two great myths. Narcissus presents the formation of the individual in terms of what *appears* to be the dyadic interaction of 'me-other' or, perhaps more pertinently, 'me/(m)other.' However, the dyadic quality of this interaction is only a matter of appearance, for the 'other' (paradigmatically the primary caretaker, or whoever performs the maternal functions of whatever natal gender) must already be located within the triangulated system of representationality (that is, oedipalized, as in a process rudimentarily foreshadowed in Hegel's discussion of the master/slave dialectic). Thus, if there could be such an entity as a 'Mother' who is not herself oedipalized (again, this is not to discount the possibility of male performance of the maternal functions), she could not possibly raise a human child. Recall Green's aphorism that 'there is no such thing as a mother-infant relationship.' As if subsequent to the dynamics of Narcissus (although such a notion of chronology is fallacious, since all psyche life is oedipalized), Oedipus then presents the formation of the individual in terms of what are explicitly triadic interactions (even though the terms of the configuration may be more imaginary than actually present in the individual's life). As I have argued in 'Oedipality and Oedipal Complexes,' there have been serious and fundamental errors in the way Oedipus has been understood.

Accordingly, I have proposed that we use the term 'oedipal complexes' for all the narratives pertaining to triangulation between the 'self' and the individual's various maternal and paternal caretakers (actively present or absent but imagined). 'Oedipality' then is to be grasped as the kernel of any and all oedipal complexes and it is to be defined in terms of the way the incest taboo (universal, albeit with many cultural variations) structures the psychic formation of every individual. In this context, we must consider how this taboo is not just a genetically encoded aversion (although in some ethologically relevant sense it may also be some sort of a 'modular action pattern' with an 'innate releaser mechanism'), but a feature of the structuration of language, the symbolic order. As Lacan correctly says, it is after all language that inducts the child into the primal sense of a forbidden, the symbolic *No!* In this sense, it is the structuration of representationality – language, in a general sense – that forms our psychic life and keeps us from the erotically compelling slide into incestuous chaos.

Thus, since the necessary avoidance of incest – the requirement of civilization that there be this ultimate 'Law' – keeps us alienated or estranged from our desire, the critique of domination cannot rest with a diligent examination of the fundamental structures by which we think (our cognition, affect and conation). This is what has been, and is being, engaged by many skilled commentators. It has also to be empowered by deeper consideration of the way in which the inescapable oedipality of all our (sociocultural, political, economic) discourse functions ideologically to perpetuate the oppressive conditions of our social arrangements. In short, what can lift us out of ideology is not so much the promulgation of 'other' ways of thinking as it is the necessity of opening thinking to otherness that is otherwise. This is a mandate for the future of critique.[92]

From transformative imprisonment to transmutative release

Surely, if there is any hope of profoundly significant change in human practices, then the centerpiece of Freud's free-associative findings must be completely and candidly addressed (namely, what is popularly called the 'discovery of the unconscious,' which is the discovery of the repressiveness of self-consciousness that entails the human condition's internal and insuperable nonidenticality). This is alienation that is different from (and perhaps more fundamental than) the theological sense in which Augustine of Hippo bewailed it, or the reparable sense in which Marx correctly diagnosed the disconnect between the worker and what s/he produces (or in the sense it was studied by academics such as Wright Mills as a phenomenon of the middle-class in twentieth century North Atlantic cultures). Rather, what has been argued throughout this trilogy (and was less directly suggested by Freud as early as 1912 in his *Totem und Tabu*), is that we examine all modes of alienation as ultimately reflecting and refracting, or as deriving from, the fundamentality of the incest taboo, as representationally conveyed bedrock of what we call 'civilization.' This is the foundational sense of alienation as the rift between the energetic motions of desire and the representational system within which we are able to articulate thoughts, feelings, wishes, fantasies and motives – the system that commits us to relations of domination/subordination-subjugation.

However, despite what might be its initial appearance, the conclusion that alienation is the inevitable condition of our humanity is not a mandate for apathy or passivity in relation to the multifarious modes by which such alienation instigates and perpetuates oppression. Whereas the nonidenticality of desire and the materiality of our biology may seem to remain untouchable (although it is a dynamic that is assured, despite its speculative-inferential status), the rupture between desire and representationality is susceptible to the sort of praxis that is epitomized by free-associative discourse. This is *not* to suggest that the alienation of desire and representationality is superable. Rather, it is to insist that their perpetual concurrence of 'con/disjunctures' (the diverse 'meetings' of this otherwise momentum of our being with what are the ongoing representational transformations of one/other) can be shifted healingly from the alienated stases of repetition-compulsivity to the dynamic kinesis of estrangement. This is the de-repressive praxis of *becoming* through a process of listening (that is not hearing-to-understand). It is an enlivening discourse that reconfigures – as it were – the relation between the *beingness* of our lived-experience and the representational domain we inhabit with all its permutations. Such a process of 'reconfiguration' is transmutative, and thus contrasts with changes that merely involve the transformative operations of representationality. It is realizable only through the negatively dialectical or deconstructive impact that such praxis has upon the law and order of representationality. This is key to the radicality of free-associative psychoanalysis, in going beyond the reformist transformations of psychotherapeutic discourse.

Thus, although the nonidenticality between desire and our capacities for thinking cannot be overcome, it can be mobilized and in this way transmuted from the stases of alienation into the kinesis of estrangement. Such a transmutation is – at least a partial or momentary – release of the subject from its imprisonment in repetition-compulsivity and the narratological-imperative. One implication of the discovery of this nonidenticality is as follows. Any method of inquiry or mode of practice that misses – presumes nonexistent or nugatory – this insuperable contradictoriness inherent in our lived-experience necessarily culminates in the ultimate bankruptcy of reformism. It culminates in an ideological distorted and perniciously conservative 'take' on the character of our humanity, as well as the betrayal of any radical possibility of liberatory release from our variously oppressive confinements. In relation to such betrayal, the theoretical edifices of ego-psychology, object-relations and all manner of self/other psychologies, are all wittingly or unwittingly collusive and culpable. Writing about psychoanalysis, Althusser argues persuasively that, given the contradictoriness of reality (psychic and sociocultural), it can only be engaged truthfully by adopting a particular – disruptive or unsettling – stance toward it. Herein lies the unique power of free-associative discourse. This praxis does not engage so much in maneuvers that *transform* our representational world, engendering improved understandings about our condition. Rather, it strikes transgressively at the cogency, coherence and continuity of our representational system in a manner that *transmutes* being and thus empowers our capacity to listen to the desirous movement of our lived-experience, motions and commotions of psychic energy that are beneath, besides or beyond what can be represented. That is, to listen and thus to become more *alive!*, but never to make-sense or to rest in the delusions and illusions of 'understanding.'

Thus, psychoanalysis points to the limitations of dialogue – in which the one and the other converse in order to resolve their differences – as a transformative procedure that necessarily remains within the imprisonment of dominative modes of discourse and that therefore can only result in a pretense of emancipation (even if the immediate effects of this are benign). To express this differently, psychoanalytic discourse does not resolve contradictions that cannot be resolved, but rather it mobilizes them and thus enlivens our thoughts (feelings, wishes, fantasies and motives) without claiming that they are any more 'correct' (correspondent, coherent, or pragmatically effective). Its liberatory impact is in its transmutative movement that truthfully conjures our being in relation to our discourse without ever arriving at the simulative 'truth' of understanding. This is the strange truthfulness of psychoanalytic praxis.

Here then we must pause to formulate some final critical comments directed against the popularity of Lacanian theorizing and to specify how Lacan himself departed decisively from any vision of radical psychoanalysis when he left behind his youthful interest in the surrealist movement and became infatuated with the scientism of structuralist thinking. Thereafter he established – from around 1936, when he was in his mid-thirties, until his death in 1981 – a monumental theoretical edifice. It is an *oeuvre* which every psychoanalyst must now study seriously and from which there is much to learn – despite the fact that, from the standpoint of radical psychoanalysis, this edifice leads us on paths that are inherently and egregiously mistaken.

As is well known, Lacan understands the world in terms of three registers: the Imaginary (which is not to be confused with imagination), the Symbolic (which I believe can legitimately be equated with the way in which representationality is discussed herein) and the Real (which is not to be confused with reality). Hereafter, with the exception of the Real, I will not follow Lacan's habit of capitalizing the imaginary and the symbolic.[93]

Dating back to 1936 (with his paper 'Beyond the "Reality Principle"'), Lacan's notion of the imaginary involves the delusional or illusory and specular – oculocentric – realm of dyadic relations and, in the third set of his annual seminars, which ran from 1955 to 1956, he links it to the precepts of ethology. The imaginary is presented as if an initiatory register somewhat distinct from the symbolic order and perhaps conditioned by the individual being biologically primed to be, as Lacan expresses it, 'captured by the image' of the other (a perceptual-behavioral mechanism that he seems to identify as the most basic 'sexual relation'). In this context, Lacan briefly alludes to the relevance of ethological findings. So here it is legitimate to consider how Lorenz's famous ducklings were shown to be primed for attachment by modal action patterns triggered by the innate releaser mechanism of the image of the parent duck (or, mistakenly, by the image of a substitute such as Lorenz himself). My underlying point here is that, from the outset, Lacan's approach ablates the possibility of psychic energy as a meaningful force that is neither identical with biological mechanisms nor assimilable within the domain of representationality (I will return to his notion of the unassimilable register of the 'Real' shortly; see Endnote 93). Thus, Lacan's allusion, in this third set of seminars, to the imaginary register as linked to 'animal psychology' tellingly preempts the vitally important point later elaborated by Laplanche. That is, concerning the function of enigmatic messages in the genesis of libidinality. As has been discussed, these are messages different from, but nevertheless lean-on – are propped-upon or follow-from – biological mechanisms such as those studied by ethologists, and they are not assimilable within the symbolic order. Such Laplanchean insights are barred from the Lacanian canon.

Indeed, in the trajectory of Lacan's theorizing, he gradually brings the imaginary register or 'plane' entirely within the grasp of the symbolic (which is partially my justification for preferring the term 'representationality'). As early as his 1949 'Mirror Stage' paper, Lacan suggested that this register involves a spatiality that is *always already structured* by the symbolic order (recall how seemingly dyadic relations that are held to occur prior to the child's negotiation of her/his 'oedipal complex' are actually, always already, oedipalized). In the 1955–1956 seminars, he speaks of 'certain functional interweavings' of what are now termed two 'planes' (the imaginary *in stricto sensu*, and the symbolic). By the time of his eleventh annual seminar in 1964, it is explicitly stated that the imaginary, and indeed the entire visual field, is structured by the law and order of the symbolic (as the whole domain of representationality). In short, the imaginary is not to be considered an autonomous register. Rather, it is a 'plane' of experience constituted by, and only accessible within, the symbolic order.

Thus, Lacan's celebrated 'return to Freud' ultimately pivots on his distinction between the symbolic order and the Real. In many ways, the latter is the most slippery or evasive of his concepts, yet it is the means by which he could be said to avoid a certain sort of linguistic idealism. It is all that is outside the domain of representationality (both imaginary and symbolic). Strikingly, the Real is thus *both* ontologically substantive (as a register in which there is no absence, even though it is elusive to the presencing of *re*-presentationality), *and* yet it also 'functions' (for want of a suitable verb) as an absolute that is empty, as the abyss of all that is unthinkable, like death itself. At various points in his teaching, Lacan suggests that the Real only 'makes itself known' as an unknowable or unfathomable force, in phenomena such as traumatic anxiety and psychotic hallucinations.[94]

It is now possible to summarize the consequences of Lacan's virtual totalization of the symbolic order (in the manner I embarked in my 1984 book) and thus to specify how radical psychoanalysis is fundamentally not Lacanian (and how Lacanian precepts amount to an effort to foreclose radical psychoanalysis, if not radical thinking in general). Although Lacan points to the existence of the Real outside the law and order of representationality, it can be argued that he merely reframes the dichotomous metaphysics that has entranced the North Atlantic world throughout the modern era (for example, meaning/matter, signification/death). Given that the Real is all that is outside the symbolic order, the Lacanian edifice disallows the possibility of a force, the psychic energy of desire, which might pervasively and meaningfully mediate and yet be otherwise than both the symbolic domain of signification, along with its imaginary plane, and the Real (whether conceived as materiality or as an abyss). There are at least three consequences to this.

First, what is 'outside' the symbolic order cannot be considered as possibly having an enigmatic and extraordinary mode of meaningfulness of its own – an elusive and exuberant meaningfulness that is interminably unrepresentable – and thus Lacan effectively denies that the nonidenticality of the Real and the symbolic could be, in any way, inherently dynamic. This denial accords with Lacan's tendency, common to the structuralist tradition, to present the symbolic order as ahistorical and immutable (a matter extensively discussed by several commentators, including by Joan Copjec in her defense of Lacan against Foucault). That is, this order is effectively a totality (not unlike the Hegelian pinnacle of *absolute Wissen*). In this respect, Lacanian doctrine poses itself as the apotheosis of the masterdiscourse of the modern era. On the one hand, the Real is discussed as if it were the Kantian thing-in-itself, entirely unknowable and inaccessible to reason. On the other hand, the Real is discussed as if vindicating the Hegelian formulae that 'the real is the rational and the rational is the real' or that 'idea or reason' – for which we may read the symbolic order – 'is the formative principle of all reality.' The latter position fosters Lacan's occasional claims, from the early 1970s onwards, that the Real might be amenable to calculation (concordant with his obsessive efforts to mathematize the operations of the unconscious). In short, *Lacanian theorizing obliterates the mysteries of life*, the dynamic mysteries of our lived-experience as the motions and commotions of psychic energy, as a nonidenticality to which we might listen but never understand.

Second, the manner in which Lacan posits the symbolic leaves little or no opening for praxis. The law and order of this register is totalizing and seemingly immutable (Lacan's explanation of historical processes and generative principles is slight and not entirely convincing). Whatever changes it might undergo historically, it is not feasible that they be due to the expressive activity of a thinking, feeling and speaking, subject. Lacanian theorizing rules this out.[95] The 'I' – as a signifier tossed about by metaphoric and metonymic transformations of representationality – is a subject completely impotent in relation to this transformativity of the symbolic order. By contrast, the praxis of radical psychoanalysis, via its commitment to free-associative discourse, 'attacks' the cogency, coherence and continuity of the stream of consciousness (and hence the totalizing implications of the representational system). It thereby opens discourse to a dimension of our being that is otherwise than the law and order of representationality. With free-association, the subject, by casting itself and its own certainties into a negatively dialectical or deconstructive momentum, empowers itself to listen to the repressed dimension of its being-in-the-world; namely, the desirous 'voicing' of a meaningfulness that cannot be (re)habilitated within the symbolic. Radical psychoanalysis is thus a de-repressive praxis that transmutes the 'encounter' – so to speak – between the subject of self-consciousness and its processes of becoming. Against this possibility, the end of Lacanian treatment seems to be some sort of enlightened resignation to the omnipotent and inescapable conditions established by the symbolic order – a submission to the totalitarian force of the system. In short, there is a profound sense in which *Lacanian theorizing leaves us immobilized*, resigned and deprived of a de-repressive praxis, as if with nothing to do and no place to go.

Third, one cannot but be impressed by the sheer fleshlessness of Lacan's theoretical edifice. The Lacanian world is nothing if not paradoxically ideocentric and ideogenic. This is 'paradoxical' only in as much as its centrism is not that of the thinking and speaking subject (as in the Cartesian or Fichtean tradition), but rather the capitalized 'Phallus' as the centripetal organizing and originary mark of the symbolic order (the originary mark that then governs the transformative possibilities of thinking and speaking within the bounds of logic and rhetoric). The Lacanian world is also oculocentric and oculogenic, specifically in the exegesis of the imaginary register that is then found to be 'always already' governed by symbolic law and order. Tellingly, sensuous and sensual experience seems to have no status, or at best a negligible or derivative status, within the Lacanian canon. For Lacan, if the enigmatic messages of our experiential embodiment are not articulable within the lawfulness of the symbolic order, they are effectively nonexistent, barred from having any effect. In his theoretical framework, the erotic is thus entirely subsumed within the symbolic order. It cannot be considered an essential dimension of embodied experience and there is no theoretical space for the 'voicing' of the yearnings for expression of our libidinality or desire, our psychic energy.[96] Psychic energy of this sort has been expunged from the Lacanian vision (only to be resuscitated by Laplanche's post-Lacanian theorizing), and embodied experience is subsumed within the imaginary (and thence the symbolic register). With Lacan, sexuality disappears both into the specular imaginary (a phenomenon with ultimately biological determinants) and then into the stratagems of the symbolic order (the significations of the Phallus and the *manqué-à-être* or 'want-to-be' of this register).[97] There is no listening to the murmurings of psychosexual energies that are recondite, yet powerfully within us. Such listening would surely be dismissed by Lacan as mystical absurdity and, for him, it seems that to 'lovemake' is to dominate. In the masculinist idiom, it is to 'fuck' the other that is woman.[98] In short, *Lacanian theorizing nullifies the erotic desire of our embodied experience as the source of life's lifefulness and deathfulness* (as well as pleasure/unpleasure).

Radical psychoanalysis is about accessing (listening to, without pretense of hearing-to-understand) the vitality of libidinal energies that are repressed by the logical and rhetorical law and order of our thinking, feeling and speaking. By contrast, practices based on the Lacanian theoretical edifice could be said to take intelligence to its limit, and not to allow any opening to the otherwise. They thus forestall the potential *becoming* of our being through a free-associative 'attack' on our imprisonment within the symbolic register.

On the nonviolent power of transgressive praxis

If discovery of the repressiveness of self-consciousness implies the human condition's insuperable nonidenticality, then the only viable method of liberatory movement from our imprisonment within the system entails a shift from our alienation in repetition-compulsive transformations into a praxis of aware vivacity in the transmutative kinesis of estrangement. That is, liberation not as any sort of endpoint, nor as radically achievable by transformations within the 'system.' Rather liberation is the process of embracing an incessant movement of freeing and truthfulness that requires the praxis of nonviolently 'attacking' the repressive (and suppressive) character of the system within which our thinking, feeling and speaking, are established and imprisoned by repetition-compulsivity (and the narratological-imperative).

One might well wish that Lacan had applied his brilliance to a deeper examination of the significance of the surrealist movement and its existential implications, rather than to the heady exaltation of structuralist scientism and the dissemination of an attitude of resignation that is surely symptomatic of the exhaustion of the modern era. Although one must protest the grievous sexist, patriarchal and somewhat misogynist values espoused by many of the leaders of this movement (now well exposed by recent feminist critique), the surrealists must be credited for a certain sort of recognition *both* of the futility of laboring within the conventions of the prevailing discourse (that is, the futility of opposition within the 'system' or of the attendant hope of its fundamental transformation thereby) *and* of the potentially transmutative power of a discursive praxis that rips into the fabric of precepts ordained by this hegemony.[99] Like the method of psychoanalysis, the surrealists deploy and celebrate the margin of potency that the subject might have in relation to the inescapably totalitarian force of the system within which (and by which) it is constituted. The method of free-association is an 'attack' on the repressive enclosure of the representational system. Surrealism is a protest against the constraints and restraints of the prevailing modes of discourse. This crucially important impulse to protest radically was initiated during and immediately after World War I. That is, just a decade after Bergson's celebration of the *élan vital*, yet in the midst of one of the most ghastly testimonies to the human capacity for butchery and death-dealing destructiveness. Also notable is that the impulse emerged just at the time when Freud started to retreat from psychoanalytic praxis into a preoccupation with speculative theorizing and the construction of objectivistic models of the mind – a direction entirely contrary to that which inspired both dadaist and surrealist activities.

As the 'war to end all wars' came to an end, what emerged was a disorganized and disorganizing momentum, largely based upon inchoate and contrariwise insights as to the limits of transformation within the 'system' (or at least upon skepticism about the ends of such reformism). Attempting to conjoin psychoanalytic insights, anthropology and art, the surrealists (and their dadaist predecessors) thus aspired to a revolution that would seek novel modes of expression demonstrating the salutary possibilities of 'systemic trespass' and transgression. That is, they sought modes of discourse that, by attempting to rupture the hegemonic enclosures of the 'system,' might succeed – as does free-associative thinking and speaking – in opening discourse itself to otherwise ways of being. Such a revolutionary movement depended on the discoveries of psychoanalysis. This is because, with this discipline's disclosure of the repressiveness of self-consciousness within the logical and rhetorical conventions of 'making-sense,' we come to appreciate how almost inevitably the transformation of the one into an 'other' (re)produces, within the system, more of the 'same.' The danger of any method that limits itself to the goals and ideals of transformation is thus that the resultant procedures can end up significantly contributing to the ideological reproduction of the system itself.

To learn from the insights that surrealism drew from psychoanalysis as it was promulgated out of World War I is to grasp the revolutionary significance of psychoanalysis anew. Traditionally, these implications have been comprehended in terms of sociopolitical and cultural theory, exemplified by efforts to synthesize Marxist and Freudian insights about the human condition (literature in this lineage is ably discussed by Bruce Brown, by Eugene Wolfenstein, and several others). This worthy and powerful tradition of leftist theorizing proceeds – somewhat erratically – from the early Freudians, through the Frankfurt School, to the contemporaneity of Lacanian and post-Lacanian criticism (see Endnote 92). What is suggested here is that the revolutionary significance of Freud's discipline might be found not so much in theorizing, but in what the discipline teaches us about praxis in relation to the ideological enclosures of discourse. The surrealists followed Nietzsche's ambition to release thinking, feeling and speaking from the constraints of understanding in order to engage in the poetics of a certain sort of listening (perceiving or experiencing, in which formative constructs do not emerge as staging posts but as transient moments to be swept into the playful and workful momentum of further praxis). In the context of sociopolitical and cultural change, what is called for is nothing less than activities of unsettling, dismantling or decomposing – negatively dialectical and deconstructive action upon the systemic enclosures of everyday life.

The call for a revolution in consciousness is longstanding. In addition to writers already mentioned, consider the classic writings of György Lukács, Karl Korsch or Antonio Gramsci (see Endnote 89). The focus on everyday life surfaces only in the twentieth century and it is a call not merely for 'ideology-critique' as the aspiration to amplify reason against the pervasiveness of mystification, but for an 'attack' on the enclosive foundations and the hegemony of – bourgeois – rationality. This amounts to guerilla activity (as introduced in Chapter 3) in relation to the conventions and procedures of everyday life, endemic to which are the everyday installations of domination/subordination-subjugation. It initiates, or aspires to, a permanent revolution of everyday life.[100] The friendly – nonviolent – guerilla is one who acts in response to suffering, and does so by treating everything familiar as if nothing is alien and everything is strange. The action is undertaken against the mechanisms of reification, mystification and alienation. It is 'negative' in the sense that 'carnivalesque' discourse, as discussed by Mikhail Bakhtin, might be effective as a charge against the prevailing context's authoritarianism (for example, in using the public expression of the erotic as an indictment of hypocrisy). Here the friendly guerilla is Freud's *Boshafter* (discussed in Chapter 3), who undertakes an insurgent act that implodes a particular convention pivotal to the hegemony and the maintenance of a sociocultural setting: S/he broadcasts that women at a bourgeois picnic, who announce that they are wandering off to 'pick flowers,' are actually retreating into seclusion in order to piss or shit. Thereafter, this nicety is no longer viable. The guerilla's disclosure is thus a processive moment of truthfulness that frees the subjects involved, at least for a while. It is a freeing from the oppressive constraints and restraints, the law and order, of the setting and it is profoundly significant that the hypocrisy thus imploded concerns a matter of bodily – erotic – activities. The voicing of embodied experience will thereafter be expressed with truthfulness and it will be honored.

The irreverent and insubordinate activities of the friendly guerilla – friendly, yet ruthlessly adverse to the hegemony of an oppressive system – must perhaps be defined in terms of what they are not. As an 'attack' on the suppressive and repressive functioning of the mechanisms of everyday life – an effort to unveil being-as-becoming through contrariwise thinking, speaking and acting – it operates against both empiricism and mystification. These are the very practices that Marx condemned as the twin sides of bourgeois ideology. In defiance of predetermined conceptual schemes, the 'attack' cannot take facts as facts, and thus cannot be objectivistic nor can it be submissive to the apparently apodictic certainties of subjectivity. Such an 'attack' is spiritual-existential, yet not mystical in the sense that mysticism appeals to gnosis or to absolute authority. To listen to the mysteries of one's being is not equivalent to believing that they have been apprehended either by intuition or by authority. In this respect, gnosis, as Enrique Dussel wrote, 'is the perfect act of the ontological oppressor.' It must finally be added that this praxis of subversive sociopolitical and cultural discourse – a discourse that brings together personal and systemic change – is far from utopian, for it acknowledges the pervasive and inexorable operation of contradictoriness. Moreover, to pursue the truthfulness of our everyday being by praxis that is freeing of awareness (from the constraints and restraints, the delusions and illusions, of suppression and repression) is not to imagine that there is some 'truth' of our being to eventually be attained, but rather to invite the processes of being-becoming out of their immanence.

* * *

Humanity is in dire need of radical changes in the sociocultural, political, economic and ecological arrangements by which we all live. At least in its radicalized version, psychoanalysis surely offers insights into the way in which such need might be addressed and also into the limitations of many of the traditional or conventional approaches to personal and social change. This discipline presages and joins forces with those contemporary philosophical movements that demonstrate how issues of ethicality are the basis of all human activity – that is, of epistemology and ontology, as well as the politics of all our individual and collective arrangements. It shows that what is of fundamental significance to the conduct of all human life is how one is oriented to what is *other* as well as – the crucial contribution of psychoanalytic praxis – to what is *otherwise*. This is surely because Love – which is, when genuine, never without a certain species of terror – is a process of receptivity and responsiveness to the otherness *both* of what is other *and* of what is otherwise. In the sense in which I capitalize the term, Love is not like the 'love' that we equate with attachment. Rather, it is a sacred process of orientation and opening to otherness – a radical mode of vibrationality, rather than any specifiable positionality. To be receptive and responsive to the otherness of whatever is other is to workplay against our captivation within the structures of oppression. That is, the structures of domination/subordination-subjugation. To be receptive and responsive to the otherness of whatever is enigmatically and extraordinarily otherwise is to workplay against the repressiveness of the law and order of representationality. It is to engage a derepressive praxis that mobilizes the relation between our being and our thinking, feeling and acting. It is *not* to imagine that a life entirely without repression is feasible or that it would be beneficial. This is transgressive, negatively dialectical or deconstructive praxis, the unsettling, dismantling or decomposing of our egotism, in a movement that is both truthful and freeing. It is an engagement with the prevailing discourse that discloses the limitations of transformative practices that fail to confront forcefully the manacles of repetition-compulsivity and the narratological-imperative.

It is evident (although frequently disregarded) that psychoanalysis subverts the monadological doctrines of personhood through the discoveries of its method. It does so *both* by showing how each individual's psyche is constituted by the representational system into which s/he is inducted *and* by intimating how we may all be connected by the enigmatic energies of desire that flows and ebbs within each of our embodied experiences (and also that circulates through, around and between us). As is well known, but insufficiently acknowledged, every moment of life and every molecule in the universe, past and present, is interconnected with every other – different, nonidentical, but interconnected. As has been extensively discussed in this trilogy, the unique effect of the free-associative method is the power to live without the ambition to rebut the ubiquity of connectivity *and* nonidenticality. In everyday terms, this means to live without accepting suffering, yet also without the ambition to achieve some sort of delusional or illusory state of settlement, unity, wholeness, finality or integration. That is, to live very much *alive!* yet to live within an awareness of the inescapability of contradictoriness. As praxis of passion and poetry, the discourse of unsettling, dismantling or decomposing that is initiated by the advent of psychoanalysis brings an acute awareness of the insuperable rupture and the inevitable inadequacy endemic to our life of thinking, feeling and acting. It offers us insight into how freeing and truthfulness are always contingent upon this awareness of the multiple modes of our imprisonment – awareness that a processive movement of freeing and truthfulness is desirable and attainable, whereas a stasis of 'freedom' or 'truth' is not. In this way, free-associative praxis empowers us to grasp how the truthfulness of the being-becoming of our lived-experience is always a freely desirous subject-in-process (at least when it is not caught in the stagnancy of repetition-compulsivity and the narratological-imperative).

Contrary to the opinions of many, psychoanalysis is not an ideocentric or ideogenic doctrine. Rather it is a praxis that illuminates the somatocentric and somatogenic composition of human life through the way in which the mediative flow and ebb of the energies of desire ceaselessly and concomitantly, 'condisjoin' our biological functioning with our psychological system (commonly called our 'mind'). Given the dynamic nonidenticalities both of biology and desire, and then of desire and representationality, what psychoanalysis teaches us concretely is that profound change – a transmutative change in the conditions of human self-consciousness – entails nothing less than a revolutionary awareness of the role that sexuality and death play in each moment of our everyday lives.[101] This is the key reason why the 'psychoanalytic movement' has betrayed the radicality of psychoanalysis – the fundamental key to all resistance to the prioritization of free-associative praxis.

There is no anthropological evidence that disputes the centrally significant tenet of psychoanalysis, namely that any possibility of a civil collectivity – any possibility of compassion and community, indeed any hope of civilization – ultimately depends on the maintenance of the foundational taboo against incest. This tenet is entailed by the discovery of the repression-barrier, which enabled Freud to extrapolate from his clinical labors to this fundamentally important generalization about our humanity. The incest taboo – notwithstanding the cultural variations in its performance – is the 'law of laws' that secures all possible organization of human conduct. The psychic formation of our humanity requires it. In this respect, repression is necessary (and a representational system that effects such repression is necessary). But the gravity of this tenet – the crucial importance of upholding the fundamentality of the prohibition against incest – must not be taken to imply that the liberatory power of de-repressive praxis is anything other than profoundly desirable for our vitality. That we can never ultimately arrive at that which we most desire should not be taken to imply that opening our discourse to the movement of our desire is anything other than essential for liberation from our multiple imprisonments.

Politically and pragmatically, if oppression is to be undone, there is little more important that the provision of sexual freedom. The freeing of our erotics from the governance of the discourse of domination/subordination-subjugation is essential to the overthrow of imperialism, colonialism, sexism, racism and other modes of oppression. Only if it is engaged playfully – in a transgressive effort to transcend its malignant power over us – can sexual activity under the motif of domination ever contribute to overcoming the pervasiveness of human relations founded in oppression. The licentiousness of otherwise sexual activities, nonviolent and risk-reductive, is essential for human emancipation from all the relations in which one individual or one group exploits, abuses and diminishes, its various others. In this sense, sexual freedom is necessary if we are to escape venality and dehumanization, the exploitation, brutality, genocide, ecocide and cyclical horror of all that currently engulfs us. The licentious enjoyment of nonviolent and risk-reductive erotics is a requirement if we are ever to exit the ubiquitous ideologies of domination, fanaticism, abusive capitalization and other modes of violence.

This enjoyment of licentious sexual activity opens us to an acute awareness of death – both the disavowal of death as foundational to our egotism, and the pervasiveness of deathfulness within the liveliness of life itself. Much of the mechanics of domination are fueled by the repudiation of death as the end of the self-conscious 'I.' Master and slave commit themselves in a struggle to appropriate the life-blood of the other, as if one could, by its acquisition, avoid one's own mortality. Fantasies of an afterlife, of 'leaving a legacy' and of other tokens of immortality fill the breach of an abyss imparted by each self-consciousness' dim acknowledgment of death as the terminus toward which its life is bound. Additionally, an awareness of libidinal turbulence, which is incessantly within us, composing us with the lifefulness of each moment of its flow, bestows a sensual intimation of the deathfulness of life itself. Can it be doubted that the grip of oppressive structures over us would be voided if we were to embrace this deathfulness within each moment of the liveliness of life itself – if we were to accept, embody and caress, our life as the necronautical journey that it is?

Ultimately the reformist procedures of psychotherapy can neither accept nor contribute to the necessity for an emancipative drive against our imprisonment in repetition-compulsivity and the narratological-imperative. By contrast, radical psychoanalysis offers a processive invitation to liberation from the shackles of domination and oppression. It points to a human future of liberation. That is, a future for a humanity that is now perilously close to extinction. But the path of radical psychoanalysis is profoundly frightening, perhaps terrifying. This is because – to paraphrase the insight of Georges Bataille – it takes an iron nerve to experience within us, within every moment of our embodied experience, the perpetual conjugation of life's promise with the sensuous and erotic dimension of death.

NOTES

1 Karl Marx's aphorism advocating change as a priority over interpretation is to be found in his *Ludwig Feuerbach and the End of Classical German Philosophy*. The notion of 'praxis' that accompanies this advocacy is discussed in my *Radical Psychoanalysis* (and in an academic context, the anthologies edited by Robin Nelson, and by Estelle Barrett with Barbara Holt, discuss the recent developments in 'practice-as-research'). Perhaps trickling down from Heraclitus' notion of change as the only permanent quality of being, Marx's idea of permanent revolution appears in his 1844, *Holy Family*, but is first used as a consistent strategy for change in his 1850 *Address of the Central Committee to the Communist League* and was notably developed by Leon Trotsky in 1929. My own early efforts to assess the philosophical implications of psychoanalysis are to be found in my 1984 and 1993 books. In a 1995 interview with Anthony Molino (in Molino's anthology *Freely Associated*), Christopher Bollas argued that:

> There is a fundamental divergence between analysts or schools who see the analysand's free expression of thought and feeling as a priority and those who don't. There are, in a certain sense, two paths. Along the first, this fundamental expression would have to take priority over the psychoanalyst's interpretation: without this freedom of mood, of thought, of feeling, without this density, the analysand is not going to issue a license to the unconscious; s/he is not going to find a voice in the context of the analytical situation ... On the other path, which is very different but very popular at this time, is the patient who speaks about his/her life to an analyst, who then translates that speech in a metaphor of the patient's relation to the analyst [and, it should be added, to the world in general]; of a part of the patient's self in the here-and-now relation to a part of the analyst ... This, I believe, forecloses free association in the analysand ... the difference between that analysand and the one who's freely speaking is enormous ...

In many respects, Bollas' description foreshadows the need for this book. I have deliberately chosen to cast the divergence in terms of the first path being the radicality of genuine psychoanalysis and the second path being psychotherapeutic (even if practiced according to some sort of 'psychoanalytically-informed' third-person theoretical framework, and even if practiced by a card-carrying 'psychoanalysts'), because it sharpens the pertinent issues. As will become evident, I stand firmly on the first of Bollas' two paths. However, I believe that scarcely anywhere in the literature has there been a clear exposition as to how this path heals and how the latter path (which prioritizes therapeutic interpretation modifying patients according to a preordained scheme) actually aborts the healing that comes from genuine psychoanalysis. The intent of this book is to provide such an exposition.

2   The movement against psychiatric treatment and its political abuses gained momentum in Europe around the late eighteenth century, as documented in Micale and Porter's 1994 anthology and elsewhere. The term 'anti-psychiatry' was coined by David Cooper in 1967 (and expounded both in his 1968 anthology and in his 1971 book). Such as it is, the movement includes various lines of protest against specific treatments of an inhumane character (e.g., electroconvulsive therapy, insulin shock therapy and brain lobotomy), against the medicalization of 'madness' and deviance, against the biomedical stigmatization and psychosocial labeling of non-normativity, against involuntary hospitalization and against the politicized use of the psychiatric system as a coercive instrument of oppression. These issues will be touched on further in Chapter 2. Michel Foucault's books of 1954, 1961 and 1963, as well as his lectures of 1973–1974, continue to be indispensable reading on this topic. Georges Canguilhem's 1966 exposition of the history of the distinction between normality and pathology is also invaluable.

3   Although we may all cling to Humpty-Dumpty's illusion that a thing 'means just what I choose it to mean,' the entire drift of twentieth century philosophy has undermined the apparent prerogatives of the Cartesian subject as author of its own thoughts. Roland Barthes famous 1967 essay and Foucault's 1969 response to it are indicative of this dethronement, which is usually held to follow from post-Saussurean structuralism (and Marxism), but which would include diversely different tendencies including Wittgenstein's *Philosophical Investigations*. The subject – 'I' – is henceforth understood to be subjected to the system of signification within which it is articulated, rather than being considered the creator of its own meanings. Useful texts by John Sturrock and by Rosalind Coward with John Ellis document these important shifts. As will be discussed in what follows, the subject's subjection occurs semiotically both in 'primary' processes of the imposition of enigmatic messages by which the psyche is 'hailed into being' (the fate of Narcissus), and in 'secondary' processes that secure the individual's emplacement within the symbolic order of representationality (the fate of Oedipus).

4   There are exceptions to the reluctance of psychotherapists to examine their own sociopolitical position both in Europe and the USA (as well as in South America and throughout Asia). For example, the anthology produced by Jerome Agel in 1971 documents some instances of such efforts. As far as I am aware, it was – perhaps paradoxically – Dwight Eisenhower in 1961 who first coined the term 'military-industrial complex,' predicting, as did William Fulbright a few years later, that its development would be hazardous for the future of democracy. See Henry Giroux's excellent study, *The University in Chains: Confronting the Military-Industrial-Academic Complex*, which discusses the devolution of universities into 'hypermodern militarized knowledge factories.' Also in this regard, Jacques Derrida's *Eyes of the University* and Bill Readings' *The University in Ruins* are exceptionally useful.

5   The notion of rupture can here be taken to imply a 'failure of inter-translatability,' discursive hiatus or abscission in the mode of temporalization. My 1993 book presents the rupture of desire and the semiotic structuring that it infuses and disrupts. These disjunctures are then discussed in my 2013 and 2016 books. I have been consistent with this use of the term 'desire' (for the meaningfulness of psychic energy that activates representations by being invested or *cathected* into them, but is never itself representable) since 1993. This specialized usage is challenging because in the vernacular 'desire' can mean a wish or motive that can be articulated representationally. That is

not how it is used here. Rather, it is a term that replaces, at least partially and some-what uneasily, Freud's notion of psychic energy or *Trieb* (which is commonly trans-lated as 'drive'), as a force that is neither biological (that is, not to be identified with *Instinkte*, as modal action patterns, neural networks or hormonal suffusions), nor psy-chological (that is, never identical with representational forms that might point to its operation). My reason for using this terminology, rather than Freud's, is because his usage becomes entangled with his speculative tendency to give 'drives' specific qual-ities, either sexual or aggressive and so forth (as well as, in 1920, to nominate the life-fulness and deathfulness principles as drives). In my usage, desire is not equivalent to any biological operation – and here I follow Laplanche's brilliant exposition of the way desire emerges because of processes in which the infant (as a biological organism) is bombarded with 'enigmatic messages' in relation to the performance of physical functions, such as sucking (to give just a single example). Desire is thus an embodied erotic energy, which may manifest itself meaningfully but disruptively in the theater of representations (conscious, preconscious and 'deeply-preconscious,' as will later be explained). It is a mode of meaningfulness that is never to be captured representation-ally. Thus it remains an unrepresentably wild – elusive, enigmatic, excessive, extraor-dinary and exuberant – force or 'voicing' within the lived-experience of our psychic life. Any post hoc reference to it is at best an approximative formulation, a *knowing about* in the sense presented by Wilfred Bion, which is always displaced or deferred in relation to the actual motions and commotions of desire. Desire thus has – incessantly unto death – the dynamic quality of being, as Freud suggested in 1905 and again in 1915, a 'demand for work.' That is, it pressures the representational system to propel the subject – or 'I' – from one representational transformation to the next in the stream of consciousness. Some of this is discussed in my 1915 paper, 'On the Mythe-matic Reality of Libidinality as a Subtle Energy System.' This notion of 'desire' is also discussed in Ilka Quindeau's excellent 2013 text.

6 These are well presented in *The Middle Length Discourses of the Buddha*. For a more popular and contemporary rendition, see the Dalai Lama's 1996 presentation. There is, of course, an important (and perhaps burgeoning) literature conjoining the teach-ings of the Dharma with the psychoanalytic attitude and method. As is well known, Erich Fromm dips into this issue in several of his prodigious writings, but the litera-ture is more recently represented well by a 1998 anthology edited by Anthony Molino and the 2003 anthology edited by Jeremy Safran. John Suler's 1993 thoughtful examination of this area is also interesting.

7 In my *Psychoanalysis and the Postmodern Impulse*, I responded to Claude Lévi-Strauss' discussion (in his 1949 essay) of the chant used by Cuna shamans to facilitate child-birth when labor has become dangerously protracted. Although Lévi-Strauss argued for a comparison with the effectiveness of interpretation in what he calls 'psychoanaly-sis,' I suggested that the comparison might better apply to psychotherapies (despite the fact that the Cuna chant is rote), in which change depends on the exegetical expertise of the practitioner to forge a link between the individual's idiographic interpretations of the events occurring in his/her life and more socioculturally or epistemically nor-mative interpretations. For competent surveys of shamanic practices, see Thomas Dubois' 2009 work, Christina Pratt's 2007 encyclopedia or Andrei Znamenski's 2004 anthology. The essays in Art Leete and Paul Firnhaber's anthology also provide a useful interdisciplinary approach.

8 I am not going to defend this loose and somewhat polemical categorization, nor provide an extensive bibliography on these lineages (which I have done elsewhere). Obviously, there are overlaps and hybrids between these three and – equally obviously – this cat-egorization omits Lacanian and post-Lacanian trends within contemporary 'psycho-analysis' that do not fall neatly into the definition of psychotherapy. From my standpoint, today one cannot understand what is authentically psychoanalytic and what is not without seriously engaging the ideas central to Lacan's proclaimed 'return to

Freud' (even if not necessarily the entire Lacanian canon). For a sense of the diversity of what passes as 'psychoanalysis' nowadays, I think Paul Marcus and Alan Rosenberg's anthology continues to be serviceable. My 2013 and 2016 books offer some specific criticisms of each of the three main 'schools of psychoanalysis.'

9   Competent surveys of contemporary psychotherapies are provided – albeit with a North Atlantic bias – by the anthologies edited by Jay Lebow and by Jon Frew with Michael Spiegler.

10   Bodymind treatments are surveyed and discussed in my 2010 book, and also ably presented by Michael Heller in his encyclopedic 2012 volume. See also the *Handbook* edited by Gustl Marlock and his colleagues.

11   In the African context, Megan Vaughan's *Curing their Ills* and Jock McCulloch's *Colonial Psychiatry and 'the African Mind'* are valuable. Sloan Mahone and Megan Vaughan's anthology offers a wider discussion. Also of interest in this regard is Christopher Lane's anthology. For the history of slavery, which seems coextensive with the history of human 'civilization' itself, see Milton Meltzer's 1993 text.

12   A useful account of von Humboldt's ideas in English is provided by Rebekka Horlacher's *The Educated Subject and the German Concept of 'Bildung.'* On autobiography, works by Carolyn Barros, by Jerome Buckley and by Roy Pascal are useful. Derrida's essay '*Monolingualism of the Other; or, the Prosthesis of Origin*' is of great interest in deconstructing the significance of this genre and analyzing the conundrum, 'I have but one language – yet that language is not mine.'

13   As I have discussed previously (for example, the 1914 paper, 'A Practitioner's Notes on Free-Associative Method as Existential Praxis,' in my 2017 paper, 'Opening to the Otherwise,' and elsewhere), one very remarkable feature of Freud's assertion that free-association is *required* for psychoanalysis to occur is that he continued to insist upon this fundamental point even after 1914, when the focus of his labors was on the construction of theoretical edifices – conceptual systematizations – by which psychotherapeutic procedures might be governed. For example, this insistence is repeated in his 1916–1917 'Introductory Lectures,' in his 1924 'Short Account of Psychoanalysis' as well as his 1925 'Autobiographical Study,' and as late as 1937 in his 'Constructions' essay. In a letter to Stefan Zweig, written February 7th, 1931, Freud criticizes Zweig for not emphasizing free-association in his book, *Mental Healers*, and states that it is 'considered by many people' to be 'the most important contribution made by psychoanalysis, the methodological key to its results' – a verdict with which Freud is evidently very much in agreement, as am I. Given this, it is remarkable that, as Bollas wrote in 2007, 'interest in free-association has diminished historically in psychoanalysis' – a plaint previously published by Patrick Mahony in 1987, by Anton Kris in 1996, by Guy Thompson in 2004 and by several others. The effort of my work since my 2013 book has been to revivify interest in free-association as central to the psychoanalytic venture and as defining the limits of the discipline (that is, if free-association is not the priority of the method, then one can justifiably proclaim, in Rachel Blass' words, 'that's not psychoanalysis!'). As for the distinction between psychoanalytic and psychotherapeutic discourses, I suggested in my 2018 paper, 'On the Unique Power of Free-Associative Discourse,' that Freud may have had a clear sense of this prior to 1914, when the tone of his writings emphasize psychoanalysis-as-praxis, but seems to have progressively lost his grip on the significance of the distinction thereafter.

14   An important dimension of the various modes of attack on the hegemony of objectivism is the realization of the way in which it conveys the motif of domination/subordination-subjugation and an ideology that takes the hallmark of knowledge to be 'mastery over.' As analytico-referentiality with its many facets (including the masculinist birth of time and experimentalism) emerged in sixteenth- and seventeenth-century Europe as the dominant mode of discourse, sociopolitically as much as scientifically, knowledge became inextricably associated with the exercise of brute power. It is

presumed that to grasp the interiority of things, one must penetrate (and exploit) them. In more contemporary terms, this is the ideology of knowledge as prediction and control. Francis Bacon was an early advocate and exemplary representative of such logical-empiricist (or analytico-referential) discourse. For him, the purpose or ambition of knowledge is to enlarge 'the bounds of human empire' (by which we should read, then as now, an empire governed almost entirely by white and wealthy males). In such a framework of understanding knowledge ('knowledge-for-the-robber-baron'), nature is a woman to be penetrated and exploited (along with women themselves, persons of color, children, the enslaved classes, and all manner of minorities), so that 'she' will surrender herself to the governance of 'the man who holds the stronghold of wisdom' (the words are actually John Milton's). The writings of Timothy Reiss are most helpful in understanding these European developments, which are also discussed extensively in my 1993 book in which I try to assess the role of psychoanalysis in the twentieth century's crumbling of the dominance of such discourse. The advent of psychoanalysis is a major force in this crumbling – a harbinger of the collapse of the modern era – because, as Reiss expresses it, Freud's discoveries signify 'the limits *a quo* and *ad quem* of analytico-referential discourse.' More recently, with the collapse of colonialism and the emergence of new formations of neocolonialism and cultural imperialism, a sustained critique of Eurocentric modes of thinking and 'epistemic coloniality' has developed. Here one thinks of diverse writings from the 'southern periphery' by Paolo Freire, Enrique Dussel and Boaventura de Sousa Santos (see also Raewyn Connell's text). The issues of power that are bound to factors of identity and exploitation in the contemporary post-colonial world are topics of an increasingly large literature. They are discussed in the writings of such scholars as Paulin Nountondji, Ato Quayson, Achille Mbembe and Gayatri Chakravorty Spivak – to mention only the smallest sampling.

15 This sort of determination to review and discard whatever aspects of 'psychoanalysis' fail to garner support from objectivistic or third-person investigation is well exemplified in a series of books by Morris Eagle that review the state of the 'evidence.' The enterprise is, as I wish to demonstrate, fundamentally flawed in that it fails to consider the negatively dialectical and deconstructive scientificity of psychoanalytic discourse as inherently and justifiably evading the standards of an empiricist science that only counts those aspects of lived-experience that are available to third-person scrutiny. As is well known, the assumption that only the empirically provable counts as knowledge has spawned an entire lineage of attacks on psychoanalysis as 'pseudo-science' (exemplified by the diversely dismissive writings of philosophers such as Karl Popper, Adolf Grünbaum, Frank Cioffi and Frederick Crews). The resort to hermeneutic accounts of psychoanalysis, pioneered by writers such as Charles Rycroft and Paul Ricoeur, has had indisputable value in counteracting the hegemonic assumption that only objectivistic inquiry counts as a valid way of knowing or a science. For as Ricoeur once wrote, perhaps no one 'has contributed as much as Freud to breaking the charm of *facts* and opening up the empire of *meaning*' (see my 1976 essay in which I somewhat mistakenly argue for the requirement that hermeneutic and empiric accounts of phenomena should be complementary). However, the recognition that Freud's discipline is about the meaningfulness of lived-experience has paved the way for a vast array of dialogical accounts of 'psychoanalysis' – interpersonal, relational, intersubjective and so forth. This literature is too voluminous to review. However, the writings of Roger Frie, Lewis Kirschner and Jessica Benjamin, as well as several books by George Atwood and Robert Stolorow provide a sense of the theoretical underpinnings of this approach. However, as I intend to show, the significance of the doctrine of repression tends to go missing in this view of Freud's discipline.

16 Obviously, this is a very rough synopsis of the sophistication of Husserl's thinking. His own account is perhaps most accessible in his *Ideas* or the later *Cartesian Meditations*. There are also many tempered and sympathetic secondary sources (such as the

texts by Robert Sokolowski and by Herbert Spiegelberg). In my opinion, the best exemplification of the way his method might contribute remains Husserl's own *Phenomenology of Internal Time-Consciousness*. From a psychoanalytic standpoint and given what is now known about repetition and 'afterwardsness' or *Nachträglichkeit* (for example, see Green's 2002 and 2003 compilations, or Dominique Scarfone's 2006–2015 essays, as well as the series of writings by Laplanche), Husserl's contribution to our understanding of the pluritemporality of psychic life is rather unimpressive (as I discussed in my 1983 and 1994 books).

17 One of the more interesting contemporary efforts in this direction is Gunnar Karlsson's 2004 *Psychoanalysis in a New Light*. Karlsson offers a valuable critique of the current vogue for 'neuropsychoanalysis' and, in considering a phenomenological rendition of psychoanalysis, he manages to embrace the notion of libidinality as the core of the psychoanalytic unconscious. However, it remains unclear – at least to me – how he resolves the issue of the unrepresentability of the repressed in relation to the achievements of a phenomenological method. The essays in Dorothée Legrand and Dylan Trigg's anthology, which often lean heavily on the writings of Maurice Merleau-Ponty, are very sophisticated philosophically (yet tellingly, terms such as 'repression' and 'sexuality' are entirely missing from their book's index). While this argument is beyond my scope herein, I think the conclusion is warranted that, despite Merleau-Ponty's important emphasis on embodiment in his writings through the 1940s, the egological emphasis of phenomenology necessarily misses Freud's notion of desire as psychic energy and hence the unconscious-as-repressed.

18 There are, of course, problems with picking and choosing from which of Freud's ideas one wishes to learn or to build an argument, and my writings have always been vulnerable to this charge. However (and by way of a defense of such a strategy), there are at least five major misassumptions common in scholarship that focuses on Freud's writings: (i) that his ideas form a monolithic corpus of thinking about the human condition; (ii) that every pronouncement he makes on a topic must therefore, sooner or later, be relatable to every other (that is, that his edicts are never contradictory); (iii) That he always understood clearly the significance of his discoveries; (iv) that his proposals were all more or less valid and valuable (although many of his more virulent adversaries have simple trashed his work *tout court*); and (v) that his theoretical judgments are what really matter, rather than his revolutionary finding of the free-associative method. The dogma that the significance of the breakthrough implied by free-associative praxis is that of the invention of a methodological means toward interpretive ends has been widespread, as propounded by Ralph Greenson in 1967 (among many others), emphasized both appreciatively and critically by Merton Gill (in somewhat different ways in 1982, in 1994 and with Margaret Brennan in 1959), and discussed with exceptional lucidity by Guy Thompson (in 1994 and 2004). The point of my trilogy might be reduced to the tenet that free-associative discourse is not the means to an end, but is the end itself. Free-associative speaking and listening is the contemplative working-through (Freud's *Durcharbeitung*) that empowers a specific sort of access to the repressed that is such a vital dimension within psychic life. It invites the repressed to 'voice' itself in a way that is profoundly healing. As will be discussed later, *durcharbeiten* – to work-through – takes the self-conscious subject perpetually toward its own abyss and this is itself the process of emancipative healing (liberation or releasement). As Thompson discusses, there is substantial evidence that, for Freud, free-association comprised almost the entirety of his patients' treatment experiences (see the accounts of John Dorsey and also in Beate Lohser and Peter Newton's *Unorthodox Freud*). Of course, this should not be taken to mean that Freud was inactive, nor to mean that dialogue and friendly conversation were not also important aspects of Freud's relations with his patients (as has been discussed by Heinrich Racker).

19 As I hinted in my 2018 paper, I have some concerns about Bollas' wish, as he expli-
    citly wrote in 2002, to 'redefine free association as *free talking*, as nothing more than
    talking about what is on the mind, moving from one topic to another in a free-
    moving sequence that does not follow an agenda.' In my view, Bollas is unquestion-
    ably one of the truly great psychoanalytic thinkers alive today (as well as a much
    valued colleague whom I would like to think of as a friend). The books published
    in the decade from 1999 to 2009 surely establish his preeminence as an exponent of
    free-associative discourse, and I consider them indispensable reading. That said, any
    tendency to define free-association merely in terms of a lack of censorship in talking
    has to be qualified, perhaps even contested. In short, I am unclear whether Bollas
    would agree with me in the argument that now follows. Much of the literature on
    free-association (for example, papers by Leopold Bellak, Stanley Rosner, or Leo
    Spiegel) only addresses such questions tangentially.

20 The seemingly paradoxical notion that the repressed discloses itself not only in its
    opening but also in its closing needs preliminary elaboration. In his 1964 *Séminaire*,
    Jacques Lacan spoke of the ontic function of his notion of the unconscious 'some-
    thing that opens and closes' like a *fente* or slit through which something vanishes
    even as it emerges. To me, this is an apt image for the disruptive flow and occasion-
    ally more quiescent ebb of the repressed as it impacts the linguistically-structured
    representational system. What is sensed in the awareness available through the free-
    associative method is the *movement* of energies, flowing in and ebbing out of the
    formations that furnish our psychic life. The flow, the investment of psychic ener-
    gies to animate and bring into consciousness the forms of representationality, is
    Freud's 1920 'lifefulness principle' (*Lebenstrieb*), whereas the ebbing of psychic
    energy from the representational world is the 'deathfulness principle' (*Todestrieb*). In
    this understanding of these *Triebe* (which deviates from the commonplace Kleinian
    and other post-Freudian references to the 'life' and 'death instincts'), I am following
    Laplanche's excellent presentations. I believe it is in the context of what I am now
    calling the flowing and ebbing of psychic energies that Lacan came to suggest that
    the unconscious has the 'rhythmic structure' of a 'pulsation of the slit.' The point
    here is the way in which the 'absenting-presence' of the psychoanalyst (and the set-
    ting in which the sessions occur) provokes an intensification of this opening and
    closing. Much has been written on the setting of psychoanalytic discourse – for
    example, coming from the context of North American practice, Leo Stone's 1962
    book used to be a standard reference, which mentions the 'awakening' of the
    unconscious in the psychoanalytic process. However, I agree with more contempor-
    ary commentators – particularly those who have attended to developments in
    France – that Jean-Luc Donnet's *The Analyzing Situation* is now an indispensable
    text in this respect.

21 Surely one cannot but applaud Lacan's bluntness when, in his 1960–1961 *Séminaire*
    on transference, he says:

> The space occupied by not understanding is the space occupied by desire. It is to
> the extent that this is not perceived that an analysis ends prematurely and is, quite
> frankly, botched.

In terms of my emphasis on psychoanalysis as operating beyond psychotherapy, it is
noteworthy that in this *Séminaire* he adds that the psychoanalyst (to whom Lacan
refers consistently in the masculine) must:

> … know that his occupying the correct position is not contingent on the criterion
> that he understand or not understand. It is not absolutely essential that he under-
> stand. I would even say that, up to a certain point, his lack of comprehension can
> be preferable to an overly great confidence in his understanding. In other words,

he must always call into question what he understands and remind himself that what he is trying to attain is precisely what in theory he does not understand. It is certainly only insofar as he knows what desire is, but does not know what the particular subject with whom he is engaged in the analytic adventure desires, that he is well situated to contain within himself the object of that desire.

With some qualification – notably around how there is always a sense in which treatment begins in the mode of 'making-sense' and then progresses into the psychoanalytic mode of free-associative interrogation – I think Lacan's points are very pertinent. However, I have some serious and profound reservations about Lacanian 'clinical technique' and perhaps yet more about Lacanian theory – as I have discussed in my 1984 book and several times thereafter. For example, in relation to the clinical situation, I clearly, if only partially, dissent from the Lacanian characterization of the functioning of the psychoanalyst solely as a figure of absence that symbolizes the dead father. I definitely dissent from Lacan's notion of the significance of temporal pacing (the sessions of variable length and so forth), and from his thunderclap (*éclat*) vision of psychoanalytic 'cure' as like the sudden moment of *satori* in which the patient arrives not so much at the awakening of comprehension, but rather at an awakening to the impossibility of comprehension (that is, I dissent from the thunderclap characterization, not from the notion that psychoanalysis effects the aliveness of aware incomprehension). However, despite these various levels and facets of dissent, the Lacanian emphasis not on 'making-sense' of the patient's discourse, but rather on listening to its disruptions, does seem profoundly important. In his 1958 paper, 'The Direction of the Treatment and the Principles of its Power,' Lacan indicated the danger in which psychoanalysts 'because they understand a lot of things ... imagine that to understand is an end in itself, and that it can only be a happy end' (Bruce Fink's translation). In his prior paper on 'The Situation of Psychoanalysis and the Training of Psychoanalysts in 1956,' he had argued against Karl Jaspers' emphasis on the importance of understanding patients in treatment, disclosing that:

> I repeatedly tell my students: 'Don't try to understand!' ... May one of your ears become as deaf as the other must be acute. And that is the one that you should lend to listen for sounds and phonemes, words, locutions, and sentences, not forgetting pauses, scansions, cuts, periods, and parallelism ... without which analytic intuition has no basis or object. (Fink translation)

From this perspective the patient's capacity to 'make-sense' or to expand the realm in which sense can be articulated is less significant than listening to the errant signifiers, strange scansions, mistaken punctuations, malapropisms, syllepses, catachreses and so forth (here I would include and indeed emphasize the significance of disruptive bodily phenomena that occur within the patient's speech). In my opinion, Fink's various books discussing Lacanian technique have been especially valuable in bringing these ideas to the attention of anglophone readers (his 2015 translation of Lacan's 1960–1961 *Séminaire* is also to be much appreciated). Richard Boothby's writings are also very helpful.

22 In my 2015 debate with Mark Solms on the irresolvable problems of so-called 'neuro-evolutionary archaeology,' I challenge the neuroscientific tendency to reduce lived-experience to the either/or of neurobiology and what he calls 'subjectivity.'

23 I discuss the ambiguity of Freud's notion of subtle energies in my 2015 paper, 'On the Mythematic Reality of Libidinality,' and elsewhere. The ambiguity stems from Freud's clear insistence in his published writings on the endogenous character of psychic energy in relation to his more or less secret belief in telepathy. He admitted in confidence to Ernest Jones that he had had telepathic experiences which 'have attained such convincing power over me that diplomatic considerations [have] to be

relinquished' (in a letter dated March 7th 1926). But then – very oddly – he tells Jones that his 'acceptance of telepathy is [his] own affair' and that 'the subject of telepathy is not related to psychoanalysis.' Yet, one would assume that telepathy could only be explainable if there is indeed some sort of energy exchange between the participants (something immaterial must surely be 'going on' between them).

24 In relation to certain aspects of the tensions between Freudian and Jungian stand-points, some of the relevant issues are covered in my 2017 paper, 'On the Other-wise Energies of the Human Spirit: A Contemporary Comparison of Freud and Jungian Approaches.' As an aside, it may be noted that Laplanche's interpretation of the lifefulness and deathfulness principles connects interestingly with Jones' ideas (adumbrated in several papers such as those of 1927 and 1929) about *aphanisis* as the 'fading of desire.' Somewhat similar to a terror of annihilation, Jones suggests that this 'fading' is most feared by all of us. There is, of course, a connection here with Freud's 1926 assertion (in *Inhibitions, Symptoms and Anxiety*) that while death is incomprehensible, what he calls 'castration' is, for both men and women, our cen-trally motivating anxiety. In terms of the notion of 'deathfulness' as pervading ever moment of subjectivity, my 2004 paper offers a preliminary discussion – the notion is also central to tantric cosmology, as described in my 2010 book. It is not only that human subjectivity is 'deathbound' as Alphonso Lingis describes so well in his 1989 book – not only that death has to be considered by every human as the *ter-minus ad quem* – it is also that a certain *deathfulness* lies within each moment of life itself. This is, I think, what Sabina Spielrein was trying to convey, for which she received too little credit. Again, it is also an insight quite compatible with many lineages of Asian thinking – see, for example, the writings of Agehananda Bharati in 1965, Poola Raju in 1985 and Surendranath and Surama Dasgupta in 2010.

25 Of course, as far as I know, no training institute welcomes applicants merely on the basis of their prior educational qualifications. An assessment of the applicant's 'suit-ability of personality' is usually conducted. However, the literature on this topic – to say nothing of a brief albeit casual survey of so many of the individuals who have been accepted and proceed to graduate from such institutes – suggests that the cri-teria for the personal qualities of an individual appropriate for training are, to say the least, somewhat confused or at least problematic in their implementation. Cyn-ically, one might suggest that, if one wishes to pass the application interviews, one must be sufficiently bright to be able to appear pliant and idealizing of the institute itself and its senior personnel without appearing to be too pliant or too idealizing (the senior personnel responsible for admission procedures are usually not that stupid). More seriously, as I shall discuss in what follows, psychoanalysis is a 'calling' and the greatest danger, in terms of applicants who should not be accepted into training, is the individual whose ethical integrity is compromised. That is, the indi-vidual who 'fakes' the call to commit her/himself to training. Such is the individual whose personality includes more than a dash of what has been called 'psychopathy' (following Hervey Cleckley and other contributors to this concept) or perhaps also the individual whom Bollas would, in his 1987 book, diagnose as 'normotic' (that is, excessively and deceptively 'normal').

26 These insights are to be found in many places in Adorno's writings and those of his colleagues in the so-called Frankfurt School of ideology-critique. For example, in his 'Note on Human Science and Culture' (which reflects my own experience obtaining degrees in psychology), he wrote:

> The disappointment of many students of the human sciences in the first semesters is due not only to their naiveté but also to the fact that the human sciences have renounced that element of naiveté, of the immediate relation to the object with-out which spirit cannot live; the human sciences' lack of self-reflection is not less naïve.

Using the term 'spirit' in the German sense of *Geist* (roughly equivalent to the intelligence of humanity and human culture), Adorno later adds:

Even where academic culture is engaged with spiritual matters it unconsciously falls into step [here Adorno uses the 1933 Nazi term for compelling someone to follow the party] a science that takes for its standard what already exists, the factually real and its processing – that facticity with which the vital force of spirit should not content itself. Just how profoundly deprivation of spirit and scientification are intertwined at their roots is manifest in the way that ready-made philosophemes are then imported as an antidote. They are leached into interpretations made in the human sciences in order to lend them luster they otherwise lack, without such philosophemes being the result of coming to know the spiritual creations themselves. With ridiculous solemnity the same thing is read invariably, again and again, out of them. Between spirit and science a vacuum has developed. Not only specialized education but culture itself no longer cultivates … Nothing in cultural and educational institutions, not even the universities, offers any support to spirit.

As Adorno himself then notes, this is reminiscent of Friedrich Nietzsche's 1888 condemnation of universities that '*despite* themselves, are really the greenhouses for this sort of stunting of spiritual instincts.' It is also interesting to note that as early as 1919 Freud wrote that 'the psychoanalyst can dispense entirely with the University without any loss.'

27 Within the membership of the International Psychoanalytic Association, one of the most prominent critics of the training system has been, from 1986 onwards, no less than Otto Kernberg (see also his papers of 1993, 1996, 2000, 2006, 2007, 2010, 2014 and 2016, much of which is collected in his 2016 book). Then there are several studies of psychoanalytic organizations that offer important and incisive critiques – usually without the underlying conservatism and placatory tone of Kernberg's contributions. Interesting examples of these would include: Jurgen Reeder's *Love and Hate in Psychoanalytical Institutions*; Douglas Kirsner's *Unfree Associations*; Manuela Robles' *Fanaticism in Psychoanalysis*; Kate Schechter's *Illusions of a Future*; and even some of the contributions in Murray Meisels and Ester Shapiro's anthology. Peter Zagerman's anthology presents some important essays evaluating the model of training named for Max Eitingon, which has prevailed since the 1920s.

28 The five criteria are discussed in my *What is Psychoanalysis?* They are: (i) that the patient should have a sense of his/her own suffering (without an excessive commitment to externalizations); (ii) that the patient should show a readiness to form an alliance with the psychoanalyst – essentially an alliance to listen and maybe to understand; (iii) that the patient should demonstrate a capacity to regulate or modulate anxieties and difficult affects (which occur with regressive shifts) without resorting to enactments or addictive behaviors; (iv) that the patient has what might be called the 'functions of ego organization' that ensure a basic ethical integrity, as well as a capacity to eventually integrate and synthesize the thoughts, feelings, wishes and fantasies that appear to be broken-down during treatment; (v) that the patient has the ability to be a steward of the treatment – for example, to attend sessions, to contribute adequately to the practitioner's livelihood and to keep third-parties out of the treatment relationship.

29 The poem was written in 1978 during the crisis of the Vietnamese 'boat people' and in contains five particularly challenging verses:

I am a mayfly metamorphosing
on the surface of the river.
And I am the bird
that swoops down to swallow the mayfly.

I am a frog swimming happily
in the clear water of a pond.
And I am the grass-snake
that silently feeds itself on the frog.
I am the child in Uganda, all skin and bones,
my legs as thin as bamboo sticks.
And I am the arms merchant,
selling deadly weapons to Uganda.
I am the twelve-year-old girl,
refugee on a small boat,
who throws herself into the ocean
after being raped by a sea pirate.
And I am the pirate,
my heart not yet capable
of seeing and loving.
I am a member of the politburo,
with plenty of power in my hands.
And I am the man who has to pay
his 'debt of blood' to my people
dying slowly in a forced-labor camp.

This is from *Call Me By My True Names: The Collected Poems of Thich Nhat Hanh* (1999) with kind permission of Parallax Press, Berkeley, California.

30 Two not uncommon observations are relevant to this point. Some 'Training Analysts' are so convinced of their superior understanding of the discipline that they convey to their patients how impossible it would be for them to ever dare consider the path of becoming a psychoanalyst (if they dare nevertheless, they become the sort of psychoanalyst who has unresolved oedipal conflict in relation to their own psychoanalyst). There are other 'Training Analysts' who are tacitly invested in having as many of their patients as possible graduate in their institute as psychoanalysts – this being a means by which the Training Analyst accrues a certain sort of power within the organization.

31 Normality – as conventionally understood – is precisely what obstructs psychoanalysis. The individual treasuring the construct should never go beyond psychoanalytically-informed psychotherapy. This goes to the issue of the ways in which psychoanalytic discourse constitutes a critique of the *polis* – an unveiling of the ideological platforms that sustain existing cultural and sociopolitical conditions.

32 The notion of narcissism has become very confused, as is amply documented in a variety of critical studies (including Elizabeth Lunbeck's 2014 work). It can mean a personality deformation in which the individual is overly invested in either idealization or denigration (of self and sometimes of selected others). It can also mean a healthy investment of 'positive' feelings in a robust sense of self (see Lunbeck's discussion). The confusions around the term parallel – for obvious reasons – the multiple ways in which the notion of the 'self' have been used and misused. It is in this context that, in 2009 and elsewhere, I have used the term 'egotism' to stand for that dimension of self-appraisal and self-advancement that is implemented at the expense of others – that is, egotism that closes off the other, except insofar as it can admit the other for the sustenance and inflation of the self.

33 As I have done in previous writings, I use the term 'bodymind' to highlight the need to break with the Cartesian dichotomy of 'body and mind.' Other writers – such as Bollas – favor the term 'mindbody' which I have reversed in order to emphasize the priority of embodied experience, and to avoid the idea of a mind that dominates over the body. In terms of Freud's tendency to use adversarial analogies for the practitioner's relation with certain aspects of the patient's functioning, it can be noted that

he compared his methods with surgical intervention as early as 1893 and occasionally after that. In the 1913 essay, the beginning of a psychoanalytic treatment is likened to the 'opening moves' in a game of chess (an image that states well the crucial importance of the way in which the practitioner acts initially with the patient, but which nevertheless seems adversarial). In his 1926 essay on 'lay analysis,' written at the height of his enchantment with the structural-functional model, Freud's language becomes quite bellicose. In that essay, he writes of the 'main task' of the practitioner as a 'struggle against resistances,' compared with which the 'task of making interpretations is nothing.' While I am inclined, with some qualification, to agree with this viewpoint, Freud proceeds to depict it in regrettably military formulations – describing how 'the army has to overcome the enemy's resistance' which involves 'battles.' What we can surely take from the graphic quality of this essay is that resistances are the force by which suppression and repression are reinforced, and psychoanalysis is, if nothing else, a de-repressive praxis.

34 It is customary to list Freud's major interlocutors (such as Breuer, Fliess, Jung, Ferenczi) and all the others with whom he interacted collegially (one thinks here of individuals such as Max Schur) or with whom he had such prodigious correspondence (Jones, Abraham and many others). But one should also consider Freud's use of those whom he treated as interlocutors of a certain sort. While it is common to realize that patients are used by their psychoanalyst for the development of the latter's implicit and explicit theorizing (despite the fact that psychoanalysis is not about the construction of theoretical models), it is less frequently discussed how patients contribute to the psychoanalyst changing within. That is, the patient's participation in psychoanalysis prompts the reciprocal free-associative reverie of the psychoanalyst (as discussed but Bollas, Zvi Lothane and others) such that the interior world of the latter is, with every patient, transformed and transmuted, at least to some degree. Given some of the accounts we have of what it was like to be in treatment with Freud (see Hendrik Ruitenbeek's anthology), one senses that Freud may have learned much about himself from his patients (perhaps even more than they learned about themselves).

35 In a preliminary manner, the previous two volumes in this trilogy tried to show how oedipality is deeply linked to the free-associative discoveries of repression, pluritemporality and polysexuality. This is further advanced in my subsequent paper, 'Oedipality and Oedipal Complexes Reconsidered,' in which I argue that the incest taboo is key both to the distinction between oedipality and oedipal complexes, and to our understanding of the universal features of the human condition.

36 It seems imperative, whenever a non-Lacanian attempts to write about Lacanian psychoanalysis, to include the *caveat* 'as I understand it.' One is always susceptible to the charge: 'But you have *not* understood the matter, because Lacan also said this-or-that in such-and-such a place.' These defenses not only render him a sort of 'supreme master' (which is how it seems he may have wished to be viewed), but they render Lacanian ideas inaccessible to critical thinking. Although I met Lacan in person, neither of my two courses of psychoanalytic treatment were Lacanian; I have, however, struggled with his writings in the original and studied every available English translation to date (as well as not a few secondary sources); I also used to attend a seminar of Lacanian psychoanalysts who met regularly for clinical discussions. That said, I do not anticipate being exempt from the stock criticism of having caricatured Lacanian psychoanalysis, for which I am – somewhat – apologetic.

37 In my 2016 *Radical Psychoanalysis*, the nature of the psychoanalytic friendship was discussed. There I wrote that:

> … the friendly character of the psychoanalytic partnership has perhaps been obfuscated by the somewhat antiseptic or even medicalized discussion of concepts such as the 'treatment situation' and the 'therapeutic alliance.' Psychoanalysis involves

> an emotionally intimate relationship of two persons engaged in a 'shared activity' and founded on a fundamental 'bond of trust' … (even if the bond is repeatedly challenged, questioned, provoked and called into account)

These are the twin hallmarks of friendship, as discussed extensively ever since Aristotle's *Nicomachean Ethics*. On the practitioner's side, the psychoanalyst trusts the patient to remain a more or less steadfast guardian of their relationship … On the patient's side, s/he more or less consistently trusts – whatever the vicissitudes of affection and animosity in the transference – that the psychoanalyst will facilitate a beneficial process with wisdom, equanimity and love. In common with ordinary friendships, psychoanalytic processes are *like* those of a familial relationship, *like* those of a romantic relation, yet proceed in neither direction … the psychoanalytic relationship – hovering inclusively between *érōs, agápē* and *philía* – has to be scrupulously ethical and is destroyed whenever it becomes actually familial or actually romantic. Unlike many ordinary friendships, the relationship is notably lopsided, not only because the patient's psychic life is addressed more explicitly than the practitioner's (for which privilege the patient pays a fee), but also because it is exclusively the psychoanalyst's responsibility to facilitate and maintain the ethicality of the relationship as one of openness, of freedom, safety and abstinent intimacy. Herein lies the unique professionalism of the psychoanalytic partnership. Although this friendship is not one of equality (in the way that many ordinary friendships need to be), there is actually no inherent reason why friends have to be equals. Aligned with the ethicality of genuine friendship, as discussed in classic philosophy, the relationship between patient and practitioner involves virtue, utility and pleasure. The virtue of the psychoanalytic partnership is its commitment to truthfulness. Its utility lies in its healing potential. And it is – even while embracing the hatred which inevitably surfaces in the course of its journey – a relationship that is, or should ultimately become, pleasurable.

38 This is also because, while patients may quite rightly feel loved by their psychoanalyst and while indeed love is, in a certain sense, what the psychoanalyst should come to feel, the patient who has fantasies that s/he is, in some ultimate way, 'special' – a moderated fee readily being taken as evidence of this – is likely to use such fantasies to shield the necessary free-associative dismantling of her/his egotism. In short, any moderation of the fee is liable to shortchange the patient. Thus, a 'reasonable' or 'realistic' fee is always around 1/30th to 1/50th of the revenues that a psychoanalyst might 'reasonably' and 'realistically' expect to earn.

39 When supervising trainees, I sometimes offer the following – excessively cutesy – analogy. What do you do when you realize that your friend, Jill, has another friend, Jack, who is important to her yet who is pushing her toward all sorts of dangerous or deleterious activities. Most people understand that it is usually pointless merely to tell Jill that she should get Jack out of her life. She may well decide to get you out of her life instead. Rather, one tries to engage Jill in some sort of reflective conversation: What does she see in Jack? What does she think Jack contributes to her life? And so forth. Anna Freud suggested a useful illustration of this (which I will amplify and modify somewhat). She asked how one responds to a patient who begins a session by saying 'there is something on my mind today, but I am unable tell it to you.' None of the following responses (many of which would probably have been used by early practitioners) is psychoanalytic: 'You know the basic rule … you have to tell me … please tell me … how do you think I can help you if you withhold things from me … okay, if that's how you feel, let's talk about something else … let me guess what it might be and you can tell me if I'm correct' and so forth. Nor is it acceptable for the practitioner to withdraw into – petulant – silence. Of course, there is no perfect response, but three ingredients are very important, both in their content and in the attitude they convey: (i) 'I appreciate your letting me know that there is something on your mind that you feel unable to tell me … ' (after all,

resistive patients cooperate very actively with the treatment whenever they let the practitioner know that they are aware they are resisting); (ii) '... because this probably means that to some extent you would like to tell me, but only when you are ready, which is important ... ' (here the practitioner *both* addresses the patient's wish that there could be greater candor *and* commends the patient for asserting what is the patient's right, namely to remain in control of the conversation that occurs in the relationship, as well as suggesting that, when s/he is ready, the patient is welcome to change his/her decision and be disclosive); (iii) '... meanwhile could we explore why you think it is that some things feel impossible to tell me ... ' (and finally the practitioner invites the patient to reflect and speak free-associatively about why his/her resistances are important). This is, in my view, the loving incursion of the friendly guerilla addressing the patient's resistances.

40 The notion of 'volition' is, of course, problematic psychoanalytically (let alone from other standpoints). Although I think Freud's adversarial tone when writing about his labors with patients (from the chess analogy in his 1913 paper on beginnings to the battle-cries of his 1926 essay, as mentioned in Endnote 33) is regrettable, there is some usefulness in studying the literatures on change that come from outside psychoanalysis (and by this I do *not* mean the literatures of manipulative psychotherapies). As discussed by Howard Caygill and others, the guerilla strategies of Mohandas Gandhi and Mao Zedong are an instructive contrast with the classic tome of Carl von Clausewitz' *On War*. Freud had undoubtedly read, or at least knew well of, Clausewitz' ideas, but, of course, not those writings published after his death in 1939.

41 Useful introductions to irony and related devices are those by Wayne Booth, Clare Colebrook, Linda Hutcheon, John Lippitt and Douglas Muecke. Søren Kierkegaard's 1841 work is seminal and, in a rather different context, Richard Rorty's *Contingency, Irony, and Solidarity* demonstrates the power of irony to effect changes. In terms of Lacanian psychoanalysis, Gary Handwerk's *Irony and Ethics in Narrative: From Schlegel to Lacan*, is a very useful study.

42 Perhaps Lao-Tzu's major text should be on every candidate's reading list, for its precepts exemplify in so many ways the 'spirit' with which the psychoanalyst should conduct her/himself. Thomas Cleary's and Stephen Mitchell's translations are very accessible, although I am told that Robert Henricks' is more faithful to the original. In a context different from psychoanalysis, Greg Johanson and Ron Kurtz's *Grace Unfolding* should be inspiring for any psychotherapist.

43 There is a contemporary philosophical background to the notion of the *caress* and its fundamental significance in human functioning. This cannot be reviewed within the scope of this text, for it requires an extensive examination of discussions by Emmanuel Levinas, Jacques Derrida, Jean-Luc Nancy, Luce Irigaray and others. Some references are given in the bibliography, but the philosophical discussion of these that is required has to be left for a later occasion. It might be noted, however, that the most erotically powerful mode of caress occurs not only when the caresses are willingly received (if they are not, then it is really a coercion and not a caress at all), but also when they arrive in a spatiotemporal rhythm that is unanticipated (concretely in relation to massage practices, this was elucidated briefly in my 2005 description of Juliet Anderson's work).

44 This probably accords with Freud's own – narcissistic – view of himself. On the one hand, he remained skeptical as to whether 'civilization' could ever hold sway over the baser nature of humanity. On the other hand, he seemed, sometimes in a disarmingly humble manner, to see himself as the ultimately rational man, leading the 'chosen ones' out of their 'mental slavery.' The problem with the notion of sublimation is exactly illustrated when it comes to the calling of psychoanalysis. It is easy to say that, *among other factors* (that is, without being absurdly simplistic), actors sublimate their exhibitionism in their craft, physicists expert in nuclear fission are no doubt sublimating some sort of primal scene fantasy, gynecologists sublimate their anxious fantasies about castration, surgeons their sadism, and so forth. But what do

psychoanalysts sublimate? One only goes into psychoanalysis because one suffers, one may or may not emerge from such treatment as a practitioner. The issue of the psychoanalyst's motivation is complex and should not be judged as simple as altruism.

45 This is not to discount Bollas' interesting contributions on the reciprocal functioning role of 'reverie' nor Lothane's ideas about the mutuality of free-association, but such orientations require care as to what the practitioner might be unwittingly introducing into the relationship. Perhaps a rather trite example would be helpful here. As I listen to a patient, although not hungry, I drift into fantasies of a lavish breakfast. Am I to take this foremost as a lapse in my clinical functioning, an intrusion of my own dynamics into my workplay as a psychoanalyst? Or am I to take this as my 'unconscious' response to 'unconscious phantasies' within the patient, such as her hunger for me, wish to be greedy with me, demand to suckle at my breasts and so forth? Either answer might lead to a substantive interpretation, which is not the priority of radical psychoanalysis. Perhaps more significant is the way in which these phenomena express resistances to ongoing free-associative praxis *both* on the part of the listening practitioner *and* on the part of the patient. Thus, we ask what next event in the free-associative chaining, which occurs aloud on the part of the patient and silently on the part of the psychoanalyst, is being avoided by the limitations of the psychoanalyst's voiding of his inner responsiveness? It must be emphasized here that when psychoanalysts such as Bollas write about reverie, or when I describe psychoanalytic listening as radically different from hearing-to-understand, this is *not* what Lacan means when he said 'I don't attend, which is the height of bliss. Absence. A strange absence … ' By this, it is implied that he gave himself license to exit the consulting room even while the patient was speaking (in his proclamation of the 9th October, 1967, he insists that 'the authorization of an analyst can only come from himself'). However, such dereliction surely cannot be justified by this sort of theoretical rigmarole, in which one imagines that one is oneself no less than the *Grand Autre* because one has bestowed upon oneself *la passe* (for further commentary on this, see Jacques-Alain Miller's 1977 article and Elisabeth Roudinesco's 1986 text).

46 Both in its popular and in its professional philosophical renderings, the history of ideas about morality and ethicality has been terminologically confused. Here I follow a – perhaps slightly modified – rendition of this distinction that is articulated well by Gilles Deleuze. Simply put, *morality* is a set of rules, a moral code, by which actions (as well as thoughts, feelings, wishes, fantasies and motives) can be subjected to *judgmental evaluation* as to their positive or negative – 'good' or 'bad' – implications or consequences. Such judgments are invariably made by explicit or implicit reference to some sort of system of transcendent or allegedly universal values, which inevitably has ideological implications. By contradistinction, in a move that draws upon writings from the pre-Socratics to Nietzsche and Foucault, as well as by Levinas most notably, *ethicality* is the *facilitative process* (tied to a quite different mode of 'regulation') that orients us toward a responsive openness to all that is other and otherwise (see also my 2017 article, 'Opening to the Otherwise'). In this sense, ontology is always 'preceded' by an ethics. Moreover, bypassing the post-Socratic insistence on the priority of epistemology, ethics becomes the 'first philosophy' (as made clear by Levinas, and embodied in the writings of Foucault, Deleuze and others). Whether morality is subsumed by ethicality or is profoundly different from the latter's implications is a matter of debate that I will sidestep, except to reiterate my insistence that the moral codes underpinning the enterprises of psychotherapy are inevitably steeped in ideology to the extent that, in the very foundation of their procedures, the values of adjustment both to pre-existing concepts of 'reality' and to conventional moralities are prioritized. In short, psychotherapy reproduces the dominant culture at the level of individuality. Psychoanalysis engages the individual in the ethicality of a 'breaking-loose.'

47 Much of my understanding of 'ontoethics' owes to Elizabeth Grosz' 2017 *The Incorporeal: Ontology, Ethics, and the Limits of Materialism*. She writes that:

> When epistemology questions itself and its own conditions of knowledge, its own lacunae and places of nonknowing, there is a residue or remainder of ontological issues and concerns that is untouched by epistemology and that may not always be submitted to existing schemas of knowledge, existing forms of grammar and syntax or forms of representation.

Despite having studied Grosz' writings, I am unclear why her cautiously qualified 'may not always' is in this sentence (because, in psychoanalytic terms, it would imply that desire might sometimes be fully captured in representational form, which I question). Nevertheless, the argument made throughout my trilogy (and even before that, with a different tone, in my 1993 book) is that the repressed unconscious, the desirous turbulence and disruptiveness of psychic energies, is, from the standpoint of epistemological operations, precisely an exuberant and excessive 'residue' or 'remainder' that 'gives the lie' to the enclosures of (re)interpretation. Yet this is, in Freud's 1900 words, the unconscious 'core' or heart of our being-becoming (*der Kern unseres Wesens*), which he also alludes to, most interestingly and seemingly under the influence of Philippe Tissié, as our 'visceral self' (*das 'moi splanchnique'*). The idea that it might not only be that desire *cannot* be captured by knowledge, but also that it might *refuse to be* thus captured is intimated in Freud's 1900 writing about the returning force of the repressed in dreams, as their 'unfathomable navel' of what he would later call 'thing-presentations.' The latter constitute the dream's ultimate energy or 'wish' that forever evades translation into proper representational form (as Derrida aptly discussed in a 1996 essay on the resistances *of* psychoanalysis). It is also suggested in Freud's rather awkward suggestion (in a 1916 footnote to his 1900 text) that 'the dream does not intend to say anything to anyone, and is not a vehicle of communication; rather, it intends to remain ununderstood' (*der Traum will niemandem etwas sagen, er ist kein Vehikel der Mitteilung, er ist im Gegenteile darauf angelegt, unverstanden zu bleiben*). This will be developed further as I come to discuss what, in 1913, Freud called the frontier in which psychoanalysis operates as being 'between psychology and biology' (*zwischen psychologischer und biologischer Auffassung*).

48 The term, 'modern era,' here refers to the – mostly Eurocentric – discourse that has dominated 'reason' since the medieval era's commitment to theocratic-theological knowledge. This is identitarian discourse, which emerges from Hellenic, Hebraic, Christic and Islamic cosmologies, and is characterized by the metaphysics of presence and the masterdiscourse of the analytico-referential episteme (sometimes equated with logical-empiricism), as well as the patriarchal authoritarianism inscribed by a certain sort of symbolic law and order. In my 1993 book, I argued that the modern era begins to crumble in the course of the twentieth century and that, although 'postmodern' discourse is far from established (despite impulses toward such discourse), Freud's revolutionary discoveries stand at the head of this crumbling (as does the subsequent Heideggerian turn toward ontology and the movement of post-structuralist critique, including that of deconstruction). The free-associative praxis of psychoanalysis is a methodical subversion of the hegemony of modern discourse. As an aside, it might be noted that it is significant that the term 'ontoethics' has been coined by contemporary scholars both of Taoic philosophy and of some strands within Confucian and neo-Confucian studies (see Chung-Ying Cheng's 2004 and 2010 papers). It is also aligned with many strands of South Asian philosophy, as described not only in the previously mentioned works by Bharati in 1965, Raju in 1985 and Surendranath and Surama Dasgupta in 2010, but also in the writings of Jonardon Ganeri (see also the various essays on Derrida's relation with South Asian thinking such as Harold Coward's 1990 thesis). However, as previously indicated, my adoption of the term

owes much to Grosz's brilliantly useful 2017 book. In this context, Jean-François Lyotard's essay. 'Can Thought go on without a Body?' (in his 1988 collection of essays) is quite amusingly provocative.

49 As I have argued here and previously, the generation of these *Hilfsvorstellungen* (which can also be considered as *notions-for-praxis*) 'starts' with the free-associative discovery of the repressiveness of self-consciousness. The associated notions of the repression-barrier and the pervasiveness of psychic energy or desire led Freud to assert the pluritemporality and polysexuality of psychic life. These notions then generate, as if derivatively, the tenet of the universality of oedipality in the constitution of the human condition. These 'fundamental coordinates' are introduced and discussed in my *What is Psychoanalysis?* It is important to recognize (as explained in *Radical Psychoanalysis*) that the auxiliary role of such 'provisional notions' or helpful ideas in a *praxis* is significantly different from the development of theoretical concepts in an analytico-referential or logical-empiricism science. Such a notion is, as it were, an incentive to commence the labor of praxis and one that then justifies or 'explains' the route that praxis has taken.

50 See my recent paper on 'Oedipality and Oedipal Complexes: On the Incest Taboo as Key to the Universality of the Human Condition,' as well as my 2015 paper 'Boundaries and Intimacies: Ethics and the (Re)Performance of "The Law" in Psychoanalysis.'

51 This, of course, is precisely the juncture at which so many 'psychoanalysts' have actually departed from psychoanalysis, favoring a psychotherapy that only discusses that which can be represented (as well as typically entertaining an enthralled interest in the findings of neuroscience). The literature 'against energy' is sizable. An example would be Robert Galatzer-Levy's 1976 discussion. He musters three criticisms. One is that the notion of energy is irrelevant to clinical labors. The arguments herein and in several of my preceding writings are intended to demonstrate precisely why this is not the case. Without the notion-for-praxis of repression (that is, both the repressiveness of consciousness and the notion that repression decomposes meaning, taking it from its representational form and rendering it into 'proto-meaningful' flashes, fluxes, traces, sparks or waves of eruptive and disruptive energy), there is no psychoanalysis. Galatzer-Levy, in line with so much of the writing of his time, seems to assume that repression is merely what Freud called a deeper 'gradation in the clarity of consciousness' (*Deutlich-keitsskala der Bewußtheit*) than suppression. That is, merely a disorganization of representations from 'secondary' to 'primary' process. With a vitiated or evacuated concept of 'repression' such as this, Galatzer-Levy is thus able to claim the irrelevance of any notion of psychic energy, other than as a reference to biological mechanisms. What differentiates psychoanalysis from psychotherapy has, inevitably, now gone missing. His second criticism of psychic energy is that it is an unscientific concept because it is not operationally definable, not measurable and therefore untestable. This is, of course, a 'righteous argument,' as far as it goes. But it shows, very pertinently, how grasping 'psychoanalysis' within the framework of conventional epistemologies misses the revolutionary momentum of psychoanalysis itself (that is, comprehending psychoanalysis as an ontoethical discipline actually undercuts the argument that a discipline should be dismissed if it fails to be 'operationally testable'). Galatzer-Levy's third criticism is that the notion of psychic energy implies a mechanistic model of human functioning. This is, of course, quite incorrect. Even a cursory review of the concept of energy, for example as conscientiously provided by Jennifer Coopersmith (and especially considering the opening of our vision of energy that has been impelled by quantum science) indicates that energy does not necessarily function as if in a closed system. The very diverse writings of such commentators as Stuart Kauffman, Alexander Koyré and Roger Penrose are provocatively convincing on this point.

52 For pre-Socratic philosophy, see Richard McKirahan's *Philosophy before Socrates* and Patricia Curd's 2011 *Reader*. For Stoicism, see George Tanner's 2017 introduction

or, for a more scholarly treatment, the first volume of Anthony Long and David Sedley's *The Hellenistic philosophers*.

53 It is obviously beyond the scope of this book to explore in more detail the importance of Spinoza's philosophy of immanence (the issues surrounding his expressionism, as Deleuze discusses it in 1968 and again two years later), nor to discuss Irigaray's suggestion in 1984 that Spinoza retains the phallocentric tendency to exclude women. However, what will be questioned shortly is how Spinoza's philosophy might respond to the distinctively psychoanalytic idea that there are two *irreparable ruptures* (limiting inter-translatability): between biological operations and desire or psychic energy (as illuminated by a Laplanchean reading of *Urverdrängung*), and then between representationality and desire or psychic energy (which is asserted by Freud's definition of *eigentliche Verdrängung*as involving failures in translation). It would seem, *prima facie*, that for Spinoza (in Grosz's words) 'neither mind nor body are separate from each other or form substance itself. As attributes of and in substance, they are two orders that *do not require mediation* [my emphasis] to act together, for the always accompany each other.' This suggests that Freud – against the happy rhetoric of 'consilience,' which was propounded by William Whewell in the mid-nineteenth century and which today mandates the enterprise of 'neuropsychoanalysis' – has something profound to add, or even contradict, the assumptions of Spinoza.

54 Much has been written about Nietzsche's notion of the 'eternal return' and Freud's *Wiederholungszwang* (repetition-compulsion) as articulated in his 1914 essay on 'Remembering, Repeating and Working-through' – for example, Paul-Laurent Assoun's 1980 study or that offered by Danielle Chapelle in 1993. Irigaray has, of course, aptly suggested that the enclosive move of Nietzsche's 'return' implies the exclusion of womanliness and a disdain for embodiment, even while Nietzsche proclaims an affirmation of the impersonal forces of the body (see Irigaray's 1980 *Marine Lover*).

55 This quote is from *The Will to Power*, the manuscript edited posthumously by Nietzsche's sister. However, the writings from 1876 until Nietzsche's death in 1900 are all, directly or indirectly, pertinent to our understanding of the revolutionary dimensions of psychoanalysis.

56 Schopenhauer's book is alleged to have aroused Nietzsche's interest in philosophy and its influence is explicitly indicated in his 1874 essay, 'Schopenhauer as Educator,' which is in his *Untimely Meditations*. Freud was quite forthright as to how Schopenhauer had impressed him, as documented in several biographies – although there is some evidence that, in later life, he tried to minimize Schopenhauer's influence on him, perhaps to emphasize his own scientific originality. The influence of Schopenhauer on Bergson is less emphasized in commentaries on the latter's philosophy, although it has been suggested recently by several scholars, including Peter Sjöstedt-H. In Grosz's words, Bergson 'perhaps more than any other philosopher in the last 150 years, aimed to link our thinking about ontology, ethics, and collective existence together.' Influenced by the Stoic philosopher, Posidonius, and by Zeno of Elea, and taking-off from his studies of duration and intuition, Bergson developed his *lebensphilosophie* in 1907, by positing the force of *élan vital* – the vital impetus that he recruits in order to critique mechanistic visions of evolution and the doctrine of finalism. Although Bergson denied that his philosophy is a version of vitalism, arguing that his notion is not intended to encompass 'the whole of life in one indivisible embrace,' he has routinely been criticized on this basis. The possible parallels and conjunctions between desire (*Trieb*, psychic energy, libidinality) for Freud and *élan vital* for Bergson have been discussed by Brigitte Sitbon (and others). Such discussions are pertinent to the argument being made herein. In the context of Grosz' thesis, Bergson is discussed fully, but Schopenhauer is barely mentioned, and Freud not at all – yet the extension of her notion of incorporeality into a study of these thinkers would surely be invaluable for our further understanding of psychoanalysis.

57 Although Freud could quote from the Upanishads, had a statue of Vishnu on his desk, is known to have been excited by Yaekichi Yabe's presentation of Buddhism and communicated with Hindus and Hindu scholars such as Girindrasekhar Bose and Romain Rolland, it would be too bold to claim that he was directly influenced by Asian ideas about subtle energies. His connection to Kabbalist Judaism is far more extensively documented. I discussed this previously both in *What is Psychoanalysis?* and in my 2015 paper on the 'mythematic reality' of libidinality as a subtle energy system. Subtle energy, in these teachings, is usually thought of as being in everything and the existence of everything depends upon it – the precondition of the becoming of existents. Yet it is neither purely matter nor purely mind (at least in many of these teachings). Rather, it is a sort of virtuality or incorporeality in Grosz' terminology. In a less cosmological frame, Coopersmith reviews the concept of energy within the history of physics from Leibniz to Einstein and Feynman. Interestingly, she falters when she finally attempts to provide a definition. Favoring Feynman's *Lectures on Physics*, she emphasizes the defining properties as *that-which-is-conserved*, even while readily admitting that frequently energy is not conserved (and subtle energy in these eastern traditions is more likely to be defined as *that-which-is-inexhaustibly-invested-and-expended*). Coopersmith eventually – perhaps with a note of understandably irony – defines energy as 'the ceaseless jiggling motion … the curvature of spacetime, the foreground activity, the background hum, the *sine qua non.*'

58 In insisting on the endogenic character of psychic energy, Freud succeeds in rendering psychoanalysis the somatocentric discipline that it is. However, the insistence skips over the way in which each individual is – to use Louis Althusser's term – *interpellated.* That is, 'hailed into being-becoming' by process of interpellation, which is 'a form of address that has conditioning effects on the child's nervous system.' Many aspects of this are brilliantly discussed in Judith Butler's *The Psychic Life of Power.* It seems that this is very much what Laplanche attempts to explicate under his notion of our 'fundamental anthropological situation' – the way in which the child's psychic energy is formatively molded by a bombardment of enigmatic messages that affects the way in which biological forces and mechanisms morph into a libidinal constitution.

59 The notion of a 'libidinal economy' has been very usefully explored, with quite diverse emphases and purposes, by so many commentators that a satisfactory survey of this literature is beyond my scope herein. The term was popularized by Jean-François Lyotard and the associated work of Jean Baudrillard, as well as of Deleuze and Guattari. From a psychoanalytic standpoint, the diverse contributions of Norman O. Brown, Michel Foucault, Alphonso Lingis, Herbert Marcuse and now Giorgio Agamben, as well as many others including Trevor Pederson, have all been very influential.

60 'Consilience' has become the buzzword of neuropsychoanalysis as explained, for example, by Jaak Panksepp both in his 1999 article and in his major books. Preceded by terms such as 'concomitancy' – fashionable in neuropsychology – it rests on assumptions compatible with Spinoza's unitarian notion of substance. Panksepp's ideas were criticized in Green's commentary in the same debut issue of the journal, *Neuropsychoanalysis.* They have also been criticized, in a somewhat different vein, in my 2015 papers on the so-called 'neuro-evolutionary archaeology of affective systems.'

61 This is *not* to suggest that interdisciplinary dialogue is entirely without interest or value. The problem throughout the twentieth century is that such dialogues have invariably been part of an effort to assimilate psychoanalysis to some other discipline (mainstream psychology, sociology, ethology, textual hermeneutics, neuroscience and so forth) and/or to validate psychoanalysis by referring it to modes of investigation (logical-empiricist or conventionally interpretive epistemologies) that are not its own. That is, there has been a retreat from the radicality of psychoanalysis and a lack of courage in asserting the unique character of its discipline. Again, this is not to imply that interdisciplinary dialogue should not take place, but that it need not take place with psychoanalysis on the defensive; rather the reverse. Other disciplines

should be held to account for their insistence on subject/object epistemology and their avoidance of the ontoethical implications of their ways of knowing. Currently, there is much to be gained by efforts to relate psychoanalysis (by which I mean for psychoanalysis to contribute to, not to be appropriated by) to three recent intellectual developments. The first is the so-called 'affective turn' in the human sciences – see, for example, the anthology edited by Patricia Clough and Jean Halley, as well as that edited by Melissa Gregg and Gregory Seigworth. The second is the development dubbed the 'new feminist materialism' – see, for example the anthologies edited by Annette Kuhn and AnnMarie Wolpe, by Diana Coole and Samantha Frost and by Stacy Alaimo and Susan Hekman. The third is the so-called 'object-oriented ontology' – represented in the anthology edited by Levi Bryant, Nick Srnicek and Graham Harman, as well as in the writings of Quentin Mellasioux or of Ian Bogost.

62 Here it should be recalled that, as discussed in Chapter 1, I defined free-associative discourse as 'the complexly dynamic process in which the individual voices, aloud and without any censorship, her/his streaming of consciousness in the silent presence of a psychoanalyst.' Unfortunately, the term is often used today both for any sort of uncensored expression, including the 'free talking' of unexpurgated story-telling, and for any sort of impromptu contribution to a discussion, in which the speaker does not prepare his or her remarks. For example, at a recent professional meeting that I attended, the (pretentious or unthinking) chairperson asked members of the audience to offer their 'free-associations' to a particular idea that had been presented. Nothing that is forthcoming under such circumstances could possibly count as a free-association (at least under my radical definition). This must be emphasized because, as I am defining it, a patient, who tells the story of how he met his neighbor at a bar the previous evening and who completes the story relatively coherently, is not really free-associating (if one truly speaks one's stream of consciousness, no narrative is going to be completed without insistent and persistent interruptions). Relinquishing what Freud called the 'connecting thread' that allows discourse to 'stick to a point,' results in discourse that expresses far less cogency, coherence or continuity. Retaining the ordinary requirement to maintain a 'connecting thread' holds discourse to what I call the narratological-imperative, and thus sustains the repressiveness of self-consciousness.

63 In a recent paper ('The Erotics and Poetics of *Freier Einfall*: On the Necessary "Femininity" of Free-Associative Discourse for Listening to the Repressed'), I have elaborated this issue of Freud's shift and the unfortunately historical turn toward considering 'free-association' to be equivalent to any comparatively uncensored talking, including a somewhat free-wheeling sequence of story-telling that is still governed by the narratological-imperative (a term I introduced in *Psychoanalysis and the Postmodern Impulse*).

64 To elaborate this point and give it some historical markers: First, the idea that free-association is replaceable by any other technique that can elicit 'data' for an inferential procedure by which unconscious factors can be inferred (and thence interpreted) is common to a broad range of psychotherapies, but notably arises from ego-psychological theories (from Anna Freud and Heinz Hartmann to the heirs of Charles Brenner and Jacob Arlow), as well as the exponents of attachment theories and mentalization-based treatments. Second, the idea that the products of 'active imagination' can be used to elucidate the unconscious (having the patient tell stories, respond to projective test materials, visualize and describe images and narratives, as well as the expressive use of 'automatic writing,' and so forth) is strongly influenced by Carl Jung and his successors (see, for example, Jung's 1913–1916 and his 1957–1961 writings, as well as expositions by Barbara Hannah or by Anthony Stevens). As I argued in *Radical Psychoanalysis*, such techniques access the descriptive unconscious, but are minimally useful in terms of the challenges of listening to the repressed. Some exceptions to this argument may come from the use of the body in treatment (methods of movement and *prāṇāyāma,* for example) as will be discussed in what follows. Third, the use of 'deep' interpretations

that skip over the patient's ongoing free-associative speaking (as well as the patient's necessary resistances) belongs distinctively to Melanie Klein and has been criticized extensively, including by Lacan. One cannot shrink from condemning the violence done to the patient by such methods of 'direct' or 'deep' interpretation, regardless whether the content of the interpretation is 'right' or 'wrong' (on this point Piera Aulagnier has an interesting perspective particularly in relation to psychosis). Fourth, there is, of course, an irony to the Lacanian critique of Kleinian techniques, given that the Lacanian use of 'short sessions' and other techniques merely for the purpose of dramatically disturbing or coercively destabilizing the patient is equally abusive (by which I mean violent and anti-psychoanalytic) in as much as such techniques entirely circumvent the personal and interpersonal dynamics that free-associative discourse engages. Fifth, contemporary or neo-Kleinians usually do not follow the technique of 'deep interpretations' of the patient's anxieties and affects without regard to the patient's expressivity. However, rarely does the notion of resistance feature in contemporary Kleinian writings and especially not to resistance to free-association. Rather, this group of writers seems to regard the back-and-forth of transference and counter-transference experiences as equivalent to the flow of free-association. This is, of course, a somewhat flawed idea in that it limits the discourse to experiences that are, sooner or later, representable (see my 2017 paper, which challenges some Kleinian tenets). Finally, the idea that dialogue is sufficient (and free-association dispensable) is endorsed by a broad swath of psychotherapists, both psychoanalytically-informed and not. Here one might start by considering the techniques of Alfred Adler and Harry Stack Sullivan, but also all the contemporary social, interpersonal-relational and self-psychological schools. Dialogue can, of course, access what is other than those representations that are within the purview of immediate self-consciousness, but it necessarily sustains the repressiveness of representationality. Note that it is not that any of these methods is ineffective in terms of the goals of psychotherapy, but rather that none of them allow for listening to the voicing of the unrepresentable repressed. Indeed, by focusing merely on the representable other – the merely descriptive unconscious, the deep-preconscious or selectively unattended material – such techniques usually reinforce the ongoing repressiveness of self-consciousness.

65 My 2013 paper ('Free-associating with the Bodymind') did not address visual phenomena. However, even if the eyes are closed there are not only differential sensations of light and dark, but also afterimages and the sensation of other images as if on the inner surface of the eyelids. It is very advantageous for patients to close their eyes while free-associating on the couch. There are, however, many patients who do not do this – often because it compromises their sense of safety. For them, the distractions of the consulting room's ceiling, as they lie on the couch, is often quite an interference with the stream of consciousness (and not usually a particular helpful one, as it takes such patients away from the occurrences inside).

66 As mentioned in Endnote 10, there are several competent introductions to the rather diverse field of bodymind healing. Many of the approaches in this field are decidedly not psychoanalytic, or even psychodynamic. Some are even constituted anti-psychoanalytically. However, there are also some approaches that are important for psychoanalysts to know. One example might be the 'movement in depth' program which Mary Starks Whitehouse (and others) called 'authentic movement,' conceiving of this method as a type of embodied free-association (see Patrizia Pallaro's useful anthologies, as well as Janet Adler's introductory text). The way in which some practitioners have synthesized Asian principles with 'western' body-based psychotherapeutic practices is also interesting (see, for example, the writings of Halko Weiss and of Greg Johanson). In relation to tantric methods of 'meditating with the body,' my 2006 book provides an introduction as does the very accessible text by Reggie Ray.

67 Regrettably, the issue of the translation of *freie Einfall* has been too little discussed in the small but burgeoning literature on translating Freud, exemplified by Darius Gray Ornston's anthology and, before that, Bruno Bettelheim's plea for a more human-ized understanding of Freud's ideas.

68 The book of *Eichah* or 'Lamentations' (verse 26) enjoins us to 'wait quietly' for salvation, which one might interpret as waiting quietly − contemplatively or meditatively − for messaging that comes from elsewhere. In some scriptural translations (notably the Froschauer Bible translated by Huldrych Zwingli) this is rendered as waiting *in Gelassen-heit*. This means a surrendering of the will, a submission as in *'islam* (as I have mentioned in previous writings), to messages that come from elsewhere, from the divine or, more mundanely, from the *anderer Schauplatz* of the unconscious (as Lacan's riff on Freud's pronouncements in *Die Traumdeutung*). This 'elsewhere' might be the externality of the absolute (as in most of the Judeo-Christian-Islamic tradition) or the internality of a deeply inner voice (as George Fox's posthumously published declarations would have it, along with many strands of the Sanātana Dharma and Taoic traditions). Such receptive-ness is surely pertinent to how we understand the significance of the praxis of *freier Ein-fall*. The development of Heidegger's notion of *Gelassenheit* has been much discussed, including Barbara Dalle Pezze's interesting exegesis of his 'Conversation on a Country Path about Thinking,' written between 1944 and 1945; see also John Caputo's *The Mys-tical Element in Heidegger's Thought*, as well as William Lovitt and Harriet Brundage's 1995 discussion. For Meister Eckhart see the 1981 collection of his writings from the end of the thirteenth to the beginning of the fourteenth centuries, which evidently influenced Heidegger significantly.

69 The distinction between meditative and contemplative practices varies with different traditions and has often been blurred. In my 2013 book (see also Endnote 45 herein), I suggested that Bollas' description of the *reverie* in which he and his patient are immersed during the psychoanalytic session might best be called contemplative in the manner dis-cussed by Thomas Merton and others (Bollas refers to it as meditative). Perhaps the issue is nugatory. However, the pivotal issue is what the thinking and speaking subject *does* in order to enter the process of *releasement* that Heidegger describes and advocates. This is a process that can readily be compared, or even equated, with the notions of 'samadhi' or 'samāpatti' in the Dharmic traditions (see the excellent *Encyclopedia* pro-duced by Ingrid Fischer-Schreiber and her colleagues). That is, in a certain sense, a pro-cess that releases the thinker from the repetition-compulsivity of representationality and the narratological-imperative. Aside from the totalizing issue of his hermeneutics and his cosmology, my concern with Heidegger (as will be mentioned here) is that, even in his later writings, such as those collected in *Poetry, Language, Thought* or in *On the Way to Language*, there is little sense of a *method* by which, as it were, ordinary thinking may be required or enticed to cease and desist its hold over us. Although his 1954 lectures can be read as an effort in this direction, we are still left with the paradoxical activity of a 'willing' that 'willingly renounces willing' in order to be receptive to whatever comes from elsewhere, and with the question how this is to be effected (although Heidegger would certainly object to my phrasing of this question).

70 I explored how the action upon self-consciousness that is effected by psychoanalytic dis-course could be understood in terms of a negatively dialectical movement in my 1984 book, and how it might be understood in terms of deconstruction in my 1993 book. In his 'Conversation on a Country Path about Thinking' (the second part of his *Discourse on Thinking*), Heidegger applauds a figure who says that what is needed is 'a non-willing in the sense of a renouncing of willing, so that through this we may release, or at least prepare to release, ourselves to the sought-for essence of a thinking that is not a willing.' It seems entirely apposite to argue, as I do throughout this trilogy, that perhaps the only way this can be done is via the discourse of free-associative speaking, thinking and lis-tening. It is well known that Heidegger openly expressed antipathy toward Freud's writings − I am not familiar with the details of his biography, so it is unclear to me

whether Heidegger's dismissiveness was actually based on any scholarly appraisal or familiarity whatsoever of the issues at stake.

71 When I write that psychotherapy avoids sexuality and death, 'even when it appears not to do so,' I intend to convey something quite specific. There is, of course, a beleaguered group of psychotherapists ('sexuality counselors'), who bravely help clients and patients improve their sexual lives (bravely, that is, in the face of many cultural forces). But, for the most part, they talk *about* sexual functioning. My point here is that such a valuable mode of professional help is nevertheless quite different from experiencing – becoming aware of – one's sexual energies and one's body as a field of psychic-erotic energy as occurs through an immersion in free-associative discourse. Sexuality counseling does not usually 'return the patient to' an awareness of embodied experience as erotic, so much as it assists the patient or client with insights and information as to how to construct a more satisfying sexual life in the everyday world. Similarly, many psychotherapists and thanatologists help their clients and patients to talk *about* their mortality and the associated processes of mourning. But again, as valuable as this often is, it is nevertheless quite different from experiencing – becoming aware of – the deathfulness of one's inner being, such as occurs through an immersion in free-associative discourse (as will shortly be discussed). Counseling around issues of loss and mortality does not usually facilitate the patient's or client's awareness of the momentum of *Todestrieb* within every pulse of their lived-experience, and thus falls short of facilitating their becoming, in the here-and-now, more *alive!*

72 The recent writings of Rocco Gennaro competently survey some of the challenges of the conceptualizations of consciousness that have characterized the 'western' philosophical tradition. See also Susan Blackmore's introductory texts, as well as Susan Schneider and Max Velmans' anthology. In terms of less mainstream approaches, Ken Wilber's 1977 book offers a popular comparison of 'western' and 'eastern' perspectives, which is also the focus of Prem Saran Satsangi and Stuart Hameroff's 2016 anthology. Günther Nitschke's illustrated discussion (of a tantric movement from transpersonal to what he calls 'transparent' or meditational consciousness) provides an lively exposition of some eastern models of consciousness (including the Vedantic, the Vajrayāna model of the bardo, various yogic ideas and other Mahāyāna doctrines) and he briefly compares these with 'western' models (here his emphasis might seem strongly 'new age' oriented, relying as it does on writers such as David Bohm, Fritjof Capra, Jean-Émile Charon, Stanislav Grof, George Leonard, Erich Neumann, Bhagwan Shree Rajneesh, Alan Watts and Ken Wilber). There is an enormous literature in this somewhat esoteric area; for example, the remarkable range of experiences gathered under the topic of 'cosmic consciousness' (from Gautama to Henry David Thoreau and beyond) is evident in Richard Bucke's anthology.

73 In so far as twentieth century phenomenology calls for us to arrive at the essential structures of consciousness by means of the method of epoché (the bracketing-out, withholding or suspension of judgments and presuppositions), one might erroneously imagine it the ideal method for an exploration of the relationship between primary and secondary modes of consciousness (see Endnotes 16 and 17). Here one might consider a sizable literature from Merleau-Ponty to the contributions in Legrand and Trigg's anthology, including Karlsson's arguments for comprehending psychoanalysis in terms of phenomenology. However, as I see it, the problem is that, as Heidegger intimates, 'the nature of thinking can be seen only by looking away from thinking,' by which he surely implies the significant limits of thinking that attempts to look more deeply into thinking. Additional weight to this argument surely comes from the insights of psychoanalytic praxis that demonstrate how a method that starts with consciousness, in the affirmative manner to which phenomenology is committed, cannot grasp the possibility of a dynamic of conflict or contradictoriness as inherent in the

relations between different modes of consciousness (primary and secondary). This indicates the essential significance of free-associative discourse as negatively dialectical or deconstructive in relation to the law and order of representationality. A somewhat different and more clinical literature that touches, albeit indirectly, on this issue are clinical writings that extol the virtues of unknowing and not-knowing. Examples of this are Stephen Kurtz's 1989 book or the anthology edited more recently by Jean Petrucelli. The provocative and highly interesting writing of Danny Nobus and Malcolm Quinn addresses similar issues albeit in a Lacanian vein. On this issue, one can also be reminded of Donald Winnicott's pronouncement in his very important 1969 paper that he intervenes in order to let the patient know where his ignorance begins. In a rather different vein, Estelle Frankel draws from spiritual traditions to discuss how general health is deeply influenced by, and our psychological, emotional and spiritual health is radically influenced by, a capacity to tolerate and navigate uncertainty.

74 The relation between what I am calling 'awareness' and what Ganeri calls 'attention' (in his brilliant 2017 book, *Attention not Self*) begs for elucidation, which would require detailed further study that is beyond the scope of this text. With exemplary skill, Ganeri weaves 'western' philosophy with analytic-referential (logical-empiricist) and phenomenological traditions, with cognitive psychology (and contemporary neuroscience) and with various dharmic lineages (mostly within the Mahāyāna, and specifically the teachings of the fifth century Theravadan scholar, Buddhaghosa). In so doing, he manages to move beyond both the now unfashionable philosophy of 'agent causalism' (the idea of a self that produces mental activity) and the 'causal theory of action' that characterizes many of the cognitive psychology models currently in vogue. Instead, Ganeri makes the notion of attention fundamental to his sophisticated exposition of psychic life. From a psychoanalytic standpoint, it is regrettable that Ganeri, like Heidegger before him, seems to eschew any interest in psychoanalysis. Not only is the unconscious never discussed in any sense, but one searches *Attention not Self* in vain for any indication as to where dynamic conflict might be accommodated within his perspective. Even the Sullivanian notion of 'selective inattention' seems to have no place in Ganeri's thinking, although he gives very brief mention to what he calls 'inattentional blindness' (but again, this does not seem to be the result of a dynamic of intentionality or of competing transpersonal forces). Thus, although Ganeri provides an extensive discussion of the definition of consciousness, it would require careful elucidation to grasp how his notion of 'attention' might overlap with what I am calling primary awareness.

75 In relation to these notions of the primacy of the caress, one must also follow Irigaray's other writings, including her 1991 essay, 'Questions to Emmanuel Levinas' (see also Tina Chanter's very valuable, *Ethics of Eros*). In an important sense, of course, Levinas is a provocative philosopher of the primacy of the caress. There are parallel threads in Nancy's writings and Derrida's 2000 essay on touching and related topics, as well as the extraordinarily valuable explorations of Lingis.

76 Since 2005 (and polemically in 2009), I have argued the thesis that we are actually all inherently – or 'constitutionally' – *polysexual* or 'queer,' at least in our erotic potentialities. This is a more acceptable – 'sex-positive' – rendering of Freud's notion that we are all start from experiences of 'polymorphous perversity.' That is, we are all born with polysexual potential and what sexologists call the 'development of an individual's sexual patterning' is mostly formed by suppression of diverse erotic potentialities (a heterosexual path develops with the suppression of homosexual inclinations, and so forth). I first encountered the term 'polysexuality' in a 1981 issue of *Semiotexte* edited by François Peraldi. Since my development of the notion it has been picked up by several other authors (usually without attribution). The term 'pansexuality' (discussed as early as 1980 by William Stayton, and currently a rather fashionable designation in some cultural arenas) emphasizes the emotionally-charged 'object' of sexual desire (as potentially male, female, inanimate or abstract

and so forth), whereas the emphasis of polysexuality is not on the 'object' so much as the erotic-experiential movement of desire (the internal pathways of energetic motion and commotion).

77 'Lovemaps' is John Money's rather unfortunate term, which he uses as more or less equivalent to the commonly accepted notion of 'sexual patterning.' Its flaw is that it conflates the object of sexual inclinations and the object of emotional intimacies. As every psychotherapist knows, lust and love (in the sense of emotional connectedness) do not always, and for many people rarely, coincide. The psychoanalytic literature, from Freud's 1910 writings on men's 'object choice' and the Madonna/Whore complex onwards, documents how this lack of coincidence readily results from our oedipality – as indicated in my 2019 paper.

78 To advocate for awareness that returns us to the sensuous basis of our lived-experience risks the same sort of misreading to which Norman O. Brown's important texts were sometimes treated (in which he was charged with promoting irresponsible licentiousness and so forth). To assert the primacy of embodied experience as opened to us via the ethicality of free-associative discourse is indeed a call for de-repressive praxis. It is a call for liberation – *eleutheria!* – erotically and otherwise. However, unlike some images of Dionysian madness, entailing unrestrained indulgences that are routinely borne of latently hostile impulses (indulgences fueled as an aggressive reaction against the forces of suppression), this is a praxis regulated by a specific mode of ethicality – an opening to what is already otherwise that insists on being given voice.

79 This definition of the ontology of sexual energy, as the pervasive movement of subtle energies in pleasure and unpleasure that sustains the being-becoming of our lived-experience, is – I am arguing – directly or indirectly propounded by Freud and is surely discovered by his distinctive method of free-associative interrogation. It serves to focus how radical psychoanalysis differs from the reading of Freud's significance presented by the Lacanian lineage. For example, writing brilliantly in her 2017 *What is Sex?*, Alenka Zupančič defines sexuality, in a Lacanian vein, as 'not some being that exists *beyond* the symbolic; it "exists" solely as the contradiction *of the symbolic space that appears because of the constitutively missing signifier, and of what appears at its place (enjoyment).*' In what she calls a 'para-ontology,' she discusses how 'being is collateral … to its own impossibility,' which leads her to present sexuality linked to the unconscious as 'the point of a short circuit between ontology and epistemology' and then 'it is because of what is missing ("fallen out") from the signifying structuring of being that the unconscious, as a form of knowledge, relates to the impossibility of being involved in, and "transmitted" by, sexuality.' In such a line of theorizing, which insists that the sexual is the irreducibly 'Real' in the Lacanian sense, the possibility of erotic energy being a substantive force is expunged. In its refusal of erotic ontology, Lacanian thinking can only focus on the signification of relation and the ubiquity of non-relation. Herein lies the sheer fleshlessness of Lacanian psychoanalysis. Could it not be concluded that much Lacanian thinking is predicated on a determination to deny, or to expunge, the erotic mysteries of life? This issue is well exemplified in the recent theorizing of other exceptionally talented scholars such as Slavoj Žižek, Mladen Dolar and Lorenzo Chiesa. This is not to demean their provocative and most interesting contributions to our thinking, but it seems to remain more or less accurate to state that sexuality is now considered by these writers entirely within the – phallic – organization of the symbolic, the imaginary and the 'Real.' This positions the Lacanian appreciation of sexuality against any ontoethical project of erotic emancipation, which is where the awareness opened by free-associative discourse leads. It is possible that Chanter's worthy effort to read Levinas in relation to Lacan might go some way toward a remedy for the implications of this verdict, especially in relation to Levinas' emphasis on the ontology of the caress (and Chanter's exemplary exegesis of the importance of Irigaray's contributions). But the sense of abstraction in Lacanian thinking remains. A similar

charge might be made – paradoxically – against Butler's prioritization of performativity over expressivity, in that the ontology of sexuality is sidelined in relation to the focus on performance as that which creates the erotic and the identifications that surround it. The question of what Lacanians call *jouissance*, of what pleasure and unpleasure might (as well as the clinical conundrum of the path by which pain can become pleasure), has yet to be adequately resolved and is beyond the scope of the current text. Although some claim (almost entirely on the basis of Lacan's twentieth set of seminars in 1972 and 1973, which refers to *jouissance* as 'bodily substance' and admits the possibility of a specifically 'feminine *jouissance*' that is 'supplementary' but 'beyond the Phallus') that Lacan's notion is akin to Freud's notion of libidinality, this claim seems stretched, to say the least. What is required here (and is beyond my present scope) would also be a critique of Lacan's use of the notion of the 'sinthome' (and the Borromean knot) in his seminars from 1974 to 1976, which raise issues about the singularity of being that have been examined by Mari Ruti and others. Suffice it to add, at this juncture, that the issue is provocatively confronted by Aaron Schuster's dazzling effort to read Lacan in conjunction with Deleuze. However, his brief comments on the notion of *energeia* seem symptomatic of his distance from the ontology of erotic energy that is discussed herein (and seem to indicate his Lacanian commitments). Despite his acknowledgment of Deleuze's 'interest in deviant currents of psychoanalysis' as exemplified by his mention of Wilhelm Reich and his quotation from Alexander Lowen's 1970 text, Schuster seems uninterested in where such ideas might lead. For example, it is indicative that vitalism is more or less dismissed summarily as a 'formula of the superego.' Lacanian thinking, as is well known, discounts (and even tends to disparage) the power of the feminine, and thus the possibility of an emancipative receptivity to its forces. In this respect, it seems regrettably symptomatic that Schuster disregards entirely the writings of Irigaray (or other feminist critique of Lacan, such as Julia Kristeva's), which are in closer alignment to what is advanced in this text (see also Ashmita Khasnabish's excellent study of *Jouissance as Ānanda*).

80 The 'madness' of listening to movements of a subtle energy, the meaningfulness of which cannot be represented, is essentially what makes psychoanalysis radical, as well as incomprehensible to outsiders (see also, Endnote 20). As I previously quoted, Freud asserted in his 1916 lectures that 'the talk of which psychoanalytic treatment consists brooks no listener and cannot be demonstrated.' Perhaps most significantly in the present context, Nancy's 2002 essay leads an important discussion of listening that is not hearing-to-understand. Although his exploration is most focused on listening to music, he introduces a notion of the 'resonant subject' that seems profoundly important for our thinking about the listening mode engaged by the patient and the psychoanalyst. In this context, we must begin to grasp the significance in any radical psychoanalytic process of 'listening-receptively' or 'listening-resonantly,' as a release (*Gelassenheit*) from ordinary thinking or hearing-to-understand (see Endnote 68). The patient and psychoanalyst listen in an energetic field (that is both individual and bipersonal) and their listening is surely a resonating process in relation to energetic or libidinal events, as much as, or more than, it is a procedure of cogitation. This resonant-listening is an embodied listening – a matter that is hardly ever discussed in the psychoanalytic literature. The topic is admirably broached by Katya Bloom, and also addressed by some contributors to the body psychotherapy and somatic psychology literatures (see, for example, Nancy Mangano Rowe's contribution in Mark Brady's anthology). One implication of all these isues is that the conventional literature on listening (for instance, Michael Nichols' manual on how to do it, or the scholarly studies of 'hearer creativity' sampled in Graham McGregor and R. S. White's anthology) is not particularly helpful to the psychoanalyst. Theodor Reik's writings remain classics within the field (although they scarcely address the embodied resonance of listening). Subsequent contributions (for example, Robert Langs' 1978 tome) seem useful clinically although comparatively

uninspiring. Perhaps it is not surprising that some of the material coming from spiritual and mystical traditions is often more helpful to the aspiring psychoanalyst (for example, the contributions in Brady's anthology, or even Kay Lindahl's very basic orientation). It is evident that, in making these assertions, the notion of energy movements and that of inchoate yet meaningful messages – the enigmatic yet relational semiotics about which Laplanche writes – are not distinguishable. Although written from a different perspective, Paul Bains' discussion of the primacy of semiosis is useful in this regard, as are, of course, the writings of Kristeva on the distinction between symbolic representationality and the semiotic relationality of the 'maternal' *chora* (as I have discussed more extensively in previous volumes). Within Asian traditions, the breath (used in both a literal and a figurative sense) has always been taken as the most evident indicator of the movement of subtle energies, which has given rise to sophisticated methods of workplaying or meditating with the breath (a preliminary sampling of such methods is to be found in the texts by Takashi Nakamura, by Yogi Ramacharaka and by Richard Rosen).

81 The literature coming mostly from South Asian traditions on the movement of *prāna* has been overrun by popular publications (mostly published in the USA) on chakras and the channels or nādis running between them (for example, the writings of Anodea Judith). My 2006 book attempted to provide an antidote to all the western-ized misunderstandings of the rigor and spiritual orientation of tantric and yogic practices. Although much of the serious literature in this field remains in Sanskrit, the authoritative text on this topic in English is John Woodroffe's (also known as Arthur Avalon) now classic *The Serpent Power*, which is oriented to *kundalinī-yoga* (from shaktist and tantric traditions). His *Garland of Letters* is also a useful introduction to the *advaita-vedānta* or non-dual philosophy of these traditions (with their attendant yogic practices). More contemporary than Woodroffe's writings, Satyananda Saraswati, who founded the Bihar School of Yoga in the 1960s, wrote a very comprehensive guide to the tantric practices of kriya and yoga, with an extensive discussion of the astral qualities of the prānic body. For a mapping of the channels through which *ch'i* moves, along with the meridian points used by healers who come mostly from the East Asian traditions, the pictorial atlas produced by Yu-Lin Lian and his colleagues offers a graphic and authoritative introduction. Harriet Beinfield and Ephraim Korn-gold provide a very readable introduction to Chinese medicine for those entirely unfamiliar or skeptical about this field. Other reasonably informative introductions for westerners are provided by Daniel Keown and by Misha Ruth Cohen. In relation to the discussion of subtle energy from a psychoanalytic standpoint, the perspectives on understanding *ch'i* articulated by the Confucian scholar, Chu Hsi, are particularly interesting in that he discusses the energy as having both inner and outer 'aspects' – which bears upon Freud's controversial insistence on the endogenous character of drive or desire. The literature in these areas is voluminous and the bibliographies (of both primary and secondary sources) in the Fischer-Schreiber *Encyclopedia* remain exceptionally useful. In a very different vein, there is an accumulation of writings on the electromagnetic fields within and surrounding the physical body – although now somewhat outdated, Robert Becker and Gary Selden provided an introduction to these phenomena.

82 In the psychoanalytic context, Jerry Piven's excellent writings offer us some of the most useful thinking about this topic. On the one side, humans may be all too aware of what Kamo-no-Chomei called our 'fleeting evanescent nature' (cited by Piven in his 2004 book), but that does not obviate the limitations I experience in thinking about *my* death, which can only be experienced as a sort of 'unreality' (the descriptor used by Georg Hegel in 1807). For as soon as 'I' think about my absence, 'I' am necessarily asserting my presence (as Maurice Maeterlinck and many others have discussed). In this sense, the challenge – explicitly confronted by Franco de Masi – is that of 'making death thinkable,' which is a response to Freud's repeated assertions that our unconscious 'does not believe in its own death' (in his 1915

paper on war and death), that 'death is an abstract concept with a negative content for which no unconscious correlate can be found' (in 1923), and that 'the unconscious seems to contain nothing that could give any content to our concept of the annihilation of life' (in the 1926 *Inhibitions, Symptoms and Anxiety*). Against this trend within the literature generated by Freud's successors, Masi discusses how 'the fear of dying is ineliminable and is with us all our life.' Prior to Masi's essay, Irvin Yalom suggested that 'the terror of death is ubiquitous and of such magnitude that a considerable portion of one's life energy is consumed in the denial of death.' Long before that, Heidegger wrote in 1927 about the anguish we experience when we are aware that the nothingness of our being is the truth of our being-in-the-world (a theme taken up extensively in the motley literatures of what is loosely called 'existentialism'). As is well known (especially since it was discussed so powerfully by Ernest Becker in 1973), almost all humans seem to deny death by making it, in William Shakespeare's words, 'the undiscovered country, from whose bourn no traveler returns.' Imaginative portrayals of an afterlife seem operative in every known human culture (and are interestingly discussed by Edgar Herzog). The creation of such reassuring meanings stands, as John Bowker ably discusses along with many other commentators, at the very origins of religion (see Mircea Eliade's 1986 *Encyclopedia*). Freud resolves the paradox of death being both terrifying and unthinkable by suggesting that the fear of death is a manifestation of anxieties over guilt, castration or mutilation. In this vein, Otto Fenichel writes that 'every fear of death covers other unconscious ideas' (see also the essays in Hendrik Ruitenbeek's 1969/1983 anthology). However, as writers such as Harold Searles, John Frosch, Thomas Ogden, Michael Eigen, Marvin Hurvich and others have suggested, it is not clear that this resolution actually covers the depth and ubiquity of anxieties over annihilation (see also the extensive documentation on 'death anxiety' that is presented in the anthologies edited by Robert Neimeyer and Hannelore Wass, as well as in Robert and Beatrice Kastenbaum's *Encyclopedia*). In a somewhat different vein, Michel de M'Uzan provides some interesting observations on the way in which encounters with dying are disquieting – specifically in the context of psychoanalytic praxis.

83 At the end of Chapter 2, I documented some of the ways in which Freud's epigones read and misread this 1920 contribution, providing alternative formulations as well as one-sided interpretations. Havi Carel provides one of the most scholarly and extensive discussions of Freud's *Todestrieb*, although – as will become evident – I disagree with her privileging the aspect of aggressivity over what she calls the 'Nirvana Principle.' Additionally, Karlsson's 2004 discussion is interesting (although, again, I am not in agreement with the direction in which he proceeds). In a Lacanian vein, Ellie Ragland's *Essays on the Pleasures of Death* is also very scholarly and an important contribution. The writings of Rob Weatherill are also valuable in this context. Derrida's writings of 1987, 1992, and with Maurice Blanchot in 1998 are also, in certain respects, indispensable in terms of their decipherable significance for psychoanalysis.

84 Kurt Eissler, in his work with dying patients, followed Jones in arguing that what is feared is not so much death as the extinction of pleasure. However, the most theoretically important successor to Jones' discussion of *aphanisis* has been Lacan's. In his 1964 *Séminaire* (*The Four Fundamental Concepts of Psychoanalysis*), Lacan modifies Jones's idea substantially, suggesting that it is not the fading of desire that is the relevant dynamic, but the fading of the subject which initiates the dialectic of desire (the subject's effort to appropriate the desire of the other, or neurotically to shield her/himself from desire itself, which he had discussed in his 1960–1961 *Séminaire*). As I have indicated previously (see Endnote 79), the Lacanian determination to render drive as merely a symbolic construct, and thus to formalize desire – to deny its fleshliness and to render a theory of desire that is devoid of any sense of energetics – is central to the way in which radical psychoanalysis is not Lacanian.

85 In his provocative texts of the 1950s in which he contemplated the connections
    between erotics and death, Georges Bataille characterizes our 'necronautical journey'
    (to borrow terminology from Tom McCarthy and Simon Critchley) from cradle to the
    grave as a period of discontinuity. We emerge from and return to the great continuity
    of beingness. For each of us the discontinuities of 'me-my' identities being only what
    Kamo-no-Chomei might have called the 'fleeting evanescence' of what is considered
    'my life' – the life of *me*. In very different ways both Bataille and Heidegger suggest that
    deathfulness is a release from the 'mineness' of lived-experience, and it would be foolish
    to imagine that such a release is necessarily without its specific mode of pleasure.

86 Orgasmic release – in its most intensified renditions – is feared for the loss of ego
    functioning that accompanies such experiences. The latter may include loss of ordin-
    ary consciousness, the dissolution of body boundaries and the sense of selfhood,
    accompanied by blissful feelings of oceanic transcendence. In the psychoanalytic litera-
    ture – from Michael Balint's 1948 paper onwards – this tends to be discussed in an
    object-relational context that distinguishes 'genital love' from phallic–clitoral sexuality.
    The conflation of genitality with a specific object-relational pattern has led some
    commentators to take a stand against orgasmic intensification, because of the de-dif-
    ferentiation that may accompany such experiences. Kernberg, for example, whose
    1995 *Love Relations* appears, at least if read superficially, to be moderately sex-positive,
    seems to assume that such experiences will necessarily precipitate an overwhelming
    expression of aggressive-destructive impulses (see Arthur Efron's excellent commentary
    on the ways various 'psychoanalytic' lineages are sex-negative, avoiding the sexuality
    of our embodied experience and specifically his critical assessment of Kernberg's atti-
    tudes). Outside of the psychoanalytic field, there is a sizable literature on the use of
    'body meditation' – with or without activity that would commonly be referred to as
    sexual – to achieve transcendent moments of consciousness. The serious aspects of the
    literature on tantric meditation would be included in this (see my 2006 and 2009
    books), and Reggie Ray provides a very helpful introduction coming from the
    Tibetan tradition of *Vajrayāna* (*Tángmi* or *Mikkyō* in East Asia). Georg Feuerstein's
    writings also provide useful introductions to these practices, and a scholarly survey, in
    the South Asian context, is provided by Bharati's 1965 text.

87 An adequate examination of the cultural, sociopolitical and economic positioning of
    psychoanalytic doctrines is, of course, beyond the scope of this trilogy's final
    remarks, the distinctiveness of which is that I intend to open debate on these issues
    specifically from the standpoint of *radical* psychoanalysis. Eli Zaretsky's outstanding
    2007 book, *Secrets of the Soul* (as wells his more recent, *Political Freud*), very compe-
    tently addresses, from a social and historical perspective, the paradox wherein psy-
    choanalysis could be

>   a great force for human emancipation, [playing] a central role in the modernism
>   of the 1920s, the English and American welfare states of the 1940s and 50s, the
>   radical upheavals of the 1960s, and the feminist and gay-liberation movements of
>   the 1970s … [simultaneously becoming] a fount of antipolitical, antifeminist, and
>   homophobic prejudice …

    Zaretsky's thorough scholarship is invaluable and what is offered in this Chapter is
    perhaps accurately characterized as little more than a footnote that addresses the spe-
    cific implications of the radicalization of psychoanalysis presented in this trilogy – and
    even at that does so in a fashion that requires further development.

88 It is important to remember that, as a species of idealist, Hegel is discussing a move-
    ment of self-consciousness and not literally a struggle at the political level. His descrip-
    tion concerns the way in which 'a self-consciousness exists in and for itself, when and
    through the process whereby it exists for another; that is, it exists only in being rec-
    ognized, known or established, by another self-consciousness' (my translation of *das*

Selbstbewußtsein is an und für sich, indem und dadurch, daß es für ein anderes an und für sich ist; d.h. es ist nur als ein Anerkanntes). Thus, Hegel is describing not only how self-consciousness requires the 'gaze of the other' (to borrow the oculocentric account given by many contemporary enthusiasts for 'attachment theories') in order to come into existence, but also how its reflective capacity is only generated by recognizing that it is itself an 'other' for another self-consciousness (that is, contrary to the claim made in Johann Fichte's *Wissenschaftslehre*, self-consciousness cannot establish itself by itself). That this requires the triangulated cognitive capacities endowed by an induction into some sort of representationality, structured as a language, has been appropriately elaborated by many theorists who followed Alexandre Kojève's brilliant exegesis.

89 Here it seems irresistibly tempting to consider how Hegel must have had a certain sort of political awareness in order to generate this narrative of the development of self-consciousness. As is well known, Marx opened the possibility that Hegel's master/slave dialectic might have a literal application in the materialist realm of political economy – the capitalist class would necessarily eventually be overthrown by those performing the work of production. The failure of this vision is one of the central stories of the twentieth century. The literature addressing why 'communist' revolutions egregiously eventuated in what are effectively capitalist nation states is voluminous and well beyond the scope of this text to review. However, it may be noted that often the 'blame' for these miscarriages is directed at the nationalist constitution of such revolutions. That is, communism could only have come into bloom if it were to be pervasively international in its operations, rather than circumscribed by the artifices of state boundaries (and thus culminating in the impossible challenge of nurturing communism in nation states that cannot avoid integration into the world economy of capitalism). However, there is also the vitally important question as to how capitalist structures of domination are subjectively internalized (and become a value system passionately adhered to) even in individuals whose objective interests would be the overthrow of this system. This conundrum is addressed by the literature on ideology, some of the best contributions to which might have benefited greatly from psychoanalytic insight. Perhaps it is no more than an idly regretful fantasy to consider how the crucially significant endeavors of György Lukács or Antonio Gramsci (let alone other brilliant contributors such as István Mészáros, Bertell Ollman, George Lichtheim, Richard Schacht and Rahel Jaeggi) might have been amplified and empowered were they not so variously dismissive of psychoanalytic insight (although Ollman's use of Reich's bioenergetic theories make him an interesting exception to this statement).

90 Throughout history, the frequency with which change, whether bloody or seemingly bloodless, appears to result in what is, most regrettably, an inversion of power is quite compelling: the leaders of the peasant revolt become the new regime (frequently, it would seem, as oppressive as its predecessor); workers unite to overthrow the capitalist elite and then find themselves installing their leadership as the bureaucracy of state capitalism (different structures of ownership, same structures of exploitation); anti-colonialists fight to expel their oppressors and then establish a nation that suffers, within its own borders, many of the features of colonialism; women fight for, and achieve a certain amount of, economic or political parity, to find either that they are still second-class citizens or that, to be successful, they must mimic the worst characteristics of men; and so on. As the satirical pessimism of Jean-Baptiste Karr famously expresses it, *plus ça change, plus c'est la même chose*. This is, of course, an oversimplification, but the accumulation of evidence pertaining to it is alarming. This is *not* to suggest that these struggles are worthless – I am entirely against any such cynical message. But it is to suggest that men, women and children have too often fought, shed blood, been tortured and died for righteous causes that are then systemically subverted, and in this respect yet more needs to be learned from Hegel's dialectic. Clearly, the 'system' of domination/subordination-subjugation is

often sufficiently durable to outlast changes in the *dramatis personae*. Although somewhat dated, Trent Schroyer's discussion of the development of critical thinking about domination, at least in a Eurocentric context, remains valuable and does Ben Agger's subsequent treatment of this topic (and as do the writings of those thinkers on whom they focus, such as Adorno, Horkheimer and Marcuse). In a more contemporary context, Anita Chari's *A Political Economy of the Senses* addresses forms of domination that have arisen in neoliberal capitalism. She skillfully develops a critique of reification (which Lukács diagnosed the central social pathology of capitalism) that brings together more traditional Marxist approaches (exemplified by David Harvey) and theorists of radical democracy (exemplified by Ernesto Laclau and Chantel Mouffe). From the present standpoint, it is so regrettable that Chari's text avoids psychoanalytic ideas entirely and, although providing a most interesting discussion of current trends in artistic praxis, does not connect these trends to the surrealist movement that was so influenced by psychoanalytic insights.

91 In addition to Marx's political use of Hegel's master/slave narrative, this dialectic has been extensively and quite impressively used by theorists of colonial and sexist oppression to explain how the system constitutes the self-consciousness of the oppressor and the oppressed. Some of the literature on anti-racist and anti-colonialist struggles – great writings exemplified by Aimé Césaire, by Albert Memmi, by Franz Fanon and by Malcolm X – was greatly empowered both by some appreciation of Hegel and also, at least slightly in the case of Memmi and Fanon, by the influence of psychoanalytic insight. The way in which post-colonial societies often mimic the corruptions of the colonizer is, of course, a highly sensitive topic, as is the question of the way in which white racism might beget other forms of racism. A final example of the way in which the master/slave dialectic is exemplified is offered by a study of the political struggles around feminist emancipation: 'first-wave feminists' (such as Mary Wollstonecraft) hoped that securing enfranchisement democratic societies would be sufficient to produce equality; the 'second-wave' (see Linda Nicholson's anthology) recognized that suffrage was insufficient to secure liberation given the deep-rooted cultural oppression of women; the controversies of the 'third-wave' (discussed by Elizabeth Evans) and the most recent 'fourth-wave' (see discussions by Prudence Chamberlain and by Nicola Rivers) have been somewhat empowered by the contributions of notable psychoanalytic, specifically post-Lacanian, feminists trained in France (most notably by Irigaray and by Kristeva). Thus, there is perhaps an increasing awareness that women cannot 'liberate' themselves by emulating men. The general lesson of all these struggles is that the 'underdog' can indeed take over as the dominant power, but the structures of domination/subordination-subjugation are far more challenging to dismantle. This is a lesson that a study of the notion of oedipality should have already taught us.

92 I am of course aware of the extent to which my formulation of this mandate both coincides, extends and deviates from some of the best contemporary writing on the topics of alienation and reification. Here I am thinking of a very wide range of publications, not only of the writings of commentators such as Axel Honneth, Rahel Jaeggi and so many others (including the heirs to the Frankfurt School, such as Raymond Geuss), but also all the furor around Žižek's prodigious output, as well as scholarly work of thinkers such as Nikolas Kompridis. Perhaps more pertinently – for those more parochially interested in the discipline of 'psychoanalysis' – what I am suggesting is significantly different from the approach taken by most 'leftist Freudians.' Here I am not so much referring to the efforts of socialists of a liberal-humanist persuasion (Marie Langer's career, with her essay on 'Psychoanalysis without the Couch,' is a sterling example), but to the distinguished and more radical tradition of 'Freudo-Marxism' from Wilhelm Reich to Erich Fromm, Herbert Marcuse and Louis Althusser (again along with Žižek), as well as the theoretical groundwork of 'psychoanalytic-Marxism' (as ably discussed by

Bruce Brown, by Eugene Wolfenstein and others), but also some valiant, even if less than successful, efforts from related traditions. For example, Stephen Frosh's critical examination of identity politics, which draws on relational perspectives, remains useful. Within the Jungian lineage, Andrew Samuels' writing is important. In the Kleinian lineage, Fred Alford has attempted to counter its retrogressive implications (and Michael Rustin examines some of the challenges in this direction). Perhaps more influentially, some very significant works of Lacanian social criticism have emerged – a few examples of which are books by Mark Bracher, Todd McGowan, Yannis Stavrakakis and Samo Tomšič. However, as I read them, none of the above writings draw, in the manner I am proposing, on the discovery of oedipality as basis for a critique of dominative relations in human affairs.

93   I will continue to capitalize the 'Real' not only to emphasize how little this has to do with reality in the ordinary sense, but also because, as will become evident, its conceptualization is crucial to the way in which Lacan disavows the radicality of psychoanalytic discourse. This is obviously not the place to explore in exegetical detail the confusions and controversies surrounding Lacan's concept of the Real. Using only the English literature, such an exploration would require, at the very least, not only a deep familiarity with Lacan's own, often conflicting, pronouncements in translation, but also a study of the debates between commentators such as David Macey, Peter Dews, Malcolm Bowie, Marc de Kesel and Tom Eyers (even the brief entry in Dylan Evans' *Dictionary* illustrates some of the concept's confusional complexity). Starting with his 1936 paper's reference to the earlier writings of Émile Meyerson, Lacan poses the Real as being-in-itself, an ontological absolute. By the time of his famous paper, 'The Function and Field of Speech and Language in Psychoanalysis' (later published in the *Écrits*), and his first set of seminars in 1953, the Real has become a fundamental concept for Lacan's version of psychoanalysis. Located behind, beneath or beyond the symbolic order, it is undifferentiated and unassimilable to representation – the realm of whatever exists outside this order. In the next set of seminars (1954–1955), Lacan tells us there is no absence in the Real (despite the fact that it is absolutely elusive to the presencing of *re*-presentation). By the time of his eleventh set of seminars in 1964, the Real is emphatically defined as an impossibility. Although *real* (at least in a certain sense), it cannot be imagined, represented or attained. For Lacan it often seems to entail the material substrate of the imaginary and the symbolic. However, on the one hand, he stresses the indeterminacy of the Real in its being unassimilable to representation (and as such it functions as an abyss, unthinkable and thus akin to death), whereas, on the other hand, Lacan wants to assert a relationship between the Real and what we think of as ordinary reality, insofar as he requires that the former be rationally amenable to calculation. This sketch of his use of the concept of the Real is, I think, sufficient to show how distant Lacan is *both* from any notion that what is outside, or otherwise than, the symbolic order of representationality might engage with this order in a dynamic of nonidenticality, *and* from any notion that what is substantively otherwise than representationality might indeed be the fleshly embodied movements of desire as psychic energy.

94   The idea of the unfathomable links this discussion to Freud's 1900 assertion that every dream has 'at least one locus at which it is unfathomable, like a navel, a passage through which its meaningfulness is connected to the unknown' (and unknowable ... *mindestens, eine Stelle, an welcher er undergründlich is, gleichsam einen Nabel, durch den er mit dem Unerkannten zusammenhängt*). This is discussed in Chapters 6 and 7 of my *Radical Psychoanalysis*, as well as in my 2017 paper ('Opening to the Otherwise'). The point to be emphasized in the present discussion is that, for Lacan, there is no process that can be engaged within the symbolic order that might empower the subject to listen to what might be compelled into exile by that order – the enigmatic meaningfulness of the unknowable. That is, in his terms, everything that is effectual must be

within the law and order of the representational – and the totality of this system is, to all intents and purposes, immutable. In short, the theoretical edifice of Lacanian psychoanalysis allows no praxis. 'Cure' is not a becoming, an opening to being that is otherwise-yet-within. Rather, it is a satori-like realization that the symbolic, with all its entrapments in repetition-compulsivity and the narratological-imperative, is 'all that is the case.' Lacanian practice emanates from a doctrine of acquiescence, a submission to the 'will' of the symbolic order.

95 Despite Lacan's much touted sympathies with the revolutionary activities of 1968, about which Frosh's essay (in Gurminder Bhambra and Ipek Demir's 2014 anthology) is thoughtful, Lacanian psychoanalysis remains resolutely and endemically apolitical (and thus wields the conservative force accorded to the bystander). One cannot avoid this conclusion despite the fact that Lacan articulated a valid critique of ego-psychological, object-relational and other 'psychoanalytic' ideologies, and despite the fact that he chastised so many of his 'psychoanalytic' peers as 'guarantors of the bourgeois dream' – sociocultural engineers contributing to the perpetuation of the system. However, it must be noted how little Lacan had to say about imperialism, colonialism, sexism, racism and other modes of oppression. As is often the case, such indifference grievously devolves into the collusion of the bystander (as discussed, for example, in Mary Watkins and Helene Shulman's text). All this is *not* to suggest that Lacanian thinking, mostly after Lacan's voguish years of productivity, has not resulted in some outstanding sociopolitical criticism. Here I think both of the development of post-Lacanian feminism (exemplified by the writings of Irigaray and Kristeva), which could not have occurred without Lacan's insights even while proceeding against many of his precepts, and of the development of post-Lacanian critique of capitalism (mentioned in Endnote 92). To give just a single example, McGowan's 2016 book is exceptionally clear in its most interesting use of Lacanian theory of desire (which in a Lacanian context does not mean psychic energy or libidinality, but rather the surplus generated when a need is articulated as a demand). McGowan shows how capitalism mimics the Lacanian structure of desire by offering the public incomplete satisfactions that hide the suffering capitalism inflicts while leaving the public longing for more (cultivating the ethos of consumerism). He convincingly demonstrates how this ideological 'strategy' recruits our desires, giving them the illusion of corresponding to our 'nature,' and thus renders us addictively attached to the images of a better future under capitalism. This is critique at its best – reminiscent of the great writings of the Frankfurt School – and yet, for all its merits, one cannot accept the framework of Lacanian thinking *tout court*.

96 Lacan seems candid on these matters. The body appears only in the imaginary register and, for example, in his twentieth set of seminars (1972–1973) he condemns any idea of the speaking body as 'mystery' and thus he precludes the liberatory power of listening to mysteries. But in these seminars, Lacan also suggests that the body 'enjoys itself' (*il se jouit*) although, given his definition of desire in terms of lack (see Endnote 97), this enjoyment cannot be said to have desirous effects. For Lacan, the possible connection between 'speech' and embodiment belongs to the register of the Real and is thus an impossibility. Essentially he argues, for example both in his 1964 set of seminars and later in his *Autres Écrits* (published after his death by Éditions du Seuil), that flesh is only of interest as a medium that can bear the imprint of the sign (that is, not the meaningfulness of enigmatic messages, but the symbolizable sign). It seems safe to conclude that the very promising methods of treatment currently being developed by 'bodymind' healers (see Endnote 10) would be summarily dismissed by Lacan. For him, pleasure – and the 'painful pleasure' involved in the suffering of enjoyment or *jouissance* – seems to have little or nothing to do with embodied experience, except almost serendipitously. See also Endnote 79 on the issue of pleasure and how Lacan counterposes it to *jouissance*.

97 Unlike the free-associative praxis of radical psychoanalysis as a process of listening to the motions and commotions of desire (as a substantive erotic energy within and perhaps all around us), Lacanian theorizing subsumes the notion of 'desire' within his general theme of *lack* or *manqué-à-être* (want-to-be, want-of-being, lack-of-being, or failure-to-be). Like most of Lacan's concepts, the notion of lack shifts in the course of his writings and seminars. The notion first appears influenced by Jean-Paul Sartre's *Being and Nothingness* and, by the time of his 1954–1955 set of seminars, desire is formulated in terms of the 'lack of being whereby the being exists.' For Lacan, the speaking subject's 'desire is the metonymy of the want-to-be' – lack of being produces desire, whereas lack of having produces demands. In his fourth set of seminars of 1956–1957, he elaborates the notion of lack, such that there can be lack as symbolic castration (the subject can never speak from the locus of the Phallus), lack as imaginary frustration (deprivation of the breast) and lack as real privation (in relation to the symbolic). All these are, in a sense, reflections or refractions of the symbolic register's lack of being. The premise that this register and its speaking subject lack being (and that this is the major motor for representational transformations) is central to Lacanian theorizing.

98 See my 2013 essay on the eroticism of slowness for a discussion of the ontoethical distinction between 'fucking' as a dominative act that adheres to the – illusory or delusional – superiority of the phallic and 'lovemaking' as a mutual interchange of erotic energies. The latter, with its potential for ecstatic release (exiting from the static) is also explored in my 2009 *Liberating Eros,* as well as in a variety of tantric and Taoic texts that present such praxis as meditation.

99 There is no space here for an exegetical or critical review of the literature on surrealism or its parentage in the dada movement (David Hopkins provides a brief but accessible introduction). For dada, Robert Motherwell's anthology is an excellent resource, as is that edited by Dawn Ades, and Richard Sheppard's collection of essays is informative. The 'philosophical' writings of Hugo Ball, Walter Serner and Tristan Tzara are still provocatively worthy of consideration (as is the literary productions of Emmy Hennings). For surrealism, André Breton's 1925 and 1930 *Manifestoes of Surrealism* (see also his 1934 *What is Surrealism?*), as well as some of Roger Callois' writings, are still necessary reading. Breton's essays on automatic messages perhaps show most explicitly the influence of psychoanalytic ideas on his artistic practices. See also the 2015 anthology edited by Dawn Ades and Michael Richardson (as well as their 2015 collection of documents relevant to Bataille and surrealist ideas). Although his connection with surrealism is somewhat controversial, the writings of Bataille (see his anthology, *The Absence of Myth*) are in many ways more directly pertinent to the challenges of psychoanalytic discourse, than those of the earlier leaders of the movement. For the issues of sexism within the surrealist movement, see Whitney Chadwick's 1991 text, as well as Penelope Rosemont's anthology.

100 The idea of permanent revolution comes notably from Marx in 1844, Trotsky in 1929 and from Zedong in 1937. The focus on everyday life was pioneered by Henri Lefebvre (and taken up subsequently by Michel de Certeau). What is advocated here has a somewhat tangential kinship with the anti-authoritarian and anti-capitalist philosophies of autonomist Marxism (about which, at least in a European context, see Georgy Katsiaficas' *The Subversion of Politics*, as well as Sylvère Lotringer and Christian Marazzi's important anthology). Perhaps more clearly, it is not unlike the philosophy of situationism, with its focus on attacking the mechanisms of alienation, as presented by Guy Debord and Raoul Vaneigem (see also the anthology edited by Ken Knabb). The heir to these tendencies is the brilliant sociopolitical philosophy of Antonio Negri and his collaborator, Michael Hardt.

101 Of all the early psychoanalysts, perhaps no one was more aware of these implications of Freud's findings than Otto Gross. In 1913, he wrote that the psychoanalytic exploration

of the unconscious is the philosophy of revolution. That is, it is destined to ferment revolt within the domain of psyche towards the liberation of each individual fettered by the repressiveness of her/his self-consciousness. Psychoanalysis is a calling to create our capacity for the process of freedom, which is the prologue for revolutionary change. The incomparable transmutation of all our values in the future begins today with Friedrich Nietzsche's thinking about the hidden foundations of our soul, and with Sigmund Freud's discovery of the psychoanalytic method … with that, a new ethicality is born. (my translation)

BIBLIOGRAPHY

Abram, D. (1996). *The spell of the sensuous: Perception and language in a more-than-human world*. New York, NY: Vintage.

Ades, D. (ed.) (2006). *The dada reader: A critical anthology*. Chicago, IL: University of Chicago Press.

Ades, D. & Baker, S. (eds.) (2006). *Undercover surrealism: Georges Bataille and 'Documents.'* Cambridge, MA: MIT Press.

Ades, D. & Richardson, M. (eds.) (2015). *The surrealism reader: An anthology of ideas*. Chicago, IL: University of Chicago Press.

Adler, A. W. (1898–1937). *The collected clinical works of Alfred Adler* (12 volumes, edited by H. T. Stein). Bellingham, WA: The Alfred Adler Institute of Northwest Washington, 2005.

Adler, J. (2002). *Offering from the conscious body: The discipline of authentic movement*. Rochester, NY: Inner Traditions.

Adorno, T. W. (1951). *Minima moralia: Reflections from damaged life* (translated by E. F. N. Jephcott). London, UK: Verso, 2006.

Adorno, T. W. (1963–1969). *Critical models: Interventions and catchwords* (translated by H. W. Pickford). New York, NY: Columbia University Press, 2005.

Adorno, T. W. (1965–1966). *Lectures on negative dialectics: Fragments of a lecture course 1965/ 1966* (edited by R. Tiedemann, translated by R. Livingstone). Cambridge, UK: Polity Press, 2008.

Adorno, T. W. (1966). *Negative dialectics* (translated by E. B. Ashton). New York, NY: Seabury, 1973.

Adorno, T. W., Frenkel-Brunswick, E., Levinson, D. J. & Sanford, R. N. (1950). *The authoritarian personality*. New York, NY: Harper & Row.

Agamben, G. (1980). *Language and death: The place of negativity* (translated by K. Pinkus & M. Hardt). Minneapolis, MN: University of Minnesota Press, 2006.

Agamben, G. (2009). *Nudities* (translated by D. Kishik & S. Pedatella). Stanford, CA: Stanford University Press, 2011.

Agamben, G. (2014). *The use of bodies* (translated by A. Kotsko). Stanford, CA: Stanford University Press, 2015.

Agel, J. (ed.) (1971). *The radical therapist* (by the Radical Therapist Collective). New York, NY: Ballantine.

Agger, B. (1992). *The discourse of domination: From the Frankfurt School to postmodernism.* Evanston, IL: Northwestern University Press.

Alaimo, S. & Hekman, S. (eds.) (2008). *Material feminisms.* Bloomington, IN: Indiana University Press.

Alexander, F. G. (1963). *Fundamentals of psychoanalysis.* New York, NY: W. W. Norton.

Alexander, F. G. (1966). *The history of psychiatry: An evaluation of psychiatric thought and practice from prehistoric times to the present.* New York, NY: Harper & Row.

Alford, C. F. (1989). *Melanie Klein and critical social theory: An account of politics, art, and reason based on her psychoanalytic theory.* New Haven, CT: Yale University Press.

Althusser, L. (1964–1973). *On ideology.* London, UK: New Left Books, 1971.

Althusser, L. (1968). *For Marx* (translated by B. Brewster). London, UK: Verso, 2006.

Althusser, L. (1971). *Lenin and philosophy and other essays.* New York, NY: Monthly Review Press, 2001.

Althusser, L. (1993). *Writings on psychoanalysis: Freud and Lacan* (translated by J. Mehlman). New York, NY: Columbia University Press.

Anselm of Aosta. (c. 1077–1098). *Anselm: Basic writings* (edited by T. Williams). Indianapolis, IN: Hackett, 2007.

Anzieu, D. (1975). *Freud's self-analysis* (translated by P. Graham). London, UK: Hogarth Press, 1986.

Aristotle (c. 364–322 B.C.E.). Nicomachean ethics. *The complete works of Aristotle* (2 volumes, edited by J. Barnes), *2*, 1729–1867. Princeton, NJ: Princeton University Press, 1984.

Assoun, P.-L. (1980). *Freud and Nietzsche* (translated by R. L. Collier). New York, NY: Continuum, 2002.

Atwood, G. E. & Stolorow, R. D. (2014). *Structures of subjectivity: Explorations in psychoanalytic phenomenology and contextualism* (2nd edition). Hove, UK: Routledge.

Aulagnier, P. (1975). *The violence of interpretations: From pictogram to statement* (translated by A. Sheridan). Hove, UK: Brunner-Routledge, 2001.

Bachelard, G. (1934). *The new scientific spirit* (translated by A. Goldhammer). Boston, MA: Beacon Press, 1984.

Bachelard, G. (1938). *The formation of the scientific mind* (translated by M. McAllester Jones). Bolton, UK: Clinamen, 2002.

Bachelard, G. (1940). *The philosophy of no: A philosophy of the new scientific mind* (translated by G. C. Waterson). New York, NY: Orion, 1968.

Badiou, A. (1997). *Deleuze: The clamor of being* (translated by L. Burchill). Minneapolis, MN: University of Minnesota Press, 1999.

Bains, P. (2006). *The primacy of semiosis: An ontology of relations.* Toronto, Canada: University of Toronto Press.

Bakhtin, M. M. (1919–1921). *Toward a philosophy of the act* (translated by V. Liapunov). Austin, TX: University of Texas Press, 1993.

Bakhtin, M. M. (1970–1975). *Speech genres and other late essays* (translated by V. W. McGee). Austin, TX: University of Texas Press, 1986.

Baktin, M. M. (1937–1941). *The dialogic imagination* (translated by M. Holquist & C. Emerson). Austin, TX: University of Texas Press, 1983.

Ball, H. (1920–1921). *Flight out of time: A dada diary* (edited by J. Elderfield, translated by A. Raimes). Berkeley, CA: University of California Press, 1996.

Barratt, B. B. (1976). Freud's psychology as interpretation. *Psychoanalysis and Contemporary Science, 5*, 443–478.

Barratt, B. B. (1984/2016). *Psychic reality and psychoanalytic knowing.* Hillsdale, NJ: Analytic Press. [Republished by Routledge in 2016]

Barratt, B. B. (1993/2016). *Psychoanalysis and the postmodern impulse: Knowing and being since Freud's psychology.* Baltimore, MD: Johns Hopkins University Press. [Republished by Routledge in 2016]

Barratt, B. B. (2004). Desire and death in the constitution of I-ness. In: J. Reppen, J. Tucker & M. A. Schulman (eds.). *Way beyond Freud: Postmodern psychoanalysis observed.* London, UK: Open Gate Press, pp. 264–279.

Barratt, B. B. (2005). *Sexual health and erotic freedom.* Philadelphia, PA: Xlibris/Random House.

Barratt, B. B. (2006). *What is tantric practice?* Philadelphia, PA: Xlibris/Random House.

Barratt, B. B. (2009). *Liberating eros.* Philadelphia, PA: Xlibris/Random House.

Barratt, B. B. (2010). *The emergence of somatic psychology and bodymind therapy.* Basingstoke, UK: Palgrave Macmillan.

Barratt, B. B. (2013a). Free-associating with the bodymind. *International Forum of Psychoanalysis, 22,* 161–175.

Barratt, B. B. (2013b). Sensuality, sexuality, and the eroticism of slowness. In: N. Osbaldiston (ed.), *The culture of the slow: Social deceleration in an accelerated world.* Basingstoke, UK: Palgrave Macmillan, pp. 136–153.

Barratt, B. B. (2013c). *What is psychoanalysis? 100 years after Freud's 'Secret Committee.'* London, UK: Routledge.

Barratt, B. B. (2015a). Boundaries and intimacies: Ethics and the (re)performance of 'The Law' in psychoanalysis. *International Forum of Psychoanalysis, 24(4),* 204–215.

Barratt, B. B. (2015b). On the mythematic reality of libidinality as a subtle energy system: Notes on vitalism, mechanism, and emergence in psychoanalytic thinking. *Psychoanalytic Psychology, 32,* 626–644.

Barratt, B. B. (2015c). Critical notes on the neuro-evolutionary archaeology of affective systems. *Psychoanalytic Review, 102,* 183–208.

Barratt, B. B. (2015d). Rejoinder to Mark Solms' response to 'Critical notes on the neuro-evolutionary archaeology of affective systems'. *Psychoanalytic Review, 102,* 221–227.

Barratt, B. B. (2016). *Radical psychoanalysis: An essay on free-associative praxis.* London, UK: Routledge.

Barratt, B. B. (2017a). Seven questions for Kleinian psychology. *Psychoanalytic Psychology, 34(3),* 332–342.

Barratt, B. B. (2017b). Opening to the otherwise: The discipline of listening and the necessity of free-association for psychoanalytic praxis. *International Journal of Psychoanalysis, 98 (1),* 39–45.

Barratt, B. B. (2017c) On the otherwise energies of the human spirit: A contemporary comparison of Freudian and Jungian approaches to 'spirit.' In R. S. Brown (ed.) *Re-encountering Jung: Analytical psychology and contemporary psychoanalysis.* London, UK: Routledge, 2017, pp. 47–67.

Barratt, B. B. (2018a). On the unique power of free-associative discourse: Notes on the contributions of Henry Lothane and Christopher Bollas. *Psychoanalytic Inquiry, 38(6),* 478–487.

Barratt, B. B. (2018b). *The erotics and poetics of Freier Einfall: On the necessary 'femininity' of free-associative discourse for listening to the repressed.* Johannesburg, South Africa: Parkmore Institute.

Barratt, B. B. (2019). Oedipality and oedipal complexes reconsidered: On the incest taboo as key to the universality of the human condition. *International Journal of Psychoanalysis, 100(1).*

Barrett, E. & Holt, B. (eds.) (2010). *Practice as research: Approaches to creative arts enquiry*. London, UK: I. B. Tauris.

Barros, C. (1998). *Autobiography: Narrative of transformation*. Ann Arbor, MI: University of Michigan Press.

Barthes, R. (1967). Death of the author. In: *Image-music-text* (translated by S. Heath). New York, NY: Hill & Wang, 1978, pp. 142–148.

Bataille, G. (1945). *On Nietzsche* (translated by B. Boone). London, UK: Continuum, 2004.

Bataille, G. (1954). *Inner experience* (translated by S. Kendall). Albany, NY: State University of New York Press.

Bataille, G. (1957). *Erotism: Death and sensuality* (translated by M. Dalwood). San Francisco, CA: City Light Books, 1986.

Bataille, G. (1961). *The tears of eros* (translated by P. Connor). San Francisco, CA: City Lights Books, 2001.

Bataille, G. (c. 1925–1961). *The absence of myth: Writings on surrealism* (edited & translated by M. Richardson). London, UK: Verson, 1994.

Baudrillard, J. (1983). *Fatal strategies* (translated by P. Beitchman & W. G. J. Nieslu-chowski). New York, NY: Semiotext(e), 2008.

Baudrillard, J. (1987). *The ecstasy of communication* (translated by B. Schütze & C. Schütze). New York, NY: Semiotext(e), 2012.

Baudrillard, J. (1992). *The illusion of the end* (translated by C. Turner). Stanford, CA Stanford University Press, 1994.

Baudrillard, J. (2008). *Radical alterity* (translated by M. Guillaume & A. Hodges). New York, NY: Semiotext(e), 2008.

Beauvoir, S. de (1947). *The ethics of ambiguity* (translated by D. Frechtman). New York, NY: Citadel.

Beauvoir, S. de (1949). *The second sex* (translated by C. Borde & S. Malovany-Chevallier). New York, NY: Vintage.

Becker, E. (1973). *The denial of death*. New York, NY: Free Press.

Becker, R. O. (1985). *The body electric: Electromagnetism and the foundation of life*. New York, NY: William Morrow.

Beinfield, H. & Korngold, E. (1992). *Between heaven and earth: A guide to Chinese medicine*. New York, NY: Ballantine.

Bellak, L. (1961). Free-association: Conceptual and clinical aspects. *International Journal of Psychoanalysis*, *42*, 9–20.

Benjamin, J. (2017). *Beyond doer and done to: Recognition theory, intersubjectivity and the third*. Abingdon, UK: Routledge.

Bergson, H.-L. (1889). *Time and free will: An essay on the immediate data of consciousness* (translated by F. L. Pogson). Minneola, NY: Dover, 2001.

Bergson, H.-L. (1896). *Matter and memory* (translated by N. M. Paul & W. S. Palmer). New York, NY: Zone Books, 1990.

Bergson, H.-L. (1907). *Creative evolution* (translated by A. Mitchell). Scotts Valley, CA: CreateSpace, 2011.

Bergson, H.-L. (1919). *Mind-energy* (translated by H. W. Carr). Scotts Valley, CA: Create-Space, 2013.

Bergson, H.-L. (1934). *The creative mind: An introduction to metaphysics* (translated by M. L. Andison). Minneola, NY: Dover, 2010.

Bettelheim, B. (1983). *Freud and man's soul: An important re-interpretation of Freudian theory*. New York, NY: Vintage.

Bhambra, G. K. & Demir, I. (eds.) (2014). *1968 in retrospect: History, theory, alterity.* Basingstoke, UK: Palgrave Macmillan.

Bharati, A. (1965). *Tantric traditions.* Kolkata, India: Hindustan Publishing Company, 1993.

Black, R. (ed.) (2013). *Practice as research in the arts: Principles, protocols, pedagogies, resistances.* Basingstoke, UK: Palgrave Macmillan.

Blackmore, S. (2011). *Consciousness: An introduction* (2nd edition). Oxford, UK: Oxford University Press.

Blackmore, S. (2018). *Consciousness: A very short introduction* (2nd edition). Oxford, UK: Oxford University Press.

Blanchot, M. (1994). *The instant of my death* (translated by E. Rottenberg). Stanford, CA Stanford University Press.

Blass, R. B. (2010). Affirming 'That's not Psychoanalysis!' – On the value of the politically incorrect act of attempting to define the limits of our field. *International Journal of Psychoanalysis, 91(1)*, 81–99.

Bloch, E. (1938–1947). *The principle of hope* (3 volumes, translated by N. Plaice, S. Plaice & P. Knight). Cambridge, MA: MIT Press, 1986.

Bloch, E. (1961). *Grundfragen der Philosophie: Ausgewählte Schriften, Band 1.* Frankfurt, Germany: Suhrkamp.

Bloom, K. (2006). *The embodied self: Movement and psychoanalysis.* London, UK: Karnac.

Blumgart, L. (1916). Abstracts from the 'Jahrbuch für psychoanalytische und psychopathologische Forschungen'. *Psychoanalytic Review, 3*, 90–114.

Bogost, I. (2012). *Alien phenomenology – or what it's like to be a thing.* Minneapolis, MN: University of Minnesota Press.

Bohm, D. (1983). *Wholeness and the implicate order.* London, UK: Ark.

Bollas, C. (1987). *The shadow of the object: Psychoanalysis of the unthought known.* London, UK: Free Association Books.

Bollas, C. (1995). Interview with Anthony Molino. In: A. Molino (eds.) *Freely associated: Encounters in psychoanalysis with Christopher Bollas, Joyce McDougall, Michael Eigen, Adam Phillips, Nina Coltart.* London, UK: Free Association Books, 1997, pp. 5–51.

Bollas, C. (1999). *The mystery of things.* London, UK, Routledge.

Bollas, C. (2002). *Free association: Ideas in psychoanalysis.* Cambridge, UK: Icon.

Bollas, C. (2007). *The Freudian moment.* London, UK: Karnac.

Bollas, C. (2009a). *The evocative object world.* Hove, UK: Routledge.

Bollas, C. (2009b). *The infinite question.* Hove, UK: Routledge.

Booth, W. C. (1975). *A rhetoric of irony.* Chicago, IL: University of Chicago Press.

Boothby, R. (1991). *Death and desire: Psychoanalytic theory in Lacan's return to Freud.* London, UK: Routledge.

Boothby, R. (2001. *Freud as philosopher: Metapsychology after Lacan.* London, UK: Routledge.

Bowie, M. (1993). *Lacan.* Cambridge, MA: Harvard University Press.

Bowker, J. (1991). *The meanings of death.* Cambridge, UK: Cambridge University Press.

Bracher, M. (1993). *Lacan, discourse and social change.* Ithaca, NY: Cornell University Press.

Brady, M. (ed.) (2003). *The wisdom of listening.* Boston, MA: Wisdom Publications.

Brentano, F. C. H. H. (1887). *Descriptive psychology* (translated by B. Müller). Abingdon, UK: Routledge, 1995.

Breton, A. (1925–1930). *Manifestoes of surrealism* (translated by R. Seaver & H. Lane). Ann Arbor, MI: University of Michigan Press, 1972.

Breton, A. (1934). What is surrealism? In: *What is surrealism? – Selected writings* (edited by F. Rosemont). Atlanta, GA: Pathfinder Press, 1978, pp. 151–187.

Breton, A., Eluard, P. & Soupault, P. (1919–1933). *The automatic message, the magnetic fields, the immaculate conception* (edited & translated by D. Gascoyne). Boston, MA: Atlas Press, 1997.

Brown, B. (1973/2009). *Marx, Freud, and the critique of everyday life: Toward a permanent cultural revolution*. New York, NY: Monthly Review Press.

Brown, N. O. (1959). *Life against death: The psychoanalytical meaning of history*. New York, NY: Vintage.

Brown, N. O. (1966). *Love's body*. New York, NY: Random House.

Bryant, L., Smicek, N. & Harnman, G. (eds.) (2011). *The speculative turn: Continental materialism and realism*. Melbourne, Australia: Re-Press.

Bucke, R. M. (ed.) (2010). *Cosmic consciousness: A study in the evolution of the human mind*. Mansfield, CT: Martino.

Buckley, J. H. (1994). *The turning key: Autobiography and the subjective impulse since 1800*. Cambridge, MA: Harvard University Press.

Buddha, G. (c. 500 b.c.e.). *The middle length discourses of the Buddha: A new translation of the Majjhima Nikāya* (translated by B. Ñāṇamoli & B. Bodhi). Boston, MA: Wisdom, 1995.

Burke, E. (1756). *A philosophical inquiry into the origin of our ideas of the sublime and beautiful*. London, UK: Oxford University Press, 2015.

Busch, F. (1995). *The ego at the center of clinical technique*. Northvale, NJ: Jason Aronson.

Busch, F. (1999). *Rethinking clinical technique*. Northvale, NJ: Jason Aronson.

Busch, F. (2013). *Creating a psychoanalytic mind: A psychoanalytic method and theory*. Hove, UK: Routledge.

Butler, J. P. (1997). *The psychic life of power: Theories in subjection*. Palo Alto, CA: Stanford University Press.

Caillois, R. (1934–1978). *The edge of surrealism: A Roger Caillois reader* (edited by C. Frank). Durham, NC: Duke University Press, 2003.

Canguilhem, G. (1966). *The normal and the pathological* (translated by C. R. Fawcett). New York, NY: Zone Books, 1991.

Capra, F. (1975). *The Tao of physics*. Berkeley, CA: Shambhala.

Caputo, J. D. (1990). *The mystical element in Heidegger's thought*. New York, NY: Fordham University Press.

Carel, H. (2006). *Life and death in Freud and Heidegger*. New York, NY: Rodopi (Contemporary Psychoanalytic Studies).

Carnap, R. (1935). *Philosophy and logical syntax*. Bristol, UK: Thoemmes, 1996.

Carroll, L. (1872). *Alice through the looking glass* (illustrated by H. Oxenbury). Somerville, MA: Candlewick Press, 2009.

Caygill, H. (2013). *On resistance: A philosophy of defiance*. London, UK: Bloomsbury.

Certeau, M. de (1980). *The practice of everyday life* (translated by S. Rendall). Berkeley, CA: University of California Press, 1984.

Césaire, A. F. D. (1955). *Discourse on colonialism* (translated by J. Pinkham). New York, NY: Monthly Review Press, 1972.

Chadwick, W. (1991). *Women artists and the surrealist movement*. London, UK: Thames & Hudson.

Chamberlain, P. (2017). *The feminist fourth wave: Affective temporality*. Basingstoke, UK: Palgrave Macmillan.

Chanter, T. (1995). *Ethics of eros: Luce Irigaray's rewriting of the philosophers*. London, UK: Routledge.

Chanter, T. (2001). *Time, death, and the feminine: Levinas with Heidegger*. Stanford, CA: Stanford University Press.

Chapelle, D. (1993). *Nietzsche and psychoanalysis.* Albany, NY: State University of New York Press.

Chari, A. (2015). *A political economy of the senses: Neoliberalism, reification, critique.* New York, NY: Columbia University Press.

Charon, J.-E. (1977). *The spirit: That stranger inside us.* Haverford, PA: Infinity, 2004.

Cheng, C.-Y. (2004). Dimensions of the Dao and onto-ethics in the light of the DaoDeJ-ing. *Journal of Chinese Philosophy, 31(2),* 143–182.

Cheng, C.-Y. (2010). Developing Confucian onto-ethics in a postmodern world/age. *Journal of Chinese Philosophy, 37(1),* 3–17.

Chiesa, L. (2007). *Subjectivity and otherness: A philosophical reading of Lacan.* Cambridge, MA: MIT Press.

Chiesa, L. (2016). *The not-two: Logic and god in Lacan.* Cambridge, MA: MIT Press.

Chused, J. F. (2012). The analyst's narcissism. *Journal of the American Psychoanalytic Association, 60(5),* 899–915.

Cioffi, F. L. (1998). *Freud and the question of pseudoscience.* Peru, IL: Open Court.

Clausewitz, C. V. (1816–1830). *On war* (edited & translated by M. Howard & P. Paret). Princeton, NJ: Princeton University Press, 1989.

Cleckley, H. (2015). *The mask of sanity: An attempt to clarify some issues about the so-called psychopathic personality* (2nd edition). Eastford, CT: Martino.

Clough, P. T. & Halley, J. (eds.) (2007). *The affective turn: Theorizing the social.* Durham, NC: Duke University Press.

Cochrane, K. (ed.) (2013) *Women of the revolution: Forty years of feminism.* New York, NY: Random House.

Cohen, M. R. (2015). *The new Chinese medicine handbook: An innovative guide to integrating eastern wisdom with western practice for modern healing.* Beverly, MA: Fair Winds Press.

Colebrook, C. M. (2004). *Irony.* London, UK: Routledge.

Connell, R. W. (2007). *Southern theory: Social science and the global dynamics of knowledge.* Cambridge, UK: Polity Press.

Coole, D. & Frost, S. (eds.) (2010). *New materialisms: Ontology, agency, and politics.* Durham, NC: Duke University Press.

Cooper, D. (ed.) (1968). *The dialectics of liberation.* London, UK: Verso, 2015.

Cooper, D. (1971). *Psychiatry and anti-psychiatry.* London, UK: Routledge, 2013.

Coopersmith, J. (2015). *Energy, the subtle concept: The discovery of Feynman's blocks from Leibniz to Einstein* (revised edition). Oxford, UK: Oxford University Press.

Copjec, J. (1994). *Read my desire: Lacan against the historicists.* Cambridge, MA: MIT Press.

Coward, H. (1990). *Derrida and Indian philosophy.* Albany, NY: State University of New York Press.

Coward, R. & Ellis, J. (1977). *Language and materialism: Developments in semiology and the theory of the subject.* London, UK: Routledge & Kegan Paul.

Crews, F. (2017). *Freud: The making of an illusion.* New York, NY: Metropolitan Books.

Csikszentmihalyi, M. (1975). *Flow: The psychology of optimal experience.* New York, NY: Harper & Row.

Curd, P. (2011). *A preSocratics reader: Selected fragments and testimonia* (2nd edition, translated by R. D. McKirahan). Indianapolis, IN: Hackett.

Dahl, H., Kächele, H. & Thomä, H. (eds.) (1988). *Psychoanalytic process research strategies.* Berlin, Germany: Springer-Verlag.

Damasio, A. R. (2000). *The feeling of what happens.* San Diego, CA: Harcourt Brace.

Damasio, A. R. (2003). *Looking for Spinoza: Joy, sorrow, and the feeling brain.* Boston, MA: Mariner.

Damasio, A. R. (2012). *Self comes to mind: Constructing the conscious brain.* New York, NY: Vintage.

Dasgupta, S. & Dasgupta, S. (2010). *A history of Indian philosophy* (5 volumes). Charleston, SC: Nabu Press.

Dean, J. T. (2013). 'What does not change' – Technique and effects in psychoanalysis. *Division Review: A Quarterly Forum* (of Division 39, The Division for Psychoanalysis of the American Psychological Association), 7 (Spring), 20–26.

Debord, G. L. (1967). *The society of the spectacle* (translated by F. Perlman). Detroit, MI: Black & Red Publications.

Deleuze, G. (1953). *Empiricism and subjectivity: An essay on Hume's theory of human nature* (translated by C. V. Boundas). New York, NY: Columbia University Press, 1991.

Deleuze, G. (1962). *Nietzsche and philosophy* (translated by H. Tomlinson). New York, NY: Columbia University Press, 1983.

Deleuze, G. (1966). *Bergsonism* (translated by H. Tomlinson & B. Habberjam). New York, NY: Zone Books.

Deleuze, G. (1968a). *Difference and repetition* (translated by P. Patton). New York, NY: Columbia University Press, 1994.

Deleuze, G. (1968b). *Expressionism in philosophy: Spinoza* (translated by M. Joughin). New York, NY: Zone Books, 1992.

Deleuze, G. (1969). *The logic of sense* (translated by M. Lester with C. Stivale, edited by C. V. Boundas). New York, NY: Columbia University Press, 1990.

Deleuze, G. (1970). *Spinoza: Practical philosophy* (translated by R. Hurley). San Francisco, CA: City Lights Books, 1988.

Deleuze, G. (1988). *The fold: Leibniz and the baroque* (translated by T. Conley). Minneapolis, MN: University of Minnesota Press, 1993.

Deleuze, G. (1990). *Negotiations, 1972–1990* (translated by M. Joughin). New York, NY: Columbia University Press, 1995.

Deleuze, G. (2001). *Pure immanence: Essays on a life* (translated by A. Boyman). New York, NY: Columbia University Press.

Deleuze, G. & Guattari, F. (1972). *Anti-oedipus: Capitalism and schizophrenia, volume 1* (translated by R. Hurley). London, UK: Penguin, 2009.

Deleuze, G. & Guattari, F. (1980). *A thousand plateaus: Capitalism and schizophrenia, volume 2* (translated by B. Massumi). Minneapolis, MN: University of Minneapolis Press, 1987.

Deleuze, G. & Guattari, F. (1991). *What is philosophy?* (translated by H. Tomlinson & G. Burchell). New York, NY: Columbia University Press, 1994.

Deleuze, G. & Parnet, C. (1977). Dead psychoanalysis: Analyse. In: *Dialogues: Gilles Deleuze and Claire Parnet* (translated by H. Tomlinson & B. Habberjam). New York, NY: Columbia University Press, 1987.

Dennett, D. C. (1991). *Consciousness explained.* Boston, MA: Little, Brown & Co.

Derrida, J. (1967). *Speech and phenomena: And other essays on Husserl's theory of signs* (translated by D. B. Allison). Evanston, IL: Northwestern University Press, 1973.

Derrida, J. (1987). *Of spirit* (translated by G. Bennington & R. Bowlby). Chicago, IL: University of Chicago Press, 1989.

Derrida, J. (1990). *Eyes of the university: Right to philosophy 2* (translated by J. Plug). Stanford, CA: Stanford University Press, 2004.

Derrida, J. (1992). *The gift of death* (translated by D. Wills). Chicago, IL: University of Chicago Press, 1995.

Derrida, J. (1992–2000). *On touching – Jean-Luc Nancy* (translated by C. Irizarry). Stanford, CA: Stanford University Press, 2005.

Derrida, J. (1994). *The politics of friendship* (translated by G. Collins). London, UK: Verso, 1997.

Derrida, J. (1996a). *Monolingualism of the other; or, the prosthesis of origin* (translated by P. Mensah). Stanford, CA: Stanford University Press, 1998.

Derrida, J. (1996b). *Resistances of psychoanalysis* (translated by P. Kamuf, P.-A. Brault & M. Naas). Stanford, CA: Stanford University Press, 1998.

Derrida, J. (1998). *Demeure: Fiction and testimony* (translated by E. Rottenberg, including M. Blanchot's *The instand of my death*). Stanford, CA: Stanford University Press, 2000.

Derrida, J. (2000). *On touching – Jean Luc Nancy* (translated by C. Irizarry). Stanford, CA: Stanford University Press, 2005.

Descartes, R. (1637). *Discourse on the method* (translated by P. J. Olscamp). Indianapolis, IN: Hackett, 2001.

Descartes, R. (1641). *Meditations on first philosophy* (translated by J. Cottingham). Cambridge, UK: Cambridge University Press, 1996.

Descartes, R. (1644). *Principles of philosophy* (translated by V. R. Miller). Dordrecht, The Netherlands: Reidel, 1983.

Dews, P. (1987). *Logics of disintegration: Post-structural thought and the claims of critical theory.* New York, NY: Verso, 2007.

Dolar, M. (2006). *A voice and nothing more.* Cambridge, MA: MIT Press.

Donnet, J.-L. (2005). *The analyzing situation* (translated by A. Weller). London, UK: Karnac, 2009.

Dorsey, J. (1976). *An American psychiatrist in Vienna, 1935–1937, and his Sigmund Freud.* Detroit, MI: Center for Mental Health.

Dubois, T. A. (2009). *An introduction to shamanism.* Cambridge, UK: Cambridge University Press.

Durkheim, É. (1912). *The elementary forms of religious life* (translated by C. Cosman). London, UK: Oxford University Press, 2008.

Dussel, E. (1977). *Philosophy of liberation* (translated by A. Martinez & C. Morkovsky). Eugene, OR: Wipf & Stock, 2003.

Dussel, E. (2011). *Politics of liberation: A critical global history* (translated by T. Cooper). Norwich, UK: SCM Press.

Eagle, M. N. (1984). *Recent developments in psychoanalysis: A critical evaluation.* New York, NY: McGraw-Hill.

Eagle, M. N. (2011). *From classical to contemporary psychoanalysis: A critique and integration.* London, UK: Routledge.

Eagle, M. N. (2013). *Attachment and psychoanalysis: Theory, research, and clinical implications.* New York, NY: Guilford Press.

Eagle, M. N. (2017). *Core concepts in classical psychoanalysis: Clinical, research evidence and conceptual critiques.* London, UK: Routledge.

Eagleton, T. (1991/2007). *Ideology: An introduction* (updated edition). London, UK: Verso.

Eagleton, T. (2011) *Why Marx was right.* New Haven, CT: Yale University Press.

Eckhart, M. (c. 1300). *Meister Eckhart: The essential sermons, commentaries, treatises and defenses* (edited & translated by B. McGinn & E. Colledge). New York, NY: Paulist Press, 1981).

Edelman, G. M. (1993). *Bright air, brilliant fire: On the matter of mind.* New York, NY: Basic Books.

Edelman, G. M. (2007). *Wider than the sky: The phenomenal gift of consciousness.* New Haven, CT: Yale University Press.

Eigen, M. (1986). *The psychotic core.* Northvale, NJ: Jason Aronson, 1993.

Eigen, M. (1996). *Psychic deadness.* Northvale, NJ: Jason Aronson.

Einstein, A. (1934–1955). *The world as I see it* (translated by A. Harris). New York, NY: Citadel Press, 2006.

Eissler, K. R. (1955). *The psychiatrist and the dying patient*. New York, NY: International Universities Press.

Eitingon, M. (1922) Zur psychoanalytischen Bewegung. *Internationale Zeitschrift für Psychoanalyse, 8,* 103–106.

Eliade, M. *et al.* (eds.) (1986). *The encyclopedia of religion* (10 volumes). London, UK: Macmillan Reference Library.

Eliot, T. S. (1942). Little Gidding. In: T. S. Eliot (ed.) *Collected poems: 1909–1962.* New York, NY: Harcourt Brace, 1963.

Ellenberger, H. (1970). *The discovery of the unconscious: The history and evolution of dynamic psychiatry*. New York, NY: Basic Books.

Evans, E. (2015). *The politics of third wave feminisms: Neoliberalism, intersectionality, and the state in Britain and the US*. Basingstoke, UK: Palgrave Macmillan.

Eyers, T. (2012). *Lacan and the concept of the 'real.'* Basingstoke, UK: Palgrave Macmillan.

Fanon, F. (1952). *Black skin, white masks* (translated by C. L. Markmann). New York, NY: Grove Press, 1967.

Fanon, F. (1961). *Wretched of the earth* (translated by R. Philcox, with commentary by J.-P. Sartre & H. K. Bhabha). New York, NY: Grove Press, 2004.

Federn, P. (1936). Zur Unterscheidung des gesunden und krankhaften Narcissmus. *Imago, 22,* 5–38.

Fenichel, O. (1945). *The psychoanalytic theory of neurosis*. New York, NY: W.W. Norton, 1995.

Ferenczi, S. (1926–1933). *Final contributions to the problems and methods of psychoanalysis* (edited by M. Balint). London, UK: Hogarth Press, 1955.

Ferenczi, S. & Rank, O. (1924). *The development of psychoanalysis*. New York, NY: International Universities Press, 1986.

Feuerstein, G. (1998a). *The yoga tradition: Its history, literature, philosophy and practice*. Prescott, AZ: Hohm Press.

Feuerstein, G. (1998b). *Tantra: The path of ecstasy*. Boston, MA: Shambhala.

Feyerabend, P. K. (1978). *Science in a free society*. London, UK: Verso, 1982.

Feyerabend, P. K. (1981a). *Realism, rationalism and scientific method: Philosophical papers, volume 1* (revised edition). Cambridge, UK: Cambridge University Press, 1985.

Feyerabend, P. K. (1981b). *Problems of empiricism: Philosophical papers, volume 2*. Cambridge, UK: Cambridge University Press, 1985.

Feyerabend, P. K. (1975). *Against method: Outline of an anarchistic theory of knowledge* (4th edition, introduced by I. Hacking). London, UK: Verso, 2010.

Feyerabend, P. K. (2011). *The tyranny of science*. Cambridge, UK: Polity Press.

Feynman, R. P., Leighton, R. B. & Sands, M. (1961–1963). *The Feynman lectures on physics* (the New Millenium edition in 3 volumes). New York, NY: Basic Books, 2011.

Fichte, J. G. (1794–1802). *Fichte: Science of Knowledge/Wissenschaftslehre* (translated by P. Heath & J. Lachs). Cambridge, UK: Cambridge University Press, 1982.

Fink, B. (1997). *A clinical introduction to Lacanian psychoanalysis: Theory and technique*. Cambridge, MA: Harvard University Press.

Fink, B. (2011). *Fundamentals of psychoanalytic technique: A Lacanian approach for practitioners*. New York, NY: W.W. Norton.

Fink, B. (2014a). *Against understanding, volume 1: Commentary and critique in a Lacanian key*. London, UK: Routledge.

Fink, B. (2014b). *Against understanding, volume 2: Cases and commentary in a Lacanian key*. London, UK: Routledge.

Fischer-Schreiber, I., Ehrhard, F.-K., Friedrichs, K. & Diener, M. S. (1986). *The encyclopedia of eastern philosophy and religion: Buddhism, Hinduism, Taoism, Zen – A complete survey of the teachers, traditions, and literature of Asian wisdom.* Boston, MA: Shambhala, 1989.

Fonagy, P. (2003a). Genetics, developmental psychopathology, and psychoanalytic theory: The case for ending our (not so) splendid isolation. *Psychoanalytic Inquiry, 23,* 218–247.

Fonagy, P. (2003b). Some complexities in the relationship of psychoanalytic theory to technique. *Psychoanalytic Quarterly, 72,* 13–47.

Foucault, M. (1954). *Mental illness and psychology* (translated by A. M. Sheridan). New York, NY: Harper & Row, 1976.

Foucault, M. (1961). *Madness and civilization: A history of insanity in the age of reason* (translated by R. Howard). London, UK: Tavistock, 1965.

Foucault, M. (1963). *The birth of the clinic: An archaeology of medical perception* (translated by A. S. Smith). New York, NY: Pantheon, 1973.

Foucault, M. (1966). *The order of things: An archaeology of the human sciences* (translated by A. S. London). New York, NY: Pantheon, 1970.

Foucault, M. (1969). What is an author? In: *Language, counter-memory, practice: Selected essays and interviews* (edited & translated by D. F. Bouchard). Ithaca, NY: Cornell University Press, 1977, pp. 113–138.

Foucault, M. (1969–1971). *The archeology of knowledge* (translated by A. M. Sheridan Smith). New York, NY: Pantheon, 1972.

Foucault, M. (1973–1974). *Psychiatric power: Lectures at the Collège de France, 1973–1974* (translated by G. Burchell). New York, NY: Picador, 2008.

Fox, G. (1694). *The journal of George Fox* (edited by R. M. Jones). Philadelphia, PA: Friends United Press.

Francoeur, R. T. (ed.) (1997). *The international encyclopedia of sexology* (3 volumes). New York, NY: Continuum.

Francoeur, R. T., Cornog, M., Perper, T. & Scherzer, N. A. (eds.) (1995). *The complete dictionary of sexology* (New Expanded Edition). New York, NY: Continuum.

Frankel, E. (2017). *The wisdom of not knowing: Discovering a life of wonder by embracing uncertainty.* Boulder, CO: Shambhala.

Freire, P. (1968). *Pedagogy of the oppressed* (30th anniversary edition, translated by M. B. Ramos). New York, NY: Bloomsbury, 2000.

Freire, P. (1973). *Education for critical consciousness.* New York, NY: Bloomsbury, 2013.

Freud, A. (1936–1980). *The writings of Anna Freud* (8 volumes). New York, NY: International Universities Press, 1974–1981.

Freud, S. (1873–1939). *The letters of Sigmund Freud* (selected & edited by E. L. Freud, translated by T. Stern & J. Stern). New York, NY: Basic Books, 1960.

Freud, S. (with J. Breuer, 1893). Studien über Hysterie. *Gesammelte Werke, 1,* 79–251. [Translated as: Studies on hysteria. *Standard Edition, 2,* 1–305.]

Freud, S. (1895). Entwurf einer Psychologie. In: M. Bonaparte, A. Freud & E. Kris (eds.) *Aus den Anfängen der Psychoanalyse.* London, UK: Imago, 1950, 371–466. [Translated as: Project for a scientific psychology. *Standard Edition, 1,* 295–397.]

Freud, S. (1900). Die Traumdeutung. *Gesammelte Werke, 2–3,* 1–642. [Translated as: The interpretation of dreams. *Standard Edition, 4–5,* 1–627.]

Freud, S. (1901). Zur Psychopathologie des Alltagslebens. *Gesammelte Werke, 4.* [Translated as: The psychopathology of everyday life. *Standard Edition, 6.*]

Freud, S. (1905a). Drie Abhandlungen zur Sexualtheorie. *Gesammelte Werke, 5,* 29–145. [Translated as: Three essays on the theory of sexuality. *Standard Edition, 7,* 130–243.]

Freud, S. (1905b). Bruchstück einer Hysterie-Analyse. *Gesammelte Werke*, *5*, 163–286. [Translated as: Fragment of an analysis of a case of hysteria. *Standard Edition*, *7*, 7–122.]

Freud, S. (1908). Die 'Kulturelle' Sexualmoral und die Moderne Nervosität. *Gesammelte Werke*, *7*, 143–167. [Translated as: 'Civilized' sexual morality and modern nervous illness. *Standard Edition*, *9*, 177–204.]

Freud, S. (1909). Analyse der Phobie eines Fünfjährigen Khaben. *Gesammelte Werke*, *7*, 243–377. [Translated as: Analysis of a phobia in a five-year-old boy. *Standard Edition*, *10*, 1–149.]

Freud, S. (1910a) Über Psychoanalyse. *Gesammelte Werke*, *8*, 3–60. [Translated as: Five lectures on psychoanalysis. *Standard Edition*, *11*, 1–56.]

Freud, S. (1910b). Beiträge zur Psychologie des Liebeslebens: Über einen Besonderen Typus der Objektwahl beim Manne. *Gesammelte Werke*, *8*, 66–77. [Translated as: A special type of choice of object made by men (contributions to the psychology of love I). *Standard Edition*, *11*, 163–176.]

Freud, S. (1910c). Die zukünftigen Chancen der psychoanalytischen Therapie. *Gesammelte Werke*, *8*, 104–115. [Translated as: The future prospects of psychoanalytic therapy. *Standard Edition*, *11*, 139–151.]

Freud, S. (1910d). Über 'Wilde' Psychoanalyse. *Gesammelte Werke*, *8*, 118–125. [Translated as: 'Wild' psychoanalysis. *Standard Edition*, *11*, 219–230.]

Freud, S. (1912a). Zur Dynamik der Übertragung. *Gesammelte Werke*, *8*, 364–374. [Translated as: The dynamics of transference. *Standard Edition*, *12*, 97–120.]

Freud, S. (1912b). Zur Einleitung der Behandlung. *Gesammelte Werke*, *8*, 454–478. [Translated as: On beginning the treatment. *Standard Edition*, *12*, 121–144.]

Freud, S. (1912c). Totem und Tabu. *Gesammelte Werke*, *9*, 1–205. [Translated as: Totem and taboo. *Standard Edition*, *13*, 1–162.]

Freud, S. (1913). Zur Einleitung der Behandlung. *Gesammelte Werke*, *8*, 454–478. [Translated as: On beginning the treatment. *Standard Edition*, *12*, 121–144.]

Freud, S. (1914a). Zur Geschichte Der Psychoanalytischen Bewegung. *Gesammelte Werke*, *10*, 44–113. [Translated as: On the history of the psychoanalytic movement. *Standard Edition*, *14*, 1–66.]

Freud, S., (1914b). Erinnern, Widerholen und Durcharbeiten. *Gesammelte Werke*, *10*, 125–136. [Translated as: Remembering, repeating and working-through. *Standard Edition*, *12*, 145–156]

Freud, S. (1914c). Zur Einführung des Narzissmus. *Gesammelte Werke*, *10*, 138–170. [Translated as: On narcissism: An introduction. *Standard Edition*, *14*, 67–102.]

Freud, S. (1915a). Triebe und Triebschicksale. *Gesammelte Werke*, *10*, 210–232. [Translated as: Instincts and their vicissitudes. *Standard Edition*, *14*, 109–140.]

Freud, S. (1915b). Die Verdrängung. *Gesammelte Werke*, *10*, 248–261. [Translated as: Repression. *Standard Edition*, *14*, 146–158.]

Freud, S. (1915c). Das Unbewusste. *Gesammelte Werke*, *10*, 264–303. [Translated as: The unconscious. *Standard Edition*, *14*, 166–204.]

Freud, S. (1915d). Zeitgemässes über Krieg und Tod. *Gesammelte Werke*, *10*, 324–355. [Translated as: Thoughts for the times on war and death. *Standard Edition*, *14*, 273–300.]

Freud, S. (1915/1916–1917). Vorlesungen zur Einfürung in die Psychoanalyse. *Gesammelte Werke*, *11*. [Translated as: Introductory lectures on psychoanalysis. *Standard Edition*, *15 & 16*.]

Freud, S. (1918). Aus der Geschichte einer Infantilen Neurose. *Gesammelte Werke*, *12*, 29–157. [Translated as: From the history of an infantile neurosis. *Standard Edition*, *17*, 1–124.

Freud, S. (1919a). On the teaching of psychoanalysis in universities. *Standard Edition, 17*, 169–174.

Freud, S. (1919b). Wege der Psychoanalytischen Therapie. *Gesammelte Werke, 12*, 183–194. [Translated as: Lines of advance in psychoanalytictherapy. *Standard Edition, 17*, 57–168.]

Freud, S. (1920a). Jenseits des Lustprinzips. *Gesammelte Werke, 13*, 3–69. [Translated as: Beyond the pleasure principle. *Standard Edition, 18*, 1–64.]

Freud, S. (1920b). Zur Vorgeschichte der analytischen Technik. *Internationale Zeitschrift für Psychoanalyse, 6(1)*, 79–81. [Translated as: A note on the prehistory of the technique of psychoanalysis. *Standard Edition, 18*, 261–265.]

Freud, S. (1921). Psychoanalyse und Telepathie. *Gesammelte Werke, 17*, 27–44. [Translated as: Psychoanalysis and telepathy. *Standard Edition, 18*, 173–194.]

Freud, S. (1922). Traum und Telepathie. *Gesammelte Werke, 13*, 165–191. [Translated as: Dreams and telepathy. *Standard Edition, 18*, 195–220.]

Freud, S. (1923). Das Ich und das Es. *Gesammelte Werke, 13*, 237–289.[Translated as: The ego and the id. *Standard Edition, 19*, 12–66.]

Freud, S. (1924). Kurzer Abriss der Psychoanalyse. *Gesammelte Werke, 13*, 403–427. [Translated as: A short account of psychoanalysis. *Standard Edition, 19*, 189–210.]

Freud, S. (1925). Selbstdarstellung. *Gesammelte Werke, 14*, 33–96. [Translated as: An autobiographical study. *Standard Edition, 20*, 7–74.]

Freud, S. (1926a). Hemmung, Symptom und Angst. *Gesammelte Werke, 14*, 113–205. [Translated as: Inhibitions, symptoms and anxiety. *Standard Edition, 20*, 75–176.]

Freud, S. (1926b). Die Frage der Laienanalyse. *Gesammelte Werke, 14*, 209–286. [Translated as: The question of lay analysis. *Standard Edition, 20*, 183–250.]

Freud, S. (1937a). Konstruktionen in der Analyse. *Gesammelte Werke, 16*, 43–56. [Translated as: Constructions in analysis. *Standard Edition, 23*, 257–269.]

Freud, S. (1937b). Die endliche und unendliche Analyse. *Gesammelte Werke, 16*, 59–99. [Translated as: Analysis terminable and interminable. *Standard Edition, 23*, 209–254.]

Freud, S. & Ferenczi, S. (1908–1933). *The correspondence of Sigmund Freud and Sándor Ferenczi* (3 volumes, edited by E. Falzeder & E. Brabant, translated by P. Hoffer). Cambridge, MA: Belknap Press, 1994–2000.

Freud, S. & Fliess, W. (1887–1904). *The complete letters of Sigmund Freud to Wilhelm Fliess, 1887–1904* (edited & translated by J. M. Masson). Cambridge, MA: Belknap Press, 1986.

Freud, S. & Jung, C. G. (1906–1914). *The Freud/Jung letters* (edited by W. McGuire, translated by R. F. C. Hull & R. Mannheim). Princeton, NJ: Princeton University Press, 1994.

Frew, J. & Spiegler, M. (2013). *Contemporary psychotherapies for a diverse world* (revised edition). London, UK: Routledge.

Frie, R. (1997). *Subjectivity and intersubjectivity in modern philosophy and psychoanalysis: A study of Sartre, Binswanger, Lacan, and Habermas.* Lanham, MD: Rowman & Littlefield.

Fromm, E. S. (1947). *Man for himself: An inquiry into the psychology of ethics.* New York, NY: Holt, Rinehart & Winston, 1976.

Fromm, E. S. (1950). *Psychoanalysis and religion.* New Haven, CT: Yale University Press, 1959.

Fromm, E. S. (1955). *The sane society.* New York, NY: Holt, Rinehart & Winston, 1976.

Fromm, E. S. (1957). *Psychoanalysis and zen Buddhism* (with D. T. Suzuki & R. De Martino). New York, NY: HarperCollins, 1970.

Fromm, E. S. (1960). *Let man prevail: A socialist manifesto and program.* New York, NY: Socialist Party USA, 1967.

Fromm, E. S. (1960–1967). *On disobedience: Why freedom means saying 'no' to power*. New York, NY: Harper Perennial, 2010.

Fromm, E. S. (1976). *To have or to be?* London, UK: Bloomsbury, 2013.

Frosch, J. (1983). *The psychotic process*. New York, NY: International Universities Press.

Frosh, S. (1991). *Identity crisis: Modernity, psychoanalysis, and the self*. London, UK: Routledge.

Frosh, S. (2010). *Psychoanalysis outside the clinic: Interventions in psychosocial studies*. Basingstoke, UK: Palgrave Macmillan.

Gandhi, M. K. (1909–1948). *'Hind Swaraj' and other writings* (edited by A. J. Parel). Cambridge, UK: Cambridge University Press, 2010.

Gandhi, M. K. (c.1920–1947). *Satyagraha: Nonviolent resistance* (edited by B. Kumarappa). Ahmedabad, India: Navajivan Publishing House, 1951.

Gandhi, M. K. (1928). *Satyagraha in South Africa* (translated by V. G. Desai). Ahmedabad, India: Navajivan Publishing House.

Gandhi, M. K. (1942–1948). *Gandhi on nonviolence* (reprint edition, edited by T. Merton). New York, NY: New Directions, 2007.

Ganeri, J. (2001). *Philosophy in classical India: The proper work of reason*. London, UK: Routledge.

Ganeri, J. (2003). *Philosophy in classical India: An introduction and analysis*. London, UK: Routledge.

Ganeri, J. (2006). *Artha/meaning: Testimony and the theory of meaning in Indian philosophical analysis*. Oxford, UK: Oxford University Press.

Ganeri, J. (2007). *The concealed art of the soul: Truth, concealment and self in Indian thought*. Oxford, UK: Clarendon Press.

Ganeri, J. (2015). *The self: Naturalism, consciousness, and the first person stance*. Oxford, UK: Oxford University Press.

Ganeri, J. (2017a). *The Oxford handbook of Indian philosophy*. Oxford, UK: Oxford University Press.

Ganeri, J. (2017b). *Attention not self*. Oxford, UK: Oxford University Press.

Garvey, M. M. (1914–1940). *The philosophy and opinions of Marcus Garvey* (Centenntial Edition, edited by A. J. Garvey). Dover, MA: Majority Press, 1986.

Gennaro, R. J. (2012). *The consciousness paradox: Consciousness, concepts, and higher-order thoughts*. Cambridge, MA: MIT Press.

Gennaro, R. J. (ed.) (2015). *Disturbed consciousness: New essays on psychopathology and theories of consciousness*. Cambridge, MA: MIT Press.

Gennaro, R. J. (2017). *Consciousness*. London, UK: Routledge.

Geuss, R. (1981). *The idea of a critical theory: Habermas and the Frankfurt School*. Cambridge, UK: Cambridge University Press.

Geuss, R. (2017). *Changing the subject: Philosophy for Socrates to Adorno*. Cambridge, MA: Harvard University Press.

Gill, M. M. (1982). *Analysis of transference: Theory and technique*. New York, NY: International Universities Press.

Gill, M. M. (1994). *Psychoanalysis in transition: A personal view*. Hillsdale, NY: Analytic Press.

Gill, M. M. & Brenman, M. (1959). *Hypnosis and related states*. New York, NY: International Universities Press.

Giroux, H. A. (2007). *The university in chains: Confronting the military-industrial-academic complex*. Boulder, CO: Paradigm.

Giroux, H. A. (2016). *The Giroux reader* (edited by G. Robbins). Abingdon, UK: Routledge.

Gramsci, A. (1914–1926). *Gramsci: Pre-prison writings* (edited by R. Bellamy, translated by V. Cox). London, UK: Cambridge University Press, 1994.

Gramsci, A. (1926–1934). *Prison notebooks* (3 volumes, translated by J. A. Buttigieg). New York, NY: Columbia University Press, 2010.

Green, A. (1974). Surface analysis, deep analysis: The role of the preconscious in psychoanalytical technique. *International Review of Psychoanalysis, 1*, 415–423.

Green, A. (1991). On thirdness. In: *André Green at the Squiggle Foundation* (edited by J. Abram). London, UK: Karnac, 2000, pp. 39–68.

Green, A. (1999a). The greening of psychoanalysis: André Green in dialogue with Gregorio Kohon. In: G. Kohon (ed.) *The dead mother: The work of André Green*. London, UK: Routledge, pp. 10–58.

Green, A. (1999b). Consilience and rigour: Commentary by André Green. *Neuropsychoanalysis, 1(1)*, 40–44.

Green, A. (2002). *Time in psychoanalysis: Some contradictory aspects* (translated by A. Weller). London, UK: Free Association Books.

Green, A. (2003). *Diachrony in psychoanalysis* (translated by A. Weller). London, UK: Free Association Books.

Greene, B. R. (1999). *The elegant universe: Superstrings, hidden dimensions, and the quest for the ultimate theory*. New York, NY: W. W. Norton, 2010.

Greene, B. R. (2004). *The fabric of the cosmos: Space, time, and the texture of reality*. New York, NY: Vintage, 2005.

Greene, B. R. (2011). *The hidden reality: Parallel universes and the deep laws of the cosmos*. New York, NY: Vintage, 2011.

Greenson, R. R. (1967). *The technique and practice of psychoanalysis*. New York, NY: International Universities Press.

Gregg, M. & Seigworth, G. J. (eds.) (2010). *The affect theory reader*. Durham, NC: Duke University Press.

Groddeck, G. (1923). *The book of the it* (translated by V. M. E. Collins). London, UK: Vision Press, 1979.

Grof, S. (1988). *The adventure of self-discovery*. New York, NY: State University of New York Press.

Gross, O. (1913). Zur Überwindung der lulturellen Krise. In: *Otto Gross: Ausgewählte Texte* (edited by L. L. Madison). Hamilton, NY: Mindpiece, 2012, pp. 297–299. [Translated as: On overcoming the cultural crisis. In: *Otto Gross: Selected works, 1901–1920* (edited & translated by L. L. Madison). Hamilton, NY: Mindpiece, 2012, pp. 257–259.]

Grosz, E. (2017). *The incorporeal: Ontology, ethics, and the limits of materialism*. New York, NY: Columbia University Press.

Grünbaum, A. (1984). *The foundations of psychoanalysis: A philosophical critique*. Oakland, CA: University of California Press.

Guattari, F. (1955–1970). *Psychoanalysis and transversality: Texts and interviews, 1955–1971* (translated by A. Hodges). South Pasadena, CA: Semiotext(e).

Handwerk, G. J. (1986). *Irony and ethics in narrative: From Schlegel to Lacan*. New Haven, CT: Yale University Press.

Hanh, T. N. (1978). Please call me by my true names. In: *Call me by my true names: The Collected Poems of Thich Nhat Hanh*. Berkeley, CA: Parallax, 1999.

Hannah, B. (2001). *Encounters with the soul: Active imagination as developed by C. G. Jung*. Brooklyn, NY: Chiron.

Hardt, M. & Negri, A. (1994). *Labor of Dionysus: A critique of the state-form*. Minneapolis, MN: University of Minnesota Press.

Hardt, M. & Negri, A. (2000). *Empire*. Cambridge, MA: Harvard University Press.

Hardt, M. & Negri, A. (2004). *Multitude: War and democracy in the age of empire*. London, UK: Penguin.

Hardt, M. & Negri, A. (2009). *Commonwealth*. Cambridge, MA: Harvard University Press.

Hardt, M. & Negri, A. (2017). *Assembly*. London, UK: Oxford University Press.

Harvey, D. (2007). *A brief history of neoliberalism*. Oxford, UK: Oxford University Press.

Hazlitt, W. (1821). *On going on a journey: Table talk, volume 1*. London, UK: John Warren.

Hegel, G. W. F. (1807). *Phänomenologie des Geistes*. Hamburg, Germany: Verlag von Felix Meiner, 1952. [Translated as: *Hegel's phenomenology of spirit* (translated by A. V. Miller). London, UK: Allen & Unwin, 1969.]

Heidegger, M. (1927). *Being and time* (translated by J. Macquarrie & E. Robinson). New York, NY: Harper & Row, 1962.

Heidegger, M. (1943). The word of Nietszche: 'God is dead.' In: *The question concerning technology and other essays* (edited by J. Macquarrie & E. Robinson). New York, NY: Harper & Row, pp. 53–114.

Heidegger, M. (1944–1955). *Discourse on thinking: A translation of Gelassenheit* (translated by J. M. Anderson & E. H. Freund). New York, NY: Harper & Row, 1966.

Heidegger, M. (1950–1960). *Poetry, language, thought* (translated by A. Hofstadter). New York, NY: Harper & Row, 1971.

Heidegger, M. (1954). *What is called thinking?* (translated by J. G. Gray). New York, NY: Harper & Row, 1968.

Heidegger, M. (1959). *On the way to language* (translated by P. Hertz & J. Stambaugh). New York, NY: Harper & Row, 1971.

Heidegger, M. (1969). *On time and being* (edited & translated by J. Stambaugh). New York, NY: Harper & Row, 1972.

Heisenberg, W. (1958). *Physics and philosophy: The revolution in modern science*. New York, NY: Harper Perennial, 2007.

Heller, M. C. (2012). *Body psychotherapy: History, concepts, and methods* (translated by M. Duclos). New York, NY: W. W. Norton.

Helmholtz, H. V. (1847/1895). *On the conservation of force* (edited & translated by 'The Perfect Library'). Scotts Valley, CA: CreateSpace, 2015.

Hennings, E. (1920). *Das Brandmal: Ein Tagebuch*. Frankfurt, Germany: Suhrkamp, 1999.

Heraclitus of Ephesus (c. 500 b.c.e.). *Fragments* (translated by B. Haxton). London, UK: Penguin.

Herbart, J. F. (1824–1825). *Psychologie als Wissenschaft*. Charleston, SC: Nabu Press, 2013.

Herzog, E. (1983). *Psyche and death: Death-demons in folklore, myths and modern dreams* (translated by D. Cox & E. Rolfe). Dallas, TX: Spring Publications.

Hofstadter, R. (1966). *Anti-intellectualism in American life*. New York, NY: Vintage.

Holveck, E. (2002). *Simone de Beauvoir's philosophy of lived experience: Literature and metaphysics*. Lanham, MD: Rowman & Littlefield.

Honneth, A. (2012). *Reification: A new look at an old idea* (with J. Butler, R. Geuss, J. Lear & M. Jay). Oxford, UK: Oxford University Press.

Hooks, B. (1994). *Teaching to transgress: Education as the practice of freedom*. London, UK: Routledge.

Hopkins, D. (2004). *Dada and surrealism: A very short introduction*. London, UK: Oxford University Press.

Horkheimer, M. (1947). *Eclipse of reason*. Eastford, CT: Martino, 2013.

Horkheimer, M. (1967). *Critique of instrumental reason*. London, UK: Continuum International, 1983.

Horkheimer, M. (1968). *Critical theory* (partially translated by M. J. O'Connell). New York, NY: Seabury Press, 1972.

Horkheimer, M. & Adorno, T. W. (1944/1947). *Dialectic of enlightenment* (translated by G. F. Noerr & E. F. N. Jephcott). Stanford, CA: Stanford University Press, 2007.

Horlacher, R. (2017). *The educated subject and the German concept of Bildung: A comparative cultural history*. London, UK: Routledge.

Hountondji, P. J. (ed.) (1999). *Endogenous knowledge: Research trails*. Dakar, Senegal: Council for the Development of Social Science Research in Africa.

Hountondji, P. J. (2002). *Struggle for meaning: Reflections on philosophy, culture, and democracy in Africa* (translated by J. Conteh-Morgan). Columbus, OH: Ohio University Press.

Hsi, C. (c. 1160–1200). *Learning to be a sage: Selections from the 'Conversations of Master Chu'* (arranged topically & translated by D. K. Gardner). Berkeley, CA: University of California Press.

Hume, D. (1748). *An enquiry concerning human understanding* (edited by E. Steinberg). Indianapolis, IN: Hackett, 1993.

Hurvich, M. S. (2018). *Annihilation anxieties: Clinical, theoretical, and empirical aspects*. London, UK: Karnac.

Husserl, E. (1904–1910). *The phenomenology of internal time consciousness* (translated by J. S. Churchill). Bloomington, IN: Indiana University Press, 1964.

Husserl, E. (1913–1923). *Ideas: General introduction to pure phenomenology* (translated by W. R. B. Gibson). London, UK: Allen & Unwin, 1969.

Husserl, E. (1929). *Cartesian meditations* (translated by D. Cairns). The Hague, The Netherlands: Martinus Nijhoff, 1960.

Husserl, E. (1935). *The crisis of European sciences and transcendental phenomenology* (translated by D. Carr). Evanston, IL: Northwestern University Press, 1974.

Hutcheon, L. (1994). *Irony's edge: The theory and politics of irony*. London, UK: Routledge.

Hyppolite, J. (1946). *Genesis and structure of Hegel's 'Phenomenology of Spirit'* (translated by S. Cherniak & J. Heckman). Evanston, IL: Northwestern University Press, 1974.

Illich, I. (1971). *Deschooling society*. New York, NY: Harper & Row.

Irigaray, L. (1974). *Speculum of the other woman* (translated by G. C. Gill). Ithaca, NY: Cornell University Press, 1985.

Irigaray, L. (1977). *This sex which is not one* (translated by C. Porter). Ithaca, NY: Cornell University Press, 1985.

Irigaray, L. (1980). *Marine lover* (translated by C. G. Gill). New York, NY: Columbia University Press, 1991.

Irigaray, L. (1984). *An ethics of sexual difference* (translated by C. Burke &G. C. Gill). Ithaca, NY: Cornell University Press, 1993.

Irigaray, L. (1991). Questions to Emmanuel Levinas: On the divinity of love (translated by M. Whitford). In: R. Bernasconi & S. Critchley (eds.), *Re-reading Levinas*. Bloomington, IN: Indiana University Press, pp. 109–118.

Isaacs, S. (1948). The nature and function of phantasy. *International Journal of Psychoanalysis*, *29*, 73–97.

Jacoby, R. (2000). *The last intellectuals: American culture in the age of academe*. New York, NY: Basic Books.

Jaeggi, R. (2014). *Alienation* (translated by F. Neuhouser & A. E. Smith). New York, NY: Columbia University Press.

Jakobson, R. & Halle, M. (1956). *Fundamentals of language*. The Hague, The Netherlands: Mouton.

James, W. (1890). *The principles of psychology* (2 volumes). Mineola, NY: Dover, 1950.

James, W. (1892). *Psychology: Briefer course*. Mineola, NY: Dover, 2001.

Jaspers, K. T. (1938). *Philosophy of existence* (translated by R. T. Grabay). Philadelphia, PA: University of Pennsylvania Press, 1971.

Jaspers, K. T. (1957/1964). *Spinoza: From 'The Great Philosophers,' Volume 2* (edited by H. Arendt, translated by R. Mannheim). London, UK: Harvest/HBJ, 1974.

Johanson, G. & Kurtz, R. S. (1991). *Psychotherapy in the spirit of the Tao-te ching*. New York, NY: Bell Tower.

Johnston, A. & Malabou, C. (2013). *Self and emotional life: Philosophy, psychoanalysis, and neuroscience*. New York, NY: Columbia University Press.

Jones, E. (1927). The early development of female sexuality. *International Journal of Psychoanalysis, 8*, 459–472.

Jones, E. (1929). Fear, guilt and hate. *International Journal of Psychoanalysis, 10*, 383–397.

Judith, A. (1987). *Wheels of life: A user's guide to the chakra system*. Woodbury, MN: Llewellyn.

Judith, A. (2004). *Eastern body, western mind: Psychology and the chakra system as a path to the self* (revised edition). New York, NY: Celestial Arts.

Jung, C. G. (1906). Studies in word association. *Collected works, 2*. [See also: *Studies in word association* (translated by M. D. Eder). New York, NY: Moffat, Yard & Company, 1919.]

Jung, C. G. (1912). Wandlungen und Symbole der Libido [Transformation and symbolism of the libido]. Published as *Psychology of the unconscious: A study of the transformations and symbolisms of the libido – A contribution to the history of the evolution of thought* (translated by B. M. Hinkle). New York, NY: Dodd, Mead & Co., 1947.

Jung, C. G. (1913–1916). *Jung on active imagination* (edited by J. Chodorow). Princeton, NJ: Princeton University Press, 1997.

Jung, C. G. (1957–1961). *Memories, dreams, reflections* (edited by A. Jaffe, translated by R. Winston & C. Winston). New York, NY: Vintage.

Kant, I. (1764). *Observations on the feeling of the beautiful and sublime* (translated by J. T. Goldthwait). Oakland, CA: University of California Press, 2004.

Kapp, A. (1833). *Platon's Erziehungslehre, als Pädagogik für die Einzelnen und als Staatpädagogik*. Liepzig, Germany: Verlag Ferdinand Eßmann.

Karlsson, G. (2004). *Psychoanalysis in a new light*. Cambridge, UK: Cambridge University Press, 2010.

Karr, J.-B. A. (1923). *Les guepes* (4 volumes). Charleston, SC: Nabu Press, 2011–2012.

Kastenbaum, R. & Kastenbaum, B. (eds.) (1989). *Encyclopedia of death: Myth, history, philosophy, science – The many aspects of dying*. New York, NY: Avon.

Katsiaficas, G. (2006). *The subversion of politics: European autonomous social movements and the decolonization of everyday life*. Oakland, CA: AK Press.

Kauffman, S. A. (2008). *Reinventing the sacred: A new view of science, reason, and religion*. New York, NY: Basic Books.

Kennedy, R. (2002). *Psychoanalysis, history and subjectivity: Now of the past*. Hove, UK: Brunner-Routledge.

Keown, D. (2014). *The spark in the machine: How the science of acupuncture explains the mysteries of western medicine*. London, UK: Singing Dragon.

Kernberg, O. F. (1986). Institutional problems of psychoanalytic education. *Journal of the American Psychoanalytic Association, 34*, 799–834.

Kernberg, O. F. (1993). The current status of psychoanalysis. *Journal of the American Psychoanalytic Association, 41*, 45–62.

Kernberg, O. F. (1996). Thirty methods to destroy the creativity of psychoanalytic candidates. *International Journal of Psychoanalysis, 77*, 1031–1040.

Kernberg, O. F. (2000). A concerned critique of psychoanalytic education. *International Journal of Psychoanalysis, 81(1),* 97–120.

Kernberg, O. F. (2006). The coming changes in psychoanalytic education: Part I. *International Journal of Psychoanalysis, 87(6),* 1649–1673.

Kernberg, O. F. (2007). The coming changes in psychoanalytic education: Part II. *International Journal of Psychoanalysis, 88(1),* 183–202.

Kernberg, O. F. (2010). A new organization of psychoanalytic education. *Psychoanalytic Review, 97(6),* 997–1020.

Kernberg, O. F. (2014). The twilight of the training analysis system. *Psychoanalytic Review, 101(2),* 151–174.

Kernberg, O. F. (2016a). A proposal for innovation in psychoanalytic education. *Division Review: A Quarterly Forum* (of Division 39, The Division for Psychoanalysis of the American Psychological Association), *15,* 13–16.

Kernberg, O. F. (2016b). *Psychoanalytic education at the crossroads: Reformation, change and the future of psychoanalytic training.* London, UK: Routledge.

Kesel, M. de (2009). *Eros and ethics: Reading Jacques Lacan's Seminar VII.* Albany, NY: State University of New York Press.

Khasnabish, A. (2003). *Jouissance as ānanda: Indian philosophy, feminist theory, and literature.* Lanham, MD: Lexington.

Kierkegaard, S. (1841). *The concept of irony with continual reference to Socrates/Schelling lecture notes: Kierkegaard's writings, volume 2* (translated by E. H. Hong & H. V. Hong). Princeton, NJ: Princeton University Press, 1992.

Kierkegaard, S. (1843). *Fear and trembling/Repetition: Kierkegaard's writings, volume 6* (translated by E. H. Hong & H. V. Hong). Princeton, NJ: Princeton University Press, 1983.

Kirshner, L. (2017). *Intersubjectivity in psychoanalysis: A model for theory and practice.* Abingdon, UK: Routledge.

Kirsner, D. (2009). *Unfree associations: Inside psychoanalytic institutions.* Lanham, MD: Jason Aronson.

Klages, L. (1926). *Die Psychologischen Errungenschaften Nietzsches.* Leipzig, Germany: J. A. Barth.

Klein, M. (1921–1960). *The writings of Melanie Klein* (4 volumes). London, UK: Hogarth.

Knabb, K. (ed.) (2006). *The situationist international anthology* (revised & expanded edition). Berkeley, CA: Bureau of Public Secrets.

Knowles, M. S. (1980). *The modern practice of adult education: From pedagogy to andragogy.* Englewood Cliffs, NJ: Prentice Hall.

Kohon, G. (ed.) (1999). *The dead mother: The work of André Green.* London, UK: Routledge.

Kojève, A. (1933–1939). *Introduction to the reading of Hegel* (lectures assembled by R. Queneau, edited by A. Bloom, translated by J. H. Nichols). New York, NY: Basic Books, 1969.

Kolakowski, L. (1972). *The presence of myth* (translated by A. Czerniawski). Chicago, IL: University of Chicago Press, 1989.

Kompridis, N. (2006). *Critique and disclosure: Critical theory between past and future.* Cambridge, MA: MIT Press.

Korsch, K. (1923). *Marxism and philosophy* (translated by F. Halliday). London, UK: Verso, 2013.

Koyré, A. (1957). *From the closed world to the infinite universe.* Radford, VA: A & D (Wilder), 2008.

Kravis, N. (2013). The analyst's hatred of analysis. *Psychoanalytic Quarterly, 82(1),* 89–114.

Kris, A. O. (1996). *Free association: Methods and process.* London, UK: Routledge.

Kristeva, J. (1974). *Revolution in poetic language* (translated by M. Waller). New York, NY: Columbia University Press, 1984.

Kristeva, J. (1975). *The system and the speaking subject*. Lisse, The Netherlands: Peter de Ridder.

Kristeva, J. (1977a). *Polylogue*. Paris, France: Seuil. [Partially translated as *Desire in language*.]

Kristeva, J. (1977b). *Desire in language* (translated by L. S. Roudiez). New York, NY: Columbia University Press, 1980.

Kuhn, A. & Wolpe, A. (eds.) (1988). *Feminism and materialism*. London, UK: Routledge.

Kuhn, T. S. (1962). *The structure of scientific revolutions* (3rd edition). Chicago, IL: University of Chicago Press, 1996.

Kurtz, S. (1989). *The art of unknowing: Dimensions of openness in analytic therapy*. Northvale, NJ: Jason Aronson.

Lacan, J. (1953). The function and field of speech and language in psychoanalysis. In: *Écrits: The first complete edition in English* (translated by B. Fink). New York, NY: W.W. Norton, 2005.

Lacan, J. (1953–1954). *Le séminaire de Jacques Lacan, livre I: Les écrits techniques de Freud*. Paris, France: Seuil, 1975. [Translated as: *The seminars of Jacques Lacan, Book I: Freud's papers on technique, 1953–1954* (translated by J. Forrester). New York, NY: W.W. Norton, 1988.]

Lacan, J. (1954–1955). *Le séminaire de Jacques Lacan, livre II: Le moi dans la théorie de Freud et dans la technique de la psychanalyse*. Paris, France: Seuil, 1978. [Translated as: *The seminars of Jacques Lacan, Book II: The ego in Freud's theory and in the technique of psychoanalysis, 1954–1955* (translated by S. Tomaselli). New York, NY: W.W. Norton, 1988.]

Lacan, J. (1955–1956). *Le séminaire de Jacques Lacan, livre III: Les psychoses*. Paris, France: Seuil, 1966. [Translated as: *The seminar, book III: The psychoses, 1955–1956* (translated by R. Grigg. London, UK: Routledge.]

Lacan, J. (1956). The situation of psychoanalysis and the training of psychoanalysts in 1956. In: *Écrits*. Paris, France: Seuil, 1966, pp. 459–492.

Lacan, J. (1956–1957). *Le séminaire de Jacques Lacan, livre IV: La relation d'objet*. Paris, France: Seuil, 1994.

Lacan, J. (1958). The direction of the treatment and the principles of its power. In: *Écrits*. Paris, France: Seuil, 1966, pp. 585–646.

Lacan, J. (1959–1960). *Le séminaire de Jacques Lacan, livre VII: L'éthique de la psychanalyse*. Paris, France: Seuil, 1986. [Translated as *The ethics of psychoanalysis: The seminar of Jacques Lacan, Book VII* (translated by D. Porter). New York, NY: W.W. Norton, 1992.]

Lacan, J. (1960–1961). *Le séminaire de Jacques Lacan, livre VIII: Le transfert*. Paris, France: Seuil, 1991. [Translated as *Transference: The seminar of Jacques Lacan, Book VIII* (translated by B. Fink). Cambridge, UK: Polity Press, 2015.]

Lacan, J. (1964a). *Le séminaire, livre XI: Les quatre concepts fondamentauxde la psychanalyse*. Paris, France: Seuil, 1973. [Translated as: *The four fundamental concepts of psychoanalysis* (translated by A. Sheridan). London, UK: Hogarth, 1977.]

Lacan, J. (1964b). Founding act. In: *Television: A challenge to the psychoanalytic establishment* (translated by D. Hollier, R. Krauss, A. Michelson & J. Mehlman). New York, NY: W. W. Norton, 1990.

Lacan, J. (1966). *Écrits*. Paris, France: Seuil. [Partially translated as: *Écrits: A selection* (translated by A. Sheridan). London, UK: Tavistock, 1977. Also translated as: *Écrits: The first complete edition in English* (translated by B. Fink). New York, NY: W.W. Norton, 2005.]

Lacan, J. (1967). Proposition du 9 Octobre 1967 sur le psychanalyse de l'École. *Scilicet*, *1*, 14–30, 1968.

Lacan, J. (1972–1973). *Le séminaire, livre XX: Encore*. Paris, France: Seuil, 1998.

Laclau, E. (1996). *Emancipation(s)*. New York, NY: Verso.

Laclau, E. (2014). *The rhetorical foundations of society*. London, UK: Verso.

Laclau, E. & Mouffe, C. (1985). *Hegemony and socialist strategy: Towards a radical democratic politics*. New York, NY: Verso, 2001.

Laing, R. D. (1968). The obvious. In: D. Cooper (ed.), *The dialectics of liberation*. London, UK: Verso, 2015, pp. 13–33.

Lama, D. (1996). *The four noble truths*. London, UK: Thorsons, 1998.

Lane, C. (ed.) (1998). *The psychoanalysis of race*. New York, NY: Columbia University Press.

Langer, M. (1981). *From Vienna to Managua: Journey of a psychoanalyst* (translated by M. Hooks). London, UK: Free Association Books, 1989.]

Langer, M. (1985). Psicoanálisis sin divan. Paper presented to Cuba's Academy of Sciences. [Translated as: Psychoanalysis without the couch. *Free Associations, 15*, 60–66.]

Langs, R. (1978). *The listening process*. New York, NY: Jason Aronson.

Lao-Tzu (c. 500 b.c.e.). *Te-tao ching: A new translation based on the recently discovered Ma-wang-tui texts* (translated by R. G. Henricks). New York, NY: Ballantine, 1989.

Lao-Tzu (c. 500 b.c.e.). *The essential Tao* (translated by T. Cleary). San Francisco, CA: HarperCollins, 1991.

Lao-Tzu (c. 500 b.c.e.). *Tao te ching* (translated by Stephen Mitchell). San Francisco, CA: Harper Perennial, 1994.

Laplanche, J. (1970). *Life and death in psychoanalysis* (translated by J. Mehlman). Baltimore, MD: Johns Hopkins University Press, 1985.

Laplanche, J. (1981). *The unconscious and the id* (translated by L. Thurston & L. Watson). London, UK: Rebus Press, 1999.

Laplanche, J. (1987). *New foundations for psychoanalysis* (translated by D. Macey). Oxford, UK: Basil Blackwell, 1989.

Laplanche, J. (1992). *Seduction, translation and the drives* (edited by J. Fletcher & M. Stanton, translated by M. Stanton). London, UK: Institute of Contemporary Arts.

Laplanche, J. (1992–1993). *Essays on otherness* (edited by J. Fletcher). Abingdon, UK: Routledge, 1999.

Laplanche, J. (1993). *The temptation of biology: Freud's theories of sexuality* (translated by D. Nicholson-Smith). New York, NY: The Unconscious in Translation, 2015.

Laplanche, J. (1994). Psychoanalysis as anti-hermeneutics. *Radical Philosophy, 79*.

Laplanche, J. (1997). Aims of the psychoanalytic process. *Journal of European Psychoanalysis, 5* (Spring-Fall).

Laplanche, J. (1999). *Between seduction and inspiration: Man* (translated by J. Mehlman). New York, NY: The Unconscious in Translation, 2015.

Laplanche, J. (2000–2006). *Freud and the 'Sexual' – Essays 2000–2006* (translated by J. Fletcher, J. House & N. Ray). New York, NY: International Psychoanalytic Books, 2011.

Laplanche, J. (2006). *Après-coup – followed by 'Time and the other' and 'Temporality and translation'* (translated by L. Thurston & J. House). New York, NY: The Unconscious in Translation, 2017.

Laplanche, J. & Pontalis, J.-B. (1967). *The language of psychoanalysis* (translated by D. Nicholson-Smith). New York, NY: W. W. Norton, 1973.

Laplanche, J. & Pontalis, J.-B. (1968). Fantasy and the origins of sexuality. *International Journal of Psychoanalysis, 49*, 1–18.

Lebow, J. L. (ed.) (2008). *Twenty-first century psychotherapies: Contemporary approaches to theory and practice*. New York, NY: Wiley-Blackwell.

Leenhardt, M. (1909/1922). *La grande terre*. Paris, France: Société des missions évangéliques. [Expanded as: *Gens de la Grande Terre*. Paris, France: Gallimard, 1937.]

Leete, A. & Firnhaber, R. P. (eds.) (2004). *Shamanism in the interdisciplinary context.* Boca Raton, FL: Brown Walker Press.

Lefebvre, H. (1940). *Dialectical materialism* (translated by J. Sturrock). Minneapolis, MN: University of Minnesota Press, 2009.

Lefebvre, H. (1947–1981). *The critique of everday life* (3 volumes, translated by J. Moore & G. Elliott). London, UK: Verso, 2008.

Lefebvre, H. (1974). *The production of space* (translated by D. Nicholson-Smith). London, UK: Wiley-Blackwell, 1992.

Legrand, D. & Trigg, D. (eds.) (2017). *Unconsciousness between phenomenology and psycho-analysis.* Cham, Switzerland: Springer.

Leibniz, F. W. (1678–1716). *G. W. Leibniz: Philosophical essays* (edited & translated by R. Ariew & D. Garber). Indianapolis, IN: Hackett, 1989.

Leibniz, G. W. (1675–1716). *G. W. Leibniz: Philosophical essays* (translated by R. Ariew & D. Garber). Indianapolis, IN: Hackett, 1989.

Leonard, G. (1978). *The silent pulse.* New York, NY: E. P. Dutton.

Levinas, E. (1961). *Totality and infinity: An essay on exteriority* (translated by A. Lingis). Pittsburgh, PA: Duquesne University Press, 1969.

Levinas, E. (1974). *Otherwise than being, or beyond essence* (translated by A. Lingis). The Hague, Netherlands: Martinus Nijhoff, 1981.

Levinas, E. (1991). *Entre nous: Thinking-of-the-other* (translated by M. B. Smith & B. Harshaw). New York, NY: Columbia University Press, 1998.

Levinas, E. (1995). *Alterity and transcendence* (translated by M. B. Smith). New York, NY: Columbia University Press, 2000.

Lévi-Strauss, C. (1949). The effectiveness of symbols. In: *Structural anthropology* (translated by C. Jacobson). New York, NY: Basic Books, 1963, pp. 186–205.

Levy, R. A., Ablon, J. S. & Gabbard, G. O. (eds.) (2008). *Handbook of evidence-based psycho-dynamic psychotherapy: Bridging the gap between science and practice.* New York, NY: Humana Press.

Levy, R. A., Ablon, J. S. & Kächele, H. (eds.) (2011). *Psychodynamic psychotherapy research: Evidence-based practice and practice-based evidence.* New York, NY: Humana Press.

Lian, Y.-L., Cchen, C.-Y., Hammes, M. & Kolster, B. C. (2012). *Pictorial atlas of acupuncture: An illustrated manual of acupuncture points.* New York, NY: H. F. Ullman Publishing.

Lichtheim, G. (1963–1966). *The concept of ideology and other essays.* New York, NY: Vintage/Random, 1967.

Limentani, A. (1986). Variations on some Freudian themes: Presidential address. *International Journal of Psychoanalysis, 67,* 235–243.

Limentani, A. (1989). *Between Freud and Klein: The psychoanalytic quest for knowledge and truth.* London, UK: Free Association Books.

Lindahl, K. (2002). *The sacred art of listening.* Woodstock, VT: Skylight Paths Publishing.

Lingis, A. (1983). *Excesses: Eros and culture.* Albany, NY: State University of New York Press.

Lingis, A. (1985). *Libido: The french existentialist theories.* Bloomington, IN: Indiana University Press.

Lingis, A. (1989). *Deathbound subjectivity.* Bloomington, IN: Indiana University Press.

Lingis, A. (1996). *Sensation: Intelligibility in sensibility.* Atlantic Highlands, NJ: Humanities Press.

Lippitt, J. (2000). *Humor and irony in Kierkegaard's thought.* Basingstoke, UK: Palgrave Macmillan.

Lohser, B. & Newton, P. M. (1996). *Unorthodox Freud: The view from the couch.* New York, NY: Guilford Press.

Long, A. A. & Sedley, D. N. (1987). *The Hellenistic philosophers: Volume 1, Translations of the principal sources with philosophical commentary*. Cambridge, UK: Cambridge University Press.

Lothane, Z. (2010). The analysand and the analyst team practicing reciprocal free association. *International Forum of Psychoanalysis*, 19(3), 155–164.

Lotringer, S. & Marazzi, C. (eds.) (2007). *Autonomia: Post-political politics*. Los Angeles, CA: Semiotext(e).

Lovitt, W. & Brundage, H. (1995). *Modern technology in the Heideggerian perspective*. Lewiston, NY: Edward Mellen Press.

Low, B. (1920). *Psychoanalysis: A brief account of the Freudian theory*. London, UK: Routledge, 2014.

Lowen, A. (1970). *Pleasure: A creative approach to life*. Hinesburg, VT: Alexander Lowen Foundation, 2013.

Lowen, A. (1975). *Bioenergetics*. New York, NY: Coward, McCann & Geoghegan.

Lowen, A. (1995). *Joy: The surrender to body and to life*. New York, NY: Penguin.

Lukács, G. (1919–1923). *History and class consciousness: Studies in Marxist dialectics* (translated by R. Livingstone). Cambridge, MA: MIT Press, 1972.

Lunbeck, E. (2014). *The americanization of narcissism*. Cambridge, MA: Harvard University Press.

Luxemburg, R. (1899). *Reform or revolution and other writings*. New York, NY: Dover, 2006.

Lyotard, J.-F. (1974). *Libidinal economy* (translated by I. H. Grant). Bloomington, IN: Indiana University Press, 1993.

Lyotard, J.-F. (1988). *The inhuman: Reflections on time* (translated by G. Bennington & R. Bowlby). Stanford, CA: Stanford University Press, 1991.

Macey, D. (1988). *Lacan in contexts*. New York, NY: Verso, 1988.

Maeterlinck, M. P. M. B. (1923). *Death* (translated by A. T. de Mattos). Lexington, KY: Bibliolife, 2009.

Mahone, S. & Vaughan, M. (eds.) (2007). *Psychiatry and empire*. Basingstoke, UK: Palgrave Macmillan.

Mahony, P. J. (1987). *Psychoanalysis and discourse*. London, UK: Tavistock.

Malabou, C. (2004). *What should we do with our brain?* (translated by S. Rand). New York, NY: Fordham University Press, 2008.

Malabou, C. (2007). *The new wounded: From neurosis to brain damage* (translated by S. Miller). New York, NY: Fordham University Press.

Malabou, C. (2009). *Ontology of the accident: An essay on destructive plasticity* (translated by C. Shread). Cambridge, UK: Polity Press, 2012.

Malcolm, X. (1963–1965). *Malcolm X speaks: Selected speeches and statements* (edited by G. Breitman). New York, NY: Grove Press, 1994.

Malcolm, X. (1964–1965). *The autobiography of Malcolm X (as told to Alex Haley)*. New York, NY: Ballantine, 1992.

Marcus, P. & Rosenberg, A. (eds.) (1998). *Psychoanalytic versions of the human condition: Philosophies of life and their impact on practice*. New York, NY: New York University Press.

Marcuse, H. (1929–1969). *Marxism, revolution and utopia* (edited by D. Kellner & C. Pierce). London, UK: Routledge, 2014.

Marcuse, H. (1932–1992). *Philosophy, psychoanalysis and emancipation* (edited by D. Kellner & C. Pierce). London, UK: Routledge, 2011.

Marcuse, H. (1955). *Eros and civilization: A philosophical inquiry into Freud*. London, UK: Allen Lane, 1969.

Marcuse, H. (1964). *One-dimensional man: Studies in the ideology of advanced industrial society*. Boston, MA: Beacon Press.

Marcuse, H. (1968). *Negations: Essays in critical theory* (translated by J. J. Shapiro). London, UK: Penguin.

Marley, B. (1979/80). Redemption song. Track on: *Uprising* (released 1980). London, UK: Island Records.

Marlock, G., Weiss, H., Young, C. & Soth, M. (2015). *Handbook of body psychotherapy and somatic psychology.* Berkeley, CA: North Atlantic Books.

Marx, K. (1844). Holy family. In: *Collected works of Marx and Engels, Volume 4.* New York, NY: Lawrence & Wishart, 1975.

Marx, K. (1845). *Ludwig Feuerbach and the end of classical German philosophy* (revised and edited by F. Engels). Scotts Valley, CA: CreateSpace, 2016. [Also in: *Collected works of Marx and Engels, Volume 5.* New York, NY: Lawrence & Wishart, 1975.]

Marx, K. (1850). Address to the Central Committee of the Communist League. In: *Collected works of Marx and Engels, Volume 10.* New York, NY: Lawrence & Wishart, 1978.

Masi, F. de (2004). *Making death thinkable* (translated by G. Antinucci). London, UK: Free Association Books.

Matthews, J. D. (n.d.). *Toward the destruction of schooling.* Santa Cruz, CA: Quiver Distro.

Mauss, M. (1924). *The gift: The form and reason for exchange in archaic societies* (translated by W. D. Halls). New York, NY: W. W. Norton, 2000.

Mbembe, A. (2015). *On the postcolony.* Johannesburg, South Africa: Wits University Press.

McCarthy, T., Critchley, S. *et al.* (1999–2010). *The mattering of matter: Documents from the archives of the 'International Necronautical Society.'* Berlin, Germany: Sternberg Press, 2013.

McCulloch, J. (1995). *Colonial psychiatry and 'the African mind.'* Cambridge, UK: Cambridge University Press.

McGowan, T. (2016). *Capitalism and desire: The psychic cost of free markets.* New York, NY: Columbia University Press.

McGregor, G. & White, R. S. (eds.) (1990). *Reception and response: Hearer creativity and the analysis of spoken and written texts.* London, UK: Routledge.

McKirahan, R. D. (2001). *Philosophy before Socrates: An introduction with texts and commentary* (2nd edition). Indianapolis, IN: Hackett.

Meisels, M. & Shapiro, E. R. (eds.) (1990). *Tradition and innovation in psychoanalytic education.* Hillsdale, NJ: Lawrence Erlbaum.

Mellasioux, Q. (2006). *After finitude: An essay on the necessity of contingency* (translated by R. Brassier). London, UK: Bloomsbury Academic, 2010.

Meltzer, M. (1993). *Slavery: A world history.* New York, NY: Da Capo Press.

Memmi, A. (1957). *The colonizer and the colonized* (translated by H. Greenfeld). Boston, MA: Beacon Press, 1991.

Memmi, A. (1959). *Dependence: A sketch for a portrait* (translated by P. A. Facey). Boston, MA: Beacon Press, 1984.

Memmi, A. (2004). *Decolonization and the decolonized* (translated by R. Bononno). Minneapolis, MN: University of Minnesota Press.

Merleau-Ponty, M. (1942). *The structure of behavior* (translated by A. Fisher). Boston, MA: Beacon Press, 1963.

Merleau-Ponty, M. (1945). *Phenomenology of perception* (translated by C. Smith). New York, NY: Humanities Press, 1962.

Merleau-Ponty, M. (1948). *Sense and non-sense* (translated by H. Dreyfus & P. A. Dreyfus). Evanston, IL: Northwestern University Press.

Merleau-Ponty, M. (1949). *Consciousness and the acquisition of language* (translated by H. J. Silverman). Evanston, IL: Northwestern University Press, 1973.

Merton, T. (1959/1968). *Inner experience: Notes on contemplation* (edited by W. H. Shannon). San Francisco, CA: Harper, 2004.

Merton, T. (1962). *New seeds of contemplation.* New York, NY: New Directions, 2007.

Mészáros, I. (1970). *Marx's theory of alienation.* London, UK: Merlin Press, 2006.

Meyerson, E. (1925). *La deduction relativiste.* Paris, France: Payot.

Micale, M. S. & Porter, R. (eds.) (1994). *Discovering the history of psychiatry.* London, UK: Oxford University Press.

Miller, J.-A. (1977). Introduction aux paradoxes de la passé. *Ornicar, 12–13.*

Mills, C. W. (1951). *White collar: The American middle classes.* Oxford, UK: Oxford University Press.

Molino, A. (ed.) (1997). *Freely associated: Encounters in psychoanalysis with Christopher Bollas, Joyce McDougall, Michael Eigen, Adam Phillips, Nina Coltart.* London, UK: Free Association Books.

Molino, A. (1998). *The couch and the tree: Dialogues in psychoanalysis and Buddhism.* New York, NY: North Point Press.

Money, J. (1977). *Principles of developmental sexology.* New York, NY: Continuum.

Money, J. (1986). *Lovemaps: Clinical concepts of sexual/erotic health and pathology, paraphilia, and gender transposition in childhood, adolescence, and maturity.* New York, NY: Irvington.

Motherwell, R. (ed.) (1989). *The dada painters and poets: An anthology* (2nd edition). Cambridge, MA: Belknap Press.

Mouffe, C. (2005) *On the political.* London, UK: Routledge.

Muecke, D. C. (1969). *The compass of irony.* London, UK: Methuen.

Nagel, T. (1979). *Mortal questions.* Cambridge, UK: Cambridge University Press, 1991.

Nagel, T. (1986). *The view from nowhere.* London, UK: Oxford University Press.

Nagel, T. (2012). *Mind and cosmos: Why the materialist neo-Darwinian conception of nature is almost certainly false.* London, UK: Oxford University Press.

Nakamura, T. (1981). *Oriental breathing therapy.* Tokyo, Japan: Japan Publications.

Nancy, J.-L. (1988). *The experience of freedom* (translated by B. McDonald). Stanford, CA: Stanford University Press, 1993.

Nancy, J-L. (1993). *The sense of the world* (translated by J. S. Librett). Minneapolis, MN: University of Minnesota Press, 1997.

Nancy, J.-L. (2000–2006). *Corpus* (translated by R. A. Rand). New York, NY: Fordham University Press, 2008.

Nancy, J.-L. (2002). *Listening* (translated by C. Mandell). New York, NY: Fordham University Press, 2007.

Nancy, J-L. (2003). *Noli me tangere: On the raising of the body* (translated by S. Clift, P-A Brault, & M. Naas). New York, NY: Fordham University Press, 2008.

Negri, A. (1992). *Insurgencies: Constituent power and the modern state* (translated by M. Boscagli). Minneapolis, MN: University of Minnesota Press, 1999.

Negri, A. (2005). *The politics of subversion: A manifesto for the twenty-first century.* Cambridge, UK: Polity Press.

Neimeyer, R. A. (ed.) (1994). *The death anxiety handbook.* Washington, DC: Taylor & Francis.

Neumann, E. (1954). *The origins and history of consciousness.* Princeton, NJ: Princeton University Press.

Nichols, M. P. (2009). *The lost art of listening.* New York, NY: Guilford Press.

Nietsche, F. (1901–1906). *The will to power* (edited by W. Kaufman, translated by W. Kaufman & R. J. Hollingdale). New York, NY: Random House, 1973.

Nicholson, L. (ed.) (1997). *The second wave: A reader in feminist theory.* London, UK: Routledge.

Nietzsche, F. (1873–1876). *Untimely meditations* (2nd edition, edited by D. Breazeale, translated by R. J. Hollingdale). Cambridge, UK: Cambridge University Press, 1997.

Nietzsche, F. (1878). *Human, all too human* (2nd edition, edited by R. Schacht, translated by R. J. Hollingdale). Cambridge, UK: Cambridge University Press, 1996.

Nietzsche, F. (1881). *The dawn: Thoughts on the presumptions of morality* (translated by B. Smith). Stanford, CA: Stanford University Press, 2011.

Nietzsche, F. (1882). *The gay science: With a prelude in rhymes and an appendix of songs* (translated by W. Kaufmann). New York, NY: Vintage, 1974.

Nietzsche, F. (1883). *Thus spoke Zarathustra: A book for everyone and no one* (translated by R. J. Hollingdale). London, UK: Penguin, 1961.

Nietzsche, F. (1886). *Beyond good and evil: A prelude to the philosophy of the future* (translated by J. Norman). Cambridge, UK: Cambridge University Press, 2001.

Nietzsche, F. (1887). *On the genealogy of morality* (translated by M. Clark & A. J. Swensen). Indianapolis, IN: Hackett, 1998.

Nietzsche, F. (1888a). Twilight of the idols, or how to philosophize with a hammer. In: *Twilight of the idols and The anti-Christ* (translated by R. J. Hollingdale). London, UK: Penguin, 1990.

Nietzsche, F. (1888b). *Ecce homo: How one becomes what one is* (translated by R. J. Hollingdale). London, UK: Penguin, 1992.

Nitschke, G. (1995). *The silent orgasm: From transpersonal to transparent consciousness.* Köln, Germany: Taschen.

Nobus, D. & Quinn, M. (2005). *Knowing nothing, staying stupid: Elements for a psychoanalytic epistemology.* London, UK: Routledge.

Ogden, T. H. (1989). *The primitive edge of experience.* Northvale, NJ: Jason Aronson.

Ogden, T. H. (1994). *Subjects of analysis.* Northvale, NJ: Jason Aronson.

Ollman, B. (1971–1979). *Social and sexual revolution: Essays on Marx and Freud.* Cambridge, MA: South End Press, 1979.

Ollman, B. (1977). *Alienation: Marx's conception of man in capitalist society.* Cambridge, UK: Cambridge University Press, 1977.

Ornston, D. G. (ed.) (1992). *Translating Freud.* New Haven, CT: Yale University Press.

Otto, R. (1904). *Naturalism and religion* (translated by J. A. Thomson & M. B. Thomson). London, UK: Williams & Norgate, 1907.

Pallaro, P. (ed.) (1999/2012). *Authentic movement: Essays by Mary Starks Whitehouse, Janet Adler and Joan Chodorow* (Volume 1, 2nd edition). London, UK: Jessica Kingsley.

Pallaro, P. (ed.) (2007/2014). *Authentic movement: Moving the body, moving the self, being Moved* (Volume 2, 2nd edition). London, UK: Jessica Kingsley.

Panksepp, J. (1999). Emotions as viewed by psychoanalysis and neuroscience: An exercise in consilience. *Neuropsychoanalysis, 1(1),* 15–38.

Parmenides of Elea. (c. 500 b.c.e.). *The fragments of Parmenides: A critical text with introduction and translation, with ancient testimonia and a commentary* (edited & translated by R. McKirahan, revised & expanded edition by A. H. Coxon). Las Vegas, NV: Parmenides Publishing, 2009.

Pascal, R. (1960). *Design and truth in autobiography.* Cambridge, UK: Harvard University Press.

Pederson, T. C. (2015). *The economics of libido: Psychic bisexuality, the superego, and the centrality of the oedipus complex.* London, UK: Karnac.

Peirce, C. S. (1931–1958). *Collected papers of Charles Sanders Peirce* (8 volumes, edited by C. Hartshorne, P. Weiss & A. W. Burks). Cambridge, MA: Harvard University Press, 1965.

Penrose, R. (1989). *The emperor's new mind: Concerning computers, minds, and the laws of physics*. London, UK: Oxford University Press.

Peraldi, F. (ed.) (1981). *Polysexuality* (special issue of *Semiotexte, 4–1*). New York, NY: Columbia University Press.

Petrucelli, J. (ed.) (2010). *Knowing, not-knowing and sort-of-knowing: Psychoanalysis and the experience of uncertainty*. London, UK: Karnac.

Pezze, B. D. (2006). Heidegger on Gelassenheit. *Minerva – An Internet Journal of Philosophy, 10*.

Piven, J. S. (2003). Death, repression, narcissism, misogyny. *Psychoanalytic Review, 90(2)*, 225–260.

Piven, J. S. (2004). *Death and delusion: A Freudian analysis of mortal terror*. Greenwich, CT: Information Age Publishing.

Piven, J. S. (ed.) (2004). *The psychology of death in fantasy and history*. Westport, CT: Prager.

Popper, K. R. (1974). *The philosophy of Karl Popper* (2 volumes). La Salle, IL: Open Court.

Pratt, C. (2007). *An encyclopedia of shamanism* (2 volumes). New York, NY: Rosen.

Pythagoras of Samos (c.570–495 b.c.e.). *The Pythagorean sourcebook and library: An anthology of ancient writings which relate to Pythagoras and Pythagorean philosophy* (edited & translated by K. S. Guthrie & D. Fideler). Grand Rapids, MI: Phanes Press, 1987.

Quayson, A. (2000). *Postcolonialism: Theory, practice, or process?* Cambridge, UK: Polity Press.

Quindeau, I. (2013). *Seduction and desire: The psychoanalytic theory of sexuality since Freud* (translated by J. Bendix). London, UK: Karnac.

Quine, W. V. O. (1969). *Ontological relativity and other essays*. Cambridge, MA: Harvard University Press.

Racker, H. (1968). *Transference and countertransference*. New York, NY: New York University Press.

Ragland, E. (1995). *Essays on the pleasure of death*. London, UK: Routledge.

Rajneesh, B. S. (1979). *The tantra vision: Talks on the Royal Song of Saraha* (2 volumes). Pune, India: Rajneesh Foundation.

Rajneesh, B. S. (1989). *Meditation: The first and last freedom*. Köln, Germany: Rebel.

Raju, P. T. (1985). *Structural depths of Indian thought*. Delhi, India: South Asian Publishers.

Ramacharaka, Y. (1904–1905). *Science of breath: A complete manual of the oriental breathing philosophy of physical, mental, psychic and spiritual development*. Ocean Shores, WA: Watchmaker Publishing, 2011.

Rancière, J. (2010). *Jacques Rancière: Key concepts* (edited by J.-P. Deranty). Abingdon, UK: Routledge, 2014.

Rancière, J., Bingham, C. & Biesta, G. (2002–2010). *Jacques Rancière: Education, truth, emancipation*. New York, NY: Continuum, 2010.

Rank, O. (1924). *The trauma of birth*. Eastford, CT: Martino, 2010.

Rank, O. (1929–1931). *Will therapy*. New York, NY: W.W. Norton, 1978.

Ray, R. A. (2008). *Touching enlightenment: Finding realization in the body*. Boulder, CO: Sounds True Publishing.

Readings, B. (1997). *The university in ruins*. Cambridge, MA: Harvard University Press.

Reich, W. (1927). *Genitality in the theory and therapy of the neuroses* (translated from *The function of the orgasm* by P. Schmitz, edited by M. Higgins & C. M. Raphael). New York, NY: Farrar, Straus & Giroux.

Reich, W. (1927–1953). *Selected writings: An introduction to orgonomy*. New York, NY: Farrar, Straus & Cudahy, 1960.

Reich, W. (1933). *Character analysis* (translated by T. P. Wolfe). London, UK: Vision Press, 1950.

Reik, T. (1937). *Surprise and the psychoanalyst: On the conjecture and comprehension of unconscious process.* New York, NY: E. P. Dutton.

Reik, T. (1948). *Listening with the third ear: The inner experience of a psychoanalyst.* New York, NY: Farrar, Straus & Giroux, 1983.

Reiss, T. J. (1982). *The discourse of modernism.* Ithaca, NY: Cornell University Press.

Reiss, T. J. (1988). *The uncertainty of analysis: Problems in truth, meaning, and culture.* Ithaca, NY: Cornell University Press.

Ricard, M. (2013). *Altruism: The power of compassion to change yourself and the world* (translated by C. Mandell & S. Gordon). New York, NY: Little, Brown & Co.

Ricoeur, P. (1970). *Freud and philosophy: An essay on interpretation* (translated by D. Savage). New Haven, CT: Yale University Press.

Ricoeur, P. (1974). *The conflict of interpretations: Essays in hermeneutics* (edited by D. Ihde). Evanston, IL: Northwestern University Press.

Rivers, N. (2017). *Postfeminism(s) and the arrival of the fourth wave: Turning tides.* Basingstoke, UK: Palgrave Macmillan.

Robles, M. U. (2010). *Fanaticism in psychoanalysis: Upheavals in the institutions* (translated by E. N. Domínguez & C. Lichtschein de Sueldo). London, UK: Karnac, 2013.

Rogers, C. R. (1951). *Client-centered therapy: Its current practice, implications and theory.* London, UK: Constable.

Rogers, C. R. (1961). *On becoming a person: A therapist's view of psychotherapy.* London, UK: Constable.

Rogers, C. R. (1980). *A way of being.* Boston, MA: Houghton Mifflin.

Rorty, R. (1989). *Contingency, irony, and solidarity.* Cambridge, UK: Cambridge University Press.

Rosemont, P. (ed.) (1997). *Surrealist women: An international anthology.* Austin, TX: University of Texas Press.

Rosen, R. (2002). *The yoga of breath: A step-by-step guide to prānāyāma.* Boston, MA: Shambhala.

Rosner, S. (1973). On the nature of free-association. *Journal of the American Psychoanalytic Association, 21,* 558–575.

Ross, A. R. (2017). *Against the fascist creep.* Chico, CA: AK Press.

Roudinesco, E. (1986). *Jacques Lacan & co. – A history of psychoanalysis in France* (translated by J. Mehlman). London, UK: Free Association Books, 1990.

Rowe, N. M. (2003). Listening through the body. In: M. Brady (ed.), *The wisdom of listening.* Boston, MA: Shambhala, 157–166.

Rubin, G. S. (1975–2011). *Deviations: A Gayle Rubin reader.* Durham, NC: Duke University Press.

Ruitenbeek, H. M. (ed.) (1969/1983). *The interpretation of death.* New York, NY: Jason Aronson.

Ruitenbeek, H. M. (ed.) (1973). *Freud as we knew him.* Detroit, MI: Wayne State University Press.

Rustin, M. J. (1985). *For a pluralistic socialism.* London, UK: Verso.

Rustin, M. J. (1991). *The good society and the inner world.* London, UK: Verso.

Rustin, M. J. (2001). *Reason and unreason: Psychoanalysis, science and politics.* Middletown, CT: Wesleyan University Press.

Ruti, M. (2012). *The singularity of being: Lacan and the immortal within.* New York, NY: Fordham University Press.

Ruyer, R. (1937). *La conscience et le corps.* Paris, France: Alcan.

Ruyer, R. (1952). *Neofinalism* (translated by A. Edlebi). Minneapolis, MN: University of Minnesota Press, 2016.

Ruyer, R. (1956). *La genèse des forms vivantes*. Paris, France: Flammarion.

Rycroft, C. (1966). *Psychoanalysis observed*. London, UK: Constable.

Safran, J. D. (ed.) (2003). *Psychoanalysis and Buddhism: An unfolding dialogue*. Boston, MA: Wisdom.

Samuels, A. (1993). *The political psyche*. London, UK: Routledge.

Samuels, A. (2001). *Politics on the couch: Citizenship and the internal life*. London, UK: Karnac.

Samuels, A. (2015). *A new therapy for politics?* London, UK: Routledge.

Saraswati, S. S. (1981). *A systematic course in the ancient tantric techniques of yoga and kriya*. Munger, India: Yoga Publications Trust.

Sartre, J.-P. (1943). *Being and nothingness: An essay on phenomenological ontology* (translated by H. E. Barnes). London, UK: Methuen.

Satsangi, P. S. & Hameroff, S. (eds.) (2016). *Consciousness: Integrating eastern and western perspectives*. Boca Raton, FL: New Age Books.

Saul of Tarsus (c. 53–54). First epistle to the Corinthians. In: *New English Bible*. London, UK: Oxford University Press, 1970.

Saussure, F. de (1906–1911). *Course in general linguistics* (edited by C. S. Bailey & A. Sechehaye, translated by W. Baskin). New York, NY: McGraw-Hill, 1966.

Scarfone, D. (2006–2014). *The unpast: The actual unconscious*. New York, NY: The Unconscious in Translation, 2015.

Schacht, R. (1970). *Alienation*. New York, NY: Doubleday.

Schacht, R. (1994). *The future of alienation*. Urbana, IL: University of Illinois Press.

Schechter, K. (2014). *Illusions of a future: Psychoanalysis and the biopolitics of desire*. Durham, NC: Duke University Press.

Schneider, S. & Velmans, M. (eds.) (2017). *The Blackwell companion to consciousness* (2nd edition). Malden, MA: Wiley-Blackwell.

Schopenhauer, A. (1818/1844). *The world as will and representation* (2 volumes, translated by E. F. J. Payne). Mineola, NY: Dover, 1966.

Schrödinger, E. & Penrose, R. (1944/2012). *What is life?* Cambridge, UK: Cambridge University Press.

Schroyer, T. (1975). *The critique of domination: The origins and development of critical theory*. Boston, MA: Beacon Press.

Schuster, A. (2016). *The trouble with pleasure: Deleuze and psychoanalysis*. Cambridge, MA: MIT Press.

Searles, H. F. (1951–1964). *Collected papers on schizophrenia and related subjects*. London, UK: Routledge, 1986.

Segal, H. (1969–2006). *Yesterday, today and tomorrow* (edited by N. Abel-Hirsch). London, UK: Routledge, 2007.

Sellars, W. (1956). *Empiricism and the philosophy of mind* (2nd edition). Cambridge, MA: Harvard University Press, 1997.

Serner, W. (1920). *Letzte lockerung: Manifest dada*. London, UK: Forgotten Books, 2018.

Shakespeare, W. (1601). *Hamlet*. Cambridge, UK: Cambridge University Press, 1990.

Sheppard, R. (1999). *Modernism – dada – postmodernism*. Evanston, IL: Northwestern University Press.

Simondon, G. (1964). *L'individu et sa genèse physico-biologique (l'individuation à la lumière des notions de forme et d'information)*. Paris, France: Presses Universitaires de France.

Simondon, G. (1989). *L'individuation psychique et collective*. Paris, France: Aubier.

Sitbon, B. (2014). *Bergson et Freud*. Paris, France: Presses Universitaires de France.

Sjöstedt-H, P. (2015). *Neo-nihilism: The philosophy of power*. Seattle, WA: Amazon.

Sokolowski, R. (2000). *Introduction to phenomenology.* Cambridge, UK: Cambridge University Press.

Sousa Santos, B. de (ed.) (2007). *Another knowledge is possible: Beyond northern epistemologies.* London, UK: Verso.

Sousa Santos, B. de (2014). *Epistemologies of the South: Justice against epistemicide.* London, UK: Routledge.

Spiegel, L. A. (1975). The functions of free-association in psychoanalysis: Their relation to technique and theory. *International Review of Psychoanalysis, 2,* 379–388.

Spiegelberg, H. (1972). *Phenomenology in psychology and psychiatry: A historical introduction.* Evanston, IL: Northwestern University Press.

Spiegelberg, H. (1983). *The phenomenological movement: A historical introduction* (3rd edition). The Hague, The Netherlands: Martinus Nijhoff.

Spielrein, S. (1912). Die Destruktion als Ursache des Werdens. *Jahrbuch für psychoanalytische und psychopathologische Forschungen, 4,* 465–503. [Translated as: Destruction as the cause of coming into being. *Journal of Analytical Psychology, 39,* 155–186. Also translated as: Destruction as cause of becoming. *Psychoanalysis and Contemporary Thought, 18,* 85–118.]

Spinoza, B. de (1677). *Ethics* (translated by E. Curley). London, UK: Penguin, 1996.

Spivak, G. C. (1998). *In other worlds: Essays in cultural politics.* London, UK: Methuen.

Spivak, G. C. (1999). *A critique of postcolonial reason: Toward a history of the vanishing present.* Cambridge, MA: Harvard University Press.

Stavrakakis, Y. (1999). *Lacan and the political.* London, UK: Routledge.

Stayton, W. R. (1980). A theory of sexual orientation. *Topics in Clinical Nursing, 1*(4), 1–7. [Cited in Francoeur, R. T., Cornog, M., Perper, T. & Scherzer, N. A. (eds.) (1995). *The complete dictionary of sexology* (New Expanded Edition). New York, NY: Continuum.]

Stekel, W. (1911–1927). *Twelve essays on sex and psychoanalysis* (edited & translated by S. A. Tannenbaum). New York, NY: Critic & Guide, 1932.

Stekel, W. (1921). *The beloved ego: Foundations of the new study of the psyche* (translated by R. Gabler). London, UK: Kegan Paul, Trench, Trubner & Co.

Sterba, R. F. (1934). The fate of the ego in analytic therapy. *International Journal of Psychoanalysis, 15,* 117–126.

Sterba, R. F. (1982). *Reminiscences of a Viennese psychoanalyst.* Detroit, MI: Wayne State University Press.

Stevens, A. (1999). *On Jung.* Princeton, NJ: Princeton University Press.

Stolorow, R. D., Brandchaft, B. & Atwood, G. E. (2000). *Psychoanalytic treatment: An intersubjective approach.* London, UK: Routledge.

Stone, L. (1962). *The psychoanalytic situation: An examination of its development and essential nature.* New York, NY: International Universities Press, 1977.

Sturrock, J. (2003). *Structuralism* (2nd edition). London, UK: Wiley-Blackwell.

Suler, J. R. (1993). *Contemporary psychoanalysis and eastern thought.* Albany, NY: State University of New York Press.

Sullivan, H. S. (1953). *The interpersonal theory of psychiatry.* London, UK: Routledge, 2003.

Sullivan, H. S. (1953–1956). *The collected works of Harry Stack Sullivan* (2 volumes). New York, NY: W. W. Norton, 1956.

Swanson, C. V. (2007). *The synchronized universe: New science of the paranormal.* Tucson, AZ: Poseidia Press.

Swanson, C. V. (2009). *Life force: The scientific basis.* Tucson, AZ: Poseidia Press.

Szasz, T. (1988). *The myth of psychotherapy: Mental healing as religion, rhetoric, and repression.* Syracuse, NY: Syracuse University Press.

Tanner, G. (2017) *Stoicism: A detailed breakdown of Stoicism philosophy and wisdom from the greats.* Scotts Valley, CA: CreateSpace.

Thompson, M. G. (1994). *The truth about Freud's technique: The encounter with the real.* New York, NY: New York University Press.

Thompson, M. G. (2004). *The ethic of honesty: The fundamental rule of psychoanalysis.* New York, NY: Rodopi (Contemporary Psychoanalytic Studies).

Thoreau, H. D. (1863). *Excursions.* Scotts Valley, CA: CreateSpace, 2018.

Tiller, W. A. (2007). *Psychoenergetic science: A second Copernican-scale revolution.* Walnut Creek, CA: Pavior Publishing.

Tissié, P. (1890). *Les rêves: Physiologie et pathologie.* Charleston, SC: Nabu Press, 2012.

Tomšic, S. (2015). *The capitalist unconscious: Marx and Lacan.* London, UK: Verso.

Torsti-Hagman, M. (2003). *Harvesting free association.* London, UK: Free Association Books.

Trotsky, L. D. (1929). *The permanent revolution: Results and prospects* (translated by J. G. Wright et al.). Seattle, WA: Red Letter Press, 2010.

Tzara, T. (c. 1915–1924). *Seven dada manifestos and lampisteries* (translated by B. Wright). London, UK: John Calder, 1977.

Uexküll, J. V. (1934/1940). *A foray into the worlds of animals and humans* with *A theory of meaning* (translated by J. D. O'Neil). Minneapolis, MN: University of Minnesota Press, 2010.

Vaneigem, R. (1967). *The revolution of everyday life* (translated by D. Nicholson-Smith). Berkeley, CA: PM Press, 2012.

Vaughan, M. (1991). *Curing their ills: Colonial power and African illness.* Stanford, CA: Stanford University Press.

Wass, H. & Neimeyer, R. A. (1995). *Dying: Facing the facts* (3rd edition). Washington, DC: Taylor & Francis.

Watkins, M. & Shulman, H. (2008). *Toward psychologies of liberation.* Basingstoke, UK: Palgrave Macmillan.

Watts, A. (1971). *Erotic spirituality.* New York, NY: Collier Macmillan.

Weatherill, R. (1998). *The sovereignty of death.* London, UK: Rebus Press.

Weatherill, R. (ed.) (1999). *The death drive.* London, UK: Rebus Press.

Weiss, E. (1935). Todestrieb und Masochismus. *Imago, 21,* 396.

Weiss, H., Johanson, G. & Monda, L. (2015). *Hakomi mindfulness-centered somatic psychotherapy: A comprehensive guide to theory and practice.* New York, NY: W. W. Norton.

Whewell, W. (1837–1860). *Theory of scientific method* (edited by R. E. Butts). Indianapolis, IN: Hackett, 1989.

Wilber, K. (1977). *The spectrum of consciousness* (20th anniversary edition). Wheaton, IL: Quest Books, 1993.

Wilber, K. (ed.) (1985). *The holographic paradigm and other paradoxes.* Boston, MA: Shambhala.

Winnicott, D. W. (1955). Metapsychological and clinical aspects of regression within the psychoanalytical set-up. *International Journal of Psychoanalysis, 26,* 16–26.

Winnicott, D. W. (1965). *The family and individual development.* London, UK: Tavistock.

Winnicott, D. W. (1969). The use of an object. *International Journal of Psychoanalsyis, 50,* 711–716.

Wittgenstein, L. (1945–1949). *Philosophical investigations* (translated by G. E. M. Anscombe). New York, NY: Macmillan, 1968.

Wollstonecraft, M. (1792). *A vindication of the rights of women.* Mineola, NY: Dover, 1996.

Woodroffe, J. G. (1919). *The serpent power.* Madras (Chennai), India: Ganesh.

Woodroffe, J. G. (1922). *The garland of letters.* Madras (Chennai), India: Ganesh.

Yalom, I. D. (1980). *Existential psychotherapy*. New York, NY: Basic Books.

Young-Eisendrath, P. (2009). Psychoanalysis as inquiry and discovery, not suspicion. *Contemporary Psychoanalysis, 45(3)*, 363–369.

Zagermann, P. (ed.) (2017). *The future of psychoanalysis: The debate about the training analyst system*. London, UK: Karnac.

Zaretsky, E. (2005). *Secrets of the soul: A social and cultural history of psychoanalysis*. New York, NY: Vintage/Random House.

Zaretsky, E. (2017). *Political Freud: A history*. New York, NY: Columbia University Press.

Zedong, M. (1937a). *On guerilla warfare* (translated by S. B. Griffith). Eastford, CT: Martino, 2017.

Zedong, M. (1937b). *On practice/On contradiction* (edited by S. Žižek). London, UK: Verso, 2007.

Žižek, S. (1989). *The sublime object of ideology*. London, UK: Verso.

Žižek, S. (1992). *Enjoy your symptom*. London, UK: Routledge.

Žižek, S. (1994). *The metastases of enjoyment*. London, UK: Verso.

Žižek, S. (2003). *Organs without bodies*. London, UK: Routledge.

Žižek, S. (ed.) (2006). *Lacan: The silent partners*. London, UK: Verso.

Žižek, S. (2008). *Living in the end times* (revised updated edition). London, UK: Verso.

Žižek, S. (2013). *Demanding the impossible*. Malden, MA: Polity Press.

Znamenski, A. A. (ed.) (2004). *Shamanism: Critical concepts* (3 volumes). London, UK: Routledge.

Zupančič, A. (2017). *What is sex?* Cambridge, MA: MIT Press.

Zweig, S. (1931). *Mental healers: Mesmer, Eddy, Freud* (translated by E. Paul & C. Paul). London, UK: Pushkin Press, 2012.

Zwingli, H. (1531). *Froschauer Bible* (also known as the *Zürcher Bibel*). Zurich, Switzerland: Protestant Reformed Church, 2007.

INDEX

Abraham, K. 141n34
Abram, D. 105
'absenting-presence' 35, 70–71, 74–77
Ades, D. 163n99
adjustment 83, 95–96
Adler, A. 79, 150n64
Adler, J. 150n66
Adorno, T. 37, 49, 87, 138n26, 160n90
'affective turn' 148n61
Agamben, G. 109, 148n59
Agel, J. 131n4
Agger, B. 160n90
al-Rāzī, A. 12
Alaimo, S. 149n61
Alexander, F. 13, 75
alienation 24, 118–119, 160n92
alleviation 8–11
aloneness 81
Althusser, L. 78, 119, 148n58, 160n92
'analysis' 25, 28, 50
analytic-referential discourse 87, 133n14
Anaximander 89
ancient wisdom 111–112
Anderson, J. 143n43
andragogic training 50–51
'anti-psychiatry' 131n2
anxiety 68–69, 156n82
Anzieu, D. 82
aphanisis 110, 157n84
Aristotle 15, 142n37
Arlow, J. 149n64
Asian thinking 92, 108, 148n57, 150n66,
    151n68, 152n72, 155n80

'association' 98; see also free-association
Assoun, P.-L. 147n54
'attention' 153n74; see also Ganeri
Atwood, G. 134n15
Augustine of Aosta 18
Augustine of Hippo 118
authority of psychoanalyst 60–61, 69
autobiography 17, 133n12
Avalon, A. see Woodroffe
Avicenna see Ibn Sīnā
awareness: 'attention' 153n74; defining
    104–105; free-associative 102–110;
    lived-experience 154n78;
    psychoanalytical praxis 111–112; see also
    consciousness
ayurvedic system 14

Bachelard, G. 178
Bacon, F. 134n14
Badiou, A. 91
Bains, P. 156n80
Bakhtin, M. 126
Balint, M. 158n86
Ball, H. 163n99
'banking system' of education 48
Barrett, E. 130n1
Barros, C. 133n12
Barthes, R. 131n3
Bataille, G. 91, 158n85, 163n99
Baudrillard, J. 148n59
Beauvoir, S. 2
Becker, R. 156n82
behavior modification 11–13

Beinfeld, H. 156n81
being-as-becoming 84, 103
being-in-the-world *see* lived-experience
Bellak, L. 136n19
Benjamin, J. 134n15
Bergson, H.-L. 86–87, 92–93, 147n56
Bettelheim, B. 151n67
Bhambra, G. 162n95
Bharati, A. 138n24, 145n48,
    158n56
biological mechanisms 94–95,
    121, 128
Bion, W. 132n5
Blackmore, S. 152n72
Blanchot, M. 157n83
Blass, R. 133n13
Bloch, E. 31, 38
Bloom, K. 155n80
Blumgart, L. 41
body memories 77–78
bodymind: chakras 108; free-association
    100, 105, 107; healing 150n66;
    treatments 133n10, 162n96; use of term
    140n33
Bogost, I. 149n61
Bohm, D. 152n72
Bollas, C. 33, 130n1, 133n13, 136n19,
    138n25, 140n33, 141n34, 144n45
Booth, W. 143n41
Boothby, R. 137n21
Bose, G. 148n57
Bowie, M. 161n93
Bowker, J. 157n82
Bracher, M. 161n92
Brady, M. 155n80, 156n80
breath & breathing 89–95, 107–110,
    156n80; *see also* psychic energy
Brennan, M. 135n18
Brenner, C. 149n64
Brentano, F. 29
Breton, A. 163n99
Breuer, J. 12, 141n34
Briggs, K. 14
Brown, B. 125, 161n92
Brown, N. O. 148n59, 154n78
Brundage, H. 151n68
Bryant, L. 149n61
Bucke, R. 152n72
Buckley, J. 133n12
Buddha, G. 8, 37, 92
Buddhagosa 153n74
Burke, E. 72
Busch, F. 32
Butler, J. 148n58, 155n79

'calling' to psychoanalysis 52–58, 138n25
Caillois, R. 91, 163n99
Canguilhem, G. 131n2
capitalism 48, 112–113, 114
Capra, F. 152n76
Caputo, J. 151n68
Carel, H. 157n83
'caress' 70, 143n43, 153n75
caring role 74
Carnap, R. 86
'carnivalesque' discourse 126
Carroll, L. 30
catharsis 16–18
Caygill, H. 143n40
censorship, speaking without 33–34
Certeau, M. 163n100
certitude, 'attacks' on 30–35
Césaire, A. 160n91
chakras 108, 156n81
Chakravorty Spivak, G. 134n14
Chamberlain, P. 160n91
change concepts 2–5, 16, 130n1, 159n90
Chanter, T. 153n75, 154n79
Chapelle, D. 147n54
Charaka Samhita 14
Chari, A. 160n90
Charon, J.-É. 152n72
Chiesa, L. 154n79
Chrysippus (Chrysippus of Soli) 89
Cheng, C.-Y. 145n48
Cioffi, F. 134n15
Clausewitz, C. 143n40
Cleanthes 89
Cleary, T. 143n42
Cleckley, H. 138n25
Clough, P. 149n61
Cohen, M. R. 156n81
Colebrook, C. 143n41
compulsive repetitiousness 1–2, 8, 11;
    free-associative praxis 25; present-past
    relationship 76; stases of 35–42
Confucian thinking 15n48, 156n81
Connell, R. 134n14
consciousness 29, 104, 152n73; *see also*
    awareness
'consilience' 147n53, 148n60
contemplative practices 151n69
conversational psychotherapy 11, 15,
    18–19; *see also* 'talking cures'
Coole, D. 149n61
Cooper, D. 131n2
Coopersmith, J. 146n51, 148n57
Copjec, J. 122
counter-transferential interference 73

Coward, H. 145n48
Coward, R. 131n3
Crews, F. 134n15
Critchley, S. 158n85
Csikszentmihalyi, M. 31
Cuna chants 132n7
Curd, P. 146n52
Cuvillers, E. 13

dada movement 163n99; *see also*
    surrealist movement
Dahl, H. 32
Dalai Lama (Tenizn Gyatso) 132n6
Damasio, A. 90
Dasgupta, S. & Dasgupta, S. 138n24,
    145n48
Dean, J. T. 49
'deathfulness principle'(Todestrieb)
    107–110, 138n24, 152n71, 157n83;
    'death anxiety' 156n82; free-associative
    awareness 103; necronautical journey
    158n85; repetition-compulsivity 42;
    sexuality 152n71; trainees and 78;
    transgressive praxis 129
Debord, G. 163n100
deconstruction & 'deconstructive critique'
    4–7, 16, 19, 22–25, 37–38, 44, 56–57,
    59, 74–75, 78, 87, 102, 119–120,
    123–127, 133n12, 134n15, 145n48,
    151n70, 153n73; *see also* Derrida &
    Derridean thinking
'deeply preconscious' domain 27, 104
Deleuze, G. 87, 90–93, 144n46, 147n53,
    148n59, 155n79
Demir, I. 162n95
Dennett, D. 25, 29
Derrida, J. & Derridean thinking 29, 38,
    63, 72, 87, 91, 100, 116, 131n4, 133n12,
    143n43, 145n47, 157n83, 173n75; *see
    also* deconstruction
Descartes, R. & Cartesian thinking 90–93,
    104, 131n3, 140n33
desire: biological mechanisms 94, 128;
    deathfulness principle 109; dialectic of
    157n84; force of 35–42; as imprisonment
    128–129; lack notion 163n97; lifelfulness
    of 110; master/slave dialectic 115;
    psychic energy of 88, 105–107;
    representational system 27, 94–95, 119;
    rupture of 131n5; sexual patterning
    153n76; structure of 162n95; subtle
    energies 111; transmutative change 33;
    see also 'drives'
Dews, P. 161n93

Dharma teachings 37, 92, 132n6, 151n68;
    see also Asian thinking
Diagnostic and Statistical Manual of Mental
    Disorders (DSM) 5, 15
dialectics 37–38, 157n84; *see also* master/
    slave; domination/subordination
dialogue, limitations of 120, 149n64
Dionysian madness 154n78
Dolar, M. 154n79
domination/subordination 7, 114–118,
    129, 159n90, 160n91; *see also* master/
    slave
Donnet, J.-L. 136n20
Dorsey, J. 135n18
dreams 64, 145n47
'drives': psychic energy 86, 109–110,
    131n5; representational system 108; *see
    also* desire
Dubois, T. 132n7
Durkheim, É. 17–18
Dussel, E. 126, 133n14

Eagle, M. 134n15
Eagleton, T. 113
'eastern' context: categorizations 14;
    tantric movement 152n72; *see also* Asian
    thinking
Edelman, G. 104
education 47–48, 51, 64
Efron, A. 158n86
ego-psychological model 3, 5, 12, 61, 67,
    158n86
egology 58–60, 140n32
Eigen, M. 157n83
Einstein, A. 108, 148n56
Eisenhower, D. 131n4
Eissler, K. 157n84
Eitingon, M. & 'Eitingdon Model' 46,
    139n27
Eliade, M. 157n82
Eliot, T. S. 55
Ellenberger, H. 27
Ellis, J. 131n3
embodied experience: death 129; healing
    103; psychic energy 123; *see also* lived-
    experience
Empedocles 89
energies: awareness of 109; libidinal 87–95;
    review of concept 146n51, 148n57; *see
    also* psychic energy; subtle energy
epistemological issues 60, 69, 83–87, 98
erotics: energy 105–106; impulses 53, 123;
    pleasure 40; *see also* sexuality
estrangement 24, 119

'eternal return' 147n54
ethics: as facilitation 144n46; ontological
    84–87, 91; praxis 80; psychoanalyst's 52,
    58, 80; subtle energy 89–90
Evans, D. 161n93
Evans, E. 160n91
'everyday life' 125–126, 128, 163n100
Eyers, T. 161n93
Eysenck, H. 14
'existentialism' 156n82
expressing oneself 16–19, 43

Fanon, F. 160n91
fantasies 65–66
fear, psychoanalyst's 76, 78–82
Federn, P. 41
fees 64–65, 142n38
feminism 148n61, 154n79, 160n91, 162n95
Fenichel, O. 157n82
Ferenczi, S. 32, 79, 141n34
Feuerstein, G. 158n86
Feyerabend, P. 16
Feynman, R. 87, 148n56
Fichte, J. 37, 159n88
Fink, B. 137n21
Firnhaber, P. 132n7
Fisher-Schreiber, I. 151n69, 156n81
Fliess, W. 32, 94, 106, 108, 141n34
Fonagy, P. 32
Foucault, M. 91, 122, 131n2, 131n3,
    144n46, 148n59
Fox, G. 151n68
'frame' of treatment 63–64, 66
Francoeur, R. 106
Frankel, E. 153n73
free-association: 'attacks' on certitude
    30–35, 99; awareness 102–110;
    breakthrough 135n18; 'data' 149n64;
    defining 30–35, 149n62; effects of
    127–128; epistemology 85–86;
    'freetalking' 136n19; interpretation
    against 20–45; limitations 83–84;
    listening 98, 107–110, 163n97; 'making-
    sense' 136n21; mental functioning
    models 79; notion-for-praxis 89; praxis
    of 2, 8, 20–45, 89; radical psychoanalysis
    119–120, 123–124; redefining 136n19;
    repression-barrier 87; requirement for
    psychoanalysis 133n13; resistances to
    66–70, 72–73, 75–78, 102; retreat from
    80; 'rule' of 64; rule of 33–34, 64;
    speaking 95–102; surrealist movement
    124; trainee psychoanalysts 56, 59;
    uncensored talking 33–34, 149n63

'freeing' truthfulness 24, 59, 82, 126–128
freie Einfall 100–101, 151n67; *see also*
    free-association
Freire, P. 48, 133n14
Freud, A. 47, 142n39, 149n64
Freud, S. & Freudian thinking 2–5, 12,
    25–30, 57–59, 67–72, 87–89, 135n18,
    141n34, 145n47, 147n53, 147n54,
    147n56, 151n68, 154n77, 156n82,
    161n94; Asian influence 148n57;
    discoveries 30–45, 80–86, 88, 64, 91–94,
    96–98, 100–102, 104–105, 108–109,
    111, 118, 128, 145n47, 154n79;
    dream intentions 145n47, 161n94;
    free-association 25–28, 30–34, 36,
    39–41, 96–103, 126, 133n13, 149n62;
    interlocutors 141n34; Jungian tensions
    138n24; 'mindbody' term 140n33;
    misassumptions about 135n18, 157n83;
    objectivist inquiry 134n15; psychic
    energy 131n5, 138n24, 148n58;
    revolutionary psychoanalysis 112, 114,
    117, 124–126; Schopenhauer's influence
    147n56; sublimation 143n44; subtle
    energy notion 137n23; training
    psychoanalysts 47–49, 57, 59, 62, 64,
    66–68, 70, 72–76, 79; treatment
    analogies 140n33, 143n40; universities
    139n26
Frew, J. 133n9
Frie, R. 134n15
'friendly guerrilla' 68, 70, 126, 142n39,
    143n40
friendship 63–64, 67, 80–81, 141n37
Fromm, E. 132n6, 160n92
Frosch, J. 157n82, 161n92, 162n95
Frost, S. 149n61
'fucking' 163n98; versus 'lovemaking'
    163n98; lust 154n77
Fulbright, W. 131n4
fundamentalisms 114

Galatzer-Levy, R. 146n51
Galen (Galen of Pergamon) 14
Gall, F. 14
Gandhi, M. 70, 143n40
Ganeri, J. 145n48, 153n74
Garvey, M. 59
Gelassenheit 101–102, 151n68
genitality 158n86
Gennaro, R. 152n72
genocide 113–114
Geuss, R. 160n92
Gill, M. 135n18

Giroux, H. 48, 131n4
Goethe, J. W. 17
Gramsci, A. 125, 159n89
Green, A. 27–28, 117, 135n16, 148n60
Greenson, R. 68–69, 135n18
Gregg, M. 149n61
Groddeck, G. 96–97
Grof, S. 152n72
Gross, O. 163n101
Grosz, E. 89, 91–92, 145n47, 146n48, 147n53, 148n57
Grünbaum, A. 134n15
Guattari, F. 6, 90–91, 148n59
guerrilla activity *see* 'friendly guerrilla'

Hafez (Ḥāfeẓ-e Shīrāzī) 12
Halley, J. 149n61
Hameroff, S. 152n72
Handwerk, G. 143n41
Hanh, T. N. 50, 80, 139n29
Hannah, B. 149n64
Hardt, M. 163n100
Harman, G. 149n61
Hartmann, H. 149n64
Harvey, D. 160n90
Hazlitt, William 81
healing: avoidance as 8; bodymind 150n66; embodied experience 103; self-expression 17; theorizing basis 16
'hearing-to-understand' 55; *see also* listening
Hegel, G. W. F. 8, 20, 28, 37, 115–117, 156n82, 158n88, 159n89
Heidegger, M. 38–41, 86–87, 101–102, 109, 115–116, 145n48, 151n68, 151n69, 151n70, 153n74, 156n82, 158n85
Heisenberg, W. 87
Hekman, S. 149n61
Heller, M. 133n10
Helmholtz, H. 93
Hennings, E. 163n99
Henricks, R. 143n42
Heraclitus (Heraclitus of Ephesus) 20, 31, 28, 89, 130n1
hermeneutic discourse 87
Herzog, E. 157n82
Hippocrates (Hippocrates of Kos) 14
Hofstadter, R. 48
'holding' environment 64
Holt, B. 130n1
Holveck, E. 2
Honneth, A. 160n92
Hooks, B. 48
Hopkins, D. 163n99
Horkheimer, M. 160n90

Horlacher, R. 133n12
Hsi, C. 156n81
Humboldt, W. 17, 48, 133n12
Hume, D. 86
Humpty-Dumpty 30, 131n3
Hurvich, M. 157n82
Husserl, E. 26, 28–30, 134n16
Hutcheon, L. 143n41
Hyppolite, J. 115

'I' & 'I-Now-Is' 29–30, 38, 40, 116; fragility of 117; of self-consciousness 28–31; subjection of 131n3; symbolic order 122; *see also* egology
identitarian discourse 145n48
ideocentric psychotherapies 16
Illich, I. 48
imaginary world 120–121, 123
immanence 147n53; 'plane' of 90–92; of substance 90
imprisonment, transformative 118–124
incest & incest taboo 4–5, 61, 118, 128
incorporeal force 92–93
International Federation of Psychoanalysis 54
International Psychoanalytic Association 3, 23, 46, 54, 139n27
interpellation process 148n58
interpersonalist & relational approach 62–71
interpretation 4, 10; free-associative praxis against 20–45; resistances to free-association 66–70; self-expression 17–19
Irigaray, L. 91, 143n43, 147n54, 153n75, 154n79, 160n91, 162n95
irony 69–70, 143n41
Isaacs, S. 27
Islamic Golden Age 12

Jacoby, R. 48
Jaeggi, R. 159n89, 160n92
Jakobson, R. 36
James, W. 34
Jaspers, K. 41, 91
Jena School 69
Johanson, G. 143n42, 150n66
Johnson, A. 93
Jones, E. 93, 110, 137n23, 138n24, 141n34, 157n84
jouissance 154n79, 162n96; *see also* pleasure
Judith, A. 156n81
Jung, C. S. & Jungian thinking 14, 41, 57, 79, 98, 138n24, 141n34, 149n64, 161n92

Kamo-no-Chomei 156n82, 158n85
Kant, I. & Kantian thinking 72, 122
Kapp, A. 50
Karlsson, G. 135n17, 152n73, 157n83
Karr, J.-B. 159n90
Kastenbaum, R. & Kastenbaum, B. 157n82
Katsiaficas, G. 163n100
Kauffman, S. 146n51
Kennedy, R. 75
Keown, D. 156n81
Kernberg, O. 139n27, 158n86
Kesel, M. 161n93
Khasnabish, A. 155n79
Kierkegaard, S. 57, 69, 143n41
Kirschner, L. 134n15
Kirsner, D. 139n27
Klages, L. 116
Klein, M. & Kleinian psychotherapy 12, 27, 41, 47, 60, 71–73, 116, 136n20, 150n64, 161n92
Knabb, K. 163n100
knowledge, objectivism 133n14
Knowles, Malcolm 50
Kohon, G. 27
Kojève, A. 115, 159n88
Kolakowski, L. 8
Kompridis, N. 24, 160n92
Korngold, E. 156n81
Korsch, K. 125
Koyré, A. 146n51
Kravis, N. 80
Kris, A. 133n13
Kristeva, J. 155n79, 156n80, 160n91, 162n95
Kuhn, A. 149n61
Kuhn, T. 78
Kurtz, R. 143n42, 153n73

Lacan, J. & Lacanian thinking 3, 12, 35, 120–124, 132n8, 136n20, 136n21, 141n36, 144n45, 150n64, 154n79, 157n83, 161n92, 161n93, 162n95; aphanisis notion 157n84; bodymind 162n96; desire theory 39, 41, 44, 157n84, 162n95, 163n97, 144n45; domination discourse & language 115–116; Klein critique 149n64; 'making-sense' 136n21; the Real 120–122, 161n93; sexual energy 154n79, 155n79; training 47, 55–56, 62–63, 65–66, 71, 81; transformative release 118, 120–122; transgressive practice 65, 124, 144n45, 153n73; transition, sense of 55–56; unconscious 136n20, 151n68; 'unfathomable' 161n94; *see also* 'Real'
Laclau, E. 160n90
Laing, R. 9
Lane, C. 133n11
Langer, M. 160n92
Langs, R. 155n80
Lao-Tzu 70, 143n42; *see also* Taoic teachings
Laplanche, J. 6, 40–41, 51, 72, 88–89, 94–95, 109, 121, 132n5, 135n16, 136n20, 138n24, 147n53, 156n80
Lebenstrienb *see* 'lifefulness principle'
Lebow, J. 133n9
Leenhardt, M. 116
Leete, A. 132n7
Lefebvre, H. 163n100
Legrand, D. 135n17, 152n73
Leibniz, G. 86, 90, 148n57
Leonard, G. 152n72
Lévi-Strauss, C. 116, 132n7
Levinas, E. & Levinasian thinking 41, 76, 86–87, 105, 143n43, 144n46, 153n75, 154n79
Levy, R. 32
Lian, Y.-L. 156n81
liberation 124–129
libidinality: biological operations 95; energies 87–95; 'libidinal economy' 94, 148n59; representation system 39; semiosis 40; *see also* psychic energy
Lichtheim, G. 159n89
'lifefulness principle' (Lebenstrieb) 41–42, 78, 109–110, 129
Limentani, A. 63
Lindahl, K. 156n80
Lingis, A. 138n24, 148n59
'linguistic-turn' 115–116
Lippitt, J. 143n41
listening: defining 23–24; free-associative 98, 107–110; interpretation of relations 42; listening-and-opening praxis 2, 5; 'making sense' 77; specialized process of 25; subtle energy 155n80; trainee psychoanalysts 55; versus hearing-to-understand 55 lived-experience ; alleviation tactics 9; awareness 154n78; being-as-becoming 103; conventional first-, second-, and third-person approaches 25–31; free-associative praxis 22–24, 45; libidinal energies 87–95; mysteries 122; types of 23, 31–32; use of term 2, 4–5
'logocentrism' 116

Lohser, B. 135n18
Long, A. 147n52
Lothane, Z. 141n34, 144n45
'love' & 'Love' 127, 142n38, 154n77,
    163n68
Lovitt, W. 151n68
Low, B. 109
Lowen, A. 155n79
Lukács, G. 125, 160n89
Lunbeck, E. 140n32
Luxemburg, R. 8, 10
Lyotard, J.-F. 148n59

Macey, D. 161n93
Maeterlinck, M. 156n82
Mahone, S. 133n11
Mahony, P. 133n13
'making-sense' 25, 77, 136n21; see also
    interpretation
Malabou, C. 93
Malcolm X 160n91
Marazzi, C. 163n100
Marcus, P. 133n8
Marcuse, H. 31, 148n59, 160n90, 160n92
Marley, B. 59
Marlock, G. 133n10
Marx, K. & Marxist thinking 1, 112–113,
    118, 125–126, 130n1, 159n89, 160n92,
    163n100
master/slave relations 115–117, 129,
    160n91; see also domination/
    subordination
Masi, F. 156n82
Matthews, J. 48
Mauss, M. 116
Mbembe, A. 134n14
McCarthy, T. 158n85
McCulloch, J. 133n11
McGowan, T. 161n92, 162n95
McGregor, G. 155n80
McKirahan, R. 146n52
'me' conversations & identities 26, 158n85;
    see also egology; phenomenology
medical model 16, 48
meditative practices 151n69
Meduna, L. 13
Meisels, M. 139n27
Meister Eckhart 101, 151n68
Mellasioux, Q. 149n61
Meltzer, M. 133n11
Memmi, A. 160n91
'mental health' industry 13–14
Merleau-Ponty, M. 135n17, 152n73
Merton, T. 151n69

Mészáros, I. 159n89
metaphysics 85–86
Meyerson, E. 161n93
Micale, M. S. 131n2
military-industrial-academic complex 7–8,
    14–15, 48, 131n4
Miller, J.-A. 144n45
Mills, C. W. 118
Milton, J. 134n14
'mindbody' term 140n33; see also bodymind
Mitchell, S. 143n42
modern era 112, 122, 145n48
Molino, A. 130n, 132n6
Money, J. 106, 154n77
Moniz, A. 13
Motherwell, R. 163n99
Mouffe, C. 160n90
Muecke, D. 143n41
M'Uzan, M. 157n82
Myers, I. 14
mysteries of life 122, 126

Nachträglichkeit (après coup) 41
Nakamura, T. 156n80
Nagel, T. 26
Nancy, J.-L. 143n43, 153n75, 155n80
narcissism: confusions around term 140n32;
    the 'other' 117; trainee psychoanalysts
    50–51, 56, 58, 71–72, 74, 81
narratological-imperative: concept of 19;
    listening 23–24; preservation of 36;
    speaking modes 97; see also repetition
    compulsivity
negative dialectics 4–7, 21–23, 37–38, 44,
    56–57, 74–75, 78, 102, 119–120,
    123–127, 134n15, 151n70, 153n73
Negri, A. 163n100
Neimeyer, R. 157n82
Nelson, R. 130n1
neo-Kleinian practitioners see Klein &
    Kleinian psychotherapy
Neumann, E. 152n72
neuroscience & neuropsychoanalysis
    137n22, 148n60
'new feminist materialism' 148n61
Newton, P. 135n18
Nicholson, L. 160n91
Nietzsche, F. 41, 87, 90–93, 96, 115, 125,
    139n26, 144n46, 147n54, 147n55
'Nirvana principle' 109
Nitschke, G. 152n72
Nobus, D. 153n73
nonidenticality 94–95, 112, 119
nonverbal interpretation 69

nonviolent power 124–127
normality 57, 140n31
notion-for-praxis (Hilfvorstellung) 88–89,
94, 146n49; *see also* praxis
Nountondji, P. 134n14

'object-oriented ontology' 148n61
object-relations: patient's 60–61; school of
3, 5, 12, 43, 47, 116
objectivism 26, 32, 79, 96, 133n14, 134n15
oedipality & oedipal complexes 89, 115,
117–118, 141n35
Ogden, T. 157n82
Ollman, B. 159n89
ontoethics 83–87, 91, 103, 145n47–8,
163n98
ontology, sexual energy 154n79
oppression 7, 129, 160n91
orgasmic issues 110, 158n86
Ornston, D. G. 151n67
'other' & otherness 35, 127; domination of
114–117; self-expression 19
Other (capitalized) 62

Padmasambhava (Guru Rinpoche) 12
pain 8–9
Pallaro, P. 150n66
Panksepp, J. 148n60
pansexuality 153n76
Pappenheim, B. 12
Parmenides (Parmenides of Elea) 21
Pascal, R. 133n12
'passe' 55–56, 144n45
past-present relationship 75–76
Patañjali 12
patient, psychoanalyst as 51, 55–58
patient-candidate, psychoanalyst as 57–59
Paul the Apostle (Saul of Tarsus) 112
payment for sessions 64–65
pedagogy 47, 50
Pederson, T. 148n59
Peirce, C. S. 116
Penrose, R. 146n51
Peraldi, F. 153n76
permanent revolution 163n100
Pettrucelli, J. 153n73
Pezze, B. D. 151n68
phallus & phallogocentric system 62–63, 71,
116, 123
'phantasy' 27–28
phenomenology 28–29, 135n17, 152n73;
see also egology
Piven, J. 156n82
plane of immanence 90–92

pleasure, question of 110, 174n79
pluritemporality 24, 38, 40–42, 65, 79, 88
'pneuma' 89–90, 95
polysexuality 40, 102–107, 153n76; *see also*
sexuality
Pontalis, J.-B. 72, 94
Popper, K. 134n15
Porter, R. 131n2.
Posidonius 147n56
prānā *see* breath psychic energy
Pratt, C. 132n7
praxis: change notion 130n1; de-repressive
73; ethical 80; free-associative 2, 8,
20–45, 88–89; notion-for-praxis 88–89,
94, 146n49; of psychoanalysis 1–19, 111,
116, 128; radical psychoanalysis 1–19;
transgressive 88–89, 94, 124–127, 146n49
preconscious domain 27, 104
presence, psychoanalyst's 35, 59, 70–71,
73–77
present-past relationship 75–76; *see also*
pluritemporality
primal repression 88–89
psychiatry 5, 48, 131n2
psychic energy: biological operations
94–95; criticisms of 146n51; deathfulness
109–110; of desire 88, 105–107, 131n5;
'drives' 86; embodied experience 123;
free-association 100; incorporeal force
93; interpellation process 148n58;
notion-for-praxis 94; 'plane of
immanence' similarity 91–92; regression
77–78; representationality 88; repression
88–89; 'substance' difference 95
psychotherapy 2, 11–13, 18, 60–61;
psychoanalysis differences 20–21, 55,
74–75; training 54
psychological assessment 14–15
psychopharmacology 13
psychosynthesis 57
psychotherapy, definition 11, 12–13
Pythagoras (Pythagoras of Samos) 63

Quayson, A. 134n14
Quindeau, I. 94, 132n5
Quine, W. 25
Quinn, M. 153n72

Racker, H. 135n18
radical psychoanalysis: 'calling' to 58;
capitalism 112–113; defining 22–25;
free-association 119–120, 123–124;
liberation 129; 'making sense' 77; need
for change 127; practitioners' functions

63–64, 67, 71, 74; praxis of 1–19;
    principles 84; prolegomenal notes 2–4;
    psychotherapy distinction 3–4; schools of
    3–4; symbolic order 121–122
Ragland, E. 157n83
Rajneesh, B. S. 152n72
Raju, P. 138n24, 145n48
Ramacharaka, Y. 156n80
Ray, R. 150n66, 158n86
Readings, B. 131n4
'Real' 120, 121–122, 154n79, 161n93,
    162n96
Receptivity see Gelassenheit
Reeder, J. 139n27
Reich, W. 67, 155n79, 159n89, 162n92
Reik, T. 98, 155n80
Reiss, T. 134n14
releasement 101, 118–124, 151n58,
    151n69; see also freie Einfall; Gelassenheit
repetition-compulsivity 1–2, 8, 11;
    free-associative praxis 25; present-past
    relationship 76; stases of 35–42;
    representational systems; deathfulness
    110; desire 27, 37, 39, 94–95, 119;
    'drives' 108; embodied experience 103;
    language 6; receptivity 102; repression
    26, 127; self-consciousness 30, 31;
    suppression 59–60; thinking 117;
    transformative change 44;
    'unfathomable' 161n94
repression: barrier 4–5, 26, 87–88, 128;
    disclosure of 136n20; free-associative
    praxis 26–28, 30, 32–33, 36–37, 39–40;
    life without 127; necessity of 128;
    negation and 72; notion-for-praxis of
    146n51; psychic energy 88–89;
    psychoanalyst's training 59–60, 76–77;
    self-consciousness 112
resistances: of psychoanalyst 128;
    intrapsychic & interpersonal 68;
    to free-association 66–70, 72–73,
    75–78, 102
Ricard, M. 73
Richardson, M. 163n99
Ricoeur, P. 28, 134n15
Rinpoche see Padmasambhava
Rivers, N. 160n91
Robles, M. 139n27
Rogers, C. 18
Rolland, R. 148n57
Rorty, R. 143n41
Rosemont, P. 163n99
Rosen, R. 156n80
Rosenberg, A. 133n8

Rosner, S. 136n19
Ross, A. 114
Roudinesco, E. 144n45
Rousseau, J.-J. 17
Rowe, N. M. 155n80
Rubin, G. 106
Ruitenbeek, H. 141n34, 157n82
Rūmī (Jalāl ad-Dīn Muhammad
    Rūmī) 12
Rustin, M. 161n92
Ruti, M. 155n79
Ruyer, R. 91
Rycroft, C. 134n15

Safran, J. 132n6
Sakel, M. 13
Samuels, A. 161n92
Saraswati, S. 156n81
Sartre, J.-P. 163n97
Satsangi, P. S. 152n72
Saussure, F. 116
Scarfone, D. 135n16
Schacht, R. 159n89
Schechter, K. 50, 61, 139n27
Schneider, S. 152n72
Schopenhauer, A. 72, 92–93, 147n56
Schrödinger, E. 87
Schroyer, T. 160n90
Schur, M. 141n34
Schuster, A. 154n79, 155n79
Searles, H. 157n82
Sedley, D. 147n52
'secondary' self-consciousness 104
seduction function of psychoanalyst 63
Segal, H. 76
Seigworth, G. 149n61
Seldon, G. 156n81
'self-analysis' 31–32, 59
self-consciousness: accedence 30; egological
    project 59–60; existence of 158n88;
    expression of self 16–19, 43; the 'I' of
    28–31; master/slave dialectic 115;
    negative dialectics 38; psychoanalysis'
    effects on 151n70; repression 112; types
    of 104; see also awareness
self-psychological school 3, 5, 12; see also
    interpersonalist & relational approach
Sellars, W. 25
Serner, W. 163n99
Sexuality: behavioural categories 62;
    bodymind 105–107; death and 152n71;
    defining 154n79; energy 154n79; free
    association 110; freedom 129; imaginary
    world 123; patterning 153n76, 154n77;

slowness 163n98; *see also* orgasmic issues; tantric movement; Taoic thinking
Shakespeare, W. 157n82
Shapiro, E. 139n27
Sheldon, W. 14
Sheppard, R. 163n99
Shulman, H. 162n95
Simonton, G. 91
Sīnā, I. (Avicenna) 12
Sitbon, B. 147n56
Sjöstedt-H, P. 147n56
Sokolowski, R. 135n16
Solms, M. 137n22
'somatocentric' & 'somatogenic' 12–13, 40, 78, 145n47
Sousa Santos, B. 134n14
speaking, free-associative 95–102
Spiegel, L. 136n19
Spiegelberg, H. 135n16
Spiegler, M. 133n9
Spielrein, S. 41, 138n24
Spinoza, B. 90–95, 147n53, 148n60
Srnicek, N. 149n61
Stavrakakis, Y. 161n92
Stayton, W. 153n76
Steckel, W. 79
Sterba, R. 32, 57, 73–74
Stevens, A. 149n64
Stoicism 89–90, 93, 95, 147n56
Stolorow, R. 134n15
Stone, L. 136n20
structural-functional model *see* ego-psychological model
structuralism 116
Sturrock, J. 131n3
sublimation 72, 143n44
'substances': attributes of 90, 94–95; immanence of 90
subtle energy 137n23; Asian thinking 148n57; deathfulness 108–109; listening 155n80; lived-experience 89–90, 93–94; ontology of 154n79; revolutionary psychoanalysis 111–112; suffering 8, 73
Suler, J. 132n6
Sullivan, H. S. 61–62, 150n64
supervision of trainees 46, 49–50, 142n39
surrealist movement 124–125, 163n99
symbolic order: conditions of 123; imaginary 121; lack 163n97; language 118; 'outside' of 122; 'phallus' 62; symbolic world 120; *see also* Lacan & Lacanian thinking; phallus & phallogocentric system
Szasz, T. 14

'talking cures' 11–13; *see also* conversational psychotherapy
Tanner, G. 146n52
tantric movement 92, 150n66, 152n72, 156n81, 158n86, 163n98
Taoic thinking 92, 151n68, 163n98; *see also* Asian thinking
telepathy 93, 137n23
temporality *see* pluritemporality
'thing-presentation' 26–27, 36, 38–39, 111
Thompson, G. 84, 133n13, 135n18
Thoreau, H. D. 152n72
Tissié, P. 145n47
Todestrieb *see* deathfulness principle
Tomšič, S. 161n92
Torsti-Hagman, M. 31
training: andragogic 50–51; application interviews 52–53, 138n25; components of 51; criticism of system 139n27; entering profession 51–53; sense of transition 54–57; 'training analysis' 46, 51, 54–55; 'Training Analysts' 55, 57–58, 140n30; training institutes 46–47, 49, 52, 54, 56, 138n25; vulnerability and fear 78–82
'transference': neurosis' 76; patient-psychoanalyst 74–75, 80
transformation: change 23, 43–44; goals/ideals of 125; transformative imprisonment 118–124; versus transmutative change and release 23, 33, 44, 118–124, 128
transgressive praxis 124–127
'transitional objects' 60
Trieb *see* 'drives'
Trigg, D. 135n17, 152n73
Trotsky, L. 130n1, 163n100
truthfulness: de-repressive praxis 73; 'freeing' 24, 59, 82, 126–128; versus 'truthlessness' 10
Tzara, T. 163n99

Uexhüll, J. 91
uncensored talking 33–34, 149n63
unconscious: function of 136n20; representational system 27; 'unconscious phantasies' 27–28; unconscious theme 37
understanding: belief in 44–45; limitations of 43; listening 42; understanding-by-changing 5
'unfathomable' 161n94

universities 48–49, 138n26
Upanishads 148n57

Vaneigem, R. 163n100
Vaughan, M. 133n11
Vedas 14, 92, 152n72; *see also* Asian
    thinking
Velman, M. 152n72
Vienna Psychoanalytic Society 73
visual phenomena 150n65
'voicing' truthfulness 24
'voiding' 71–72, 74, 75, 81

Wass, H. 157n82
Watkins, M. 162n95
Watts, A. 152n72
Weatherill, R. 157n83
Weiss, E. 41
Weiss, H. 150n66
Whewell, W. 147n53
White, R. S. 155n80
Whitehouse, M. S. 150n66
Wilber, K. 152n72
'will-to-life' 92
'will-to-power' 90

Winnicott, D. W. 64, 153n73
Wittgenstein, L. 116, 131n3
Wolfenstein, E. 125, 161n92
Wollstonecraft, M. 160n91
Wolpe, A. 149n61
Woodroffe, J. (Arthur Avalon)
    156n81
'workplay' 25, 64
World Association of Psychoanalysis 54
World War I 124–125

Yabe, Y. 148n57
yogic practices 156n81; *see also* Asian
    thinking; Dharma teachings
Young-Eisendrath, P. 28

Zagerman, P. 139n27
Zaretsky, E. 158n87
Zedong, M. 143n40, 163n100
Zeno (Zeno of Elea) 89, 147n56
Žižek, S. 113–114, 154n79, 160n92
Znamenski, A. 132n7
Zupančič, A. 154n79
Zweig, S. 133n13
Zwingli, H. 151n68

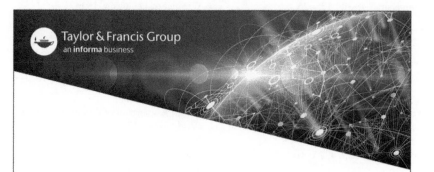